7

JOHN ALLEN FITZGERALD GREGG

1. PORTRAIT BY OSWALD BIRLEY

JOHN ALLEN FITZGERALD
GREGG
ARCHBISHOP

BY

GEORGE SEAVER

FOREWORD BY JAMES McCANN
Archbishop of Armagh

THE FAITH PRESS
7 TUFTON STREET LONDON S.W.1
1963
ALLEN *Af* FIGGIS
DUBLIN

FIRST PUBLISHED IN 1963

© *George Seaver, 1963*

PRINTED IN GREAT BRITAIN
in 10 point Times type
BY THE FAITH PRESS LTD.
LEIGHTON BUZZARD

FOREWORD

THE SUBJECT OF THIS BIOGRAPHY was a unique person. Throughout many years of public life he wielded quite exceptional influence in the Irish Church, and was a recognized leader of the Anglican Communion.

John Allen Fitzgerald Gregg won distinction as a Classical Scholar at Cambridge; as a learned writer on Biblical Theology and Church History; then as a Divinity Professor in Trinity College, Dublin; subsequently, he became Bishop of Ossory in 1915, Archbishop of Dublin five years later, and was translated to the Archbishopric of Armagh in 1939. He resigned from the Primatial See in 1959.

His leadership was destined to be spent in a period of storm and stress, during a time of social and political upheaval. Calm, wise, patient and rock-like in principle, Archbishop Gregg was held in high esteem by Irishmen of widely different outlook. His guiding hand held together the people of the Church of Ireland when the country was divided politically into two separate entities, and in later years he adapted himself in a remarkable way to the many changes that followed the ending of the Second World War.

A great man, and a great ecclesiastic, his name will be remembered as an outstanding scholar and administrator in the Succession List of the Primatial See of Armagh.

We are deeply indebted to Dr. Seaver for a life-like portrait of a distinguished Prince of the Church. This book will take its place as a model biography with the writer's earlier works on Schweitzer, Livingstone, Wilson and Younghusband.

Irish Churchmen everywhere will welcome so true a record of the life and work of one of the greatest Primates to have held the See of St. Patrick.

JAMES McCANN
Archbishop of Armagh

July 27th, 1963

PREFACE

THE WRITER'S THANKS are officially due to the Archbishops and Bishops of the Church of Ireland for entrusting him with this task, at once a great privilege and a great responsibility; and more personally to Mrs. Gregg for her constant help and encouragement, and to Mrs. Wilson and Mrs. Somerville not only for their kind co-operation but also for allowing him unreservedly the use of material indispensable for its execution. This includes diaries and manuscripts, letters and press-cuttings, which virtually cover the whole period of the Archbishop's life. Among them are certain learned papers and sermons on special occasions, too weighty for inclusion in this book, which however deserve perpetuation and will therefore, it is hoped, form the subject of a separate publication.

His personal thanks are also very specially due to his Grace the Archbishop of Dublin for invaluable help in intercepting, by his meticulous scrutiny of the proofs, the perpetuation of several errors in matters of detail which would otherwise have escaped detection.

Also to Mr. E. C. Micks, S.C., for professional help in the chapter on Ecclesiastical Courts; to Mr. MacAndrew for notes on the Reformed Churches in Spain and Portugal; and to the Very Reverend W. Corkey, D.D., for his summary of the controversy on Religious Education in the North of Ireland.

Last but by no means least to Miss Geraldine FitzGerald, formerly Librarian of the Representative Church Body, and her assistant—now successor—Miss Geraldine Willis, for countless kindnesses in tracking sources and verifying references with the utmost sureness and promptitude.

Whatever merit this book may be deemed to possess, as the memorial of an eminent Anglican churchman in Ireland in an age of transition, must be ascribed to the many contributions which have made of it a symposium rather than a monograph, and all the more valuable as such. To one and all those, whose impressions and reminiscences are recorded here, and to those who have lent letters, thanks are due: their names are asterisked in the Index. Apologies as well as thanks are offered to those other writers whose tributes have unhappily for lack of space been omitted. It is with sadness that the compiler records the deaths within the past year of the following whose contributions appear in these pages: Mr. Perrott, Canon Lyndon, Mr. Shankey, Canon Bentley, Professor Hartford, Archbishop Barton, Cardinal D'Alton.

G.S.

July 1963

CONTENTS

ILLUSTRATIONS

PART ONE

SCHOLAR, PREACHER, BISHOP

CHAPTER I

FAMILY HISTORY

THE CLAN MACGREGOR derives descent from Sir Malcolm of that name, a figure of legendary renown, who in the twelfth century defended King Malcolm (son of Duncan I, murdered by Macbeth) from the attack of a boar while hunting in a forest. Requesting permission to go to his king's aid, and receiving the reply (in old 'Scots'), 'Do so—spare naught,' he uprooted an oak sapling and with one hand bayed the beast, whilst with the other he despatched it with his sword. For this deed he was raised to the peerage of Scotland with the title 'Lord Malcolm of the Castles.' Hence the Arms of his descendants: *Argent, a sword in bend, azure, an oak-tree eradicated in bend sinister, in chief a crown, gules.* And the Motto (adopted by the Gregg branch): *E'en do bait spair nocht.* The Crest is *A lion's head, crowned with an antique crown with points.*

In 1603 was fought the battle of Glenfruin between the Macgregors and the Colquhouns, as a result of which the former were proscribed. Many sought to restore their fortunes in Ireland under the names Gregg, Greer, Greir, Gregory, and other variants; and in the same century record is found of John Gregg and of his son (or brother) Jonathan Gregg of Cappagh near Ennis in Co. Clare. Jonathan's elder son Richard Gregg of Cappagh, born about 1700, married Eliza Robinet in Cork. Their fourth son Richard Gregg of Cappagh and Ennis, born 1747 and died 1808, inherited the small family property. He married Barbara, daughter of William Vesey Fitzgerald of Ashgrove, Co. Clare,[1] and by her had twelve children. Richard Gregg died intestate and the property passed against his expressed wishes to his eldest son Richard 'in whose hands it did not increase.' (His second son, Robert, was the father of James Fitzgerald Gregg, born in Co. Meath, 1820, graduate of Trinity in 1843, ordained in 1844 and was Vicar of Yoxford in Suffolk. He was Dean of Limerick from 1899 to 1905 and was 'an eloquent preacher of evangelistic views.') His wife, who survived him, was a Roman Catholic but was converted to the Protestant form of faith by her famous son John. She was also a sister of the Right Honourable James Fitzgerald, whose two sons were in succession

[1] He was Daniel O'Connell's opponent in the Ennis election in 1829.

the first and second Lords Fitzgerald and Vesey, of whom the first especially was to prove a good friend to his cousin John.

JOHN GREGG, the fifth son of his parents, was born on 4 August 1798. He says of himself: 'I was the orphan child of the only Protestant family in one of the obscurest parishes in the most neglected county in Ireland.' Of great mental and physical vitality, he made such good use of his time at a classical school in Ennis as to win a sizarship on entrance to Trinity College, then a scholarship, and graduated second in Classical Honours, only just missing the Gold Medal. He had kept himself by taking pupils, and this he continued to do while working for ordination. An athlete as well as a scholar 'he was foremost among his fellows in every manly exercise.' After serving a short apprenticeship as a curate of Portarlington he was nominated, through the influence of his cousin the Honourable Vesey Fitzgerald, to the incumbency of Kilsallaghan near Dublin. But so forceful and eloquent was he as a preacher that in 1835 a special church—Trinity—was built for him in Dublin, near the Customs House, to accommodate 2,000 people. Crowds of cultivated folk flocked there to hear him, among them the learned Lord-Lieutenant, the Earl of Carlisle. His fluency in the Celtic language also attracted numbers among the poorer classes, many of whom were Roman Catholics. He took the degrees of M.A., B.D. and D.D. in 1860.

In the 1840s when the North Strand Chapel of Ease, as it was then called, was threatened with closure owing to the inability of its poor parishioners to maintain it, he asked his own wealthy congregation in Trinity Church for £300. They gave £900, with the result that North Strand Church, as it now is, was endowed. To this little-known fact his grandson made reference when preaching there on 10 November 1926.

On 16 February 1862 he was consecrated in Christ Church Cathedral as Bishop of Cork, Cloyne and Ross, and three days later was enthroned in the old Cathedral of St. Fin Barre. He was the last Bishop of that Diocese of the Establishment. Largely through his influence and exertions the new Cathedral was built; its design, French Gothic, is unique in the British Isles. It is further remarkable as being the only cathedral begun and completed under the same bishop; the foundation stone having been laid by him on 12 January 1865, he consecrated the building for divine worship on 30 November 1870, and lived to see the top-most stones placed on the western towers on 6 April 1878. He died on a Sunday evening, the 26th of May following, at the age of 79.

HIS FATHER

HIS MOTHER

3. ABOUT 1874. *Left to right*—Katherine, John Gregg (Bishop of Cork), Mrs. John Gregg, Revd. J. R. Gregg, Mrs. J. R. Gregg, J.A.F.G., Hilda, *(incog.)* Mary

BEDFORD SCHOOL, FORM V2, 1887. Gregg is seated on Headmaster's right

He was the greatest pulpit orator of his generation in Ireland, as well as one of the most forceful characters. His sermons, some of which appear in the 'Memorials' edited by the son who succeeded him in Cork, still please the ear by their verve and vigour; but perhaps their substance does not so please the mind of an age unaccustomed to 'evangelistic' teaching. Archbishop d'Arcy as a small boy heard him in Cork. 'He was then an old man, but the wonderful fire of his eloquence must have been as bright as ever, for I can never forget the effect he produced.' There was undoubtedly a strain of genius in him, and his fine qualities of heart and head would seem to have been transmitted, variously, to several of his descendants. A point of resemblance between himself and the grandson, who is the subject of this biography, may be seen in their familiarity with the Greek of the New Testament which to both was almost a second tongue; a point of difference in the fact that whereas John Gregg the elder loathed committee meetings, to his grandson they were as meat and drink.

John Gregg had married in 1830 Elizabeth Nichola, daughter of Robert Law, of an old and well-known family in Dublin. By her he had three sons: John Robert (of whom presently), Robert Samuel (of whom presently), and William Henry, born 1844, died 1863; and three daughters: Elizabeth, Frances Fitzgerald, and Charlotte Browne who married Samuel Owen Madden, D.D., Dean of Cork. Owen Madden was thus first cousin to the future Archbishop and of about the same age. As small boys they exchanged letters concerning their pet cats and other childish interests. It will be seen that their relationship ripened in after life when the Archbishop spent his summer holidays in Castletownshend where his cousin was Rector. It was Dr. Madden's sister Geraldine who best remembered details of the family history, and among them the interesting fact that her uncle John Robert Gregg was recognized as 'the greatest' of his father's sons, but was prevented by ill-health from attaining the distinction which fell to the lot of his younger brother.

JOHN ROBERT GREGG, the eldest son, was born 'in Co. Dublin' in 1831. He entered Trinity in 1849 at the age of 19 but his college career would seem to have been interrupted—probably by illness—since it was not till 1854 that he graduated, without honours, though having in the previous year won a Foundation Scholarship. Together with his father and his younger brother he took his M.A. in 1860. In the same year that he graduated he was ordained in Lichfield, and was curate successively of Burton-on-Trent, St. Lawrence in Reading, Sandon in Essex, and North Cerney, Glos., before be-

B

coming Vicar in 1875 of Deptford, in South London. Here he lived
in Vansittart House on the Greenwich Road. His son remembered
him coming home after a voyage to South Africa in hope of a cure
from consumption, but he died at home on 11 June 1882, aged 50,
from a pulmonary haemorrhage. He had married Sarah Caroline
Frances, daughter of the Revd. Peter French, Rector of Burton-on-
Trent, and sister of Thomas French, Bishop of Lahore. This Bishop
was remembered as standing at the gates of Lucknow during the
seige, begging for milk for his new-born child. He was a grandfather of the famous Knox brothers, sons of the Bishop of Manchester. The Revd. Peter French's wife was Mary Penelope, daughter
of Richard Valpy of Reading, the famous classicist—a connection
of which J. A. F. Gregg was always very proud.

There exists a typically mid-Victorian account of the wedding
of the Revd. J. R. Gregg and Caroline French, but unfortunately
not the date. They had four children. Hilda Caroline was an M.A.
honoris causa of London University, and the authoress of historical
novels under the pen-name 'Sydney C. Grier.' Katherine, trained in
the Royal Free Hospital, London, was one of the first women
doctors. Charming, gay, and greatly beloved, she served as a
missionary in India, where she died of cholera in 1911. Mary
Penelope Valpy, lively and good-looking, combined ultra-pietism
with a disposition to 'tease.' She trained as a nurse and went out
as a missionary to Japan. She married Martin Gurney, and left three
sons. Of his sisters it was to Mary that their young brother wrote
most often from school, as being nearest to himself in age; but it
was to Katherine that in after life he became most deeply attached,
and whose death he felt as one of his greatest sorrows.

ROBERT SAMUEL GREGG, the second son, was born at Kilsallaghan
on 3 May 1834. Like his father he graduated with honours at
Trinity, in 1857; with his father and his elder brother he took the
degree of M.A. in 1860; and B.D. and D.D. together in 1873. After a
curacy near Cork and incumbencies in Belfast and again in the
Cork diocese, he was made Precentor of St. Fin Barre's Cathedral,
and afterwards Dean. 'While still young he made his mark as a
financier in the general Synod, and took a large part in framing
the financial schemes after Disestablishment.' (Canon J. B. Leslie.)
In 1875 he was elected Bishop of Ossory and three years later, on
his father's death, the Bishopric of Cork became vacant.

In her charming *Irish Memories* published in 1917—memories
for the most part of her cousin and collaborator Violet Martin
('Martin Ross')—Miss Edith OE. Somerville relates the story of

'a Homeric battle' between her cousin's mother and one of her own
many aunts, which began with 'a suave and academic discussion of
the Irish Episcopate, and narrowed a little to the fact that the
diocese of Cork needed a bishop.'

My aunt Florence said easily, 'Oh—Gregg, of course!' My
cousin Nannie (Mrs. Martin) replied with a sweet reasonableness,
yet firmly, 'I think you will find that Pakenham Walsh is the
man.' The battle then was joined. From argument it passed on
into shouting, and thence neared fisticuffs. They advanced
towards each other in large armchairs, even as, in these later
days, the Tanks move into action. They beat each other's knees,
each lady crying the name of her champion, and then my aunt
remembered that she had a train to catch, and rushed from the
room. The air was still trembling with her departure, when the
door was part opened, the monosyllable 'Gregg!' was projected
through the aperture, and before reply was possible, the slam
of the hall door was heard.

Mrs. Martin flung herself upon the window, and was in time to
scream 'Paknamwalsh!' in one tense syllable, to my aunt's departing long, thin back.

My aunt Florence was too gallant a foe to affect, as at the
distance she might well have done, unconsciousness. Any one
who knows the deaf and dumb alphabet will realize what con-
quering gestures were hers, as turning to face the enemy she
responded

'G! R! E! G! G!'

and with the last triumphant thump of her clenched fist, fled
round the corner.

And she was right. 'Gregg & Son, Bishops to the Church of
Ireland,' have passed into ecclesiastical history.

Gregg and Pakenham Walsh (who was then Dean of Cashel)
had been sole competitors in the previous election for Ossory, as
they were now once again for election to Cork. Pakenham Walsh
succeeded Gregg as Bishop of Ossory. But Gregg was yet to be
elevated to the Archbishopric of Armagh, and his nephew, who
was in due course to follow him there, was at this time not yet
five years old. The subsequent verdict of history might therefore
have read: 'Gregg, Son & Grandson, Bishop and Archbishops to
the Church of Ireland.'

It was in December 1893 that Robert Samuel Gregg was elected
Primate of All Ireland, but his tenure of the office was short—just
over two years. He died suddenly in the Palace, Armagh, on
10 January 1896. He is remembered as a man of great stature,

fine presence, and kindly disposition, as well as the possessor of a melodious tenor voice. Though neither the scholar nor the preacher that his father had been, 'he was wise, considerate, and active, and threw his whole energy into the organization of the Church throughout his various dioceses.' (Leslie.) 'The contrast between father and son was extraordinary; for while John Gregg was all wit and fiery eloquence, Robert Gregg was singularly calm and unruffled. He had a slow, sententious style which carried weight by its very manner. He was an excellent administrator, and was one of that group of able men of affairs who took in hand the reorganization of the finances of the Church.' (Primate d'Arcy.)

He had married in 1863 Elinor, daughter of John H. Bainbridge of Frankfield, Cork, during his incumbency of that parish, and had two children: John William Robert Gregg of Athboy, Co. Meath, who married Mary Studdert; and Amy Elinor, who married the Ven. Robert Walsh, D.D., Rector of Donnybrook and Archdeacon of Dublin.

CHAPTER II

BOYHOOD AND YOUTH

JOHN ALLEN FITZGERALD GREGG, only son of the Revd. John Robert Gregg, was born at Perrott's Brook, North Cerney, Gloucestershire, on 4 July 1873, and was baptized by his father on the 24th August following. One of his earliest recollections was of being taken to Cork to see his grandfather. Another was of a trip on a paddle-steamer with his parents from Margate to the Goodwin Sands in a rough sea, when he asked his afflicted mother: 'Mama, do the little fishes have to dress and wash themselves?'

His upbringing was strict and puritanically pious. From his tender years church-going was *de rigeur,* and during Holy Communion he was left sitting in the family pew and was expected to keep quiet. He was always a lover of cats, and when a neighbour's kitten was ill he was much concerned. One Sunday morning as this kitten's mistress passed down the aisle from the altar he leaned out of his pew and asked audibly, 'How's Dingy?' The scolding that he received from his mother for this misdemeanour (he was about three) was an ineffaceable memory.

He was taught the piano by the organist in Deptford Parish Church. In the autumn of the year in which his father died, 1882, he was sent for a year as a boarder to a preparatory school in Malvern. But when her eldest daughter was threatened with symptoms of the pulmonary infection which had killed her husband, Mrs. Gregg bought a house called 'Kirkley' in Eastbourne for the sake of fresh sea air. It thenceforth became the family home, and John went as a day-boy to the 'College.' He played games with the local boys in the park, and was an eager spectator of the early South of England lawn-tennis matches. There was scarcely a year in later life when he failed to go back to Eastbourne for these annual events.

At thirteen he was sent as a boarder to Bedford Grammar School as it was then called, during the headmastership of James Surtees Phillpotts (grandson of the Bishop of Exeter). Coming from Rugby in the true Arnold tradition he was a great head, and a great man. 'The restless energy of Phillpotts came like a bracing wind, to some indeed a disturbing hurricane.' He widened and vitalized the curriculum, organized the games, established Houses, built workshops and gymnasium, inaugurated societies and debates and other

21

cultural activities. Starting with 293 boys inadequately housed, in ten years he doubled its numbers till in 1888 they had reached—including day boys—the astonishing figure of 800. 'Never was Headmaster more loved by his boys; and the entrance gates in Burnaby Road, erected in 1930 to celebrate his ninetieth birthday, express the devotion as well as the admiration he inspired.' Gregg kept in touch with his old 'chief' (as he was called) both by letters and visits till his death. Phillpotts would begin his letters, 'My dear Archbishop,' and end them, 'Yours most "chiefly," J.S.P.'

Gregg's sole surviving school contemporary with whom he was on intimate terms was a boy three years his senior, and who outlived him by two. Canon Jocelyn H. T. Perkins, C.V.O , F.S.A., D.C.L., was for more than sixty years Sacrist of Westminster Abbey and an autocratic director of its procedure and ceremonial. An accomplished musician he encouraged young Gregg's interest in music by teaching him to play the organ. They remained life-long friends, and Perkins had always a cordial welcome for him when he visited the Abbey.

Judging from his scrupulously-kept diaries and his letters home, which are normal if tinged with slight precocity, Gregg would appear to have thoroughly enjoyed his schooldays, though in a somewhat detached and desultory way. His terminal reports are more revealing, not only of his own progress and character tendencies, but of the exceptionally careful watch which the masters kept on their pupils.

From the outset he is 'a pleasant, bright, and very promising boy,' but 'a little more *pluck* is wanted in coming forward among his schoolfellows.' Again, 'Good as regards his lessons, and has done very well in form' but 'he should come out more in other ways and take an independent lead.' At the end of his first year he won the Fourth Form Prize and passed the Oxford and Cambridge Lower Certificate with distinction. At the end of his second, he won the Fifth Form Prize. He was moved up into the Sixth Form in November of 1888 when only 15 years and 4 months old—exactly two years junior to the average age of the Form. In 1890 he passed the higher Certificate with distinction, and was awarded the coveted New College Prize for Latin Verse. In the summer of this year his Headmaster has an interesting comment: 'He takes a great interest in Sophocles and works at the MSS. Doing very well. Always very pleasant to teach.' This comment is unconsciously prophetic of his pupil's future skill in textual criticism. In a paper entitled 'Manuscripts: manuscript-hunting and manuscript-finding,' which he read to the Ballymena Clerical Union in October 1898, we find:

My interest in MSS. was first aroused by the fact that when I was at school, there existed in the Sixth Form library a facsimile copy of the Laurentian MS. of Sophocles, and this MS. I used to spend a good deal of time over with a magnifying glass till at length I was able to decipher this eleventh century writing with considerable ease. My acquisition proved of considerable service to me: it was a favourite habit of my headmaster to take the Sixth Form in Sophocles, and, among other people, I did not take much trouble to prepare for him. The result was that when I was put on to construe and found a difficulty, or when the same happened to a friend, I would have recourse to the MSS. and ask to examine the readings of the original. The headmaster always jumped at the suggestion, and so it fell out that I rarely got into difficulties over Sophocles. I was celebrated in song for the achievement, when, at the end of my last term, an epilogue to the Sixth Form was written in the school magazine which ran thus:

> 'Gregg, at manuscripts a don,
> Chuckles and is not put on.'

Criticisms that recur most often in terminal reports are that he is apt to be listless, and when in 1889 he joined the volunteers his Housemaster writes: 'I am glad . . . this will brace him up.' As to games: Rugby football, though he played it, is not mentioned; at cricket 'he bowls well, is a good catch, bats straight but tamely.' Fives is his best game; and his Headmaster hopes that his success in this 'will embolden him to come out more, and exercise a good influence befitting a boy in the Sixth Form.' In his last year he is 'most energetic' as Fives Captain and 'will be greatly missed next season.' He played the organ at St. Peter's; joined the boat-club on the Ouse; discovered the merits of racquets and also of billiards; did well in the Sports in hurdles, short distances, and long jump. There were other diversions: school outings for away-matches; concerts and theatricals. He was made a Senior Monitor in 1891, but in this position 'does not sufficiently make his influence felt.' He is 'a boy of considerable ability who is doing very well but might do better if he tried harder'; his intelligence is quick, but sometimes at the cost of accuracy. In every subject of the school curriculum he is proficient: Scripture, Mathematics, History, French, Latin, Greek; but he reads no other books and has no interest in English Literature. Of temperamental defects, his House-master had written at the end of his first term in the Sixth: 'He seems to have profited by the experiences of the term, and I hope has given up the habit of finding excuses for himself by blaming others, because they play upon his weaknesses when they find him ready to play into their hands.' And at the end of his last year his Headmaster writes again:

A pleasant fellow; wants a little more strength. Should remember that true self-respect is shown by throwing oneself into the system of which one forms a part and working in small and great things in harmony with it—not in petty conflict with minor details. Has come out very much in the ways I have wished.

But in each of the moral virtues which are severally specified in the Housemaster's terminal reports—Industry, Obedience, Manners, Truthfulness, Trustworthiness, Moral Tone and Conduct—his standard is always and without exception V.G.

Having in February 1891 been awarded a Classical Scholarship for Christ's College, Cambridge, he left Bedford in the summer to his Headmaster's great regret—'a year earlier than necessary, and with the promise of being an excellent scholar.' In March he had written to his sister Mary: 'About Holy Orders—I cannot conscientiously bind myself, because I don't know how my views will stand after a few years at College.'

The finely disciplined freedom and large interests of his school life must have contrasted strangely and painfully for him with the femininely restricted and rigidly pietistic atmosphere of his home. His mother was a strict adherent of the theology commonly—and perhaps somewhat invidiously—called 'calvinistic' or 'evangelistic,' and had indoctrinated her daughters with prophecies of gloom and doom. Her daughter Mary easily absorbed these, but her son would appear to have tacitly rejected them from a quite early age. He never entered a theatre until he went to Cambridge, save once when he was taken with the other boys to see a Shakespeare play at Bedford. But he contrived to find his own amusements in other ways. Returning through London for the holidays he saw 'Panorama'—a forerunner of the cinema—at the Polytechnic; and on another occasion was shown over the Mint (this was his own enterprise; he had written in advance for permission). During his schooldays too he paid a visit to his uncle, then Bishop of Cork. Sometimes there were lighter diversions at home. His family have preserved a story of a native boy from New Guinea who, by arrangement with a missionary society, stayed with them at Eastbourne, and they all played hide-and-seek. 'The New Guinea boy always won because he tracked by scent. Father used to recall with great delight how he set off on the hunt, nose to ground.'

Dr. Phillpotts' daughter Marjorie (Mrs. Gosset) writes:

I have had an immense respect and admiration for him for some sixty-five years, though I never knew him intimately. I lived in Dublin from 1906 to 1935 and sometimes met him in connection with parochial work. Through all the 'Troubles' his wisdom, tact, foresight, and staunch upholding of our Church were indeed statesmanship of the highest order.

Gregg's name had been entered in January 1891 at Christ's College, Cambridge, as a pensioner, but having gained a Foundation Scholarship in the following month he was formally admitted as a scholar during his first term of residence, which began on 8th October (the day after Parnell's death, as he records in his diary). Joseph Armitage Robinson was then a Fellow, and to him—as also to Rendel Harris—Gregg owed not only wise advice academically but also the privilege of personal friendship. A fellow-freshman was a slight and very intelligent youth from South Africa, Jan Christian Smuts, and for a year they shared lodgings. Smuts' biographer has written:

> His fellow lodger at 13 Victoria Street was a serious and friendly young man called John Gregg, who became in later life Archbishop of Armagh. Gregg invited him in the first week or two to come for a walk and recalled in his old age that Smuts opened the conversation by giving his views on a text from St. Paul, 'Sin revived and I died.' But Smuts never proposed a second walk and Gregg got the impression that he wanted to be left to himself.[1]

From the College Magazine it appears that Gregg rowed in the Trial Eights as a freshman and again in his second year, when he secured a permanent place in the second crew. He also won two cups for sculling. In 1892 he was Hon. Sec. for the University Fives Club and took a team of six to Bedford for a match with his old school team. In 1894 he captained the College second cricket eleven. In the Easter term of that year he was elected to the first of the 'Stewart of Rannoch' scholarships in Latin and Greek, and in November read to the Classical Society a paper on the Life and Works of Isocrates which 'proved of great interest.' He gained a first class in Part I of the Classical Tripos in 1894, and a first class in Part II in 1895. In the Easter term of 1896 (being then a divinity student at Ridley Hall) he won, with W. D. Munro of Trinity, the Cambridge University Fives Tournament.

It happened that on returning home for the Easter vacation in

[1] *Smuts*, Vol. I, p. 34, by Sir W. Keith Hancock (C.U.P., 1962).

1893 he found two of his younger Knox cousins, Winifred and a brother, installed there for tuition by his sister Mary. In one of her books, *A Little Learning*, Winifred Knox (Lady Peck) recaptured her childhood's impressions of life at 'Kirkley' and of her aunt Caroline and cousin Mary. These are not flattering: they are the candid record of any normal child's reaction to such an upbringing. She does not mention her cousin John, who was seldom at home, but in a letter she writes:

> He was then a brilliant scholar at Cambridge, and though the presence of three children in the home must have been a bore he never showed it. I think he must have reacted against his mother's stern evangelicalism (what we. I fear, called her pi-jaws). She and her daughters adored John, but I vaguely felt him (even at my age, 10 to 12) a little withdrawn from all their family pietism. His eldest sister too seemed rather withdrawn from my aunt and cousin Mary. The other was a missionary and we loved her visits; she was much less given to ceaseless corrections and admonitions. I am sure we must have been great trials, but it had nothing to do with John whom I remember with awe and some admiration as a slim, dark, silent, but witty young man.

His mother had sometimes said that she wondered what would become of him, since he would certainly never become a clergyman like his father and uncle and grandfather. In extreme old age, a few months before his death, he vividly recalled the occasion of his decision, when, walking with his mother between the Town Hall and the railway station in Eastbourne sometime in 1893, it suddenly came to him to say: 'I'm going to be a parson, and I'm going to Ireland.' In the following summer he went with his sister Hilda for a visit to their uncle at the Palace in Armagh, crossing via Greenore, and thus early became first acquainted with his own future home. He took long exploratory walks in the country-side. His uncle approved of his decision for ordination but deprecated the idea of his coming to Ireland, saying, 'You'll find it very rough.'

In the following year he paid another visit to his uncle, via Belfast, this time alone, and met several of his Irish relations. In after years he recalled to his Archdeacon (later Dean), H. W. Rennison, memories of the diocese in those days:

> Once, having been to institute a new Rector at Newtown-hamilton, he commented on the smoothness and speed of motoring there that day, in contrast to driving with his uncle in an open carriage to the same place; and it had not escaped his notice that, at a certain turn, a new road now replaces what he

remembered to have been a particularly narrow stretch with a nasty hill.[2]

Another recollection was of Duncan Thackeray, Mus. Doc., then principal tenor in the Cathedral, whom he remembered in the Choir as 'a venerable figure, with long flowing beard, wearing his Doctor's hood.'

The predecessors of Robert Samuel Gregg in the See of Armagh had taken little notice of the choir-boys, but he instituted the custom of an annual tea-party for them in the Palace grounds. Himself now for some years a widower he was fortunate in having an unmarried sister to keep house for him and dispense hospitality. A small choir-boy named Henry Wood was taken in hand by this kind lady one summer afternoon and was introduced by her to a dark young man as her nephew from Cambridge, to whom she explained that Henry was a younger brother of Charles (already renowned in Cambridge as a rising musician). The dark young man fell back in astonishment and exclaimed: 'What! Is this really a brother of Charles Wood?'[3]

His own tutor in music was A. H. Mann of King's; and in Cambridge he also met Sir Charles Stanford.

His diary is a bare factual record of daily circumstance, telling of what he and others did, but nothing of what he thought or felt. It shows that at Cambridge and in the vacations too he led a full life of various activities, athletic, academic, social and cultural and, surprisingly, games take precedence. His diary too contains a meticulous account of his expenses; initials of people to whom he wrote; a list of the books he read. His Housemaster at Bedford had complained that he read nothing except his school books; his diary shows that in that latter half of the year in which he took his double first, 1895, he read no less than thirty-three books; and subsequent years show the consumption of an average of fifty solid books a year. His diary for 1895 has more than one interest: it contains quotations from the Book of Wisdom; and the statement that he invested in a Life Insurance Policy for £1,000.

On Friday, 10 January 1896, occurs this entry blacked in: 'Uncle Robert died 10.30 p.m.' On Saturday: 'Telegram came at 10.15.' On Sunday: 'Went to Church alone in morning. At night with H[ilda] and M[ary] to Rev. Wilson's.' Then:

[2] *Diary entry: Sunday, 4th August.* Drive to Newtown Hamilton with uncle. He preached. Returned 3.30.

[3] *Diary entry: Monday, 5th August.* Cathedral choir boys to tea. Played rounders and picked fruit.

13th. Left E'bourne 4.40. Travelled down w. Bp. of Derry. Good passage. *14th.* Bkf. at 5 Northbr. Road. Called 25 L.L. St. Left for Armagh 2.40. Trav. w. Archb. Plunket & Bp. of Meath. *15th.* (Residence begins R.H.) Funeral proc. began at 11. Walked with J.W.R.G. & Captain Bainbridge. Left Armagh 2.10. *16th.* Reach Cork at 2.0 a.m. Funeral in Cath. 11 a.m. Lunch w. L.A. L-N at 3.0. Called on the 2 Aunts & Rev. Powell. *17th.* Left at 10 p.m. Went to Shelbourne at 4 a.m. *18th.* Bkf. at 5 N'bk Rd. Archbp. 11.0. Lunch at Raheny. Left for Kingstown 7.0. Bkf. w. K. Reach E'brne 11.40. Very tired, bad cold.

In three days he was back to work and play again in Cambridge. He made his first journey on the Continent—Switzerland and Italy —in company with Professor Armitage Robinson and Symes Thompson (who followed his father as a leading chest specialist in London). The discovery of a Muratorian Fragment and Hexapla manuscript in the Ambrose Library in Milan, and of a Pionius manuscript and a 'curious palimpsest' in Venice were the highlights of sixteen days' strenuous and glorious travel. 'It had for him all the thrill of first adventure. I do not think,' adds Mrs. Gregg, 'that any travels ever quite came up to that first journey abroad.'

In the Michaelmas term of 1895 he had entered Ridley Hall, Cambridge. Here he was as fortunate in his preceptor as he had been at Christ's College, for the Hall's famous first Principal, Handley Carr Glyn Moule, was still in office; four years later he became Bishop of Durham. Of the subjects in the syllabus for Ordination Gregg already knew a good deal; he now set himself to learn Hebrew, and in a year acquired sufficient knowledge of a strange language to pass an elementary examination in it. Students were required to submit written sermons twice or thrice each term to the Principal for criticism, and Dr. Moule's criticisms of Gregg's early efforts may well surprise any who ever heard him preach at any time, and for whom the words 'rhetoric' or 'emotion' would be the last they would apply.

Oct. 1895. The matter is good, and the manner often good too. But you would gain greatly by two things—a definite arrangement, and somewhat shorter sentences. Both are great helps to listening and remembering.

Nov. 1895. My *one* criticism is that the style is sometimes too uniform in its rate, so to speak; too constantly rapid and (in a good sense of the word) rhetorical. It wd. be better to listen to and remember for being here and there (to quote Cicero) *sermo lenis minimeque pertinax.* The matter is very good; the style only needing more variety.

Feb. 1896. An excellent sermon. All that occurs to me as criticism is that it ends away from the text. The second part shd., I think, have been shorter, so as to allow you to return with fresh force to the subject, and to close with it. The first part is really very good. I hope it may be preached verbatim some day.

May 1896. I have little to criticize—*nothing* as to the matter of the Sermon. And the arrangement is good, clear, and 'rememberable.' But I think you will gain by deliberately aiming, as a corrective, at a style more dry and matter-of-fact! . . . The warm, moving life of your style will be the more felt for being restrained.

Whether it was by this advice that Gregg profited or not, certain it is that few pulpit utterances can have been more terse and unemotional than his.

In June 1896 he submitted to Dr. Moule a remarkable and original paper on the Greek of 1 Peter, discovering close parallels in its phrasing with those on the Person of Christ in the Nicene Creed. The Principal's comment was: 'I have read this with the greatest pleasure. The form is very good and ingenious, and the working-out just right.'

In common-room debates on the social and political problems of the day he could indulge with less restraint his flair for rhetoric in the classical mode. Such verbiage as this, for example, would have been a positive pain to him a few years later: 'To pass from a picture whose horizon is dark and lowering, but in whose gloom the weary watchers can at last descry faint streaks of a tardy sunrise, we approach the world to-day.' The cast of his mind, too, was less moulded than it became in later years. In supporting a proposal (oddly worded) 'that the formation of individualism to parties is prejudicial to the country,' he says:

> Parties political and sects religious, trusts and syndicates, cliques and sets . . . they rise and fall like corks in a pond, rising with every ripple, but moving forward never an inch. Is this life, or is it death? Some would style it the harmony of the members of a living body; I would liken it to a swarm of parasites gloating over a rotting carcase. . . .

> We rest in the privileges of one faith; but we have a curious way of promoting it. Some people won't have bishops and we call them schismatics; some ask for an infallible guide and we cry 'No Popery.' . . .

> Union is strength, and if a rallying point be sought for, we may find it in the union of all who love in the service of all who suffer.

The burden of his parable is that co-operation is more wholesome to the body politic than competition, that unity in diversity has greater coherence than uniformity. If in after years the cares of episcopal office, and therewith a certain attitude of exclusiveness, caused that early vision to be seen 'in a receding light,' it remained with him to the end as the ultimate goal of Christian endeavour, even though its realization lay beyond our present horizon. We find among his papers a scribbled note in pencil, undated: 'The order of bishops, priests and deacons represents no more than the machinery of the Church; it is ineffectual unless filled with the Spirit.' We cannot imagine that he would have expressed himself thus in later years, or at least without some qualification, when for him Order had come to stand as the sole repository—even the prerequisite—of Faith; the threefold ministry as the very being—not merely the well-being—of the Church. Christian Faith could express itself in modes so dissimilar as Eastern Orthodox and Spanish Reformed; but since both could claim historic continuity in the line of apostolic succession, the cause of both must be espoused in the World Council of Churches.

Gregg left his mark in Cambridge. He was Select Preacher to the University in 1916, 1921 and 1929, and at Ridley Hall on its fifteenth Reunion in 1926. On 22 June 1909 Dr. Moule, then Bishop of Durham, gave an address in the theological college of which he had been Principal for just under twenty years. In it he recalled the names of those who were foremost in his time as Athletes, as Scholars, and as Saints. He named four Scholars, in this order: J. A. F. Gregg, A. J. Tait (his second successor as Principal), W. F. Wright (who died young), J. L. Garland (a missionary in Persia).

The thesis for which he was awarded the Hulsean Prize, *The Decian Persecution,* was published in 1897. 'It was completed in its first form before the appearance of Archbishop Benson's great study of the life and times of Cyprian, which, however, I have frequently consulted and quoted in preparing these sheets for the press.' It is noteworthy that these two writers—the one a great church leader whose days were already numbered, the other a great church leader whose work lay in the future—were alike attracted by the heroic stature and statesmanship of this great Bishop of Carthage.

The wealth of learning that informs and the literary grace that adorns Benson's *Cyprian,* itself a labour of love and the work of a life-time, overshadow the younger scholar's first essay in the same field of historical research, yet to compare small things with great, it may be said of Gregg's work that his scholarship is matched by a style of prose-writing which is worthy of its theme. And there is about his judgments a fairmindedness not always to be found in historians who are churchmen. He sees Decius as a misguided idealist; and he is as sceptical of the vituperations of Christian writers as he is of the eulogies of those who were pagan.

With the unexpected death of his uncle at Armagh whilst he was still at Ridley Hall, Gregg had no longer an influential friend in Ireland. But there was another person outside his family to whom he had earlier confided his desire for Ordination. This was John Godfrey Fitzmaurice Day, a contemporary at Pembroke College and a fellow-member of the Cambridge University Irish Society for which they both played cricket and tennis. Godfrey Day is still and will for long be remembered as the most universally beloved personality in the Church of Ireland in his generation. The paths of these two friends were destined to cross again more than once: Day was Vicar of St. Ann's in Dublin when Gregg was a Professor of Divinity there; Day succeeded Gregg as Bishop of Ossory, and preceded him for a brief five months as Primate of All Ireland.

Day now suggested to Gregg that he must meet his father Maurice Day, then Rector of St. Matthias's in Dublin (afterwards Bishop of Clogher),[4] and by him Gregg was offered an honorary curacy in that church. But this was prevented by 'some technical hitch' and Maurice Day then introduced Gregg to Charles Frederick d'Arcy, then Vicar of Ballymena, by whom he was offered the junior curacy in that northern parish.[5] To this circumstance Gregg gratefully referred in his funeral address on Godfrey Day.[6]

---

[4] *Diary entries: Cambridge 23 June 1896.* 'Lunch with Day and his father, who came to R.H. Tea with them.' *Dublin 14 October.* 'Long talk w. Rev. Day in aft.' *Dublin, 8 November.* 'Heard Rev. M. Day and Rev. d'Arcy. Archbp's refusal.' *9th.* 'Telegr. to d'Arcy.' (Meanwhile he had been frequently to church at St. Matthias's.)

[5] *Godfrey Day: Missionary, Pastor, and Primate,* by R. R. Hartford, pp. 36–7.

[6] *ibid.,* pp. 192–8.

CHAPTER III

BALLYMENA AND CORK

IT MUST BE BORNE IN MIND that the subject of this biography, though of Irish and more remotely Scottish origins, was an Englishman born and bred; and, whether for that reason or because of individual character, was conspicuous for qualities which the English rightly or wrongly are said to possess: fair-mindedness and a sense of proportion, moderation and reserve. To the question why did he decide (after some initial hesitation) to seek Holy Orders it has been answered by his daughter that, having weighed the evidence, he became intellectually convinced of the essential truth of Christianity and of the Anglican presentation of it in particular: it seemed to him rational and right. His mind was cast in a judicial mould. Not once nor twice in after years he was to confound his legal advisers by his knowledge of points of law which had escaped their notice or remembrance. It is therefore quite understandable that, on being asked by his family what he would most have wished to be had he not been Primate of All Ireland, he replied without hesitation: 'Lord Chief Justice of England.' Perhaps he would have filled the rôle of Lord High Chancellor even better; but it is by no means improbable that, had he elected for the law, either distinction would have been within his reach.

From the year 1898 he began to compile a private Book of Quotations, dating the occasion of each entry. These are most frequent during his curate years, and when it was filled they overflowed into his diaries. As an anthology of *belles lettres* they are of very unequal value, but it is not for literary excellence that they were chosen; some indeed have emotional overtones that he would have shrunk from displaying in public. The collection, though it does no justice to the range and wealth of his learning, is valuable to a biographer as a reflex of the inner man. The quotations are such as would be made by any one with deep religious feeling and strong moral sense, but they do not evince any real profundity of thought. They are drawn almost exclusively from nineteenth century English poets and prose-writers, including fragments of translations from the Sacred Books of the East. But of European philosophers —ancient, mediaeval, or modern—there is no quotation save one from Plato in the *Gorgias* (and it by no means the best that might be chosen), and one from Epictetus. Of poets it is Browning who takes precedence, with excerpts chiefly from 'Paracelsus' (one even from the obscure 'Sordello,' and another from 'The Ring and the Book'); but the more intelligible, more meditative and less positive Tennyson is not far behind. Among moralists it is from George Eliot (a professed agnostic) that most, and indeed some of the noblest, maxims are taken both in prose and verse—as also from Matthew Arnold. One's impression is that these gleanings from the harvests of other minds are made with a view to corroborating a faith which is already assured and has never been seriously assailed by the tempests of doubt; has never known with Browning what it is to 'stoop into a dark tremendous sea of cloud,' and can never have had to confess with Tennyson, 'I falter where I firmly trod.' Another point to remark is the compiler's unexpectedly keen interest in the nature and purpose of Art, the meaning of Beauty, the function of Imagination—and here Ruskin is laid under contribution most often.

Gregg was ordained deacon and licensed as curate of the Parish Union of Ballymena and Ballyclug, Co. Antrim, on St. Thomas's Day (20 December) 1896 in St. Luke's, Belfast, by the Bishop of Down (Welland); and priest a year later in Carrickfergus by the same bishop.

Ballymena was not then the important urban centre that it since became; there were several country houses and much social activity: dinner-parties, garden-parties, amateur concerts, 'soirées' and the like, and Gregg's diary has references to 'Mr. de Pauley's Choir.' There was plenty of lawn tennis and croquet in the summer, hockey and indoor badminton in the winter. Bicycles were the main means of locomotion for week-day visiting, but an outside-car was requisitioned to convey the clergyman on duty at Ballyclug to the little church there on Sunday afternoons, and here the junior curate was very welcome since he not only officiated but played the harmonium. The lot of a country clergyman in those days was both fuller and at the same time more leisured than it is in these. Holidays were on a generous scale: a full calendar month in the summer, with ten days after Easter and again in the late autumn. Gregg would seem to have taken his duties in his stride: preparing his sermons with care, attending with regularity the meetings of the various church organizations, and visiting conscientiously— though his constitutional shyness must have been an embarrassment. He seems to have been adept at economizing time in travel. His holidays were spent mainly at home with his mother in Eastbourne, dutifully interesting himself in her concerns, with always a few days with old associates at Cambridge and sometimes at

C

Bedford, besides looking in upon various relations in England and Ireland *en route*.

There were giants in those days in the Church of Ireland and in the University of Dublin. It was an age of outstanding individuals who were also individualists, and by no means always in agreement. And one cannot feel that there was much common ground between the Rector of Ballymena and his new curate. It is known that Gregg had always an immense respect for d'Arcy's intellectual attainments, and admiration for his personal character, but little or none for his capacity as an administrator. He would surely have appreciated d'Arcy's liberalism in the realms of thought, but not the same quality when manifested in the field of practice. And indeed there was to come a day when the elder as Archbishop of Armagh and the younger as Archbishop of Dublin were to be drawn into open conflict at a General Synod. Both were temperamentally remote and withdrawn, in the sense of being unable to 'rub shoulders' with their fellows; but in all other respects they were very different. Gentle, dreamy, idealistic, d'Arcy's mental and moral virtues were of a kind more fitted to grace the Chair of a Professor of Philosophy than the rôle of a leader of the Church. His range of interests was wide: mathematician, metaphysician, religious moralist, classicist, he was also a field naturalist, an authority on birds and plants (of which latter he collected specimens in Ireland that had been believed to be extinct); a skilled mountaineer and a Shakesperian scholar. As a philosopher d'Arcy has a reputation in the academies of Europe which Gregg as a theologian never achieved; but Gregg was much the greater of the two as a Prelate.

In his autobiography *Adventures of a Bishop* (lamentably inadequate as a self-portrait) it was d'Arcy's boast that the curates of Ballymena in his day were 'hand-picked'; and two of them certainly justified that appellation. Arthur Edwin Ross, a year senior in the parish to Gregg, had been a classical scholar and theological exhibitioner at Trinity, as well as a notable athlete. He married May Hezlet, famous as the three years' woman golf champion. His Rector wrote of him: 'A man of great physical strength, a first-rate football and rowing man, his influence among men was indeed notable: and it was due not only to his splendid manhood, but to his sincere and unaffected goodness and utter straightness.' He followed d'Arcy as his curate in St. Anne's, Belfast, before becoming Rector of Portrush; returned to Ballymena as Rector, and served as an army chaplain in the Great War during which he was awarded the Military Cross with Bar; and became Bishop of Tuam in 1920.

Yet it was not he, but Gregg, who on 3 October 1897 founded the Ballymena Church Lads' Brigade with an initial muster of forty-two. Gregg often asked Ross to address the lads, and his diary notes with evident appreciation the occasions when his colleague did so. The names of visiting preachers are also noted in his diary: we find those of Canon J. B. Crozier and the Revd. J. I. Peacocke. Among other notable persons whom he met by chance in these years were Sir George White (soon after hero of Ladysmith), and Roger Casement (future Irish patriot and British traitor). The titles and authors of books read each year are sedulously entered in his diaries, but without comment except in one case, which is not without interest: 'finished Kingsley's *Hereward*: Ch. xli a very great piece of writing.'

It was during these years at Ballymena that he began his researches into the manuscripts of patristic texts. Having gone to Cambridge in March 1898 to take his M.A. degree, and having spent a day with his friend Jocelyn Perkins at Ely, he returned to the University and 'discussed "Catenae" question with J.A.R.' He then applied for and received a travel-grant from the Hort Fund enabling him to work in the Paris Library in an endeavour to restore the complete text of Origen's *Commentary on the Epistle to the Ephesians* by a study of 'Catenae.' Working concentratedly between 10 a.m. and 4 p.m. for seven days (and spending the evenings in seeing most of all the architectural and other wonders that Paris can show) he 'succeeded in restoring thirty-nine fragments which undoubtedly were Origen's; and established that Chrysostom was responsible for nearly all that were anonymous.' The result of his work under the title 'Catenae' was published in the *Expository Times* of March 1899 (Vol. X, p. 281f.). It was preliminary to a completer work under the full title 'A Reconstruction of Origen upon the Epistle to the Ephesians,' published in the *Journal of Theological Studies* serially in 1902–3 (Vol. III, pp. 233–44, 389–420, 554–76), which in 1913 gained him a Doctorate in Divinity in the University of Dublin.

In 1899 also he published in book form his translation, with introduction and notes, of the *Epistle of Clement of Rome*. He had been attracted thereto by the undoubted genuineness and antiquity of this earliest of sub-apostolic writings; by the recent discovery of MSS., including a Latin translation, corroborating and supplementing the single MS. previously known; and by the refutation which this document provides of the Tübingen hypothesis of a supposed rivalry between St. Peter and St. Paul. He thanks Professors Armitage Robinson and Rendel Harris for their advice and help.

He read several papers to the Ballymena Clerical Union, always on a high level. One of the most interesting is on Tennyson. He makes the point that there are four characteristics of this great poet to be borne in mind when reading his works: stateliness, scholarliness, sorrowfulness, speculativeness.

During the last fortnight in June 1899 he took half his summer holiday in the south-west of Ireland. It proved to be momentous. He spent the Sunday at Glengarriff 'and after aft. service went to tea at the Parsonage. Rev. Carey appointed in 1863 by John Cork.' Then to Cork where he lunched with the Bishop (Meade), visited the Cathedral, and called on the Dean (Bruce)—'and he made offer' [of post of Curate and Residentiary Preacher]. Then to Limerick where he 'had tea with cousin James [Gregg]' who took him for a walk and to the Cathedral. Thence to Kilkenny (his first visit there) where he breakfasted with the Bishop (Crozier) and 'looked at old books in [St. Canice's] Library.' Then to Dublin and back to Ballymena—'end of a most pleasant holiday.' On the following Monday—'finally accepted Dean Bruce's offer.'

He began the second part of his holidays at the end of August by briefly revisiting Cork, to inspect his future quarters in the Cathedral Library; 'took measurements, and chose wall-papers,' and played on the Cathedral organ. Then across to London and down to Eastbourne, in time to watch the tennis tournaments.

He left Ballymena on 30 September, and began his duties next day in Cork with morning Sunday School, Church Lads' Brigade, and a sermon in the evening. His diary notes: 'Income from Jan. 1, '97–Sept. 30, '99, at rate of £120 + £50 per ann. From Oct. 1, '99—at rate of £160 + £45 per ann.' He had seen a good deal of Co. Antrim during his first curacy and used to say that the experience was of great value to him when he returned to adminster the northern province.

The present Bishop of Down and Dromore (Dr. F. J. Mitchell), formerly for many years Rector of Ballymena, took occasion in 1949 to invite his Archbishop to revisit the parish. He did so; inspected the Church Lads' Brigade which he had founded; expressed pleased astonishment at the innovation of sung Communion; was presented by the parishioners with a roundel in inlaid mahogany emblazoned with the Coats of Arms of the dioceses over which he had presided. The occasion afforded an example of his spontaneous memory for names and faces. As he was going out after the service through the thronged churchyard, robed and in dignified procession, a woman, who had been a millworker and a member of his Bible Class more than forty years before, broke from the crowd and seized and vigorously shook his hand with both her own. 'Oh, *Mister Gregg!* We're quare and proud of you!' The stern, granite-like features relaxed, the large brown eyes lit up, his whole face broke into a happy smile. 'Lizzie!' he said.

Bishop Mitchell asked another woman how she remembered him as a young man, and was answered: 'He was a lovely big fella with black wavy hair and the purtiest eyes ye ever seen.'

§

Gregg's duties as Curate and Residentiary Preacher of Cork Cathedral were sufficiently onerous, especially during the winter months. On Sundays in addition to the morning routine, a young men's Bible Class at 10.15, and the evening sermon which was especially his own. At certain seasons a devotional address (the 'Thresher Lecture') at the early Celebration on Sunday, which, during Lent, would involve a special course. Each week-night, except Saturday, was occupied in some way. The Church Lads' Brigade on Monday. The Cork Young Men's Association, generally requiring an address, on Tuesday. The mid-week service and sermon on Wednesday. On Friday nights Confirmation Classes in their season. There were also occasional meetings of the Essay and Debating Club, the Choir Guild, or some other organization. He devoted Saturday to the preparation of his Sunday sermon which was always written in full, and when, as sometimes happened, he was due to preach also in the morning and had not completed the writing of it before midnight he would rise at 5 a.m. to get it done in good time.

One of his duties was the distribution of a weekly charity to certain old women who waited to receive it on a bench in a corner of the north transept. The bench it still there, and so is a small desk in the vestry, the lid of which is cut neatly into squares, now varnished all over. The squares were cut by the Curate sixty-two years ago to enclose rolled pennies—thirty in each roll—which represented the amount of alms due to each pensioner every Monday morning. He would often keep them waiting twenty or thirty minutes, for in such details he was liable to be absent-minded.

The verger, Mr. Thomas Perrott, who shows these relics, was junior verger of St. Fin Barre's then. He will say of this particular Curate that he was 'a most distant man'; he would pass one in the Cathedral grounds without noticing one or saying a word; yet one liked him when one got to know him and realized that he was a good man inside. In some ways he lacked consideration. He would pay the vergers their weekly wages, as he paid the old female pensioners, in piles of coppers taken from the collection, keeping the silver coins for deposit in the bank. The senior verger did not object to this but the junior did, and said as much; whereupon Mr. Gregg at once perceived his error and did not repeat it.

It was easy to summon him when necessary, for he was visibly either out or in. His custom was to sit hour after hour in the window (second on the right on the ground floor of the Library, and within full view from the door of the Chapter Room), wrapped in an overcoat in winter, with his back against one shutter and his feet against the other and a book propped on his bent knees between them—reading, reading, reading. If he was not to be seen there, then he was out visiting. His housekeeper used to send a boy out every evening for a pint of porter—a penny for the porter and a halfpenny for himself; which was strictly against the rules, but Mr. Gregg knew nothing of it. (In point of fact he did, as his diary shows.) People flocked to hear him when he preached those anti-Roman sermons, and the Cathedral was crowded. To the question what was he like as a preacher at other times, the reply was: 'He'd put you to sleep!' [1]

It would certainly require a wide-awake and alert intelligence to appreciate his discourses. They were too substantial in content, and also too measured in delivery, to be followed unless with full and undivided attention. They were in fact lectures in the guise of homilies. It is remarkable how very often paragraphs are introduced by the didactic conjunction 'Now.' From the outset he spoke with authority and decisiveness; and to those who listened, his sermons were as startling as they were forcible. For his teaching was and remained to the end modernist in the best sense of a word that has become, to the reactionary, old-fashioned; and there is no doubt that he must have come like a breath of fresh air, almost a tornado, into the precincts that still echoed, so to speak, with the undertone of his grandfather's minatory declamations. It is noteworthy that his texts both here and at Ballymena were taken only from the New Testament, with but two or three exceptions at most, and these from the Psalms. There are few now living who remember; but Mrs. Barry Deane is one, and she writes:

> Dr. Gregg was often a guest at my parents' house and we always attended his evening services which were crowded when he was preaching. The Dean listened with a certain amount of anxiety to the learned but often unusual sermons of his brilliant curate and, according to general report, finally insisted on these being submitted to him before being delivered.

[1] Mr. Perrott, after the best part of a life-time devoted to St. Fin Barre's, died in 1962.

His own diary bears witness to the first of these statements, but is silent as to the second. After the first two weeks he notes the congregation as 'large,' soon 'very large,' then comes the entry 'enormous.'

All his addresses, though evidently written at full speed, were very carefully prepared, with much revision. Some of the best of them were for the Young Men's Association, and actually delivered to half a dozen or less while the majority amused themselves in the adjoining gymnasium in which he himself (says Mr. Perrott) took no interest. Nevertheless his friend Hearn (later Bishop of Cork) used to say that he once watched Gregg swarm up a rope from the gym. floor to the ceiling. His addresses were certainly on a high level and far above the heads of untutored youth. The subject of the first is on the faculty of Wonder; and, though the religious *motif* is not mentioned in it, it had the effect of turning the mind of one young listener, W. C. Cooke (afterwards a well-known Cork solicitor), from agnosticism to faith. The manuscripts of his sermons and addresses are so freely interspersed with Greek, either for the sake of brevity or emphasis, and with never an accent omitted or misplaced, as to give one the impression that the New Testament was as familiar to him in the original as in translation. Sometimes too his diary entries are written in Greek, and so rapidly as to show that he could even think in that language. These entries occur when he has something private to record: as for example when his housekeeper was so drunk that he had to take his meals out or prepare them himself and fetch the water!

He had a proper sense of family pride. On 4 August 1898 his diary notes: 'Centenary of birth of John Gregg.' It notes the day on which he received from his distant cousin in Limerick 'the genealogical tables,' and on 11 November 1899: 'cousin James Gregg appointed Dean of Limerick.' In one of his addresses to young men he says that a sense of family pride may, for lack of a worthier motive, be an incentive to achievement, or a deterrent from vice.

Soon after his arrival in Cork he began taking weekly lessons in Italian. The reason for this becomes apparent in May 1900 when he joined A. E. Ross in London for a three weeks' intensive tour of Rome: and other cities containing venerated relics of antiquity. His next year's holiday was spent again in Paris, revisiting its famous galleries, completing his work on 'Origen in Eph.'; and commencing 'Origen in 1 Cor.' He was also at this time engaged on a critical comparison of the version of Origen with that of Jerome. In May 1902 he was again in Italy and Venice, repairing some omissions of his previous visits and inspecting sundry other libraries. At the Library in Venice he worked on the manuscripts of St. Bernard of Clairvaux.

Partly as pecuniary aid towards his travelling expenses, and partly for less mundane reasons, he had since his first year in Cork given private tuition in Greek to a young bank clerk named Sullivan, who had confided in him an earnest wish to become ordained. Gregg at first raised every kind of argument to dissuade him, but, finding him proof against these, promoted Sullivan's aim in every possible way. This was in fact the beginning of one of the very few friendships of Gregg's life. Long afterwards when Sullivan had served for many years as a hard-working Rector in the diocese of Dublin where his former patron was now Archbishop, it was a cause for wonder that when canonries were vacant he was passed over while those junior to him received preferment; the reason—abhorrence on the part of both of any suspicion of favouritism—was known only to a few. But when the Archdeaconry of Dublin became vacant it was no matter of surprise that Sullivan was appointed; his capacity and experience made him the obvious choice. More than once when he fell sick and was without a deputy to take the Sunday services the Archbishop stepped down to fill the breach. Sullivan loved to recall how in their younger days in Cork his tutor would end a lesson in Greek by leaning his gaunt frame against the mantelshelf in the Library and would then declaim from memory long passages of Homer, and say, 'Isn't that beautiful?'

We read in Gregg's diary of cricket and summer camps with his Lads, of tennis and croquet tournaments, and of ping-pong. In the summer of 1902 croquet is frequent at Brookfield, a house which in those days stood in splendid isolation well outside the city boundary. His partner was invariably the daughter of the house, Anna Jennings. The story of his courtship is confided to a day-to-day script in Greek and, since it was not intended for the public eye, it will not be recorded here. Suffice it that they were engaged, after some hesitation on her part, on 6 August. Her niece, Miss Margaret Jennings, now the mistress of Brookfield, relates that she and her two small brothers were so incensed by the effrontery of this tall black clergyman in coming to rob them of their beloved aunt Anna, that on the occasion of his next visit they hid in a shrubbery and pelted him with mud-pies as he came up the drive. He paused to 'reprove' them, but not severely, and mud-bespattered as he was disappeared into the house and for a while they saw him no more.

The marriage took place quietly in the Cathedral on 26 November, the Dean and the Revd. Alan Lucas officiating; and after a three weeks' honeymoon in London, having purchased furnishings, they returned to Cork to make the Library a habitable home.

Now, sixty years later, their elder daughter writes of her mother:

My father had an almost old-fashioned admiration for women who were competent, kindly, and enlightened; but silly women were beyond his comprehension. (Silly men, too—though his forbearance rarely allowed any more caustic comment than 'The man is a silly ass.') He had a really profound respect for 'the wives of the Rectory'—for their work for the Church, so often with small recognition, rearing their families and doing so much parish work while too often in a position of pitiful financial stringency. He would point out that the word 'lady' in its origin meant 'she who serves.' How true this was of clerical wives.

And more true of none than of Anna Alicia Jennings whom he married in 1902. A bright, lively, intelligent girl, the youngest of four girls in a family of seven. Her father, a not very business-like Cork business-man, had died and left his wife to repair the family fortunes by competent management. This she did, and all the family got a sound education—the boys at Cambridge, the girls at English schools. Anna went to Clifton—back and forth each term alone in the Cork to Bristol boat: there must have been many nightmare crossings in those days, with few comforts and safeguards. Anna wanted to go to a University and reached entrance standard, but was unable to continue because of eye-strain. Instead, she worked for a number of years in the Cambridge Settlement in Bethnal Green—a very courageous choice of career then for a girl used to comforts and a gay social life. So when they married she proved a wonderful complement to him; her more natural upbringing was a useful corrective to his rigid early training, and her knowledge of the depths of misery of the poor, and of the escapades and extravagances of the better-off, filled in many gaps in his experience. She was a splendid person, immensely kind and supremely sensible, efficient in daily life and unperturbed in a crisis, a most knowledgable housekeeper and admirable administrator. In those days of large households a gift for administration was invaluable, especially where an ordered household had to be run on limited means.

She had the crafts of hand and eye which he lacked. We as a family felt that his manual dexterity was tested to its limit if he so much as changed an electric light bulb. My mother was a dressmaker, embroiderer and needlewoman; a photographer, a cook, an enthusiastic and excellent amateur gardener, a painter in her younger days. Her girls she started in all these crafts—and how we have blessed her! —and in fishing, tennis, hockey, we had her encouragement. She firmly believed that every woman should have a training sufficient to enable her to earn her own living.

In spite of different temperaments Mum and Dad were a personification of love and authority, with whom there was no trifling and little fear. We were trusted, and it worked. Discipline was fair, but firm. Until later years when ill-health dogged her, Anna was the pivot of the family, splendid in her Church work, always a leader. But the family came first, and her husband first of all.

The next year passed quietly—in physical recreation with the making of a garden and croquet lawn; in mental, with organ-playing and the preparation of a critical study of 1 Corinthians 13. Concerning this he informed and consulted Dr. Armitage Robinson, now Dean of Westminster, on a special visit for the purpose. His sermons were however beginning to prove 'intractable' and required 'gouging out'—sometimes one composition is 'rejected' and torn up, and another substituted late on a Saturday night. There were anxieties too about his wife's health; but relief and thankfulness with the birth of their first child, John Francis Fitzgerald Gregg, on 21 September 1903.

His first essay in New Testament exegesis is illustrative of his critical acumen and instinct for logicality—expecting structural coherence even in the utterance of religious genius in a moment of ecstasy. It exemplifies too an attitude of mind which was to become habitual with him: a strong aversion from individualism and subjectivity, and an emphasis on the necessity of corporate or social activity in the Christian life. It speaks well for his own balanced judgment that, on receiving from his old tutor a verdict unfavourable to a paper on which he had spent such pains and which he intended for publication, he put it away and thought no more about it.

On Saturday 16 April 1904 he 'had by midday post an important letter from Dr. Peile (Master of Christ's College) causing a recrudescence of Cambridge hopes.' This was advice to apply for a vacant junior Fellowship at his old College. But the next Monday was the last date by which the application should be sent in. He therefore crossed on the Monday night, and reached Cambridge the following afternoon, dined with the Master, and 'prospects seem hopeful.' After two days there he returned (breaking the journey at Bedford) and noted: 'I am very hopeful, tho' in complete uncertainty. Neither Master, nor Dean, tho' sympathetic, would commit themselves.' For a month he 'watched with some anxiety for news of election.' Then on 19 May: 'Saw notice in

Morning Post, re Fellowship, given to A. V. Valentine Richards';
and added in Greek, 'Hopes are fled' and later, again in Greek,
'Rather grieved at what has happened.'

On 4 June came a letter from Dr. Bernard suggesting that he
apply for the Wardenship of St. Columba's College. After discussing this with his Dean he decided to do so, and sent in five
testimonials including one from Dean Armitage Robinson and
another from his old Vicar, Bishop d'Arcy. But on the 29th his
hopes were again disappointed. Next he sent in his name to the
Board of Nomination for the vacant incumbency of St. Ann's,
Shandon, to which in due course the Revd. Robert Thomas Hearn
was appointed. It completed a trio of 'possibilities withheld this
year.' Hearn had been ordained in 1898 in St. Fin Barre's for the
curacy of Youghal; he had, besides the reputation of a good pastor,
the distinction of a Doctorate in Laws. He was to continue as
Rector of Shandon for thirty-four years, when he was elected
Bishop of Cork. The appointment of his competitor for nomination
to this parish was to prove for Gregg the beginning of another of
the very few close friendships of his life. To those who knew them
both, the concord of two men with temperaments so apparently
dissimilar was always somewhat incomprehensible.

Some of the most edifying of his discourses in Cork Cathedral
are his Lenten lecture-series. He took as his subject for those in
1905, 'The Church.' Though his language is terse, it is so forceful
as to be at times almost impassioned. No high churchman could
have taken a higher view of the Church than he, as 'that wonderful
and sacred mystery,' divinely instituted, commissioned and em-
powered.

> He is not speaking [he informs his hearers] of the Church of
> England or of Ireland, or of the Roman Church or the Greek
> Church, but of *that one Holy Catholic Apostolic Church* which
> is built up of the great Society of those human souls who have
> been baptized into the three-fold Name, who acknowledge Christ
> as their Lord, and share in one Life which the Holy Spirit gives
> to the Body of Christ. For the Church *is* the Body of Christ; it
> is in truth the extension of His Incarnation. With the coming
> of the Holy Ghost at Pentecost Christ joined the Church to
> Himself in an unbreakable unity. He penetrates the Church so
> completely that there is not one of His divine attributes that it
> need lack. It is a living organism, visibly organized. An organism
> is vaster than the sum of its parts. Its parts are interrelated. It
> is not merely a place of refuge or escape for sick souls; but a
> distributing centre of radiant life-giving energy. 'Religion is the
> concern of a man with his Maker'—that slogan of the individual-

ist—is one of the most unChristian of all half-truths. Christian and Churchman are convertible terms; an unattached Christian is a monstrosity.

Baptism is placed at the forefront of every Christian life as an *assurance*: the declaration of a fact that was a fact already: 'You *are* God's child; live as such.' [It is of interest that Gregg here tacitly adopts F. W. Robertson's comparison of baptism with coronation.] Baptism *introduces* the child into the Unity, and Holy Communion *establishes* him in the Fellowship, of the whole family of God. Holy Communion is the supreme occasion which manifests the unity of the corporate life of the Body of Christ. The elements are *sacraments*—outward visible *signs* of inward spiritual grace; outward and inward are not to be confused, as in transubstantiation.

Though every member of the Church is a priest because he is a member of Christ's Body, yet the Church has commissioned official priests, as representative of them all, to conduct its forms of worship, who derive their authority in unbroken historical succession from the apostles. Though the life of the Church in its catholicity is Scriptural, Episcopal and Sacramental, yet many of its forms of worship are incidental. Not all churchmen are bound by the Book of Common Prayer or the Thirty-nine Articles, which are of local use or historic interest for us.

The authority of the Church rests on the Bible, as rule; Creeds, for faith; Observance of the Lord's day, for corporate worship; the three-fold Ministry—apostolic succession; the Sacraments—initiation and fellowship-act. Anything beyond these requisites of faith and practice is not essential. The Church is at liberty to revise its formularies.[2]

The argument proceeds with logical precision step by step. Granted the major premiss—that spiritual gifts, graces, powers, are tactually or manually conveyed—the conclusion that 'Christian and Churchman are convertible terms' is inevitable. And this was Gregg's unalterable conviction to the end of his days. He would certainly not have subscribed the document entitled 'Intercommunion' addressed by thirty-two Anglican divines to the Archbishops of Canterbury and York on 1 November, 1961, stating that the historic doctrine of episcopacy represents a serious oversimplification of a complex problem. He would probably have countered: Then what alternative, precisely, do you propose?

[2] The above is all too condensed a summary of the substance of five full lectures packed with doctrinal teaching. And although it is so very 'definite' in tone, a point worth remarking is that the books which he notes as having read while preparing them are works of some of the most 'liberal' among nineteenth century Christian writers: Stanley, *Christian Institutions;* Rashdall, *Christus in Ecclesia;* Robertson, *Life and Letters;* Hort, *Cambridge and other sermons.*

He had been in 1904 immersed in a study of the Book of Wisdom, noting especially its influence on the Christology of St. Paul and St. John, even in similarities of phrasing. He made it the theme of a course of three week-night lectures during Advent; the novelty of the subject attracted an audience of some thirty people. He also discoursed more learnedly upon the critical and theological importance of the Book, to the diocesan Clerical Society. In the following year he read through the works of Philo as a necessary side-line; and for mental recreation the whole of Diogenes Laertius (parts of which he found amusing), and of Epictetus (through life his most admired among ancient moralists).

The result of this study was the production of a solid article entitled 'The Relation of the Discourses in the Fourth Gospel to the Book of Wisdom' in which a formidable array of close parallels in phrasing are set side by side. This he submitted to the editor of the *Journal of Theological Studies,* then Professor J. F. Bethune-Baker of Pembroke College, Cambridge. On 11 December 1904 it was received and read by him with great interest, and accepted with minor and judicious suggestions as to arrangement, which Gregg adopted. Too late for publication in January the paper was deferred for insertion in the next quarterly issue, and on 22 March 1905 the first revision was corrected and passed for press. But on the 28th Bethune-Baker wrote:

I am extremely sorry to tell you that my colleague as Editor of the *Journal* has taken a violent dislike to your article on the relation between St. John's Gospel and Wisdom, and that he is supported by one of the most influential of the Oxford directors to whom I referred the matter. They both beg that it shall not appear in the *Journal,* and in view of their feeling about it I do not feel that I can publish it. . . .

He suggests its publication as a small pamphlet, and adds that he will be glad to be of any service in arranging matters with the Press. But Gregg went no further in the matter, and the corrected final proof of his paper has lain hidden till now.

One of his duties was that of chaplain to the gaol. To this was added in the spring of 1905 constant self-imposed visits to the cell of a condemned murderer. To a man of Gregg's acute sensitivity this must have been excessively painful, but he never spared himself or his feelings in the fulfilment of a recognized duty. During the last week (Holy Week) he visited the man every day, and rose on Easter Sunday at 5.30 that he might attend him for an hour before the early Celebration at 7; on Easter Monday again at 5 a.m. and again late the same night, before the execution early on the Tuesday. He wrote in his diary that he marvelled at the condemned man's composure.

The last two holidays of his curacy were spent with his wife in Switzerland and in the far south-west of County Cork. On 16 February 1906 their second son was born, and named Claude John Montgomery Gregg.

He had now been nearly ten years a curate and, conscious as he could not help being of powers far beyond those of the rank and file of the clergy, the time of his apprenticeship must have seemed to him unconscionably long. His seniors were evidently of the same opinion, but felt that he was much better qualified for academic than for parochial work. He still regarded England as his natural—or spiritual—home; he is frequently in Cambridge, 'dining at the Don's table' and meeting some of the eminent scholars of the day. But Ireland did not want to lose him. On 29 June 1906 he 'telegraphed application for Chair of Biblical Greek, on hearing fr. Dr. Gwynn.' A few days later, however, he heard that the election was postponed till October. On 18 October: 'heard from Bishop d'Arcy urging me to send name again for Prof. of Bibl. Greek. Did so.' But nine days later: 'Rec. news that Prof. Bibl. Greek goes not to me but to N. J. D. White.'

The following extracts from a prepared paper on 'The Basis of Religious Certainty,' read at a Cork Religious Meeting on 7 May 1903, are cited here to show the *aliveness* of his mind.

The basis of religious certainty is the individual consciousness. . . .

A certainty that rests on authority only, whether the authority of a book, such as the Bible, or the authority of a body such as the Church, or the authority of a fact or of a person may have a certain temporary value, but it is only temporary. It may constrain the man, but it doesn't enlarge him—at any rate, only indirectly. . . .

Spiritual teaching, taken on authority only—professed from sense of obedience and not from sense of its intrinsic worth—is a spiritual thing outside me. Faith is the individual's apprehension of truth: and where you accept a thing because you are told to do it, there is no apprehension—no personal consent, and therefore no faith, only servitude. And that is not enough: for not submission, but self-direction is the ultimate end of life. . . .

But the real faith—or the real spiritual vision—is that which sees into truth and sees through truth—which needs not to be told 'Thus saith the Lord'—which needs not to count heads or know the utterer's name before it accepts a thing—leaps at a truth

by sheer intuition, seems in league with the truth by some natural
and eternal compact. . . .

[For example,] Abraham was inspired we say, because he was
so made that he alone in a dark age was able to see that God
was a spiritual being. His distinction, his inspiration lay in that he
staked his all on a truth that was never for a moment in doubt
with him. This, of course, is no explanation of how Abraham
was what he was. It is simply a reminder that his composition
differed from that of his contemporaries, because it was ahead
of them. He had it in him to be what they had not—in his
generation, he was a spiritual freak, a sudden variation to a
higher type.

It was the same with the Isaiahs, and Hoseas, and John
Baptists: the same with Buddha and Confucius and Zoroaster,
the same with Savonarola and Luther: it was not that their
truth rested for them on an authority outside them: but, what
verified to them the message they felt impelled to proclaim was
the witness of their inner consciousness. . . .

The great aim of life is to know truth for what it is—at first
hand; to have it in you for your own. Any one who rests on
authority and lets it steer him surrenders the right of growth
which is the only justification for living.

We are put here to be educated and enhanced—and second-
hand truth will only do that in a very small degree.

We must all begin, of course, by accepting truth at second
hand, just as the child has to receive its daily bread for years
before it has strength to earn it. But once men and women receive
second-hand truth and rest in it, and think that it is enough to
accept it and that there is no necessity to interrogate it—they
have cut themselves off from real progress, and therefore from
the true end of religion. . . .

Authority is anything but discredited. It has played a stupen-
dous part in the past, because while the Newman class always
outweighs the Westcott class beyond all proportion, it helps the
intuition-obeying minds by rendering them dissatisfied, while it
rules the authority-obeying minds by taking all initiative out of
their hands. Authority has a most beneficent part to play, provided always it be remembered that it is only a temporary and
provisional makeshift.

For the postulate at the bottom of my argument is that human
nature may know itself to be a partaker of the Divine—'that
Heaven kindly gave our blood a moral flow'—that truth is not
alien to us but natural, so much so that Plato suggested that all
our learning of it was merely a recalling to memory of things
learnt before our incarnation here. . . .

Truth does not need such support as the *ipse dixit* of the
Bible. It is not the final court of appeal for us—our consciousness is gradually and rightly usurping that place for itself. The

Bible is a storehouse of spiritual truth: we can never germinate and originate truth; but our duty is to take no truth offered us without sifting and weighing and questioning it, as judges. . . .

Authority has gradually trained up the human consciousness through truth received at second hand, and pondered till it is possessed at first hand, till now the human soul is 'finding itself' in increasing numbers of people, and individuality of consciousness is asserting itself as never before. A new era is dawning. An ever-expanding largeness of nature is open to men and women, according as they employ the capacity that is in them. They will feel an added sense of responsibility, as they enter on a closer personal wrestling with truth. . . .

By no means all of us will feel the difficulty of accepting an external authority. But those of us who *do*, have one point that they can start from in their reconstruction of the spiritual fabric— a rock that is unshakable by any criticism—a single vantage-point from which they can reach out into the world of spirit and the world of matter—their own individual self-consciousness.

And in his paper on 'The Theological and Critical Importance of the Book of Wisdom' given to the Cork Clerical Society on 28 March 1905 occurs the following:

Whatever verbal definitions we have of the Person of Christ are *human* and not Divine. The Synoptic Gospels present Christ, as He presented Himself, a *life* and not a formulated dogma. It is *possible* to regard the Life there presented as not necessarily more than human. . . . The distinction must be enforced between Christ, what He said about Himself, and Christ, what His interpreters say about Him. Now where do Paul and the Fourth Gospel draw the materials of their Christology from? There is a Divine and a human source. The Divine is their personal conviction that Christ was God, wrought in them by the indwelling God; but the human source is pre-existing speculation, which suddenly found itself confronted with a reality that needed clothing in words. The Wisdom-Doctrine was waiting to be used, and Paul and John drank copiously of it.

[He ends by emphasizing the point of his paper, that any statement about the Person of Christ is really symbolic, relative, approximate, an economical formula, an accommodation, shifting, liable to be displaced.]

If Christ is to be a living Christ for us, and not merely a Christ of the Apostolic Age and of past history, we must learn to distinguish carefully between *Himself*, the Divine Figure eternal in the heavens—and the *doctrines* about Him, even Bible doctrines, which are just as likely to fetter Him as to present Him. The more completely we acknowledge the *humanness* and the *occasionalness* of the N.T. *doctrines* concerning His Person, the more completely will our soul be thrown back upon *Himself*.

CHAPTER IV

RECTOR OF BLACKROCK, CORK

BUT MEANWHILE AN EVENT of an unexpected kind had supervened. On 24 September 1906 he had been unanimously appointed by the Board of Nomination to the vacant incumbency of Blackrock, a busy suburban parish between two and three miles distant from the City, and on 28 October 'began regular Sunday duty.' This gave him perhaps a little scope for the exercise of those administrative talents for which he was afterwards conspicuous; but he was still in much demand for lectures and addresses in the Cathedral. He was frequently in the company of the Rector of Shandon.

Dr. Mary E. T. Hearn who before her marriage was an international hockey-player and had qualified as a medical practitioner and whose name as 'Doctor Mary' has ever since been a household word in Cork, says of the friendship between her husband and the future Archbishop in their young days:

They always tried to attend meetings, official or other, together. Nearly every Saturday afternoon the Archbishop used to come to Cork by train from Blackrock and meet my husband in Patrick Street. He used then to go from shop to shop paying the weekly bills. He was most punctilious about debts, and would say that no money should be owed after Saturday night. He would also wax very indignant if any one paid his fare on the train or offered him a stamp for a letter. After the shopping he would walk back to Blackrock by the river-walk called the Marina.

Unfortunately I was young when he left Cork and did not have much personal contact with him. But I know that from the first he was quite outstanding in intellectual ability. It was thought at the time that he was too scholastic for parish work, but he adapted himself very rapidly and his personality made him highly esteemed by his parishioners. He was extremely kind to any one in trouble or sorrow, but his very austere manner made young people timid in their approach to him. His brother-curates used to say that 'J.A.F.' could not help his stilted voice or his distant manner since he had an English mother and was educated at an English School and University!

He was very fond of tennis and my husband and I used often to go for a game on the court in the Rectory garden at Blackrock. He was not a strong player but made up for it by his enthusiasm

49

and would go all out to win, and would dart from one side of the court to the other, letting his partner in mixed doubles know how willing he was to do all the hard work!

Miss Grace Gloster writes from Walmer in Kent:

When the Archbishop was Rector of Blackrock we lived in Monkstown, farther down the line. My sister and I had to travel to Cork by train every day (third class), and I well remember this tall thin ascetic-looking young clergyman getting into the carriage with us at Blackrock. Years later he wrote to my mother a most judicious and sympathetic letter in reply to her request to him for advice when her daughter-in-law had joined the Roman Church and was leading her granddaughters the same way. It was characteristic of his thoughtfulness and good judgment.

His diary, though brief, is an index of certain characteristics; especially his habit of exactitude. For example, the most trifling ailment is recorded; the dates of hair-cut and shampoo (always both); the expenses of a holiday, to a penny. There are hints too of pedantry. A heated discussion or debate is 'warm'; a difficult sermon is 'refractory' and if unsuitable for delivery 'rejected.' A good game of lawn tennis (never, shortly but incorrectly, just tennis) is 'very agreeable.' The weather is 'genial' or 'inclement.' But sometimes he does not disdain the use of slang: billiards is nearly always 'pills,' and children are 'kids.'

In the matter of holidays the new Rector does himself as well as he was done by in both his curacies. Nearly always these are spent in England with his mother at Eastbourne or elsewhere. But in August 1907 he is in Portrush with Ross (for whom he preaches) and together they visit Bishop and Mrs. d'Arcy who are staying near there; go picnicking; scramble about the Causeway; and are taken for 'a drive in a motor car.' Here too he meets the new Provost of Trinity (Traill)—having previously met Mahaffy in Dublin.

On 12 November 1907 was born a daughter and christened three days before Christmas, Margaret Dorothea, but on the same night she became seriously ill. For the two following nights her parents and a doctor stayed awake beside her, 'watching and praying.' On Christmas Eve there was improvement, but on Christmas Day a sharp relapse: 'my voice broke down at end of Prayer for Ch. Militant.' For several weeks the child's life was in the balance, and for a year or more a cause for anxiety.

§

All this year and the year following in such intervals as he could afford, and sometimes 'under tremendous pressure' he was hard at work revising his commentary and writing his introduction to the Book of Wisdom.

On 28 November 1904 he had received from the Master of Selwyn, Dr. A. F. Kirkpatrick (soon to be Dean of Ely), who was general editor for the Old Testament in the Cambridge Bible for Schools and Colleges, an invitation to contribute to its series an Introduction and Notes to the Revised Version of the Book of Wisdom. The scale proposed was thirty pages of introduction; and one-third text to two-thirds notes: the whole not to exceed 200 pages, and to be of interest to the intelligent English reader. By the end of May 1906 Gregg had finished his notes and sent them for comment to the editor, who in July replied that they are much too detailed and occupy a disproportionate amount of space, but that in so difficult a book as Wisdom he is prepared to make a concession, and makes suggestions based on arithmetical calculations. Several of Gregg's notes, however, are too scholarly for the average reader, and detailed suggestions for revision are made. A year later on receipt of the Introduction which he has read with much interest, the editor queries its length and its intelligibility to the Greekless reader; and finally on receipt of the first galley-proofs, begs for further reductions where possible: 'The book has gone *far* beyond the size I originally suggested.' (In the result there are sixty-one pages on Introduction; the proportion of text to notes is approximately one-sixth to five-sixths; and yet the whole is condensed into less than 200 pages.) Several other friendly letters are exchanged before final publication early in 1909. Only Kirkpatrick's side of the correspondence is preserved. In reading it one feels that no commentator could have wished for a wiser, more discerning or more erudite director, himself well familiar with the general ground of his commentator's field of study yet willing to defer to him as a specialist. At the same time one cannot but sympathize with Gregg in the difficulty of conforming to so confined a pattern. His original work must have been more suitable for the International Critical Commentary than for the purpose for which it was designed. In its simplified and much reduced form it was praised by all the reviewers as equal in excellence to any in the series, and Kirkpatrick asked his young collaborator whether he would 'be disposed to tackle 2 Esdras next.' But this Gregg apparently declined.

Despite pressure of parochial work Gregg found time for the

exercise of his intellectual energies in other ways, and in October 1908 contributed to the *Irish Church Quarterly* another learned paper, published as a pamphlet the same year: 'Judaism and Hellenism in the Second Century before Christ.' On 20 November he was invited by Professor H. B. Swete to undertake the arduous and responsible task of general editor of a Patristic Greek Lexicon, vacant through the sudden death of Dr. Redpath who had initiated it. But since the Cork Library lacked a patristic section with recent editions, and the correspondence with scholars in England would have been too great, this proved impracticable. Early in 1909 Swete wrote again saying that the Cambridge authorities were prepared, in the case of Gregg's commentary on Wisdom, to relax their general rule of non-acceptance of contributions to the Bible for Schools series as theses for the Cambridge B.D., and would welcome the receipt of two copies for consideration.

There is no doubt that Gregg was ambitious for recognition and preferment in the Church. His diary for 1909 has a page devoted to a list of sixteen events in that year which is headed '*External progress.*' The most important are: Publication of Wisdom; Delivery of R.C. Sermons; their publication; Conferring of [Cambridge] B.D. degree; Preach in St. Patrick's Cathedral, Dublin; Repr. of Cork on Gen. Synod; Runner-up 2nd time for Dio. Council; asked by R. H. Charles to do additions to Esther [1]; Runner-up for St. Patrick's Canonry.[2] There is also this note: 'During this year Hearn and I were driven into direct opposition to the New School plans, as formulated by the "Business men's sub-committee." '

On 11 January, happening to call upon Dean Bruce, he had been asked by him to 'take a course on R.C. questions' on Sunday evenings during Lent (of which there were six that year) in the Cathedral. He had little time to prepare, but took a ten days' holiday the same month and contrived to spend a long afternoon reading in the British Museum. The result was the delivery of the six sermons on 'The Primitive Faith and Roman Catholic Developments' to an audience which filled the Cathedral to its capacity. They were published immediately with a Foreword by the Dean in response to 'the earnest desire of many who heard them, and in the hope that they may tend to the confirmation of our young

---

[1] Dr. Charles had written: 'I want a capable editor for the *Additions to Esther.* . . . The Dean of Westminster has recommended me to ask you. I have read through most of your edition of Wisdom and have gathered from it your competence to deal with your task without further guidance.'

[2] With regard to the St. Patrick's canonry his diary entries are of interest: *14 October 1909.* 'Canon Nicholson informs me that at the recent election for Canon I was nearly elected. C. Dowse eventually was appointed, I second, Hannay third.' [The famous author was elected on 11 June 1912.]

people in the primitive Catholic Faith.' In his own Preface Gregg wrote of his sermons that 'they were called forth by circumstances of a local character, which gave but little time for preparation; while a comprehensive treatment of the question was impossible within the compass of six addresses.'

Nevertheless they have become a minor classic of their kind, and are to this day set as a textbook upon which candidates for ordination in the Church of Ireland are examined, and have been many times reprinted. They have not, nor were intended to have, the weight of learning and authority that informs Salmon's *Infallibility of the Church;* but the arguments they present remain, as in Salmon's great work, unanswered because unanswerable. Gregg's sermons were devised for the comprehension of ordinarily intelligent church people, but the bibliography bears witness to the scope of his learning in this field.

His paper denouncing the 'Ne Temere' Decree on mixed marriages, promulgated by the Roman Church at Easter 1908, was delivered before the Young Men's Association in Cork on St. Patrick's Day 1911. It was subsequently enlarged for publication and is in print to this day. In it, to use a colloquialism, he 'calls the bluff' of Roman priestcraft, exposes its fallacies, penetrates its guard, and defeats it with its own weapons. Were his warnings heeded by Romans and Protestants alike, there would be less cause for those unhappy family cleavages which inevitably occur in by far the majority of these cases. Gregg quotes with approval some sentences of Cardinal Logue's pastoral letter to his own flock a few days previously; and adds whimsically on his own account that, though he too is against mixed marriages and does all he can to discourage them, he must admit that 'if a certain mixed marriage had not taken place in County Clare three generations ago, I should not be here to-night.'

His elder daughter here provides a comment explanatory of much in his view of sound churchmanship.

His attitude to the Roman Catholic Church was one of great admiration for a magnificent institution, for the devotion of so many of its sons and daughters, for the firmness of its discipline and for the unity of its teaching. But it professed so much that was incomprehensible to his rational approach: infallibility, financial extortions, reverence for relics, Mariolatry, the doctrines of purgatory and of the Real Presence—what he called 'accretions' or more politely 'developments.' The arrogance of that Church enraged him, the claim that it alone was the true church, when by contrast with the Eastern Orthodox Church it was the

Roman Church which was schismatic. The wickedness of the Ne Temere decree outraged his sense of justice and fair play. The integrity of his thinking could never forgive the Jesuitical doctrine that 'it is right to do evil that good may come.' He realized that consequences of actions are often beyond human control, so that action itself must conform to God's laws.

The effect upon himself of the publication of these Sermons was that it brought him into prominence as the foremost exponent in Ireland of the primitive faith of the Church, the defence of which could be left safely in his hands. He was well aware of his own capability; and when long afterwards, during his Primacy, the Roman Catholic Church promulgated yet another dogma, he forbade any of his clergy to controvert it, saying that he would do so himself.

§

In May of this year he took his wife to Italy, reviving memories of his previous visit and breaking fresh ground in introducing her to its treasures of architecture and art. On 27 May he preached the sermon required for the B.D. in Cambridge before the Vice-Chancellor and Dr. Swete (who was his host) and was formally admitted in Congregation. In August he made a special visit to Limerick to meet his old teacher Dr. Moule, and was very happy to hear him in the pulpit again. In the same month Mrs. Gregg won three prizes at the Cork Agricultural Show. It was a happy year, but marred in the autumn by his mother's sudden decline in health, crippled as she was also by rheumatoid arthritis.

Events listed at the end of 1910 as indicative of 'External progress' though numerous are not so impressive as in the previous year. Unnoted among them is the decision of the Dean and Chapter, on the death of Edward VII in May, to entrust all the arrangements for the Memorial Service in Cork Cathedral to the Rector of Blackrock. (He was able to produce the Form used in England on the death of the Queen in 1901.)

In his diary of the previous year there is an unusually long entry on 13 October: 'I had no expectation of Mallow, tho' people would speak to me of it. Accordingly, I felt no disappointment, rather relief, at the result. Flewett elected.' It would certainly seem strange had he accepted nomination for Mallow so soon after his appointment to Blackrock. But early in September 1910 it appears from his diary that there was a vacancy at Killiney in Co. Dublin, and that during that month the Board of Nomination met and adjourned no less than five times. He was on holiday in England most of the time, and writes: 'All this holiday somewhat disturbed by *Killiney* uncertainty.' It does not appear whether he had applied directly for this parish, or whether his name had been proposed at a meeting of the Board. He may well have been attracted by the beauty of the place and by its proximity to Dublin. A few days after his return to Blackrock, on 27 September: 'Letter arrived fr. C. D. Oliver asking for finality *re* Killiney. Decided to go to Cork and see Bp. and Dean, whom I saw. Dine at Deanery. No reasons why I should go, so posted letter by night mail train withdrawing. Believe it is right.' Next month he spoke at the Belfast Conference, visited a friend in Ballymena with A. E. Ross, and preached at the Harvest Festival in Derry Cathedral.

During these years the Rector of Shandon and the Rector of Blackrock appear constant companions. They are together at committee meetings, and tennis-parties, and walks along the Marina, are frequently in each other's houses, and are in agreement on every point of ecclesiastical or civic policy. And it is with evident delight that Gregg records in his diary (in capitals) the occasion in 1911 of his friend's engagement to Miss Mary Cummins. When Gregg is in England it is Hearn who keeps him informed of every important event. Thus it came about that Gregg, when again in Eastbourne, heard by telegram on 14 June 1911 of the election of Dr. Bernard to the see of Ossory (in succession to Bishop d'Arcy who was elevated to Dublin). Bernard's promotion left two posts vacant which he had held concurrently: that of Dean of St. Patrick's and that of Archbishop King's Professor of Divinity in Trinity College. Three days after Hearn's telegram Gregg received a letter from Professor J. P. Mahaffy (written on the same day and forwarded to him from Cork) about the latter vacancy. But a requirement for application to this post is that the applicant holds the degree of B.D. in the University of Dublin. Gregg must have telegraphed his application on receipt of Mahaffy's letter, since three days later still (20th) came 'T. K. Abbott's letter, dishing me for B.D. at T.C.D. All chance of Prof'ship seems gone. Express letter to J. P. Mahaffy by 4.40 train and exp. messenger, 2/8.' Another three days elapse (the Coronation of George V occurring on the 22nd), then: 'Heard fr. J. P. Mahaffy, more hope, and wrote *re* my published work.'

The following letters from J. P. Mahaffy, then Senior Lecturer, clarify the matter:

June 15. There will be a vacancy for our Archbp. King's Prof'ship next October, and one qualification is that the man

apptd. must be a B.D. of this Univ'ty. Now if you think of being
a candidate, it would be essential that you shd. take your *ad
eundem* B.D. here next July 6. We accept Cambridge degrees in
that way. You should write to the Sub-Proctor, who will tell you
details of fees, &c. It is not right that I should express any
further opinion.

June 21. The Sub-Proctor, whom I have since seen, was acting
upon a single case, where an Oxford B.D., got by thesis only, was
declined. But the general rule is as I said, and I trust your case
is a clear one. I shall have it settled by the Board next Saturday.
Let me have before that (at latest Sat. morning) (a) the conditions
of your Cambridge B.D., (b) what you have done in theology
since. Your case seems to me the very one to satisfy the Board.

June 26. I am glad to say the Board has agreed to your having
the *ad eundem* B.D. on July 6th.

A long letter from Hearn on 22 June ('Coronation Day—God
save the King') says:

Abbott surely is making a mistake if I judge by extract from
Calendar enclosed. I am surprised to learn that the position is
limitied to B.D.'s of Dublin University, but the history of the
Professorship more or less explains but does not justify it. At
any rate it reduces the number of *eligible* men to very few.
I cannot think that J.P.M. is acting alone in this matter—he is
a great friend of Bernard's and may in a sense be representing
his views. d'Arcy's advice will be worth having as no doubt he
and Traill wd. talk the matter over. I am frightfully excited
about it and will rejoice if such a high honour is conferred on
you. You have everything in your favour—age no block as I see
Bernard was appointed in 1888 when he was quite a young man.
Then again the University will welcome new blood. . . . On the
other hand I wd. regard Robin Gwynn as a severe competitor,
and of course being a F.T.C.D. wd. stand to him, and he is also
a man whom I have heard exercises an excellent influence on the
students. Of course I am out of touch with College now and am
merely surmising. I do hope you will be advised to let your name
go forward. Even though you shd. not be successful one must
regard it as no small mark of the appreciation of your scholarship
etc. that you shd. be asked to send in your name. From my heart
I wish you success though I cannot bear to think of you leaving
Cork. . . .

In a postcript to a circular letter thanking Gregg for congratulations, Bernard wrote: 'Thank you very much. I hope that there may
be no hitch in your *ad eundem* B.D. degree: I hoped long since
that you wd. take it out.'

And these from Bishop d'Arcy:

June 24. I was delighted to get your letter and to know that things are going the way it seems to indicate. Indeed the very thing about which Dr. Mahaffy wrote to you has been in my mind, except that I did not think about the B.D. It never occurred to me that it was a necessary condition. The one other man I thought of for it is Robin Gwynn. But I have just heard that he will not let his name be put up for it. I do not know definitely if this is strictly accurate. But, from what I know of him, I think it is very probable.

I would certainly advise your acting on Dr. Mahaffy's advice. Send in your name at once, and meanwhile I will write to Bernard about it . . . he will give a sound opinion. The fact that you have been asked to do it by a man like Dr. Mahaffy is a perfect justification of your action.

June 28. Dean Bernard tells me the B.D. is essential. He hopes you will take it *ad eundem.* But, as to this, he says an effort is being made to raise difficulties. This effort may not succeed. Gwynn will *not* be a candidate. B. hopes you will.

Whatever the difficulties may have been they were speedily overcome. (He indeed would be a bold man who would cross swords with John Pentland Mahaffy.)

He took the degree at 'Commencements' on 6 July, when the faithful Hearn met him with the necessary hood and gown; had a long talk with Dr. Bernard; and dined at the high table sitting next to Dr. Gwynn. No wonder that on his thirty-eighth birthday, two days before, he confided to his diary (in Greek): 'This year seems full of things new and strange.'

But the formality of the *ad eundem* degree was merely the handle to a door that might or might not open. Nearly four months must elapse before this could be known, and meanwhile Gregg worked hard in preparation for the much hoped-for event; and on 7 July wrote an addendum to his diary:

On Sat. June 17 I got the first intimation of summons to Archbp. K's Professorship. The idea is naturally pleasing. But subsequent reflection tends to oppress me with the burden of the first year's lectures. The attraction on the other hand is the great sphere offered by such a position in a great Divinity School.

All my friends are much more keen on my taking it, and more persuaded of my capacity for it, than I. d'Arcy, Bernard, Hearn, Archdn. Walsh all encourage. And yet I doubt the power of doing the work up to standard, up to time, without mental collapse.

A talk with J.H.B. on July 6 made the programme seem a little less severe, and the fact that I cd. get most of my first term's prep. work done during the summer made me easier in mind.

Nevertheless he contrived to take his usual holidays—to Portrush with Ross in August, to Eastbourne in September, finding his mother no worse but in constant pain. When on 30 October the election was announced he inscribed in his diary DEO GRATIAS.

For the first term he was both Rector and Professor, leaving his church to the charge of a deputy on Sunday evenings. His lectures were twice weekly, on Monday and Thursday mornings, but there was much other business connected with students, theological debates, conferences with Professors Lawlor and Newport White, sometimes too with J. P. Mahaffy. His temporary *pied à terre* in College was in the rooms of R. M. Gwynn. He would return to Cork by the afternoon train on Thursday if possible and was generally met at the station by Hearn who would walk with him part of the way to Blackrock, and with whom during the last weeks his contacts were more frequent than ever. On 16 December 1911 Mrs. Gregg bore her second daughter, Barbara Fitzgerald.

This double duty continued till 11 February 1912 when he preached his farewell sermon in Blackrock, and a few days later his wife brought her young family to the house which he had bought in Dublin—31 Leeson Park. From now on he becomes increasingly involved with affairs in Trinity College and with church life in Dublin. On 27 June there is another addendum to his diary:

> I write this, having just finished my first year's work.
> The pressure was very great, but I was wonderfully sustained. I enjoyed the first year's work, and the life generally, more than I can say. To few does it fall to be called to do their bread-winning in a manner so congenial. The only way, humanly speaking, in which I could have got through my work was by systematically mapping out what had to be done, and adhering to a rule very strictly. . . . I am wonderfully little tired at the end of the year's work, though I know I need a rest.
> Never have I had so much occasion to acknowledge the support of God: He called and He enabled.

To an outsider it would rather seem that Gregg brought to his task in a junior Professorship an equipment and capacity which many a Regius Professor might have envied. But his self-criticism here is illustrative of a quality which he possessed in an exceptional degree and which would have insured for him success in any walk of life, namely the quality of absolute *thoroughness* in everything that he undertook. He was never satisfied with less than the best possible.

The last words are indicative of his life-long belief in a special Providence overruling the course of events in the lives of the faithful. It is not indeed given to all such to identify their personal inclinations with the divine Will. Yet he must have felt the 'call' not only as the opening of a door to a larger field of activity, but as a veritable reprieve from the petty routine of parochial work for which he was temperamentally unfitted and to which he need never return. Not least had been the burden of his weekly sermons, each one of which was *original*, substantial in content and memorable in composition. During the long years of his curacy he would seem to have almost preached himself out. He is an example of one whose genius as a preacher flowered early and was succeeded by the devolopment of endowments of a quite different kind. He came to Cork as a young man with an authentic strain in him of the prophetic fire; it is seldom that we discern in his later sermons the same inspirational quality. But for the next four years he was to show his calibre as a lecturer and teacher of exceptional power. Three stars were now visible in the Irish firmament which were destined to follow one another in approximately the same orbit: d'Arcy, Bernard and (some fifteen years their junior) Gregg.[3]

[3] The sole word of criticism which Dr. Newport White wrote in his fine tribute to Bernard might with equal propriety have been written of Gregg:
   'Any public duty which he undertook was always performed to the best of his ability; but his whole training had been such as to make 'the pastoral care' uncongenial to him. He could give excellent instruction to the shepherds; but the actual work of feeding lambs and tending sheep did not come easy to him.'

CHAPTER V

PROFESSOR OF DIVINITY

THE *Cork Examiner* prefaced its valediction to the departing clergyman who had shed fresh lustre on his name in that city with a well-phrased tribute.

> Mr. Gregg is a scholar, a dreamer, and a thinker. His sermons are invariably brilliant, sound, erudite, eloquent, and stamped with the individuality of a man who is above all a thinker. And he possesses, in a very marked degree, that power, without which the orator is ineffectual, of enmeshing his audience in the magnetic net of his personality; of getting at the very pith of his subject, and holding it aloft, a nude, unassailable reality, for every eye to dwell upon. His cogency of argument, his breadth of outlook, his broad and deep human sympathy, the magnetism of his nature, and the incontestable accuracy of his knowledge, make of him a man who can, at once, appeal to the heart of the commoner, and to the head of the critical intellectual.

It is notoriously difficult to be both a philosopher and a theologian: to decide between the claims of first principles that are axiomatic to reason, and the postulate of a divine Personality apprehensible by faith. Many who decide in favour of the latter are prone to attempt to rationalize the experience which is born of faith and thus to make of it an intellectual abstraction. Gregg was first and foremost a theologian, but never one of the purely academic type: for him theology must be related to life. He had less interest in philosophy for its own sake; it was no more than an ancillary to theological thought.

In a masterly exposition of the trend of theology in our times [1] the Archbishop of Canterbury has shown how, since towards the end of the nineteenth century, its concern had been to recover the Doctrine of the Incarnation as central to the faith; and this at the expense of the Atonement (a doctrine eluding definition, at least by our formal categories of thought). But 'the formulation of the Doctrine of the Incarnation had sprung, alike in the apostolic age and in the patristic period, from out of the experience of Redemption: the saving act had been the key to the Church's faith in the divine Christ.'

The older methods of expounding the Atonement has fallen into

[1] *From Gore to Temple*, A. M. Ramsey, 1960.

disrepute. Concepts of penal expiation, substitution, satisfaction—derived as they were from the Judaic sacrificial system or from ancient Roman juridical process or from Teutonic codes of chivalry—had proved repugnant to a more enlightened age, and as a consequence the subject of the Atonement was becoming tacitly dropped in many pulpits. Gregg was concerned about this lapse, and from the first years of his ministry had been urging upon his colleagues a return to the Doctrine of the Cross as the central, because the religious, principle of Christianity; discountenancing those scholastic interpretations which had made it discreditable and emphasizing the truly spiritual significance of it in the teaching of St. Paul. There can be no doubt that he had read all that had been written on the subject in recent years, and most probably R. C. Moberly's *Atonement and Personality* (to which his own thought would seem to be most akin). But there is no mention of this or of other books in his own sermons and addresses; these bear the unmistakable stamp of convictions reached by an independent and original mind after study of the New Testament and personal reflection upon the meaning of its message.

A human being (he begins by affirming in a paper given at the Cork Clerical Meeting in April 1904, entitled 'Psychology in Doctrine or The Personal Element in Theological Ideas') is a *vital organism*—an agent, not a thing to be 'acted upon' like a pawn in chess. 'We have in man the only thing in the world than can be known from *the inside*. If doctrine is to ring real for us to-day, we must state it in terms of man, even as in the Incarnation God has stated Himself in terms of man.' What positive content, he asks, are we to give to such abstract terms as atonement, forgiveness, salvation, grace and the like—what concrete connotation? 'All these, as commonly stated, strike me as *pagan* ideas, and would long ago have driven me out of the fold, had I not found refuge in a restatement. Unless the "plan of salvation" is stated in terms of the relation of Person to person, or rather Divine spirit to human spirit, thinking men and women *must* treat it as unreal, and are bound in honesty to reject it.'

Then he goes on:

> To talk of God giving grace, granting forgiveness, inflicting punishment—ignores completely the human side of the question. These things are processes, not results; and processes must grow. Further, they depend not merely on God's action, but on man's reaction. Grace, forgiveness, punishment are merely local external ways of picturing what are really psychological states and attitudes. There is no such *thing* as grace, or forgiveness—these

are *relations* of person to person: take away the persons, and grace and forgiveness are mere ghosts. Grace and punishment are not givable or withholdable at God's pleasure: they are inevitable consequences of man being in or out of harmony with God. . . .

'Do you believe in the Atonement?' said someone to me. 'Well,' I was bound to answer, 'if you mean—do I centre all my hopes on some release from punishment that a dying Christ is supposed to have secured for me 2,000 years ago, I am bound to say I want more than that: but if you mean—do I believe that through fellowship with a living Christ, I am being made "at one" with God, and hope to be more "at one" with Him to-morrow, such a fact I profoundly believe in. But I am not called to believe in the atonement—I believe in an Atoning Person, Jesus Christ, and I believe in my at-one-ment with God.'

There is something too cut and dried, too institutional, too mechanical, and therefore psychologically unreal, in the idea that belief in a 2,000 years old fact saves, or can save: the Cross of Christ, the Blood of Christ mean a person crucified: the only thing that can save is a living person, fellowship with Him who lives for evermore. For this reason the object of all atonement is Salvation. And what is Salvation? not the getting off of punishment, not the going to a place called heaven when we die, but the healing, the restoration of our soul—the revitalizing of it. A 'saved' soul is not like a bundle taken out of a train that is going the wrong way, relabelled, and thrown into a train that will take it the right way. A saved soul is one that is made to perform its proper functions, that is galvanized out of paralysis, that is released from its frozen arrest of growth, and so once more lives. A soul's 'life' consists in harmony with the soul's environment, and that is God. To be a lost soul is to be outside God, i.e. alienated, out of tune, and therefore impenetrable to God—to be a saved soul is to become pervious once more, to find correspondences, to ripen in the sun of His felt presence—and generally to realize that fellowship for which the human soul is constituted.

Salvation, he continues, is a process, a growth, a deepening of personality here and now—not the assurance of future reward in an 'everlasting' state of bliss. Grace is not something instilled into us from outside: it is simply the result of fellowship with God—that is, a personal relation. Forgiveness must be understood also in personal terms.

Can God forgive *sin*? No. Can God let a man off punishment, even if he repents? No. God forgives the sinner: man punishes himself. His *sin* cannot be forgiven. There is in reality no such thing as a sin—there is only a sinning man. His deeds cannot be

undone: they have become fossilized in the rocks of history. . . .
The only thing we have to reckon with is the alienated man and
the forgiving God. God's forgiveness is the restoration of His
love, His own *loving self,* to the heart that wronged Him. For this
reason, the extent of the *receiving* of forgiveness, which means
the receiving of God, is absolutely conditioned by the state of
the sinning and repenting man . . . he remains punished in the
exact measure in which he is out of tune with God. And so, for
God to let a man off his *punishment* would be to let a man off
his own self, which is absurd.

The processes of forgiving love are occupied with the renewing
of the self, and forgiveness advances and punishment diminishes
according as the indwelling God neutralizes and replaces the
God-resisting tendencies the man developed in his days of sin.

It is God's nature to forgive: He sweeps into your nature
when you repent, just as the sunshine sweeps into a dark room
and floods it when you throw the shutters back.

Heaven and Hell are not future abodes of the saved and
damned: they are present states of being. Both have begun now.
The godless man is in hell, frost-bound within the vicious circle
of his own self-absorption. He probably does not know it, as long
as he is in the body. Paralysis is none the less a living death,
because it is not painfully felt.

Then comes the question of eternal annihilation—'Can a soul
that has once existed cease to exist, be blown out like the flame of
a candle?' Psychology teaches that unused faculties atrophy: thus
eternal apathy *might* result in the awful doom of cessation from
existence. But perhaps 'the horror of its self-chosen isolation and
lovelessness' must ultimately dawn upon the soul.

I believe the Bible points to an universal restoration, and that
the path to this is through a repentance that comes hereafter to
souls who have lived for self here, and who in another world
when the deceptions of sense have been swept aside have come
to realize the hideousness of self, and the anguish of a life
alienated from a loving God.

In all this are echoes of the doctrine of Clement of Alexandria,
according to whom the key to the moral history of mankind and of
each soul in particular lies in the movement of free response on the
part of man to the unchanging 'saving righteousness' of God,
which is never punitive but always disciplinary. There are echoes
too of the daring speculation of Origen that all souls will ultimately
be saved; for though, says Gregg, the 'equal reasonableness' of the
views for and against universal salvation leaves him with 'a com-

pletely open mind,' there can be no doubt—to judge from the
underlining in his script—upon which side his private sympathies
lay.

Another paper read at the Cork Clerical Meeting in February
1907, entitled 'Atonement and Forgiveness,' shows that his convictions on the cardinal doctrine of the Christian faith are un-
changed:

> I never could find any force whatever in the argument that
> Christ had to die, in order to make some adequate reparation
> for our sins. This always seems to me an argument drawn from
> a somewhat unworthy type of human transactions. The supreme
> fact of the Divine character is His free forgiveness: it is His for-
> givingness in Christ that Christians are exhorted to copy. If God
> only forgave because Christ gave Him the satisfaction needed,
> why then God's forgiveness is not free at all; it is bought: and
> God's character is shown to be, far from merciful, sternly and
> inexorably unyielding. God surely desires no reparation: it is
> enough for Him to show that He hates sin, and condemns it, by
> showing through the Cross that though He endures sin, He is
> far from making light of it. Thus instead of vindicating His
> honour, He makes men see that His honour has never even been
> tarnished.
>
> It is, I hold, one of the cardinal mistakes to believe that God
> requires changing in any way. Just as the way to resolve a discord
> in music is to change one of the dissonant notes and not both:
> so the want of *rapport* between God and man requires only the
> changing of man, and not of both God and man. God is the
> author of atonement, and He who supplied it requires no urging
> to be sympathetic towards a work which proceeds from Himself.
> Atonement is God's gift to man, and it is in man that the change
> produced by it must be sought. . . .
>
> Imputed righteousness, e.g., is a theological figment, which
> neither finds support in the Bible, nor corresponds to any reality
> affirmed by the moral sense: the very essence of God's desire
> for 'righteousness in us' is that we should be individually authors
> of righteousness: how either His desire for us or our demand
> upon ourselves can be satisfied by clothing us in a righteousness
> the very essence of which is that it is another's, it is very hard to
> see. . . .
>
> Is it possible logically, and psychologically, to forgive sins?
> Does such a thing really exist as a sin? If I have done a sinful
> deed, can that deed ever be forgiven? . . .The deed can be no
> more forgiven than it can be undone: only the sinful will which
> did it can be forgiven, as it alone can be undone. . . .
>
> What the Atoning principle had to work upon, was not crimes
> and sins and evil deeds, but rebellious wills. Men are not to be

thought of as each having a burden of sins, like Christian's bundle upon his back, the cords of which only needed snapping for it to drop into the sepulchre—such forgiveness is mechanical.

In a course of sermons upon the same theme in Lent, 1908, he tells his hearers that Atonement is to be understood—not as satisfaction for sins nor as expiation for guilt nor as appeasement of an angry God—but as Reconciliation: 'God was in Christ, reconciling the world unto Himself.' The 'Cross of Christ' and the 'Blood of Christ' have no efficacy in themselves. They are 'things outside us.' They are no more than symbolic terms (just as we speak of the King as 'the Crown' or of Judges as 'the Bench'). The Cross means *Christ* as crucified: the Blood means *Christ* who shed His blood.

The *Cross* of Christ is (or was) a piece of wood, and has long ago passed into dust: the *Blood* of Christ fell upon the hill of Calvary and was absorbed by the earth on that first Good Friday. And these two things, sacred and precious though they are to our thought, were merely natural substances, subject to the ordinary physical laws of corruption and decay, and in themselves could never take away sin.

We are reconciled to God through conscious fellowship with a Living Person; this is a personal relationship, an inward experience, and—because we are creatures in process of growth—a continually progressive one.

It has been felt necessary to dwell thus long upon this theme, if only to show that Gregg's theology was not (as it is for many theologians) the attempted solution of an intellectual conundrum, but the direct expression of religious experience. He recurred to it in course of sermons which he was invited to give during Lent in 1912 in Christ Church, Leeson Park, on the text, 'We are reconciled to God through the death of His Son.' [2] He never (or very seldom) preached the same sermon twice; there was always a freshness in his exposition. As late as March 1952 we find among his papers another sermon preached on the same text in Armagh Cathedral; it has all the vigour of conviction of his younger days.

The anomaly of describing Theology as a science becomes apparent as its sphere extends into Christology, and it is here that Gregg's unpublished writings are valuable because they lift the whole subject from the aridity of doctrinal formulas into the realm of living experience. It is customary in academic studies to divide this

[2] Of these sermons unfortunately only the first and last appear to be extant.

E

subject into the Person of Christ and the Work of Christ. But in Gregg's presentation these are to be seen as a unity. Christ's being and his doing are one—in His act of self-giving He is what He does because He gives Himself.

It is thought better to present these homiletical aspects of Gregg's theological thinking than to refer to the substance of his professorial lectures, since the former are interpretative and are his own whereas the latter are informative and are largely derived, reflecting ideas which were current half a century ago and which are considered by many to-day to be outdated. Authorities whom he most frequently quotes, for example, are: Harnack, Dorner, Pfleiderer, Westcott, Lightfoot, Sanday, Ottley, Swete—to name but a few of those best remembered; but there are others among his contemporaries such as Fairbairne, Shairp and Forrest, now half forgotten; and it is of interest to remark that among Church historians, though he often has recourse to Gwatkin, it is the anti-Romanist Schaff to whom he is most indebted and whom he always recommended to divinity students.[3]

Of the lectures themselves (written in full) it is sufficient to say that they are exhaustive, and it is to be hoped that they were dictated slowly since to take notes of them would have been as difficult as to memorize them. They are on a high level of scholarship and would have been more suitable for candidates for the B.D. degree than for the ordinary divinity student. Specimens of pedantic phrasing are not absent—for example: 'And it must be remembered that the Johannine authorship of the fourth Gospel is not irrefragably demonstrated as yet.' Problems raised by the higher criticism of the Bible are frankly stated and as frankly discussed; notions of its verbal inspiration are shown to be fallacious. More than one student, nurtured from boyhood on such beliefs, is said to have come away from the first few of Gregg's lectures with his faith shattered, and afterwards re-established on a firmer basis than ever. The lecturer would say quietly: 'Now, gentlemen, put away your pens; I want to talk to you for a few minutes.'

Of those who remember him in those days, one is the present Bishop of Cashel, Dr. Cecil de Pauley, who says:

Even as a young don he appeared a somewhat remote and

[3] Philip Schaff (1819–93), German-American theologian and church historian, *History of the Christian Church* in 12 volumes: 'a popular work from the standpoint of evangelical liberalism, hortatory rather than scientific in tone' (from the *Oxford Dictionary of the Christian Church*, ed. by F. L. Cross, D.D., 1957).

awesome figure, though in fact he was kindly and amenable. One foggy winter's day I had occasion to visit him in college. On opening the door I descried him at the far end of the long room, seated at his desk, his severe hatchet-like face framed between the light of two candles which were the sole illumination through the gloom. It was a vivid but rather eerie impression.

Canon Walter Bothwell, B.D., writes:

My first contact with him was in June 1912 when he examined me in the New Testament for Divinity Testimonium. He was a stiff examiner. Having a remarkable memory himself, he expected a high degree of accuracy and fullness of quotation; and even a slight omission lost you a quarter of a mark!

The reminiscences of Canon Charles H. P. Lyndon, O.B.E., have a pathetic interest:

I was one of his pupils in 1912–13. When awarding the Butcher Exhibition he gave one to me although I never approached him and was a poverty-stricken Masonic pupil taking an extern B.A.—Typical.

Nearly 50 years later—though I had never seen or spoken to him in the meantime—as a superannuated cleric I was doing duty in Rostrevor to which he had retired; and after Service he got his wife to lead him (for his sight was failing) to the vestry door to shake hands with me. Guess my pleasure and amazement when he addressed me as 'C.H.P., isn't it?'—Equally typical.

Miss Geraldine FitzGerald, a graduate of Trinity, recalls the series of Biblical lectures which he gave to women students of the University on Saturday mornings:

The new Professor was a tall handsome man of 38, dignified and austere, who kept us all mute and attentive as he walked to and fro, expounding his points with little or no reference to notes, in his light clear voice and a perfect choice of the exact words to convey the precise shade of meaning he required. He was able to hold our complete attention at once. I only realized then for the first time that the Book of Genesis was not written by Moses. It was a great surprise to me—it could have been a great shock. But the points were so simply, calmly, and clearly made, the conclusion that the multiple authorship did not lessen the essential truth of the narrative was brought home with the utmost conviction and lucidity, but with no over-emphasis. I felt that this man's faith was founded on a Rock, and that a first class intellect was able to give a reason for the faith that was in

him. . . . A few years later, looking back, I realized what a master
of exposition he must have been to hold the concentrated attention of feminine Junior Freshman on such a subject.

An amusing, and in one aspect a revealing, description of the
Professor's family life—or lack of it—is given by Mr. B. R. Long,
a cousin of his wife on her mother's side. In 1909 he was an undergraduate at Trinity, living with his widowed mother in Chelmsford
Road, just round the corner from 31 Leeson Park.

My memories are negative and distant, and are of 'Jeff' and
Claude rather than of their parents. Soon after our arrival in
Dublin my mother and I went to tea at the Greggs. Dr. Gregg
made a brief appearance only, pleading pressure of work, and
this was the case on all my other numerous visits. The two boys
appeared at tea, but they did not particularly strike me; they
were evidently on their best behaviour. But it seems that I had
favourably impressed them; a few days later Anna Gregg told my
mother they were always asking when I was coming again. So I
arranged to call for them that afternoon and take them for a
walk. I found them waiting for me at the hall-door, and as soon
as we were out of the house they gave me a shock.
    'Jeff' (in conspiratorial tones): 'Do you know any good swear
words?' I replied: 'Well, yes, I do.'
    'Jeff': 'We know *damn* and *blast.'*
    Claude: 'Cook says *blast*. Blast is a *lovely* word.'
    We then set off on our walk. As they obviously expected a
reply, and pressed the question whether I knew any other words
as good, I got round the matter by telling them that, as Jeff would
soon be going to school, he would learn more there. I also
advised discretion! But I fished for information about Cook.
She was the great personality in their lives; evidently a somewhat
explosive character, but very fond of children. Her favourite
reading was of ghost stories, on which she regaled them in her
spare time. So now I, having successfully shelved the awkward
subject of swear words, was lured into entertaining them with
ghost stories.
    But in taking them out for walks, I found that they had not
been adequately 'walked' at all. It seemed their father never
took them out, their mother seldom; they had been left almost
entirely to servants. The ironic incongruity of their father lecturing
students in divinity while his children were deriving dubious
knowledge from the cook, struck me forcibly, much the same
thing having happened to myself when a child. So I 'walked'
Jeff and Claude more widely than they had ever been walked
before, taking them out by train to seaside places and elsewhere,
which was much better fun and better exercise than being trailed

round suburban roads. But here I ran into a difficulty; there was an obsessional fear about their catching cold, and I must certainly never take them bathing (though I happened to be Captain of the Trinity Swimming Club). But now, of course, no matter how fine the day or how warm the sea, I could not go in myself when I had them with me. I did take this up with their father, but—though I am sure *he* would have made no objection—he was not prepared to intervene.

Another matter akin to this is the fact that Jeff had no bicycle. The first bicycles for small boys had been put on the market ten years before, and any child of middle-class parents expected a bicycle at an earlier age than 8. But in the Gregg household this was considered too dangerous, though motors were still too few to matter; horse-drawn vehicles were too familiar to be feared; tram-lines were nasty but easily avoidable.

In the winter I saw little of them, as my time was rather fully taken up in college, but I did continue occasionally to take them out. I also saw very little of their father, but my brother who was a divinity student told me that he was rather unapproachable as a Professor since he seemed to be absorbed in other matters if one tried to speak to him. But on the very few occasions when we met he was always very pleasant to me. I do not think, however, that the thought ever crossed his mind that I had stepped into shoes which he had failed to wear.

When not required in the College Chapel he was in constant demand during his first year to officiate or preach in Christ Church, Leeson Park, the most fashionable church in Dublin. Canon Ernest Barker was then a young curate there, and now writes:

> As I remember him then, though he was rather an awe-inspiring personality, he was always gracious to us younger men and ready to encourage. In spite of his voice, to which you had to get accustomed, his sermons, though always demanding full attention, appealed strongly to a very mixed congregation. As a man in those early days he was shy and reserved, lacking perhaps experience in the rough and tumble of life. His upbringing had much to say to this. But it did make him, combined with his striking appearance, a rather unapproachable person to many. But beneath the shyness and austerity, his was a very natural and humble spirit. It was a delight then and in later years to sit over the fire alone with him. His humility led him to respect and value the opinions of others and to learn from them.

In March 1912 a small Committee of the Divinity School, of which R. M. Gwynn was the chief instigator, met in the latter's rooms to sponsor the formation of the Trinity Mission to a slum

quarter of Belfast, already militant under the inspiring leadership
of the Revd. A. W. Barton. 'R. M. Gwynn sat and talked with me
re Belfast scheme for nearly two hours in the Common Room' is
one of Gregg's diary entries. Then the Committee met to hear the
Revd. A. W. Barton who came down from Belfast to speak to them.
Finally Gregg is appointed Hon. Treasurer to the Committee.

On 20 March 'I was elected at last, D.G.' to a vacant stall (that
of Maynooth) in St. Patrick's Cathedral; and the same evening he
dines with three Bishops (Keene, Day, and Bernard). Exactly
recorded are his duties during residence, even to the reading of
lessons; and the date on which he 'had rosettes put on tall and felt
hats.' So too is the date when he is elected a member of the
University Club, sponsored by two Bishops. He is beginning to
move in the high circles of Church life, is a member of several
committees and is chaplain to the Lord Lieutenant. On 17 May
his friend Canon Charles Dowse is elected to the Bishopric of
Killaloe, and on the 25th, 'C. Dowse calls and asks if I will accept
nomination to Xt. Ch. Leeson Park. *No*.' A few days later he himself suggests both to Bishop d'Arcy and to Dowse the name of
A. E. Ross to that vacancy. But Ross was appointed Vicar of
Ballymena on 28 June.

He had taken his wife to Eastbourne in the spring, where his
sister Hilda was in attendance on their invalid mother. In the
summer they went to Switzerland, via Eastbourne both ways. In
August he took duty at Aghade in the Leighlin diocese and thus
became acquainted with part of his future See. Then back to Eastbourne for the tennis tournaments. On return he visits Glastonbury
and takes the long sea route from Bristol to Cork, calls on the
Bishop and Dean and sees much of the Hearns. Thence back to
Dublin for the Michaelmas term.

But on 12 October: 'News reached me from Hearn of *death
of Bishop Meade*. Had seen him at Palace Sept. 26.'

In a Church where bishops are elected by clerical and lay representatives, rather than appointed (as in the Church of England)
by higher authority, the rein is given to invidious gossip in the
interregnum and, if it be unduly prolonged (as is generally the case),
to canvassing also. The system is also an encouragement to the
ecclesiastically ambitious. The present vacancy in the See of Cork
was no exception, as Gregg's diary reveals:

> I gathered at once that among other names mine was soon
> mentioned for succession. But the chief name was of course
> Bernard's; Abbott also, and Plunket. Bernard declined (so I

heard on Oct. 27). The field is left proportionately more open, and any result may ensue.

I hear that if my age were greater, I might count on great support from both orders. How far this will weigh, if other v. strong candidates are absent, I cannot guess. Every one mentioned seems to have some disability or other; the question is, which is worst.

I myself realize how difficult it would be for senior men to relish the election of a man of only 16 years' standing, and shall not be in the least degree surprised if it finally prevails against me.

I am trying to see all sides of the question, and to realize that there are many others likely to be preferred before me. I hope to be ready for either event, and to be pleased myself with whatever pleases God. It is hard to keep an absolutely unperturbed mind in view of all the possibilities, but I have many duties and interests and so am perforce largely diverted. May God direct the minds of the electors to make choice of a man who shall be really fitted for the work.

Oct. 30. Hearn's letter reached me, saying that C. Dowse is ready to leave Killaloe, if elected. This after being bp. there for 3 months! I cannot believe that Cork will allow itself to be led by Dean Bruce, whose nominee he is, into electing a man with so small a sense of responsibility. This I wrote to Hearn, in a letter I tossed off on receipt of his to-night.

Other competitors now enter the field. Hearn is his indefatigable informant, by post and telephone, of their prospects and of his. His diary reflects his agitation. On the eve of the election:

> In my own mind I cannot quite give up all hope, tho' I cannot see how there is any chance for me except in a completely abortive election. I do not feel at all sure that Dowse will get his $\frac{2}{3}$ majority, but I don't see how any one else can get even a clear majority of both orders. But I imagine a tremendous effort will be made to keep the election from the Bishops.

The election results were announced on 22 November. He records the votes, clerical and lay respectively, of each competitor. Dowse —the favourite—was elected by an overwhelming majority in both orders; Abbott, the only other name on the select list, was very far behind. Of those who 'also ran' (his words) Latham and Plunket came very near to Abbott; Gregg himself came next, with Flewett close behind; the rest—four of them—were nowhere.

I am quite content to be beaten, but what annoys me is:

    i. Dowse's consenting to stand.

    ii. The Dean's canvassing.

    iii. Cork's complete subserviency.

But, as time passes, we shall see things in a new light, and probably will be very thankful that things so fell out.

The soliloquy continues into the next year:

Jan. 19, 1913. I am a great deal calmer than I was a few weeks ago, but still at times the affairs of Cork trouble me. Not so much the loss, as the way in which things were done. But still, tho' I cannot see how it will come about, I have not the least doubt that one day I shall be very thankful that my way was ordered otherwise. After all, even as things are, I have a delightful sphere in Dublin. I have only been here 12 months, and it is absurd to be restless already. The opportunities, both in College and in preaching, are endless. When I look around and think of the future, I confess I do not see any way out. I have no immediate prospect of D.D., and Dr. Gwynn's life is frail and may cease at any time, and I could not compete for his post. The election to Killaloe takes place on Feb. 7, but I do not think there is the least likelihood of my being seriously thought of. [He ends, as before, with the Homeric, 'These things lie on the knees of the gods'—substituting God for gods.]

This year was without much 'external' incident. But it saw the production of another learned article for the *Irish Church Quarterly* on the *Odes of Solomon;* and of his additions to the Book of Esther in *Apocrypha and Pseudepigrapha of the Old Testament,* a weighty tome in two volumes, the work of chosen scholars, edited by R. H. Charles, Dean of Westminster. Gregg's contribution is in the best traditions of British scholarship. And on 26 June he took the Dublin D.D. degree which was awarded (apparently to his surprise) for his previous work on the Commentary of Origen on the Epistle to the Ephesians.

Early in February, Gregg and Newport White are in consultation in R. M. Gwynn's rooms with the Bishops of Meath and Clogher concerning the formation of a Hostel for Divinity students, and later in the same month he alone confers with Archbishop Peacocke and Bishop Maurice Day in the University Club. This idea, which had Gregg's active interest and support from the outset, had been unobtrusively sown, like many another valuable seed which bore fruit, by R. M. Gwynn.

His diary reveals a temperamental weakness: a habit of undue self-concern. His sense of proportion in public affairs failed him when personal considerations were in the foreground. So important a project as the above, for example, occupies no more space in his record of events than details of his visits to his tailor or dentist, or the fact that on one Sunday afternoon in St. Patrick's he, being the senior of the only two dignitaries present, received the alms and pronounced the Benediction.

On 1 July his soliloquy is resumed:

> Restlessness has largely passed off. I am thoroughly at rest in my work. I have taken the D.D., but I cannot say that I am conscious of any desire to exchange my post for the higher Professorship.
>
> I have had a very happy 6 months, and am gradually becoming consolidated in my position. I am becoming drawn into many activities in Dublin, and ought to be very happy that I have so many pleasant duties to be happy in, without having to brood over a distant future.
>
> God has been very good in carrying me so far upon my way, and in giving me a position of such consideration in Dublin. Within 3 days I shall be 40. I have everything that I could ask for—God give me grace to be contented, and to use all His gifts to good effect.

He spent the first part of the summer holidays with his wife and children in Achill and Connemara, and with his sister Hilda in Eastbourne—their mother being in a condition of complete collapse, and he was there again in September for the tennis. In October he was preaching in St. Nicholas, Cork, on the subject of Church Defence to an audience of some 600.

> It is strange how utterly disassociated from the place and its interests I feel myself. I might be in a dream and hear voices talking around me. Every one very friendly and yet I *feel* I do not belong to them.
>
> Even Hearn and his plans and schemes seem distant from me.
>
> Whether it is a mere psychological trick, or whether 18 months are really enough to break the old . . . [*illeg.*], I cannot say.
>
> But I was as glad to go off to Dublin as in 1911 I was glad to leave Dublin and hasten back to Cork. This train of feeling made me quite satisfied with the way things had gone last year. I did not *want* to stay.

§

Late on 21 October he received a telegram from his sister. He had spent the morning in preparing addresses for a Quiet Day for

Women Workers; it was conducted in his absence by Godfrey Day. He reached Eastbourne late the following evening to find his mother just alive; she died peacefully the same night.

> So it has come at last, and the 4 years of terrible pain are over. Five years and a day from K[atherine]'s death.
> . . . But the first stage of the separation of death had begun long ago. It is strange how little this has affected my power of feeling: the sense of gap or void can hardly be said to exist. Real intercourse, on full human terms, had been so long in abeyance. Of course, the dying wakes up the embers of old associations, and makes one recall this and that, but (except when standing by her bed as she lies dead) it is sad how little real *feeling* I am conscious of . . .

There is more to this effect, and it is followed by details of the course of his mother's physical and mental decline from the day, four years before, when she last wrote to him. But there is no mention of the many long months of strain and distress that his sister, upon whom fell all the responsibility, must have endured. He was obliged to return to Dublin at once for divinity examinations, and made arrangements for the funeral with the Rector of Eastbourne.

He had ever been an affectionate and (in so far as circumstances permitted) a dutiful son. His Book of Quotations has more than one comment by modern writers concerning filial relationships; but perhaps the one which he would most wish to be inscribed in his own biography is this, dated 22 July 1899: 'This only would I request, that you would remember me at the Altar of the Lord, wherever you be.' St. Monica to St. Augustine. (*Conf.* B. x. 29.)

The close of the year brought news (from Hearn by telephone) of the death of Dean Bruce, and a week later a direct invitation from the chief nominators to Gregg to accept nomination. (This would have ensured the almost certain succession, eventually, of the third bishop of his name to the diocese of Cork.) Some pages of his diary are filled with an introspective balancing of *pros* and *cons*.

> . . . Here is the thing dreamed of, during many years in Cork, come at last. And yet I feel that I must refuse it. . . . My *heart* draws me for many reasons; my *mind* says No. . . . There *are* drawbacks in Dublin. I belong to nobody—I have no pulpit— I am on the surface of life. But I am at the centre of Church organization. . . . Still, there is a home feeling about Cork. . . . And it would appeal more to be a Dean in Cork than (say) in time Bishop of a remote country Diocese.

But I must not forget my work . . . and it is easier to find a
Dean of Cork than to pick up a successor here. Here again . . .
I *can* exercise great influence. What a stimulus to future faithful-
ness!

I feel little doubt in mind as to duty. . . . But though I feel
little doubt, I do feel some regrets. . . .

To close the episode he quotes Acts 16: 7, in the Greek of the
'western' text.[4] This mingling of prudential considerations with a
sense of divine direction seems strange. Canon Babington of
Omagh, whom Gregg himself suggested, was appointed to the
Deanery and remained there for thirty-seven years.

The year 1914 opens without incident. Three persons of note
with whom he is in frequent touch are d'Arcy (soon to be Primate),
Bernard (soon to be Archbishop of Dublin), and Mahaffy (who
later this year succeeded Traill as Provost of Trinity). Of the more
active Dublin clergy, E. H. Lewis-Crosby of Drumcondra had more
than once 'sat with me in my rooms,' and after his institution to
Rathmines in April 'asks me to preach special sermon.' And
J. P. Phair of St. Catherine's, soon to be promoted to Christ
Church, Leeson Park, is the most frequent visitor to his home, for
'talks with me.'

The Right Reverend John Percy Phair, for twenty years Bishop
of Ossory, Ferns and Leighlin, now writes:

My earliest association with the late Primate dates back to
the years when, on his appointment as Archbishop King's Professor in Trinity College, he took up residence in my Parish of
Christ Church, Leeson Park, in a house which was afterwards
purchased as a Rectory. He took the keenest interest in everything that concerned the Parish and, although he regularly
attended Divine Service in the College Chapel, he gave me considerable assistance by undertaking to preach on one Sunday
each month at Matins in my Church. This kept him in close
touch with our parochial life, and his sermons, characterized by
deep thoughtfulness and instruction, were greatly appreciated.

When in after years I succeeded to the see of Ossory he would
often speak to me of the years he had spent in Kilkenny as
among the happiest of his life. I was greatly impressed by his
intimate knowledge of many families in the diocese and the
homes in which they lived.

It is generally acknowledged that he was at his best as presi-

---

[4] 'They essayed to go into Bithynia, but *the Spirit of Jesus* suffered
them not.'

dent of his own Diocesan Synods and at the General Synod. He
had a remarkable knowledge of his fellow-members and never
made a mistake when he called upon any of them to speak.
Legal questions and questions of procedure presented no difficulty to him, and he was always ready to give clear guidance on
any matter that came forward.

I had a great admiration for his ability, both intellectual and
administrative, as well as for his spiritual stature and single-
minded devotion to the Church, but I felt that he could never
inspire affection. For that reason his Confirmation addresses,
although on a very high level as regards instruction and duty,
lacked the human touch and the affection which are so necessary
in appealing to the young. So far as I could see, he was a very
lonely man, but he was so completely self-contained that he did
not miss companionship. Yet when one made an approach, as
I often did in later years, he welcomed it. He loved to talk of
the old times and the old friends which were to him a precious,
living memory right on to the closing years of his life.

The Very Reverend E. H. Lewis-Crosby, then Rector of North
Strand, has his own place in the annals of the Church of Ireland.
He died while still in harness at the age of 96 within a few days
of the Archbishop, with whom in life he had seldom been in agreement. His memory has been perpetuated by his former curate,
Evelyn Charles Hodges, who later succeeded him as Rector of
Rathmines, and after serving as Principal of the Training College
in Dublin, was for eighteen years Bishop of Limerick. He now
writes of his early and later reminiscences of the Archbishop:

A tall, spare, commanding figure, standing in the pulpit of
North Strand Church—this was my first introduction to a personality destined to leave a lasting impression upon the Church
of Ireland and the Church as a whole, as teacher, preacher,
leader, administrator and prelate. He had recently been appointed
to a post as Archbishop King's Professor of Divinity in Trinity
College and was much in demand as a clear and forceful
preacher. I still remember his sermon preached that day. He
depicted the scene of the Cambridge boat-race, familiar to him
as a student, and emphasized the necessity laid upon each
member of the crew to pull his weight. In a vivid comparison
he carried the thoughts of his listeners to the demand laid upon
each member of that working-class parish to take his share in
the maintenance of the Church of God. His words were incisive
and compelling. His accent, clear and arresting, caught and retained attention. His words bore fruit.

As Archbishop of Dublin he was Chairman of the Diocesan
Board of Education of which I was then an official. He was much

interested in the movement towards a less mechanical method of religious teaching. While always apprehensive of untutored enthusiasm he took a leading part in effecting a balanced reconstruction of teaching methods in Day and Sunday Schools.

During my brief sojourn as incumbent of Rathmines I had few occasions for consulting him directly. The parish was in perfect order as the result of my friend and patron Canon E. H. Lewis-Crosby's incumbency. I did ask the Archbishop whether I should invite some lady to speak to the girl candidates for confirmation, to supplement my instruction—I was then a bachelor. His reply was terse and emphatic; 'You are teaching doctrine, not personal behaviour, and can well rely upon receiving the necessary guidance.' Another time a Presbyterian lady resident in the parish asked me could she attend the 8 a.m. Holy Communion service. I consulted the Archbishop. His reply was: 'Tell the lady that she is very welcome as a guest, but add that guests do not outstay their welcome, and that there is a way open to her of joining the family.'

During my term of office at the Training College as Manager, he was considerate and co-operative. Many changes had to be made to meet new conditions imposed by the Irish Government and the Education Office. One of these was the direction that in the schools the infants, and subsequently the seniors, should be taught through the medium of Irish. This was greatly resented by Church of Ireland people generally. A representative deputation met the then Minister for Education. Dr. Gregg was the leader. After considerable discussion he took leave of the Minister with these words: 'I am well aware, Mr. Minister, that you have the power of the purse and of the whip, but it shall not be said that I allowed the children of my Church to be exploited in the interests of a political policy without a protest. I wish you good day.' The rebuke had its effect, and the extreme rigours of teaching through Irish were not imposed upon Church of Ireland schools.

At one of the meetings of the Training College Board, application was made for the use of the Dining Hall for a Students' party. The Archbishop—he was chairman—apparently dozing, suddenly said (but the words lack his inimitable intonation): 'Is it for a *hooley* or a *coele*?'

When I was appointed Bishop of Limerick he wrote a friendly and appreciative letter. I was struck by one phrase: 'You have been now called to a lonely life.'

As Primate he ruled constitutionally. He did not welcome drastic changes. He was always a little suspicious of enthusiasm. Yet when once convinced that reform was necessary he gave wholehearted support in carrying it into effect. Precedent was a powerful factor in his administration. Yet when the need arose he could act individually and almost autocratically. On one occasion in the General Synod, I ventured to oppose the official policy. My speech caught the ear of the Synod, and sympathy was rising in my favour. Dr. Gregg rose from the Chair and exhorted the Synod not to be carried away by eloquence.[5] My efforts failed and official policy was preserved. At the time I was somewhat hurt. Yet subsequent events proved him to be absolutely right, and a gracious explanation—almost an apology —completely restored my good will and renewed my confidence in him.

My last conversation with him was at the conclusion of the R.C.B. meeting shortly before his retirement. I went forward to inquire about his health. His reply was: 'If you exclude my eyes and my ears and my legs, I am wonderfully well.' I said, 'Well, your Grace, there is nothing wrong with your brain.' He said, 'Thank you for saying that.' Then with a whimsical smile he added, 'I think the same.'

So we leave him. Stern but always just; aloof yet sympathetic; alone yet eager for companionship; a wise counsellor yet seeking no one's confidences. An ecclesiastic who dominated his day and generation.

In March 1914 occurred the crisis in Ulster. Gregg's political persuasions were those of a conservative Unionist. But he was opposed to threats of violence in domestic disputes, and had he been in a benefice would almost certainly have had the courage to incur unpopularity by refusal to sign the Ulster Solemn League and Covenant. At the same time, as an Anglo-Irishman and as a Protestant he viewed with grave concern the prospect of Home Rule. On 25 May (contrary to his own forecast) the Home Rule Bill passed its Third Reading; and it had seemed, before the House met again on 30 July to debate the Amending Bill, that 'Asquith must at last declare himself. But European complications intervened, and once again he is saved for the time, and we continue to "wait and see." '

He had spent July with his wife in Switzerland, and for August and September the whole family moved to Kilbride in Co. Wicklow where he took nine weeks' Sunday duty, preaching his first sermon, 2 August, on 'the war-scare.' During the following weeks news of such events as the occupation of Brussels, the Retreat from Mons, the Fall of Namur, the Battle of the Aisne, the deaths in action of

---

[5] The present writer remembers the occasion. The Bishop of Limerick's speech—clear, incisive, persuasive—evoked loud and prolonged applause. The Primate's unexpected intervention—brief, terse, trenchant—had the effect of a cold douche on the general climate of feeling.

young acquaintances, consort queerly with lawn-tennis games, pony-trap drives, bicycle rides, blackberrying expeditions. 30 September sees the end of 'a delightful two months' holiday.' It was indeed a long and lovely summer. And for a year and more the life-and-death struggle the other side of the English Channel did little to disturb the even tenor of life's way in sheltered Ireland— save in the homes of those whose sons had volunteered.

October began with a week-end in Cork to preach at the Harvest Festival, and with the company of Hearn; then north to Ballymena (on the day of the fall of Antwerp) for another such occasion. There were several other of these 'autumn manoeuvres' at which he preached. And during the ensuing year the routine of college life continued uninterrupted. Gregg's view of the war's progress at this stage was that of the general public, namely of invincible but quite unfounded optimisim, fostered as it was by the fallacious reports of the Press which minimized Allied reverses and magnified German losses. But he was becoming increasingly alive to southern Ireland's insularity and apparent indifference to the European crisis; and Canon Hannay's historic sermon in St. Patrick's Cathedral on 15 November, on Ireland's national duty and destiny, drew from him the comment, 'Hannay preaches well.'

A paper which he had read to the Dublin Clerical Society on 1 February 1915, and which was published at length in the *Irish Church Quarterly* in March entitled 'The Clergy and Recent Criticism of the Creeds,' can be but briefly referred to here. It was prompted by the controversy between Bishop Gore (representing the traditionalists) and Professor Sanday (among the modernists) as to whether certain clauses in the Creeds are to be understood literally or symbolically. This paper is characteristic of Gregg's fairmindedness as a theologian, his dislike of precipitancy in arriving at conclusions that may prove to be premature, and his willingness to suspend judgment in a debate where there is much to be said for both points of view.

Early in September the resignation after prolonged illness of the Archbishop of Dublin (J. F. Peacocke) was announced; and the Bishopric of Kilmore became vacant.

On 23 September the Dublin Diocesan Synod met for the election of an Archbishop. Two nominees only were considered: the Bishop of Down (d'Arcy), and the Bishop of Ossory (Bernard). On the first vote the figures were: Down 367, Ossory 291; on the second: Down, 312, Ossory 243; on the third: Down 301, Ossory 219. The necessary two-thirds majority going by default, the election was referred to the House of Bishops. Despite d'Arcy's seniority on the Bench, the Bishops decided in favour of Bernard; and on 7 October Gregg wrote: 'I am very glad, and believe he will make a *great Archbishop.*' He continues:

> Two b'prics are vacant—Kilmore and Ossory. I know no special reason why I shd. feel interested. But suggestions from outside and from inside put it into my mind. I want to observe, in as external a way as I can, the developments of the situation.
> *12 Oct.* Dean Ovenden says, 'I venture to prophecy that if the Bps. have to appoint, it will be you. You won't be run by Kilmore Dio., tho' you may by Ossory.'

Letters of inquiry reach him from both dioceses, and on 20 October: 'I begin to realize v. serious possibility of falling between 2 stools.' Uncertainty persists till 10 November when Archdeacon Moore is elected to Kilmore. But Archbishop Bernard doubts the prospect of agreement by the electors of Ossory, Ferns and Leighlin, and expects reference to the House of Bishops; though Gregg hears on good authority that both Ossory and Leighlin are 'solid' for him. On the 16th: 'Provost proposes Committee for rearranging Div. Sch. affairs, largely in view of replacing me w. [Newport] White. But the inner meaning of proposal not disclosed!' The Archbishop still remains doubtful. But on 24 November Gregg is elected—at the age of forty-two—Bishop of the United Diocese with the necessary two-thirds majority from both orders. On the 26th at St. Patrick's: 'Sat in Maynooth stall for last time as Prebendary in my own right.' On the 28th: '11.30 Consecration Service, Christ Church Cathedral. I am consecrated BISHOP by J. H. Dublin, assisted by C. F. Down, C. B. Cork, T. S. Killaloe. Service over by 2.0—very impressive. . . . Hearn dines alone with us.' Then, in Greek: 'God be gracious to me.' On the 28th he is enthroned in St. Canice's Cathedral, Kilkenny, staying with the Dean and Mrs. Winder—'very agreeable and friendly.'

Had the election been referred to the Bishops, instead of decided by the United Diocese, the result would almost certainly have been the same. For Gregg was already a well-known figure in Irish Church life. His position in the Divinity School had brought him into touch with the central activities and leading personalities in Dublin, and he had preached from nearly every pulpit there. Freedom from the restrictions of parish routine and the long academic vacations had given him opportunities for contacts with many parishes in town and country throughout the length and breadth of the land. He was acquainted with all the Bishops, the most

4. CAMBRIDGE IRISH LITERARY SOCIETY, 1895. Gregg is extreme left of back row. Godfrey Day fourth from left

THE PALACE, KILKENNY, 1920. *Left to right*—Margaret, Claude, J.A.F.G., John, Barbara

5. ANNA A. GREGG

influential of whom—Bernard—held him in high regard. And he took himself very seriously.

There is a story, none the less in character even if fictitious, that, in response to some one's congratulations on his election to the episcopate, he said: 'Thank you. Yes. It has come somewhat sooner than I had expected.'

CHAPTER VI

BISHOP OF OSSORY

THE UNITED DIOCESE OF OSSORY, FERNS AND LEIGHLIN, comprising in area the greater part of Leinster and in population a large proportion of the nobility and landed gentry, had, since Disestablishment, and even before it, been reckoned one of the most important dioceses in Ireland. It had become almost traditional that its Bishops, because of their capacity, should succeed to one of the Archbishoprics.[1]

The newly elected Bishop, whose immediate predecessor had been 'very agreeable to him and had answered every kind of question,' took over from him the reins of office with competence, diligence, and sober enthusiasm. It was with a very real sense of vocation that he felt himself called by Divine Providence to assume so high a dignity and discharge the duties of so weighty an office; he was in very truth an overseer of the flock of Christ committed to his charge; he was God's man and minister; God was in all his thoughts. The very way in which he pronounced the word, a cause of irreverent amusement to many, was not (as was supposed) an idiosyncrasy of which he was unaware; it was a deliberate expression of his sense of *awe* in uttering the Name which is hallowed.

And because he was a man of God, he was above all else a man of prayer. But for him prayer, like belief, must be rational—not merely emotional. An article entitled 'Prayer and Natural Law,' printed in the *Alexandra College Magazine* for June 1916, comprised the substance of addresses which he had given earlier to the senior girls of that school. He never 'talked down' to any listeners, and the argument here advanced is certainly stiff reading for teen-agers. Nevertheless it so impressed itself on the mind of one of them who heard it that in later life she recalled it as likely 'to help young people of to-day as it helped me when I was young.'

Science has taught us to recognize the ideas of continuity, evolution, uniformity, as the habitual methods of God's working in the physical universe. 'Order is heaven's first law,' we are

---

[1]

Robert Samuel Gregg	Ossory 1857;	Armagh 1893
John Baptist Crozier	Ossory 1897;	Armagh 1911
Charles Frederick d'Arcy	Ossory 1907; Dublin 1919;	Armagh 1920
John Henry Bernard	Ossory 1911; Dublin 1915	
John Allen Fitzgerald Gregg	Ossory 1915; Dublin 1920;	Armagh 1939
John Godfrey Fitzmaurice Day	Ossory 1920;	Armagh 1938

taught. Of what use then is petitionary prayer? There is no room for the accidental or arbitrary in an unbroken causal nexus. 'The very wings of prayer are broken by the category of law. . . . All that God will give us is already *in* the determining factors of the world, and no amount of praying will cause to be introduced into the world-order anything that is not there already.' [He quotes the German theologian Dorner as witness on this side; and another, Wimmer, as aware of the self-contradiction involved in petitionary prayer and yet as unable to desist: 'an inward impulse moves me.']

Against the truth of divine immanence in the cosmos must be set the counter-truth of divine transcendence. If one without the other, we would have either a closed system with God so far removed from the world that He has left it to work itself out according to its own laws—Deism; or else so inextricably implicated with the world as to be the arch-prisoner of His own cosmos—Pantheism. But if we recognize the truth of both, we accept Theism; the natural order is the normal expression of God's will, but the laws of nature do not restrain or limit Him; they are simply the paths along which His creative energy habitually discharges itself. But they do not exhaust His power. He stands behind them, not they behind Him.

What after all is natural law? It is no more than an induction based on the observation of recurrent sequences of phenomena. It is our mind that formulates the law. And by the exercise of our wills we are constantly—in our little degree—interfering with the natural order and causing sequences to occur other than they would have been had nature taken its natural course. Will—our will—is a true cause in the universe: it can initiate action. How much more can the Will of God. A new instreaming of His divine power is continually possible. The world is not a closed system of physical causes and effects, but is irradiated and vitalized by a Living Being whose creative activity is perpetually concerned to enrich and enlarge its stores. Such is the vital connection of God with His world that I can conceive of no situation in which He might not modify circumstances in answer to our need.

Such is the gist of his argument. It is of course by no means original, nor does it exhaust all that can be thought on the topic. The voluntarism of Kant, which is implicit in it, is made to point beyond itself to a religious philosophy which may perhaps be best described as Personalism. He ends the paper with a thought which is to be found very often in letters to his clergy, variously expressed: 'It is possible for the secular eye to see only a happy chance, where faith detects the finger of the living God.'

§

In June 1916 the Primate of All Ireland, John Baptist Crozier, came to preach in his former Cathedral, staying at Kilkenny Castle for the week-end as guest of the Marquis of Ormonde. It would be usual for a Bishop to invite the Primate to take precedence in ministrations at the altar, and unusual to restrict his deliverances from the pulpit. Such however was not the view of the new Bishop of Ossory.

> Trinity Sunday. 11.30 Service. Primate preached. Good congregation—soldiers there. Asked to pr. for 10 min., occupied 25. I celebrate, give benediction, etc., unchallenged.

There is no record of how this assertion of independence was viewed by his superior.

The same evening he himself preached in St. Mary's church: 'about 250 present. Before sermon, felt how dreadfully inadequate it was.'

Canon Bothwell recalls his competence as a chairman:

> I was a curate in the diocese of Ferns when he was elected to the see of Ossory in 1915. One was impressed from the first by his knowledge of affairs and swift decision, and also by his scrupulous impartiality. At the Diocesan Synod of Ferns there was a discussion about the raising of clerical stipends. And Canon Willis (afterwards Archdeacon) proposed that the clergy should withdraw, leaving the matter to be settled by the bishop and laity. The Dean of Ferns seconded. Without a moment's hesitation the Bishop said, No—for if the clergy withdrew, the Synod would automatically be dissolved! Yet the proposer and seconder were experienced men of affairs.
>
> At the same Synod an old countryman laboured rather incoherently to express himself. Most of us smiled at his efforts. But later on, when the Bishop was summing up, he clearly stated what the man had been trying to say, and even incorporated his point in the resolution which followed.

Canon Barker recalls an incident of a more pathetic kind.

> Soon after his election to Ossory a big function was held to meet him. He was standing by himself looking forlorn when a little girl ran up to him and, taking his hand, said, 'Does no one like you? I like you.' With tears in his eyes he brought the child to her mother and said, 'Your little daughter has made me very happy.'
>
> The story was told me by the little girl's grandfather, the late

Colonel Claude Lane. It illustrates his longing for affection, particularly in those early days.

The year 1916 was one of crisis in the European War, and on the eve of its most critical phase—with every able-bodied Briton worth the name engaged somehow in the conflict—there was struck by Irish patriots a blow for freedom against British rule in Ireland —known by them, without consciousness of blasphemy, as the 'Easter Rising.' A minor result of this was the cancellation at short notice of the General Synod of the Church of Ireland due to convene in the following week, and therewith of the sermon to be preached to a crowded congregation in St. Patrick's Cathedral by the junior Bishop, according to custom. The rebellion was suppressed with a severity hardly to be justified upon subsequent reflection, even by national preoccupation with the continental life-and-death struggle, but it was not regarded in that light at the time, and Gregg's diary records without comment the 'execution of the rebels' and the capture of Roger Casement. He contrived a visit to Dublin and witnessed the ruins of Sackville Street.

After the carnage of battle in the summer and autumn of 1916 the Church of England launched a great national mission of Penitence and Hope. In his presidential address to the Ossory Diocesan Synod on 5 October the Bishop drew special attention to this, adding 'and we of the Church of Ireland shall have our week of prayer . . . to draw us all to a deeper sense of our Failure as a Nation to further as we ought the purpose of God.'

. . . The result of our isolation and immunity is bound to show itself in the moral and spiritual sphere unless we are very careful. . . . Ireland stands at this moment in a position of great danger. Those who speak for her in political matters seem to admit that the complete cessation of recruiting is due to reasons of policy, and that the revival of recruiting is a matter of terms. In fact, Ireland stands aloof, self-isolated, till she gets what she wants. But the present is a moment of critical decision. Much bigger issues are at stake than those of local politics; it is not a position of Irishmen fighting for England, the question for Ireland is this: Is she going to consent to be sullenly neutral in this great struggle of civilization against barbarism? . . . But I would say that it is a very serious thing for a nation on the one hand to barter its soul, and on the other to forfeit the sympathy of its fellow nations. . . . Does Ireland possess no public man who is prepared, even at the price of his political future, to tell Ireland the truth of the matter; to tell Ireland that she is taking the wrong turn; to tell Irishmen not what they like to hear, but what it is good for them to hear? Ireland cannot have it both ways. If she has peace and prosperity within her borders she must pay the price; but if, while enjoying peace and prosperity, she says to her sons: 'You have done enough, do no more; leave it to Englishmen and Scotsmen and Canadians and Australians to defend your homes,' she must not wonder if she finds one day that she has laid up for herself a store of shame and ill-will, or that in more ways that one she deplores too late a squandered opportunity. But if the ban upon voluntary recruiting is raised without delay, there is still time for Ireland to take her place among the peoples fighting for liberty, and to claim for her sons their share in a tradition that will be glorious for ever.

But the fires kindled by the Easter Rebellion had not been quenched: their embers smouldered. Recognizing the danger of this to national unity at such a time, the new Prime Minister, Mr. Lloyd George, had proposed in the House of Commons a settlement of the Irish problem on the basis of partition. But this was repugnant to Irishmen of all persuasions, Unionist and Nationalist, Catholic and Protestant (though, of course, for dia-metrically opposite reasons), and on 19 June 1916 the Bishops met to draft a unanimous resolution of protest against this proposal. It was read to the General Synod next day, and at the Primate's request Standing Orders were suspended to allow for a discussion of political affairs. There was general agreement that Partition was unthinkable.

In May 1917 the question of Settlement by Partition was due to be raised again by the Prime Minister since the Government was convinced that, as a war-measure, an Irish Settlement was immedi-ately necessary. It is here that the Bishop of Ossory asserted his independence in another way, by publicly entering the political arena. On 2 May 1917 he received the following letter from the Roman Catholic Bishop of Derry:

My dear Lord Bishop,
    I am sending you a copy of an appeal by the Country against Partition. The intention is to have it signed by Catholic and Protestant laymen of position and by Protestant and Catholic Bishops. Bishops both Catholic and Protestant have already agreed to subscribe their names.
    Should your Lordship be willing to sign, a wire saying simply Yes would suffice. The document will probably be published before the end of the present week. Should you not see your way to sign I am sure you will regard this letter as private and confidential.

                    I am faithfully yours,
                    ✝ CHAS. McHUGH.

The Bishop of Ossory, without consultation, agreed and signed the document, 'saying that I had agreed to its purely negative, anti-partition, terms.' There were only two other signatories of the Church of Ireland: the Bishops of Tuam (Benjamin Plunket), and of Killaloe (Sterling Berry). There were eighteen signatories among the Roman Catholic hierarchy, including Cardinal Logue (Primate), Archbishop Walsh (Dublin), and Archbishop Harty (Cashel); but Archbishop Healy (Tuam) and ten other Bishops abstained. There was therefore no unanimity on the matter in either Church. The Manifesto was as follows:

TO THE PEOPLE OF IRELAND

Fellow Countrymen. As there has been no organized effort to elicit the expression of Irish opinion regarding the dismemberment of our country, it may be said that the authoritative voice of the nation has not yet been heard on this question, which is of supreme importance. Large and representative meetings in many parts of that portion of Ulster so seriously affected have, no doubt, spoken in unmistakable terms, while of individual protests there has been an immense volume. But there is still wanting the national muster-roll of adherents to the principle of an Ireland one and undivided.

At the suggestion of some prominent Irishmen, we appeal to the people without distinction, religious or political, and we ask all who are opposed to partition, temporary or permanent, to send in their names with the designation of their official positions, if any, to one or other of the undersigned at the Gresham Hotel, Dublin, or to Charles O'Neill, Esq., D.L., at the same address.

Our requisition needs no urging. An appeal to the national conscience on the question of Ireland's dismemberment should meet with one answer and one answer alone. To Irishmen of every creed and class and party the very thought of our country partitioned and torn, as a new Poland, must be one of heart-rending sorrow.

In asking these names we have no ulterior object in view, and we give an assurance that they will be used only to show to the Government and to the world that the country is unrelentingly opposed to partition.

The fact that the country was already irreconcilably divided against itself politically and religiously, as well as ethnologically and historically and in every aspect of tradition and sentiment, is not mentioned. Its geographical unity must at all costs be safeguarded.

The manifesto was hailed by a leading article in the *Church of Ireland Gazette* as 'one of the most remarkable documents in Irish political history' and by it was given unqualified and enthusiastic support. Somewhat ingenuously it claims that both camps are in the right for opposite reasons:

A Belfast daily newspaper has insulted the three Bishops of our Church who have signed this manifesto by suggesting that the object of its signatories is to put pressure upon the Government to coerce Unionist Ulster. We have no hesitation, on behalf of the three Bishops, in repudiating this gratuitous insult. We have equally no hesitation in saying that in this matter they represent the views of an overwhelming majority of Irish Churchmen. The Roman Catholic prelates signatory to the manifesto are, of course, Home Rulers; but from beginning to end of the document the larger political question of the Union or Home Rule is not once introduced. Unionist Ulster desires, and Southern Unionists desire, to maintain the unity of Ireland on the basis of the Legislative Union with Great Britain. Nationalist Ireland desires and, if Home Rule for any part of Ireland is to come, Southern Unionists desire with it, to maintain the unity of Ireland on the basis of Home Rule for all Ireland. The only common ground between them, on which the two Churches meet in this manifesto, is allegiance to the ideal of an Ireland 'One and undivided.' All that the three Bishops assert in this historic document is the principle that, under any form of Government, there shall be no 'partition, temporary or permanent.'

It warns the British Government of 'the crass folly of attempting to base a settlement upon a violation of the only ground which conflicting parties in Ireland hold in common.' And what have the three Bishops done but reassert in their own names the principle which the Bench of Bishops unanimously asserted last year?

The insolent Belfast newspaper referred to was the *Evening Telegraph*. Its attitude was perhaps what would be called nowadays 'more realistic.'

Three Bishops of the protestant Church have found strange bedfellows in their political adversity. The attitude of the Roman Catholic Bishops in this matter is perfectly plain. They are out to have Ireland converted into the sanctuary of their faith; a place where their Church will be supreme in politics and in religion. Consciously or unconsciously the other three Bishops are co-operating in that scheme. . . . Bishops Plunket, Gregg, and Berry have made an appeal to 'the national conscience'—a somewhat obscure phrase—against partition. We make this appeal to the

individual conscience of each of the three. Do they invite all
those who are pledged to partition of the six counties to commit
wholesale perjury? If not, do they ask and expect the Government to impose coercion? Only by one or other of these methods
can the aim of a solid Ireland be immediately achieved.

Comparison of partition in Ireland with the division of Poland
was, it was pointed out, a patent absurdity.

But on 9 May the manifesto became the subject of a long column
in the London *Times* by its special correspondent in Dublin, and
of its leading article. These warned the Prime Minister against
precipitate proposals for a settlement. 'It must be limited by two
strict negations: no partition and no coercion of Ulster. In other
directions true statesmanship may find its possibilities illimitable.'
To add to the complication, the Roman Catholic Archbishop of
Dublin was now suspected of having engineered the manifesto in
order to secure the election of a Sinn Fein candidate for South
Longford against a Redmondite. This prompted a statement from
Bishop d'Arcy to the *Times* written on 11 May:

> Sir,—The fact that three Bishops of the Church of Ireland
> signed the manifesto against what is termed 'the dismember-
> ment of Ireland' seems to be taken in some quarters to mean that
> these Bishops have gone over to the extreme anti-British party in
> Ireland. It is also being taken to imply that the Church of
> Ireland has changed in her attitude towards Home Rule. I assure
> you that both these inferences are mistaken. First. At three special
> Synods the Church of Ireland by overwhelming majorities regis-
> tered her conviction that Home Rule would be a danger to the
> Empire and an injury to Ireland; and she has never since given
> any sign that her opinion has changed. The loud assertions of a
> few individuals, who speak only for themselves, are of no value
> in a matter of this kind. Secondly. Last year our House of
> Bishops passed a resolution against 'a policy of dismemberment'
> but, as I understood, our reference was to the policy which
> would dismember the United Kingdom and divide Ireland at
> the same time. Many in Ireland are now coming to realize that
> if the greater dismemberment takes place the lesser is an in-
> evitable consequence, and the only way to preserve the unity of
> Ireland is to preserve the union with England.
> It is with great unwillingness that I intervene. Here in Ulster
> we are anxious to avoid political controversy as much as possible
> during the war. I write at a request which I cannot easily refuse.
> The statement which I make expresses much more than my own
> individual opinion.   Yours,
>
> CHARLES F. DOWN

On 8 May he had written privately to Gregg (and the formal
style of address, despite their former intimate association, was then
customary on the Irish Bench) as follows:

> My dear Bishop,
>   Is 'dismemberment' a fair word to use? When Ontario got a
> distinct provincial government from Quebec, was Canada dis-
> membered? The parallel is very close, and the differences of race
> and religion almost the same.
>   Of course, if those who sign this document are thinking of
> complete separation from England, I grant that the word may be
> used. Otherwise, I think it misleading.
> Yours as ever,
CHARLES F. DOWN

The Primate was in England during these events and now wrote
from Newcastle-on-Tyne to the Bishop of Ossory a tactfully
worded request to him (as secretary to the Bench) to summon a
meeting;

> *11 May.*   as from University Club, Dublin.
> My dear Bishop,
>   The joint action of three Bishops of the Church of Ireland
> with the Roman Hierarchy compels the Ulster Bishops, alas, to
> take some public action, as I hear incalculable injury is being
> done to the Church in the North. But before issuing our state-
> ment I should like, as a matter of loyalty to our Brethren, to have
> a full meeting of Bishops, and if the Archbishop of Dublin can
> attend I will be grateful if you will kindly call a meeting of
> Bishops for Wednesday next, 16th inst. at 11 o'c. I am sending
> a copy of this letter to the Archbishop of Dublin and asking him
> to telegraph to you if this day and hour will suit him.
> Yrs. faithfully,
JOHN B. ARMAGH

A wire from you would reach me on Monday at the Vicarage,
Sheffield. Alas, I must stay over Monday for 2 sermons there on
Sunday and 3 addresses on Monday, but will hasten home.

Accordingly the Bishop of Ossory (having received an affirmative
telegram from Archbishop Bernard) circularized the Bishops,
stating the agenda: 'The Lord Primate desires a meeting of the
House of Bishops before the Northern Bishops issue a public statement.' At the same time he wrote privately to Archbishop Bernard
(but the letter is not extant) and received the following reply:

13 May. The Palace, Dublin.

My dear Bishop,

Of course. There was nothing in Dr. McHugh's letter (of which I too received a copy) to suggest that the Roman Hierarchy were acting as a body. The signatures were merely those of individuals.

I do not know for what purpose the Primate wishes us to meet on Wednesday. In the face of our unanimous resolution last year against the partition of Ireland, I do not quite see what the Ulster Bishops now wish to do.

Yrs. very sincerely,

JOHN DUBLIN

Gregg's record of the event is brief. 'We meet. 9 present. Ulster Bps. will promulgate mild statement.' The next day the Prime Minister's proposal for a convention of Irishmen of all sections was announced in the Press. In his diary for this year Gregg inserted a page giving his 'Reasons etc. of signing manifesto, May 7':

(a) Only express what Bps. expressed to Synod 1916. Why is it worse to say same with R.C. Bps.?

(b) Prime Minister was to make a statement in H. of C. in a very few days.

(c) To protest against monstrous use of press by N'cliffe and his appeal to American politicians to express views on Irish question.

(d) Subsequently, I learn that manifesto was prob. intended to influence Longford election of May 9. This may have been so. But I doubt if it was sufficient reason for *not* signing.

On 21 May he wrote by request for the *Church Family Newspaper* his view of the Irish situation for which he and other Irish Church Bishops had been asked. Only three others responded to the request (Killaloe, Cashel, and Meath); but their statements are brief and insignificant in comparison with his, which occupies more than a full column. He welcomes the Prime Minister's amended proposal to seek for a settlement by consent rather than partition, but points out the insuperable difficulties at the present time of securing even a measure of agreement. He counsels delay, at least till the war is ended; deprecates any consideration of American opinion, which is based on ignorance; points out that a lasting settlement must be, not machine-made, but based on mutual confidence and confidence only comes with time.

No one can have any full understanding of the Irish problem who has not studied it on the spot and lived in both North and

South. . . . For the questions that divide Irishmen are of age-old growth, and their roots lie very deep. Ireland cannot be settled as you would settle a trades dispute. You cannot bridge the kind of gulf you find here with a fine-drawn formula.

Further, the Irish problem is not merely domestic; on its solution depends the security of the British Isles.

It must not be forgotten that, besides internal discords and suspicions, external questions are involved. Many Irish political idealists would like to see Ireland as independent of Great Britain as Belgium is of France. And why not? say some. The war has given us the answer. Ireland's geographical position determines inevitably that it can never be a sovereign State. Ireland is the key of the Atlantic, and Great Britain, whose very life is bound up with command of the sea, cannot allow the control of the coasts and harbours of Ireland to be in any but British hands. . . .

In view then of the sharp differences of race, of creed, of economic interest that separate North from South, and since any settlement must rest upon three pillar conditions—the naval security of Great Britain, the willing assent of Ulster, and the unity of Ireland—it is plain that political wisdom and skill of the highest order are called for in order first to bring together a convention of Irishmen of all camps, and then to induce them to agree upon a settlement.

He ends on a prophetic note.

The time will come when the House of Commons proceeds to formulate its plans (as it will be forced to do after the war) for the transaction of domestic as distinct from imperial business. Then let it provide for the management of specifically Irish affairs in Ireland as part of a larger scheme for that decentralization which is imperative if the clogged machinery of Parliament is ever again to work freely and the House of Commons is to be effective as the Central Council of the Empire.

Dis aliter visum. The complexity of Irish ideology proved too inextricable for peaceful settlement; history took another course when fanaticism wrested the helm from statecraft. But time and time's revenges cannot refute the essential wisdom, foresight, and moderation of Bishop Gregg's counsel.

§

He suffered from a temperamental incapacity (not uncommon to those whose primary interest is with 'the things of the mind') to understand the very young. One of his greatest admirers, the Revd. C. B. Moss, says of his addresses to Confirmation candidates that 'they were very long, excellent for candidates for Ordination, but far above the heads of children in their teens.' But now that his two little boys were of school age he made a valiant effort to associate himself with them in their holiday pursuits, playing cricket and tennis with them and their Kilkenny friends on the Palace lawn, and reading Dickens to them before bedtime. 'Jeff' at fourteen had passed from a preparatory school in Llandulas to Shrewsbury with an entrance scholarship in Classics and was showing promise also as an athlete. His father would sometimes 'do a little Latin and Greek with him' in the evenings and introduced him thus early to the Ionic Greek of Homer's *Odyssey*.

The severity of his outward appearance masked a humour and humanity, an inner tenderness and sensitivity, rarely discernible even in his own family circle. Glimpses of this are happily revealed in his younger daughter's memories of their home-life, first in Kilkenny and afterwards in Dublin:

When I was a small child I found my father very alarming. It was not so much his personality as his appearance that frightened me. He was tall and slim and seemed to me to be altogether black from head to foot, with a few white patches—his deep clerical collar and quite colourless face with a blue chin. His clothes and even his hair were as black as could be. He wore metal-rimmed spectacles, so there was no relief from the general colourlessness of his appearance. It was not until I was older that I discovered two things: one was the warmth of the eyes behind the chilling spectacles, and the other, the warmth, not merely physical, in the touch or grasp of his hand. I believe in those days, even though I was his fourth child, he had been unable to discover any means of communication with the very young, whom he regarded as unpredictable, undisciplined, and unaffected by the meaning of words.

He did, however, expect a high standard of behaviour from his children, no matter how young they might be, and it took him many years to realize that even his children had failings common to all humans. I think he imagined that the great differences between his own early home life and that of his children would automatically make us better and happier than he and his sisters had been. He was to suffer many shocks in the course of time. I remember one terrifying conversation with him in his study at Kilkenny, when I was perhaps six years old. It was the first time I remember being alone with him, and I think he was as frightened of me as I was of him. After a few stilted preliminaries he said:

'Well, you should ask God to help you.'

'Oh yes,' I replied airily, 'I always do when I'm unhappy.'

He looked at me as if I had struck him. 'Unhappy!' he exclaimed in horror. 'How can a child in a home like yours ever be unhappy?' I could see he was deeply shocked and quite unable to realize that even children in the happiest of homes have their troubles. He considered environment to be of the greatest importance and once, years later, when I was walking with him in Italy, he stopped and looked with great sadness at the truly wonderful view:

'And to think,' he said, 'that even here, people die!'

When I was about seven, I accompanied my brothers on a tour of the roof of the Palace at Kilkenny. We darted up and down the lead valleys and ended with a solemn walk along the parapet, in single file. My father and mother, walking below in the cool of the evening, in the shade of the great ilex tree—just like God in the Garden of Eden—saw us as we saw them. They stood motionless, in order not to frighten us, and we froze, petrified with guilt. Eventually, we moved forwards, shaking, all our confidence gone and in real danger. We went downstairs as slowly as possible, dreading the inevitable encounter. It could have been worse; my brothers were spoken to with great severity, but nobody was punished.

There are two stories of his time in Kilkenny which he himself used to tell. One is about the Rector of a country parish where he had gone to preach one Sunday morning. He commented afterwards to the Rector on the surprisingly large number of people in Church, and the reply was: 'Oh, there aren't generally that number, my Lord, but where the carcase is, there the eagles will gather together, if you see what I mean.'

The other concerns a Rector who was a remarkable acrobat. My father arrived early at the Church but was admitted to the vestry by the sexton, in the absence of the Rector. 'I looked round then,' said my father, unable to control his laughter, 'and saw him coming into the vestry walking on his hands.'

He suffered from certain 'blind spots' which not uncommonly afflict the over seriously-minded who are also acutely self-conscious, though this became less apparent in his later years. By way of an amusing example:

Dr. Gregg, when Bishop of Ossory, was preaching in St. Canice's Cathedral at an annual Diocesan Service of the Mothers' Union. The congregation were, for the most part, elderly, and of course eminently virtuous. His opening sentence was: 'Motherhood is a responsibility, too often, I fear, entered upon lightly, and without due thought.'

This is recorded by a member of that congregation who can vouch for its accuracy; who had the double misfortune to be sitting directly under the pulpit and to possess an unruly sense of humour, which on this occasion she found it almost impossible to control.

Besides frequent engagements in Dublin and care of all the churches in so large a diocese, the Bishop had responsibilities, civic as well as ecclesiastical, in Kilkenny. This ancient city is justly proud of containing within its walls the oldest school in Ireland. Kilkenny College was founded in 1538 by the then Earl of Ormonde for the sons of Protestant gentry. The Bishop of Ossory is *ex officio* chairman of the local committee which deals with its welfare, and also a member of the Incorporated Society for Protestant Schools in Ireland which meets in Dublin under the presidency of the Archbishop of Armagh. It happened that in 1917 the head-mastership of Kilkenny College became vacant owing to the appointment of the Revd. E. G. Seale to that of Portora Royal School. A young member of the staff, who had taken an honours degree in Mathematics in Trinity and was a graduate also in Civil Engineering, Mr. C. G. Shankey, decided to apply for the vacant post, and before doing so wrote to Bishop Gregg to inform him of his intention.

He invited me to meet him at the Palace for a talk about the matter. I went in a state of considerable trepidation, and my first impression was of an austere and unapproachable dignitary of the Church. He probably sensed this and asked me in a most kindly manner whether I would mind joining him and the children in their nursery for tea.[2] This put me completely at my ease, and afterwards we had a very long talk in his study about all sorts of things besides that about which I had come to see him. It seemed that there was little about me that he did not already know. I was struck by his interest in graphical arithmetic and he spoke about it for a long time. For a man whose interests were mainly classical it was wonderful to note the clear grasp he had of this subject and he was keenly interested to learn about the method of drawing graphs of experimental results in order to establish laws in Physics and Chemistry. He ended by telling me that he would promise no support; he must see the other candidates first. I was impressed by his absolute straightness and this was confirmed on further acquaintance. You always knew where you were with him. I learned later that he did in actual fact support me when the time came to make the appointment.

[2] The date was 12 November, which happened to be his daughter Margaret's tenth birthday. The appointment was made ten days later on the Bishop's recommendation.

Nearly forty years later they met again when, on his retirement from Kilkenny, Mr. Shankey was appointed Secretary to the Incorporated Society, and one remembers the occasion when the Primate, as he then was, introduced him to a full session of the Committee with characteristic grace: 'Mr. Shankey and I are old friends now of many years' standing. He became Headmaster of Kilkenny College during my time there as Bishop of Ossory. I am very glad that he is with us again in this capacity in which his great experience will be so valuable.' Mr. Shankey adds:

The Primate had a dry sense of humour which sometimes took people by surprise. I remember once, before one of the last meetings which he was able to attend, expressing the hope that he was keeping well. His reply was: 'I walk with difficulty, I can only see what is printed in the middle of the page, and I can scarcely hear at all. Otherwise I am pretty well.' I always thought that if he had not become a great churchman he could have been a very great judge.

An impression of another kind comes from Canon John Bentley, then Rector of Jonesborough in Co. Armagh. An Englishman born and bred, in younger days he had been a notable chorister in Armagh Cathedral, and was afterwards for several years Precentor of Durham before returning to Ireland.

Early in 1918 I went to Kilkenny to visit St. Canice's Cathedral. Taking advantage of a previous invitation I paid a courtesy call on the Bishop. Soon I was surprised to hear the sound of a gong and apologized for taking up his time, but the Bishop waved aside my apologies and said, 'You may as well stay and have a meal with us.' During dinner the talk reverted to Cathedral music, of which my host seemed to have an extraordinarily intimate knowledge. He was very interested in my personal experience of the various cathedral choirs in England in which I had sung: Durham, York, Ely, St. Paul's, Manchester.

Afterwards, in the drawing room, the Bishop opened a book of songs and said, 'Put your voice to this.' He then sat down at the piano and played the introduction to 'Where'er you walk'; then followed 'I arise from dreams of thee'; and finally 'Comfort ye' and 'Every valley' from the *Messiah*. I could not have wished for a more accurate and sympathetic accompaniment.[3]

It was his frequent recreation during these years to take solitary

[3] The Bishop's diary reads: *'30 Jan.* Walk to Talbot's Inch and back by river 7.0 to find Revd. Bentley, Jonesborough, waiting for me. Stays for dinner and sings for us after.'

6. *Left to right*—ARCHBISHOP OF WALES (EDWARDS), ARCHBISHOP OF CANTERBURY (LANG), ARCHBISHOP OF ARMAGH (D'ARCY). PRIMUS OF THE SCOTTISH CHURCH (ROBBERDS). ARCHBISHOP OF DUBLIN (GREGG)

To

Walter Joseph Mayes Burrows,
on the occasion of
his Ordination as Deacon,
with kindest wishes
from

John Allen Fitzgerald
Archbishop of Dublin.

Trinity iii, MCMXXXI.

Ταῦτα μελέτα· ἐν τούτοις
ἴσθι· ἵνα σου ἡ προκοπὴ
φανερὰ ᾖ πᾶσιν.

1 Tim. iv, 15

7. INSCRIPTION IN BIBLE OF AN ORDINAND
(*The Green Studio, Dublin*)

meditative walks along the banks of the Nore, upwards through 'Bishop's Meadows' to the suspension bridge (which then was) or downwards beneath the Castle walls—in either direction surely one of the loveliest stretches of riverside in Ireland.

§

There exists in the Diocese of Ossory a clerical office which is unique in the Church of Ireland—that of Bishop's Vicar Choral. It comprises the functions of Diocesan Registrar, which involves copying in manuscript all official records, accompanying the Bishop on formal occasions for functions throughout the United Diocese, acting as Vicar Choral of the Cathedral, and as custodian of St. Canice's Library (which is a repository of ancient books). At the same time it involves the duties of part-time curate to the Dean of Ossory who is also Rector of Kilkenny. The Bishop's Vicar Choral at this time was a man of exceptional ability in the conduct of affairs, named Mervyn Clare, who had served in the same capacity under Bishop Bernard. He had come to Ireland, as his present Bishop had, from across the Channel; admired him for his great qualities as he had admired his predecessor, and was much in his counsels. But the Bishop, presuming perhaps too arbitrarily on what he took to be his rights, had been in the habit of haling his Vicar Choral away from the parish, even on Sundays, without first consulting the Dean. (And Dean Winder, it must be added, is still remembered as the most charming, conciliatory, and friendliest of men.) This gave rise to a controversy of long continuance, the course of which can be partially traced in the Bishop's diary.

> *8 Mar. 1918.* On this day the Dean held Chapter meeting and stampeded members of Caput into a resolution to take the Bp. before the Court of the General Synod. The want of courtesy in this capitular act before we have ever even exchanged letters is inexpressible.
> *9 Mar.* My mind somewhat disturbed during day. I am gravitating towards the holding of a visitation. Write to Judge Madden, sending him copy of my letter to Dean of 28 Jan.

This disturbance persists for more than a year. Neither side will give way. Legal advice is solicited, but it appears inconclusive. Judge Madden calls at the Palace and suggests arbitration by the Archbishop of Dublin. but for some reason this is not sought. Finally the Judge's own proposal of a compromise—'eight Sundays in the year for the Bishop's use of the B.V.C.'—is agreed; and on 6 April 1919 Gregg's diary records triumphantly: 'Preach in

G

St. John's. Robinson's [curate] first day, but he was silent with laryngitis. Clare assists me. I claim him from Cathedral.'

Thus far Bishop Gregg's diary, which appears inconclusive. The present writer, having served for a short while as Bishop's Vicar under Bishop Phair during the last years of Dean J. H. Burrows, without consciousness of any friction on that score between them, though aware of the previous controversy was ignorant of its outcome. He therefore requested of Bishop Phair some definite information on the point for the purpose of this book, and received the following reply:

In the course of Bishop Gregg's episcopate a controversy arose between him and the Very Revd. Thomas Winder, then Dean of Ossory, as to the position and duties of the Bishop's Vicar in the Cathedral. The appointment to the position has always been made by the Bishop and a large portion of the stipend came from an endowment made by Bishop O'Brien in the year 1872 and from Diocesan funds. Bishop Gregg therefore claimed that when he wished to have the Bishop's Vicar for any Diocesan duty outside the Cathedral he was at liberty to call upon him without reference to the Dean and Chapter. The Dean on the other hand claimed that his permission should be asked before that course was taken. The question was placed before the Chancellor of the Diocese and before some eminent Dublin lawyers for guidance and advice. At one time there were serious thoughts of bringing it before the Ecclesiastical Court for its decision. I have seen a letter that Bishop Gregg wrote to Archbishop Bernard asking what his custom had been when he was Bishop of the Diocese. The Archbishop replied that it had been his habit always to consult the convenience of the Dean before asking the Bishop's Vicar to undertake any Diocesan duty on Sundays.

'But the legal question of my rights or of the Dean's rights was never raised. I should certainly not allow that my friendly conversations with the Dean on the subject was equivalent to any formal request for the sanction of the Chapter. My practice cannot determine the legal question which has now been raised, for as I thought it was a question of some difficulty I took pains that it should never arise in my time.'

Eventually the matter was amicably settled by the adoption of a suggestion that the Bishop should not exercise his liberty to take his Vicar away from the Cathedral more than eight times in a year at most. Archbishop Bernard's comment on this happy solution was that he rejoiced that a way had been found of avoiding legal proceedings which would be a great scandal to the Church. I may say that in my own experience, first as Dean and subsequently as Bishop, the question never arose as I was always careful to consult with the Dean before calling upon the Vicar for any occasional Sunday duty.

§

Between 8 and 13 July of 1918 he made what may well be considered his most important contribution to theological thought in a series of four lectures in Trinity College to an audience of 180 clergymen from all parts of Ireland, upon 'The Church: Creeds and Authority.' Other lecturers were the two recently appointed Professors of Divinity (McNeile and Newport White), and of Ecclesiastical History (Lawlor), and the Provost (Mahaffy). The whole course, prefaced by a sermon by the Archbishop of Dublin (Bernard) was published in the same year by the Church of Ireland Press with the uninspired and uninspiring title *Ad Clerum*. Despite this, the volume was hailed by Church of England commentators in a most complimentary fashion as 'the mature thought of men who face grave problems with open-minded honesty' and as 'masterly addresses—by far the best balanced contribution to a difficult subject that has come our way' and other l.ke enconiums. But by all of them the palm is given to the Bishop of Ossory who by one is ranked equal with Dr. Headlam (then Regius Professor of Divinity in Oxford) as an expositor of Anglican doctrine, and 'Scrutator' (the most scholarly of critics) confessed that he had never found so satisfactory a discussion of the subject. The view may here be advanced that these four lectures, and they alone in the whole collection, deserve perpetuation. The passage of years has not robbed them of their freshness, vigour and vitality. One knows not which to admire more: the substance and the erudition which unobtrusively informs them; the breadth as well as the depth with which the whole subject is handled; or the economy and felicity of its phrasing. One quotation must suffice:

Is the Church of to-day powerless in the hands of its Creed? Is the Creed irreformable? . . . Is it possible to say that any point in time can be specified before which the Creed may be enriched without objection, and after which to touch is profanity? . . .

I believe that if the Church is persuaded that its Credal statements are (a) incomplete, or wanting in balance, (b) inaccurate, or not sufficiently precise, (c) unedifying, and liable to exclude from communion on non-essential grounds, the duty rests upon it to set the matter right. Needless to say, any such attempts should be undertaken only under the pressure of grave necessity, and after long and repeated discussion, extending over a generation or a century, or more.

Such freedom and freshness of theological thought is remarkable. Though a movement for the revision of the Prayer Book was already in the air (1920), it does not appear that any alteration to the Creeds was contemplated by the revisers. Those ancient articles of the faith were still sacrosanct in the eyes of even the most revolutionary of liturgists. Yet here was a Bishop of the most conservative Church in the Anglican Communion envisaging such a possibility. Not that he positively advocated it; but he did at least ventilate it as a theme for consideration.

At the Ossory Diocesan Synod of October 1919 he thanked God for the victorious peace granted to the Allied arms. The Cathedral would shortly be enriched by a piece of sculpture worthy of the building and of those whom it commemorated. But there was now cause for anxiety at home in prospect of 'yet another effort to relieve the chronic discontent of Ireland.' He went on to speak of his hopes for Church of Ireland people.

> . . . The Church of Ireland is a very solid asset in contemporary Irish life. It does not indeed wield the secular power it might claim in virtue of its total numbers, because its adherents are to be found all over the country, and therefore always in dilution. But because of our presence even in small numbers in every part of the country, and because of what our people are, we stand for a great deal more, morally and socially, than meets the eye . . .
>
> My hope is that means may be found for giving the members of the Church of Ireland a fairer share in public affairs, municipal and Parliamentary, than is permitted to them at present. Our numbers in the Southern Province were in 1914 considerably over 170,000; and yet, just because we are found in concentration nowhere but are in dilution everywhere, this large body of Church-people, though possessed of considerable substance, education, and capacity, is to all intents and purposes a negligible and neglected quantity. This is a serious loss to the country. Such a body of citizens cannot be permanently disfranchised and reduced to silence without injury to the welfare of Ireland. The voice of criticism is stifled, the contributions which the wisdom, the experience, the intelligence of our people might make, are like the deposits in an unworked mine. . . . We ask for something more than the mere permission to live: we ask for the right to count for something in the administrative life of our country.

On 10 October 1919 he delivered to the Ferns Diocesan Synod a strikingly prophetic address. The horror of the long international war was nearly a year ended, but it had left an aftermath of national unrest. Industrial agitation had engineered the first railway strike in England and the 'go slow' slogan; political agitation was responsible for the recent police murders in Ireland. An evil spirit of Collectivism was usurping the place of the individual moral sense.

The individual is being crushed under the organization; he is not allowed to call body or mind or will his own. We are ceasing to be a free people; we are being organized until we are mere items—mute items—in the dominating mass. . . .

The individual must conform to the decree of the organization. His conscience counts for nothing, unless it happens to coincide with the conscience of the crowd. And hence come tyranny, arbitrariness, enslavement. Enterprise, initiative, higher sense of duty are ruled out. The keen bricklayer may not lay more bricks than the Union allows. The man who has no grievance against his employer must down tools with the rest. . . . He is intimidated by the policy of peaceful picketing, or by the equally effective social pressure that can be exerted on his family. In order to live, and out of desire for a quiet life, many a wage-earner who hates the system gives in and acts as a silent cog in the soulless, grinding machinery.

He turned to the same menace confronting the moral life of the Irish community in another guise.

Collectivism has found a ready home in Ireland. Individualism has always found itself faced in this country by a tendency to association in groups. There are historical explanations of a national and religious kind for this readiness to combine. But just as collectivism has been of great advantage industrially (in the past) and yet is now inflicting grave injury on those whose individuality it is crushing, so collectivism in Irish life, whether political or industrial, is inflicting serious moral injury on the individuals of the community. It is rapidly robbing the Irishman of his sense of responsibility; he is coming to allow his moral standard and his conduct to be dictated to him. . . . Here is a community knowing full well the law of God on the subject of right and wrong, and yet passively tolerating repeated acts of murder as a method of political pressure. Irishmen are allowing their consciences to be either perverted or overridden on the subject of police murder. The idea seems to be that murder is less wicked when it is done for political than for private reasons; that murder may be called by a softer name when it is done by the agents of a political society than by unorganized desperadoes. No opponent of the Legislative Union likes to express his private conviction for fear of disloyalty to the 'national' cause. 'My country, right or wrong' is the general political attitude. Independent criticism, fearless appeal to the right as against the expedient, willingness to face unpopularity or even worse consequences—where are they to be seen? Irishmen have a wonderful knack of holding together, but you may hold together at too great a cost—the cost of your independence, your character, your manhood—the cost of your country's credit. For what exalts a nation is not political combination, but righteousness.

On 14 March 1920 he was the special preacher in St. Patrick's on the celebration of the 700th anniversary of the completion of its Chapter. The sermon shows the extent and accuracy of his knowledge of Celtic and Anglo-Norman ecclesiology.

The principal transaction on the second day of the General Synod in 1920 was the passing of the Bishop of Ossory's Bill for the admission of women to serve on General and Select Vestries and as Churchwardens. On its first reading it was debated at length and with some warmth; on its second reading it was passed with a considerable majority, with the proviso that women should not be elected as Parochial Nominators. Gregg's reasoned advocacy carried the day. More than thirty years later (in 1952) it was his pleasure as Primate of All Ireland to welcome, as he did in graceful terms, the first lady member of the Synod. His elder daughter says that his early conviction of the value of women in Church government was due to his admiration of his wife's capacity and industry in several directions.

§

Two deaths—of the Provost (Mahaffy) on 30 April 1919, and of the Primate (Crozier) on 11 April 1920—set in motion a train of events which, in their impact on the course of Irish Church history in general and of Gregg's career in particular, can be followed in his diaries.

Bernard, Archbishop of Dublin, was immediately spoken of as Mahaffy's successor. His connection with the University had been of long standing; a bishopric and archbishopric seemed but as interludes in his academic career. Moreover the stormy times called for a strong hand and a sane mind at the helm of Irish youth, and no one could be considered more fitted to the task than he. When to public rumour was added strong pressure from the British Government in the person of the Lord Lieutenant (French), the issue could hardly be in doubt. 'But' (wrote Gregg) 'I did not, could not, believe he would accept. It seemed to me a loss of caste, a piece of opportunism. . . . See Browning's *Lost Leader.*'

He could not know, nor is it sufficiently told in Bernard's biography, with what 'a heavy heart' he was persuaded to relinquish his office in the Church. He did so against his better judgment and this was shown by the event: he was not so 'successful' a Provost as he had been an Archbishop.

But who would now succeed him? The *Daily Express* of 17 June (Gregg notes) spots three possibles: Down (d'Arcy), Tuam (Plunket), Ossory (himself). His forecast, giving fractional details of anticipated votes, clerical and lay, show that he expected a close-run event, with d'Arcy very slightly in the lead and himself hard on the heels of Plunket. But at the election on 30 June d'Arcy was only four votes short of the necessary majority; the matter was referred to the Bishops, by whom he was unanimously elected. Gregg writes in his diary: 'A most happy solution of a situation which threatened to send Tuam to Dublin. D.G. I am wonderfully little disappointed with the result.' (On 3 October of this year Bishop Plunket—son of Lord Plunket, former Archbishop of Dublin—was translated to the See of Meath.)

Gregg's episcopal hopes and fears at this time were interrupted by an event of importance to him as a father. His younger son Claude, a very promising lad and a general favourite, passed as a naval cadet into Osborne on 25 July. His diary entry for that date is in the Greek of the Septuagint: 'The Lord, who brought me from my youth up unto this day, bless the lad.'

The death of the Primate of All Ireland in April of the following year gave another turn to fortune's wheel. Gregg's first thought is that 'd'Arcy will go to Armagh, and Plunket be chosen for Dublin.' He thinks that his own outspokenness at an R.C.B. meeting on 17 March would make him unwelcome to voters. 'Anyhow, I would rather be free to say what I believe to be necessary, than keep quiet and upset no susceptibilities.' He was unable to attend the Primate's funeral in Armagh because of the General Strike on 13 April 'in protest against allowing Sinn Fein hunger-strikers in Mountjoy prison to die.' His second thought is:

I cannot see how d'Arcy can agree, or the Bps. ask him, to go to Armagh. But with surprise of last August before me, I am prepared for its happening.

I find, by his own answer to my question, that Dublin is ready to go to Armagh. So the question of the Primacy is simple enough, and settled in a happy way, as if d'Arcy had not gone, it wd. v. possibly have been B.J.P.!

It happened; and d'Arcy, whose tenure of Sees must be unique in Church annals, went to Armagh after only ten months in Dublin. But who would succeed him? Gregg writes in his diary on 21 April 1920:

The question will then arise *re* Dublin. It is quite conceivable
I may be taken. I had not been reckoning that it wd. be so, but
a talk w. M[ervyn] C[lare] on Ap. 24 makes me see that it is
thought to be on the cards. To go wd. be to lose much, e.g.
beautiful home, pleasant diocese, leisure, time for rest and
thought.

His diary now—from May to September—reflects a preoccupation with this question which he finds it difficult to control. He
leaves the General Synod with the impression that Meath and
Derry 'and perhaps I' will be voted on. But Meath drops out of
the running and, though McNeile (Regius Professor of Divinity) is
mentioned, the field narrows to a race between Derry and Ossory.
His friends—Hearn; Godfrey Day; Mervyn Clare; Ross, now
Bishop of Tuam; J. A. Maconchy, J.P. and Hon. Secretary of the
Dublin Diocesan Council; R. H. Murray, Litt.D., of the St. Patrick's
Chapter (afterwards biographer of Dr. Bernard); and Canon J. A.
Jennings and Canon H. B. Kennedy of Dublin—provide him with
almost day-to-day reports as to the trend of public opinion. As a
result of this information he calculates on a small clerical majority
for himself and a lay majority for Derry 'but whether small or
large I cannot tell.' The day of election by the Diocesan Synod
comes at last, 30 July.

I am happily much calmer than during some of the earlier
days of the long wait. . . . The matter will go to the Bps. who
are to meet I hear about Sept. 15. It is a very long—and seemingly unreasonable—delay. May God direct the day's doings,
and cause what pleases Him to please me.

Ossory has a small clerical majority as he foretold, but Derry's
majority among the laity is more than double Ossory's. Decision
is referred to the Bishops. In August he writes:

I am told that general outside impression is that I shall be
elected by the Bps.—Derry says: 'You are the man, I told every
one who spoke to me about it to vote for you.'(!) Could I have
been as generous?

The day of election by the Bishops comes—10 September.

9.30—D.G. I have been latterly wonderfully calm; I suppose
partly because the general idea as to the result has taken from
me some of the miserable element of uncertainty which accom-
panies a Synod election.
10.00—H.C. in Christ Church Cathedral.
10.30—Election to ARCHBISHOPRIC of Dublin. [Then in Greek]
'I am elected though most unworthy. God be gracious to me.'

A telegram home despatched at 11.45—'I have been elected'—still lies between the pages of his diary for that week.

The sermon which he preached on his enthronement in Christ Church Cathedral on 7 October 1920 is eloquent of the sense of gravity with which he entered upon his inheritance as a Chief Pastor of a Church in the constitution of which a right discrimination must be observed between historic and eternal, occasional and essential, actual and ideal, human and divine: thus facing squarely the current taunt of the cynic that the Christian faith has survived the centuries not because of, but in spite of, the Church. He ended with a reference to the political scene. 'The present situation in Ireland is a moral outrage, and it must be brought to an end by the combined efforts of the Imperial Government and all patriotic Irishmen.' 'We cannot tell what political change lies before our country; but one thing is certain, the Church of Ireland must never let itself be a stranger in Ireland.' Its function must be that of a minister of reconciliation; it must stand for righteousness and peace. His own private comment on this occasion is: 'A very nice service. Faculties mercifully a little dulled, and v. little self-conscious. D.G.'

The same thesis is expounded, but with a quite different and equally fresh manner of presentation, on his enthronement in Kildare Cathedral the next day.

He was present again in Christ Church Cathedral on All Saints' Day to consecrate his old friend Godfrey Day as his successor to the See of Ossory. It was not till early in January that he and his wife could vacate the Palace in Kilkenny, and transfer domestic staff, children and household goods to the Palace at 50 St. Stephen's Green, Dublin.

PART TWO

ARCHBISHOP OF DUBLIN

CHAPTER VII

IRISH AFFAIRS

'SOME ARE BORN GREAT; some achieve greatness; others have greatness thrust upon them.' It would be difficult to decide in which category to place the newly elected Archbishop of Dublin. Probably even in boyhood, certainly in youth, he must have felt himself destined for high office in some sphere, and this he proved in no small degree by early achievement. Yet, even though his private musings show him to have been ambitious he never sought promotion, was never ostentatiously assertive; rather, he was retiring and reserved, as far from courting popularity as from assuming dominance. He glided as it were effortlessly and of natural right into positions of authority; dignified and self-possessed he made his presence felt in any company; sure of himself and of his judgment he won the confidence of others. And he had 'an air' about him; that indefinable quality of greatness, of mental and moral superiority to the common run, which makes of its possessor a patrician. To this was added the impress of an unassailable personal integrity, from which any suggestion of the meretricious or dishonourable would shrink; and of an aesthetic sensitivity which in its turn recoiled from anything vulgar or blatant, affected or pretentious, in speech or behaviour.

Native to the leisured ways of the upper-middle classes in late Victorian England, and bred in the manners of the cultivated intelligentsia in its Augustan age, he was from youth accustomed to the respect accorded to a scholar and a gentleman, had always enjoyed their immunity from physical toil and discomfort, and had never known except by report, nor sought to experience by personal contact, anything of the hard lot of the underprivileged. Then he had become ordained in a country where his family name was already a legend, and where a clergyman's life is even more sheltered than in England. Before middle-age he was a bishop and henceforth the recipient of deference; soon he was an archbishop and the deference became reverence—a reverence which, as his stature grew with increased responsibilities, amounted to veneration.

The *Cork Examiner* recognized his qualities in an 'Appreciation.'

. . . Meteor-like as his advancement may appear, it has been rendered quite inevitable owing to his supreme gifts, his high

personal character, his quiet and steadfast courage in facing
present-day questions, and his single-minded devotion to his
duties. Ever since his ordination—only twenty-four years ago—
by his brother clergy, especially by men of his own age, whatever
clerical sphere he occupied, he has been looked upon as a
magister in the best and original sense of the term, and one who
is as just as he is fearless . . . who always has the courage of his
convictions, and who is not afraid to express them, though they
may be misunderstood or lead to some temporary unpopularity.
The new Archbishop is undoubtedly a strong man, and this is
what the present hour essentially demands. From his first days
in the ministry, Dr. Gregg has been a thoughtful and arresting
preacher, somehow or other his matter and his presentation of
the truth always compel attention; since he became a Bishop his
sermons have perhaps become simpler, but there is still the same
freshness, the same originality, the same courageous attitude in
facing disputed questions, and an additional impressiveness. . . .

'Nichevo' in the *Irish Times* gave an impression of his appearance:

Dr. Gregg is a very striking looking man. He has raven-black
hair, and the heaviness of his eyebrows gives him a sombre,
almost monastic appearance. There is something ascetic about the
Archbishop. He is tall and very thin, with a pair of piercing eyes,
which tell of a clear and incisive mind. His spectacles enhance
his look of sacerdotal austerity, and his keen, finely chiselled
face proclaims the scholar, as well as the divine.

The Bishop of Down (Dr. F. J. Mitchell) writes thus of his first
recollections of the Archbishop during his own College days:

With Dr. Bernard as Provost and Dr. Gregg as Archbishop
of Dublin the Church stood high in public esteem and was well
equipped to face the perils of political revolution. Dr. McNeile,
Dr. Newport White, and Dr. Lawlor, each in their respective
ways, shed lustre upon the Divinity School, and the Church was
strongly represented in College by Dr. Luce and the Revd. Robin
Gwynn. The Archbishop must have exerted great influence at
top levels. To me as a Divinity student he was a very distant
but highly impressive personality. Sermons in College Chapel
delivered by some of our learned men were doubtless full of good
counsel. Some, however, were bound to make the Word difficult
to the point of being neither understood, received, nor accepted.
Dr. Luce had a happy knack of dealing with contemporary
problems intelligibly to the average undergraduate. Dr. Gregg,
on the occasions when he preached, managed to overcome the

handicap of a poor delivery and to make his teaching plain. College Chapel was full on these occasions, as it was when Dr. McNeile preached. But to the ordinary Divinity student living in College or in lodgings, Dr. Gregg was a very distant person and naturally so, for it was a time when his outstanding gifts were in full demand at high levels.

His election to the See of Dublin coincided with an outburst of reprisals in the north for cold-blooded murders perpetrated by Sinn Feiners, culminating in the daylight assassination of Inspector Swanzy of the Royal Irish Constabulary on 8 August 1920; and on Saturday, 11 September 1920, the day after his consecration, a letter to him addressed 'My dear Archbishop' was in the post from the Bishop of Down (Grierson) enclosing a copy of a sermon which he had preached in Belfast Cathedral the previous Sunday calling upon Ulstermen to exercise restraint in face of such excessive provocation:

I am very anxious that you should realize how matters appear to us here. I know we were to blame as a people for the wicked outburst of wrath following the death of Mr. Swanzy—but the papers not friendly to Ulster have studiously avoided pointing out that after the first few hours' passion the loyalists were subject to concerted attacks from the Sinn Fein elements, and the 'riotings' after the first few hours were chiefly self-defence.

The outburst of passion is of course to be condemned, but we feel that there is nothing comparable between the months of assassination in the South and West and this outburst of destructive madness that attacked the community. In the South (that part which is unsympathetic with Ulster) there is a seeming delight to paint us as bad as or worse than themselves, but this seems to us so grossly untrue that we feel it bitterly. You will I know forgive me writing to you, but while we would acknowledge that we deserve severe blame, yet we cannot but feel that as a Province we have as a whole very nobly done our duty and maintained on the whole an attitude upon which we can ask God's blessing.

Yours ever in all deference and affection,

CHARLES T. P. DOWN

Dr. d'Arcy was enthroned in Armagh on 11 June 1920; and Gregg, in his first presidential address to the Joint Dublin Diocesan Synods on 22 October said:

For the first time for almost a hundred years the Archbishop of Dublin has been translated to Armagh. As one who received

his title of deacon's orders from Archbishop d'Arcy I rejoice
that the Church of Ireland has conferred upon him the highest
official recognition it is in her hands to give. An ardent advocate
for Reunion he now occupies the chair filled almost 300 years
ago by James Ussher. I pray that the twentieth century may prove
more favourable to the advancement of a cause dear to the hearts
of both, than was the seventeenth.

In a general appeal for the restoration of the reign of reason to
replace the dread arbitrament of force, he continued (the rest of his
address being reported in indirect speech):

It would be quite easy to speak in scathing terms of the
vacillating character of the policy which has reduced Ireland to
its present state of unrest. But he did not think it would help.
The Government was at present endeavouring to maintain order
so far as it could. It would again be easy to say what one felt
regarding the policy of those who had set out to make Ireland
ungovernable by Great Britain, But, again, he did not think it
would help. . . .
The fact was that the question to-day was not being argued
on moral grounds. Things had gone beyond that stage. The
conflict between the two sides was not being waged in the form
of reason or morals where Christian constitutionalists took their
stand, but in the arena of force. Appeal had been made to the
dread arbitrament of physical violence, and the verdict of
superior strength was apparently the only one that would carry
conviction. That was the dominant and terrible fact in their
country and in that city to-day. Therefore, while denunciation
could serve no good purpose every effort of right-minded men
should be bent to restoring the reign of reason and law, and the
reconciliation by reasonable discussion of opposing interests.

But worse was to come. On 21 November—'Red Sunday'—fourteen British officers in Dublin were deliberately murdered in their
beds: those who were married in the presence of their wives. This
atrocity stirred Cardinal Logue, Archbishop of Armagh, to a
denunciation which was read the following Sunday by priests in
all the churches of his See.
On the same Sunday, 28 November, Archbishop Gregg was
preaching in St. Philip's, Milltown, at the dedication of a War
Memorial, on the heroic sacrifice of those whom it commemorated.
Then he turned, by way of contrast, to the ghastly events of the
previous Sunday.

Ireland is writing its judgment upon its own being with its
own hand. The civilized world shuddered at the story of

assassination that reached it from Dublin last Monday morning. Ireland, familiar with deeds of blood, accepted it well-nigh unmoved. The greater part of the nation has taken no steps to repudiate the crime; by its silence it would seem to show that it had brought itself to hold that killing is no murder, when done for political ends. . . . Conscience has become perverted by a false notion of patriotism. . . . The law holds in the life of nations that 'as we sow, we reap'; and if Ireland employs terrorism it must pay the penalty. And the penalty is that the country's own moral sense becomes terrorized—terrorized into silence, if not complicity. Ireland will sink into being a country without a character. It would be a poor satisfaction to be a Free State and to have lost moral freedom. . . .

Prospects for 1921 appeared more hopeful with the election of Arthur Griffith, a man of moderate counsels, to lead the Sinn Fein party, and Michael Collins, a colourful buccaneer, as his adjutant; and still more so when the Prime Minister, Mr. Lloyd George, offered to meet them in Conference. When it was notified in the press that St. Patrick's Day would be observed as a day of special prayer for peace in all the churches, Cardinal Logue and both Archbishops of the Church of Ireland [1] were requested for their views of a peaceful settlement by a representative of the *Irish Times*. Archbishop Gregg said:

My view is that the Prime Minister's offer of a Conference still stands, and that those who claim to speak for Ireland should take advantage of the offer. . . . England is ready to go to the utmost limit of concession for the sake of peace and goodwill, which does not ignore the facts of geography and of national defence. What is Ireland prepared to give?

Yet this year saw the burning of every coastguard station round the Irish coasts—because they were manned by British men; the gutting of many old country houses and as a consequence the exodus of many old Anglo-Irish families; on 25 May the interior of the Dublin Customs House—an architectural masterpiece of which any city in Europe might be proud—was in flames; and on the night of Sunday, 12 June, the most brutal murder was committed. The aged and beloved Dean John Finlay of Leighlin Cathedral had with the guileless intentions of a peacemaker entertained to dinner in his home a party of Sinn Fein officers, and a few days later another party disguised in British uniforms. It was

[1] On 24 May both were elected Senators of the Parliament of Southern Ireland.

H

a trap to test his political sympathies. He was that night dragged
from his house by those who had dined at his table and done to
death on his own lawn.

The next day a bomb was thrown outside the offices of the
Representative Church Body in St. Stephen's Green, almost next
door to the Archbishop's house.

The Irish Nationalist cause was, however, seriously hampered
not only by the intractability of Ulster which remained implacably
hostile to its ideals, but the growth within it of a Republican Party
which demanded complete severance from Great Britain. This
Party and Sinn Fein now came into open conflict.

Its leader, Mr. de Valera, was emerging as the protagonist of
a United Ireland Constitution and was striving to win over some at
least of the recalcitrant Ulster Unionists. General Smuts was then
in London and on 4 July, in the person of 'Mr. Smith,' he crossed
the Channel incognito and spent the next day in conference with
the contesting parties in the rôle of a mediator. An entry in Archbishop Gregg's diary for 6 July reads:

> Hearing Smuts had been in Dublin, rang up Lord Mayor and
> asked. He said he would bring him here, when he came back.
> So postpone going away till next week. *11th*. After much in-
> decision go abroad. *Truce* between Govt. and S. Fein begins
> noon.

Both for personal and public reasons it is unfortunate that Smuts
could not meet his old friend of Cambridge days, but time was the
enemy, and Smuts was at the same time trying to bring about a
meeting with Mr. de Valera and Sir James Craig—fruitlessly, since
the Ulster leader refused to confer with the Republican unless in
the presence of the Prime Minister.

In default of a meeting Gregg wrote to Smuts.

> The Irish problem, Gregg wrote, had broken many hearts, and
> nobody could hope to make any progress at all with it unless he
> had lived in Ireland, North and South, and had drunk in some of
> its spiritual atmosphere. 'If you want to do what every one in
> British politics has hitherto failed to do, here is an opportunity.
> But the essential prerequisite is this—come and live amongst us
> for a little, and then you will learn the nature of the problem.'
> Smuts did not go and live among the Irish. He was destined,
> nevertheless, to intervene decisively in Irish affairs. But not yet.[2]

Gregg took his fortnight's holiday in Switzerland and spent a

[2] *Smuts*, by Sir W. Keith Hancock, Vol. I, p. 433, C.U.P., 1962.

notable day in Rheims on the way home. On 4 August Smuts'
Open Letter to Mr. E. de Valera was published in London. It was
a masterpiece of political sagacity and practical statesmanship.

On Monday, 15 August, Gregg wrote in his diary: 'Govt. correspondence with Sinn Fein, and Smuts' letter, published,' and a
few days later: 'This week Dail Eireann meets and de V. makes
speeches which superficially threaten breakdown of proposed
negotiations. But, *malgré tout*, the public seems hopeful.' Next
week: 'Dail Eireann's reply to L.G.'s offer published—a refusal
in terms, but evidently not shutting door. What will be the next
move in game, and whose?' On 30 September: 'de Valera accepts
L.G.'s invitation for Oct. 11.' And so matters stood in temporary
abeyance.

In a sermon after the unveiling of a war memorial at Castle-
knock on 2 October the Archbishop made clear on which side his
own sense of loyalty lay:

It is very hard not to nurse resentment against Germany, but
the nursing of resentment is bad religion and bad patriotism. It
poisons the springs of human charity. Let us clear our hearts of
hatred, spite, and ill-will, lest we become guilty of a like wickedness. . . .

A spirit of charity will help us in Ireland to-day. Nothing can
reconcile me to certain of the methods adopted by those who are
determined to make British rule in Ireland impossible. But what
is to be our attitude in face of the offer now made by Great
Britain and accepted by those who claim to speak for Ireland?
Are we to say that if Great Britain is ready to draw a veil over
the recent past, we—who, in spite of all her faults, love Great
Britain—are going to see that the past is *not* forgotten? . . .

Great Britain has chosen this course when she might have
chosen another, which would have made Ireland hideous with
hatred and bloodshed. The latter course might have gratified
instincts of revenge in a dramatic way: but can we feel that it
would have exalted God's righteousness, or have settled, in any
true sense of the word, the Irish question? . . . Let us pray and
strive that, whether as between England and Ireland, or as
between the various sections in Ireland itself, anything like a
policy of resentment and revengefulness may be resolutely put
from us.

The most important of his comments on the political situation
was that made at an annual joint meeting of the Dublin Diocesan
Synods in the Synod Hall on 17 October 1921. After expressing
thanks that there was at last a truce from fratricidal bloodshed in

Ireland—a respite of three months—and a prayer that a just peace might be forthcoming, he said that he found it hard to feel confidence in the settlement now being debated in Downing Street, though, 'as a constitutionalist, I shall with all loyalty accept it if it is imposed by lawful authority.' He would prefer to be silent, but silence was liable to misconstruction. The Protestant minority were excluded from the London Conference, and thus from a voice in the future administration of the country.

The representatives of Southern Ireland in the Conference may represent a majority of Irishmen in the twenty-six counties, but they are very far from representing that minority to which most of us in this room belong. The methods with which their party is identified, or at least which it has not repudiated, and by the use of which the cause for which they stand has exacted the hearing it is now getting, are methods, many of them, which need only be named to be condemned. And yet to them it is given apparently to speak in the name of Southern Ireland, while not one representative of the minority has a place at the council table. . . .

As a minority, we differ from the majority in religion, in politics, in *ethos* generally. Our conscientious convictions have led us to maintain an attitude of aloofness from the political movement directed against the British connection, in so far as the methods adopted by its supporters seemed to us to be wrong.

Human nature is much the same all the world over, and it is hardly to be expected that this attitude of criticism and detachment has made friends for us among those from whom we differ. I am not sanguine enough to anticipate any such appreciation of our independence, and accordingly I claim that we have a right to have our position under any new settlement safeguarded as it was safeguarded by Provisions 5 and 64 in the Government of Ireland Act, 1920. Under that Act there was a prohibition of interference with religious equality, together with protection for corporate property of religious and university bodies. Such safeguards, it may be said, are not necessary to-day. I reply that it is better to leave nothing to chance. . . .

Such safeguards are no novelty. For example, when Canada was ceded to Great Britain in 1763 the French colonists were explicitly guaranteed the free exercise of the Roman Catholic religion and equal civil and commercial privileges with British subjects. Again, when Malta was taken over by Great Britain in 1814 the Canadian precedent was followed in the interests of the Roman Catholic religion. As a minority, I said, we differ from the majority in *ethos*, and although we are as truly Irish as many in the other camp, the differences are so marked as to cause us to seem alien in sympathy from the more extreme of our fellow-countrymen.

Singularity is never popular. It arouses a certain jealousy, and very small occasions are sufficient to provoke antagonism, and we are even more fully justified in asking for safeguards to-day in the case of the proposed almost unlimited experiment of 1921 than we were when the much more restricted Bill of 1920 was passing through Parliament, and provisions for minority interests were inserted. Whatever our religious or political outlook may be, here is our home, and we have every right to be here.

And, furthermore, I say that it is a very good thing for Ireland that we should be here, and it will be a very bad day for the new Ireland if any large number of us leave the country. . . . A good many people have already left; they refuse to remain in so disturbed an atmosphere. Every such departure means loss to Ireland—moral, cultural financial. . . .

I cannot believe that if Great Britain realizes how the sons of the loyal minority in Ireland rose in their thousands in obedience to the call of the Empire in the great war—I cannot believe that Great Britain will callously forget this enthusiastic and costly devotion, and abandon us to an unrelieved political impotence. But if Great Britain is not to forget us, we must remind her of our existence. And the time is short.

The speech was interrupted by frequent bursts of applause and before the meeting ended the Archbishop received from several quarters of the House a suggestion that the relevant paragraphs of it be sent to the Prime Minister. Announcing this, the Archbishop said that he could only do so if it was the unanimous wish of the House; and when this was signified he said that he would comply with their wish. There is no record of any reply from Downing Street, and in any case the protest went unheeded. To this day their exclusion from the national Government is felt as a raw grievance by Protestants in Southern Ireland, whose view is that 'England left us in the lurch.' Certainly England seems to have had a congenital aptitude for foot-faulting on every occasion when it has intervened in Irish affairs, yet it may be wondered whether there was any in which it could have indubitably put a foot right. To an impartial surveyor of the Irish scene, if such there be, it may appear that in this political ostracism of the remnant of the old Protestant ascendency in Ireland, the wheel had turned full circle; that the sins of the fathers were visited upon their children. However that may be, this was probably the first time that a protest of the Protestants in Southern Ireland against political exclusion was publicly voiced, and Gregg's address that day—calmly and judiciously delivered—enhanced his prestige and assured for him a confidence on the part of his fellow-churchmen which remained unshaken to the end of his days. The sole reference to it in his diary is: 'Quite a harmonious Synod. Lord Glenavy assessor.'

Notes in his diary for the weeks ended on 12 and 19 November are pessimistic on the subject of the British Government's intentions regarding Ulster:

> *12th.* In early part of week all points to effort by L.G. and Cabinet to place onus of settlement on breakdown on Ulster, with determination to resign if Ulster will not fall in.
> *19th.* Irish situation very obscure. Ulster's position still in question. Shameless political effort to apply moral coercion. At present it stands unshaken. What will be the next move?

On 21 November 1921 there was held in the Royal Hospital Chapel a Memorial Service commemorating the fourteen officers shot without warning on that day in the previous year, and of all officers and other ranks who had been killed or mortally wounded while on service in Ireland. Of these, thirty-nine officers had been killed, there were six missing, and 115 other ranks had been killed or wounded. The Service was conducted by the Revd. Charles Alfred Peacock, C.B.E., Assistant Chaplain-General, Irish Command. In his sermon the Archbishop said:

> We meet on the anniversary of a day which is marked in our minds with peculiar horror. . . . The lustre of a great engagement does not surround the deaths of those whom we are commemorating. . . . We salute them as brave men who did their duty and who died in doing it . . . members of the British Army, of whatever rank, whose service in this country—since the repudiation of the authority of the Imperial Parliament over a large part of Ireland—brought them to their deaths. Their duty called them to work which must be distasteful—nay, repulsive—to any man of ordinary instincts, the bearing of arms against their own fellow-citizens. But they acted as soldiers of the Crown must act, without consulting their own private feelings. The supreme authority of the King in this land had been challenged, and as his representatives they were sent to maintain it.
> Just as truly as men who fought in the Great War, these men served their country. They did the country's work where they were put to do it, and the country was in their debt.

In a sermon in St. Luke's Church on 4 December commemorating the flight from France to Dublin of the Huguenots 'who had found there a happy sanctuary, enriching with their skill the city that had afforded them shelter'—he continued:

There is in Ireland to-day a movement which aims at an artificial uniformity of opinion. France had tried to get religious
uniformity, and when the process was completed France was
bled white. Ireland can only do it at the same price, and I hope
Ireland will be wise in time. There are many who live in Ireland,
to whom Ireland is their home and who long to serve Ireland,
but who—if Ireland is going to become a place where all freedom of thought is to be sacrificed upon the altar of a dedicated
uniformity—will seek a freer atmosphere.

On 7 December the Terms of the Irish Settlement were published; on the 9th Mr. de Valera recommended their refusal; on
the 11th the Archbishop made a public statement pledging the
Church of Ireland to loyalty to the new Irish Free State. The agreement still awaited ratification, 'but in all human probability—in
view of the remarkable unanimity with which it had been greeted
in Southern Ireland generally, arms have been laid down in Ireland
never to be taken up again.'

We may not all like the facts; many of us had no desire for a
change of Constitution. But it will be our wisdom to acknowledge
them and reckon with them. Ireland in future must depend upon
itself. Hitherto its politicians have been in opposition; their rôle
has been that of critic. They must now undertake the work of
construction, a much more testing task. If they are to succeed
they must have the support of a united people. It concerns us all
that we should have a strong, capable and wise Government.
And therefore it concerns us all to offer to the Irish Free State
so shortly to be constituted our loyalty and our good will. I
believe there is a genuine disposition on the part of those from
whom we have so differed in political outlook to make room for
us and to welcome our co-operation. And we should be wrong,
politically and religiously, to reject their advances. The new
Constitution will claim our allegiance with the same solemn
authority as the one that is now being constitutionally annulled.

On 23 December the Dail adjourned till over the New Year with
the Treaty still unratified. Nevertheless the year 1921 ended with a
feeling of hope. There is a pencilled page at the end of Gregg's
diary for this year, unhappily now indecipherable, which appears
to set forth his view of the legality of the settlement and the
morality—except in cases of conscience—of acquiescence in its
terms 'so long as no reversal of what has been done can be reasonably expected.'

Yet on 7 January 1922 he was writing in his diary:

News comes that Dail Eireann has accepted Treaty, after weeks of bitter wrangling. It is impossible yet to see whether acceptance merely sets the stage for a fierce Republic–Free State conflict. The omens are less favourable than on Dec. 7.

Mr. de Valera had resigned from the Dail the previous day. On the 16th Dublin Castle was taken over by the Provisional Government. On 30 March the Archbishop consulted the Provost, Dr. Bernard, about a proposed 'resolution of protest against violence and reprisals'; and at the end of the following week a Pronouncement to that effect by the House of Bishops appeared in the daily press. But on Easter Day (16 April) there is 'some public uneasiness as to whether there is going to be a revolution' (this in Greek).

On 12 April he had received the following letter from the Roman Catholic Archbishop of Dublin:

Dear Lord Archbishop,

I thank you for your most Christian letter. The condition of public affairs in Ireland is full of dangers. Casual local incidents might easily lead to wide-spread disturbance, deplorable bloodshed, and perhaps in the end to civil war. This state of affairs has been to me as it has been to your Grace the cause of deep and most anxious concern. Before receiving your letter the Lord Mayor and myself, feeling that something ought to be done to stay the mischief before it had passed all bounds, had invited the leaders of both parties—Free State and Republic—to meet us and make an effort to explore avenues leading towards the preservation of the public peace. Whether anything useful will come of this conference it is difficult to conjecture. 'Spes mea Dominus.'

I feel that, having this conference in view, it would not be advisable for me to join in any other public measure which might be possibly construed as bringing outside and undue influence to bear on the deliberations of the Conference. I think you will understand this position.

Again thanking you for your letter and joining with you in the hope that Easter may see the dawn of peace in our land,

I remain,

Dear Lord Archbishop,

Faithfully Yours

✝ EDWARD J. BYRNE,

Archbishop of Dublin

On 28 April news reached Dublin of the murder of Protestants in Dunmanway, Co. Cork. The Archbishop—after another private consultation with the Provost—said in a sermon in Dundrum the following Sunday:

It is no matter for wonder if the members of our Church feel deep uneasiness and positive alarm in view of these horrible events. What a tale of savage blood-lust is disclosed in the murder of eight (and it may prove to be more) members of a political and religious minority, living quietly among their neighbours! The reason for this organized massacre I cannot conceive, unless it be, indeed, as has been suggested, by way of reprisal. But I fail to see what is the connection between these residents in the west of County Cork and the troubles in the North. No; I cannot see any intelligible cause for this declaration of war upon a defenceless community.

I call upon the Government of this country to take the necessary steps to protect a grievously-wounded minority, and to defend the Protestants of West Cork from a repetition of these atrocities, and to save the Protestants there and in other parts of the South from threatened violence and expulsion from their homes.

The sentiments publicly expressed upon the subject by the political leaders of Ireland are excellent; but we need at this time not merely words, but government. They cannot give us back our dead, but they can provide against a recurrence of acts of barbarism. Our people have accepted the new conditions of government loyally, and they are entitled to throw themselves on the chivalry and good faith of their fellow-Irishmen, and ask to be made secure in the elementary rights of citizens of a Christian country.

A note in his diary six days later reads:

A week of v. great anxiety as to the Church's future. News of evictions, ejections and intimidations everywhere. Where is it all to lead to? Is it beginning of end, or a short storm? Prol. Govt. so far seems powerless to intervene.

On 9 May, at a secret session after the General Synod, he was appointed to convene a meeting of representatives from Southern Ireland and to lead a deputation consisting of himself, the Bishop of Cashel, and Sir William Goulding, to the Provisional Government 'to ask advice as to the best way in which the fears of Church people can be allayed, and to assure the authorities that the best efforts of the bishops, clergy and laity are enlisted in the support of law and order.' The deputation met Michael Collins and William Cosgrave on the 12th, and Gregg records the outcome as 'satisfactory,' but the page in his diary recording what transpired at the interview was subsequently torn out.

The text of the deputation's statement and of Mr. Collins' reply was however publicized in the daily press on 13 May.

Meanwhile hundreds of Anglo-Irish refugees—whose homes in many cases had been gutted—continued to stream across the Channel, and the British Government appointed a Committee to investigate and provide relief and assistance for immediately necessitous cases. A Central Bureau was formed in Victoria Street, and an Irish Loyalist Defence Fund opened in another office in the same thoroughfare.

On 20 May Gregg notes:

An agreement arrived at between de Valera and Collins. What does it mean? Does it portend a Republic? or attack on North? I cannot see.

On 9 June he called again on the leaders of the Provisional Government after another outrage in Castlemacadam (Avoca). On the 16th the Free State Constitution was published. On the 22nd Field-Marshal Sir Henry Wilson was assassinated in London, and the Archbishop referred to it in a sermon in St. Patrick's.

On the afternoon of the 28th a considerable force of the Republican army took possession of the Four Courts in which they were blockaded by Irish Free State troops for two days. Since they refused to surrender it was decided to burn them out, and shelling from the streets took place. The Four Courts building was not only the supreme court of justice in Southern Ireland; not only the most priceless ornament of architecture in the city; it had also served for many years as the repository of ancient documents and countless manuscripts of antiquarian value, the vast bulk of which had never been transcribed. Their destruction would prove an immense and irreplaceable national loss. Made aware of the danger impending, the Provost of Trinity College, Dr. Bernard—a well-known and universally-respected figure in Dublin—donned his academic robes and courageously intervened imploring the contestants to cease fire. His appeal was unheeded; the shelling from without and the firing from within continued; on the 30th there was a great explosion, a sheet of flame went up, and the great dome collapsed. The blockaded party emerged, but it was too late; a great part of Ireland's history went up in smoke, never to be recorded. For a week firing and sniping continued in the city; there was no free movement; one side of Sackville Street was temporarily seized by the Republicans. The insurrection was suppressed for the time being; but the flames of it smouldered, and Mr. de Valera, the

Republican leader, had made good his escape. One church had been burnt out. Others had suffered damage.

On 29 July the Archbishop had another interview with Mr. Cosgrave concerning the safety of one of the Dublin churches. On 12 August he records: 'Mr. Arthur Griffith dies—a very serious loss in this crisis. He was one of the stable and stabilizing figures of Sinn Fein.' Worse was to follow. A few days later Michael Collins was ambushed and shot by Republican irregulars in a lonely part of Co. Tipperary. On 23rd: 'News comes of Michael Collins' death; ambush. After death of Griffith a v. serious situation. Will it mean intensified fighting?' On the 31st:

> Letters etc. till 2.30—then to Club, lunch. 2.30, heard firing other side of Green. 3.5 to train. Ambush had just taken place. Saw irregulars under arrest. 4.0 Greystones, to see Townsend, Golf Hotel. Out—saw wife—mistaken by S.F. troops for de Valera.

The following is a first hand account from Mrs. Hamilton Townsend's daughter Marjorie of what actually transpired on that occasion.

In the summer of 1922 I was staying with my parents, my two brothers and my grandmother, in a hotel at Greystones. My parents had come home on leave from India, found Ireland torn by civil war between Free State and Republican supporters, and had taken refuge in this seaside suburb for the length of the school holidays. One afternoon I was with my mother in the hotel lounge, my grandmother was in bed with a cold and my father had taken the two boys into Dublin to a cinema, when the maid announced 'a gentleman to see you' and ushered in the Archbishop, Dr. Gregg. He introduced himself, as my mother had not met him before, and explained that he had sent a post-card to his old Cambridge friend, Hamilton Townsend, telling him of his proposed visit. (The post-card arrived the next day.)

My mother offered him tea and while she was pouring it out came an Irish Free State officer who went straight up to the Archbishop and said,

'Excuse me sir, but who are you?'

'I am the Archbishop of Dublin' came the reply.

The officer was momentarily taken aback—

'I beg your pardon your reverence'; then 'Can you identify him?' he said to my mother.

'Unfortunately no. The Archbishop is a friend of my husband who is in Dublin this afternoon and I had never seen him before.'

'I have some letters here,' said the Archbishop. He opened a little thin attaché case and produced some envelopes addressed to himself.

The officer turned them over thoughtfully. 'I'm afraid this isn't enough evidence.'

'There are two people in Greystones who know me, the rector and the doctor—I suggest that you send for them.'

'Very well,' said the officer. 'Meanwhile please remain in this room.'

'Can my daughter go upstairs to her grandmother?' my mother asked. Permission was given.

'Run upstairs and tell Granny what's happening' and off I went.

I found my grandmother in a state of annoyance and agitation for from her bed she could see soldiers patrolling the hotel garden.

'I think they've mistaken the Archbishop for de Valera,' I said. 'He's having tea with Mum downstairs but he's got to stay there till somebody can identify him. Oh, what the boys are missing!'

But Granny was annoyed and unable to appreciate the excitement.

I went back to the drawing-room. A sentry guarded the open door and my mother and the Archbishop were carrying on a stilted conversation over cups of tea. At last the rector and the doctor arrived together; there were identifications and apologies and the officer and his men withdrew. The hotel returned to normal.

Later we heard that the Archbishop had asked his way to the hotel from a boy at the station who was de Valera's son. This, and the extraordinary facial resemblance between the Archbishop and de Valera was enough to send rumours flying and bring out the military.

On 6 December 1922 the Irish Free State formally came into being, with Timothy Michael Healy, K.C., as Governor-General designate, under the terms of the Treaty signed in London exactly a year before. The *Irish Times* sought the views of prominent men, and the Archbishop wrote as follows:

The future of Ireland depends from henceforth upon itself. . . . If those who have hitherto repudiated the new settlement will reconcile themselves to it, all may yet be well. But if the present fratricidal strife continues the country can only go from bad to worse. Law is a sacred and inexorable thing. The organized negation of law in Ireland has worked a far-reaching social havoc. To-day the rehabilitation of the idea of law in the national consciousness constitutes the crying need of Ireland, while the teaching of obedience to law is the task imposed on the parent, the clergyman, the schoolmaster, and the statesman. In the moral as in the material sphere, years alone can restore what it has been the work of years to undo.

Mr. Cosgrave's administration of the Irish Free State is said to have retaliated against the active defiance of Republicans with measures of repression 'greater than any which Britain had ever imposed on Ireland.' Their leader Mr. de Valera, who had been arrested in 1923 and imprisoned for a year, emerged in 1927 as head of the Fianna Fail Party, and in 1932 President of the Executive Council.

On the eve of Mr. de Valera's assumption of office Dr. Gregg contributed to the *Church of England Newspaper* an anonymous article dated 26 February 1932. It shows how thoroughly informed he was on every aspect of the Irish situation—political, industrial, agrarian, economic; and also how mistaken in his forecast of the outcome (as indeed was nearly every one else).

It seems beyond doubt that the party known as Fianna Fail (the Knights of Destiny) will be called upon to provide a Government for the Irish Free State. . . . Fianna Fail, we may assume, intends to proceed along rigidly constitutional lines. . . . So far as Mr. de Valera is concerned a *coup d'état* need not be anticipated. . . . Whether it likes it or not, it will be the King's Government, and until the Constitution is changed by constitutional procedure it will have to bow to the facts of the situation which it inherits. . . . Those who look for a prompt 'set-to' with Great Britain on such questions as the oath for members of the Dail, or the withholding of the annuities paid by the farmer-purchasers by way of interest and sinking fund on the Land Loans Stock, will also be disappointed. . . .

In fact there is no ground for anxiety in any sphere. Great Britain has been generous and patient; Ireland will continue to respect the Treaty and her obligations.

In a second article, 13 January 1933, after quoting the late Provost Mahaffy's epigram that in Ireland the impossible always happens and the inevitable never, he contrasts Mr. de Valera's romantic idealism with Mr. Cosgrave's practical common sense, but rather to the advantage of the former, who has won his position by the attraction of his policy to the small farmer and by his appeal to national sentiment. Three weeks later he writes that the results of the Election, with such a landslide for Fianna Fail, have surprised

even Mr. de Valera, who has received the mandate he demanded
and whose first step will probably be to abolish the Oath and the
Land Annuities. 'It is to be hoped that Great Britain will continue
to exercise its traditional patience, and will not make his path
harder by punishing him for his obstinacy.'

He made no public comment on the political situation during the
régime of the Irish Free State under Mr. Cosgrave which took
strong measures to suppress violence, nor during that of the
Republican Party—however much he disaproved of its principles
and methods—under Mr. de Valera, save once, when he protested
against the attacks made upon Protestant Churches, homes, and
business premises at Kilmallock in Co. Limerick in July 1935. But
in this he was supported both by the vigorous denunciations of the
Roman Catholic authorities in that neighbourhood and also by the
Government's prompt reassurance that all damage would be re-
paired and measures taken to bring the offenders to justice.

In this and in all other matters where the welfare of the
Protestant minority was concerned he found in Mr. de Valera a
strong, impartial, and reliable coadjutor, and gave him in return
his personal support in all undertakings for the welfare of the
country as a whole, though in his heart of hearts he considered its
severance from Great Britain a disaster of great magnitude. His
younger daughter was one among the rising generation who did
not share her father's old-fashioned views:

> The British Government was, in his view, sacrosanct, and he
> could not imagine it acting, except from the most lofty and
> humane motives. I once exclaimed, after he had declared him-
> self to be absolutely behind the Government in some colonial
> matter where we sceptics thought we could discern signs of ex-
> ploitation cloaked by self-righteousness: 'You'd think the British
> Government were divine arbiters!' 'I believe they are,' he said
> in deadly earnest, and went on to describe how he envisaged the
> British as the trustees of Christianity in a pagan world.
> Nevertheless, as soon as the Irish Free State became a reality
> and all hope of reconciliation with the British Government was
> gone, he exhorted the people of the Church of Ireland to accept
> the new situation, to co-operate with the new government and to
> stop clinging to a way of life that had gone for ever, and set
> them an example by doing so himself. He met, knew and worked
> with all the builders of the new Ireland, and I remember a letter
> from him that reached me at school, in England, containing
> nothing but a lament on the assassination of Kevin O'Higgins.
> But I think that in 1922 he felt that he had been banished from
> the Garden of Eden.

Being aware of Mr. de Valera's long-standing acquaintance with the Archbishop, and having reason to believe that he had desired his aid in certain important matters, the present writer sought an interview with him when President many years later. This was readily granted; his reception could not have been more courteous; and the President spoke to the following effect :

He said that it was a pleasure for him to speak of his recollections of the Archbishop, since he was a man for whom he had always had the highest regard. Since Dr. Gregg had been mistaken for him at Greystones and had been placed, so he was told, in temporary confinement, he was naturally anxious to see him in the flesh. Another incident occurred bearing on the supposed resemblance between them when at the death of Lady Ardilaun on 13 December 1925, Mr. de Valera was sent, anonymously, an envelope containing a newspaper cutting of a photograph. It showed a person wearing a surplice. The likeness was so remarkable that Mr. de Valera was startled, and wondered how a photograph of himself could be faked in this way. Later, he found it was a portion of a press photograph showing Archbishop Gregg officiating at the funeral service of Lady Ardilaun. When he met the Archbishop some time afterwards he was surprised to find that the resemblance did not seem at all as striking as the incidents referred to would have suggested.

His first meeting with Dr. Gregg was at a Reception in the Castle soon after he came into office as Taoiseach in 1932. He then formed an impression of Dr. Gregg's qualities and character which subsequent meetings more than confirmed.

When framing the text of the Irish Constitution, Mr. de Valera said that he dealt first with all the other articles, and had left to the last the articles on religion, as likely to present no special difficulty. He soon found that he was mistaken. 'At the outset,' said Mr. de Valera, 'I was confronted with the question: by what names should our Church and your Church be designated? It was most desirable—indeed it was essential—that our Constitution should win the respect of all sections of the Community, and that the members of all Churches should, if possible, be satisfied. But here was my difficulty. I knew that some members of our Church objected to being called *Roman* Catholics, whilst many in your church objected to being called non-Catholics or Protestants.'

In this perplexity Mr. de Valera decided to call on Dr. Gregg.[3] He did so, and after a short preliminary discussion, the details of which he has forgotten, the Archbishop rose from his chair and took a book from his shelves. 'Let us see,' he said, 'how

[3] Diary: *12 April 1937*. '12.15 Mr. de V. calls and speaks ¾ hr. in regard to religious clauses of the new Constn.'

your Church does in fact designate itself.' The book, Mr. de
Valera thinks, contained the records or decrees of the Council
of Trent. From it the Archbishop read the phrase, 'Holy, Catholic, Apostolic and Roman Church.' 'This immediately suggested
to us both,' continued the President, 'that the proper way to deal
with the difficulty was to give to each Church the title which it
had formally given to itself; your Church being designated,
accordingly, the Church of Ireland. I was very happy that in this
way my problem had been solved.' [4]

The next occasion on which Mr. de Valera sought the Archbishop's aid was after the latter's elevation to the see of Armagh.
Representations had been made to himself as Taoiseach that the
graveyard of Clonmacnoise was in a state unworthy of its historic
significance and of the Irish nation. He had himself visited the
place and found it in a sadly neglected condition. It had been
used as a burying-ground so frequently in modern times that it
had become an unsightly expanse of tombstones. Mr. de Valera
thought that the remedy would be for the State to take over the
site so that it could be cared for properly by the Commissioners
of Public Works. But this would involve the surrender of pro-
prietary rights, some of which were held by the Representative
Body of the Church of Ireland. To secure the consent of this
Body did not seem an easy matter; and so in addition to speaking first to Dr. Barton (then Archbishop of Dublin) and to
Dr. McCann (then Bishop of Meath), Mr. de Valera sought the
support of Archbishop Gregg. This support he gave immediately
and wholeheartedly. Sometime afterwards, Clonmacnoise was
handed over to the State in a contract between the Commissioners
of Public Works and the Representative Church Body.

On another occasion the Archbishop and Mr. de Valera were
brought together once more in a co-operative effort. Dr. Lindsay, the Astronomer at Armagh, came to see the President with
a request to agree that the observatories in Armagh and Dunsink
should combine with Harvard for the installation of a planetarium in Armagh, for the comparison of observations with those
at Bloemfontein. 'I at first pointed out,' said Mr. de Valera, 'that
the expense involved might be more than our joint resources
could bear; but when Dr. Lindsay suggested the formation of a
sponsoring committee consisting of myself as President, his

---

[4] RELIGION. *Article 44.* 1. 2° The State recognizes the special position of
the Holy Catholic Apostolic and Roman Church as the guardian of the
Faith professed by the great majority of the citizens.

3° The State also recognizes the Church of Ireland, the Presbyterian
Church in Ireland, the Methodist Church in Ireland, the Religious Society
of Friends in Ireland, as well as the Jewish congregations and the other
religious denominations existing in Ireland at the date of the coming into
operation of this Constitution.

Eminence Cardinal D'Alton and Archbishop Gregg, I felt proud
to be in such good company and at once agreed.' The three came
together at the Armagh Observatory for a preliminary meeting.
Subsequently the planetarium was duly acquired and installed.

The last time that Mr. de Valera saw the Archbishop was
when, returning from a visit to Belfast a few years ago, he called
upon him in Armagh. He was sorry to find him much enfeebled
in body, though as active as ever in mind. His death not long
afterwards, said the President, 'took from us a most learned and
kindly gentleman, and from me a highly valued friend.'

I

CHAPTER VIII

SPANISH AND PORTUGUESE REFORMED CHURCHES

THE REFORMED CHURCHES in the Peninsula may be called the adopted children of the Church of Ireland, and more particularly of William Conyngham, Lord Plunket, Archbishop of Dublin from 1885 to 1897, who fought for and secured their recognition. This is the same Lord Plunket in whose company the young John Gregg had travelled to Armagh at the time of his uncle the Primate's death. It has been well said:

The one statue in Dublin erected in a public place to an ecclesiastic is that in Kildare Place, where the subscriptions of Roman Catholics and Churchmen, Methodists and Presbyterians, combined to perpetuate in bronze the life-work of the most outspoken Protestant that has ever occupied the Archiepiscopal See. Other Archbishops were Protestants, but no one by word or deed showed himself more out-and-out attached to Protestant principles than the man all united to honour as a noble Irishman, a great Christian gentleman, and a self-sacrificing Churchman.[1]

The history of these Churches is as recent as 1867 when a measure of religious liberty was granted in the Peninsula. In that year Angelo Móra, a former Roman Catholic priest from Spain who had been received into the American Episcopal Church, began to preach in Lisbon, where Portuguese evangelicals were already advocating the formation of a national reformed church. In this they were greatly encouraged by Móra who showed that there had existed both in Spain and Portugal a primitive and independent church in the seventh century, and that it was their duty to revive it. The movement was strongly supported by the British Chaplain then in Lisbon, Canon Godfrey Pope, D.D., who happened to be an Irishman. Another priest who had fled to Gibraltar was Juan Cabrera. In 1870 he returned to collaborate with another young priest who was also a doctor of medicine, Francisco Palomares, who in the following year was invited to conduct divine worship

[1] In *Light and Truth,* Vol. XLVIII, No. 4, by 'A London Incumbent.' He was the Revd. Thomas J. Pulvertaft, Hon. Secretary to the Churches, an Irishman.

in Seville. The promulgation of the dogma of Papal Infallibility at this time caused many other Catholics in the Peninsula to desert the Roman faith and join the reformers. The movement there is thus in motive similar to that of the Old Catholic Party in Holland, though more 'evangelical' in character. In 1878 the Reformed Congregations in the Peninsula jointly petitioned the Anglican Church at its first Lambeth Conference to consecrate their first Bishop. The request was coldly received: it was suggested that the American Bishop of Mexico should visit them in two years' time 'for advice and assistance.' Left to themselves, in 1880 they framed their own Constitution providing for Synodical Government in each Church, and in 1884 compiled their own prayer books. These, though based on the Protestant model of the Anglican Church, were modified for Spanish use by substantial drafts from the ancient and more elaborate Mozarabic rite, and for the Lusitanian (or Portuguese) with modifications from the simpler seventh century liturgy of Braga. In the same year two further petitions were addressed to the Anglican Church, this time separately; among the signatories from Spain was Juan Cabrera, whilst those from Portugal included Canon Godfrey Pope. Again no action was taken, and matters remained in abeyance until 1888 when the second Lambeth Conference was held and the Archbishop of Dublin, Lord Plunket, championed the appeal. The Bishops were impressed, their response was more friendly and Lord Plunket was thereby led to hope that 'by lawful and cautious means the two Churches might secure an episcopate of their own according to the principles of primitive jurisdiction, each limited to his own flock and without territorial title.' From the Irish Bench of Bishops, however, he at first won no support. They had received a petition from the Lusitanian Church for a consultative Committee of three Irish Bishops to act on its behalf pending its ability to maintain a Bishop of its own. They authorized him, on the occasion of his fourth visit to the Peninsula in 1891, to convey to the Reformers their refusal of this appeal. Despite this decision by his own Church, Lord Plunket ordained Andrew Cassels this year to the diaconate at Vila Nova de Gaia, twin-city with Oporto.

Yet in three years' time his pertinacity bore fruit. Supported by the Bishop of Clogher (Stack) and the Bishop of Down (Welland) he announced to the Irish Bench that, 'in view of altered circumstances' and unless formally forbidden either by the Bench or by the General Synod, they would consecrate as bishops for those Churches native priests elected by their own Synods if approved by the three Bishops themselves. Thus it was that in 1894 Juan

Cabrera was consecrated in Madrid first Bishop of the Spanish Reformed Church, by the Lord Archbishop of Dublin assisted by the Bishops of Clogher and Down. From that time until his death in 1916 Bishop Cabrera performed all episcopal functions in the Peninsula.[2] But—to illustrate the opposition with which Lord Plunket had to contend—Lord Halifax (a member of the Church of England) took it upon himself to write to the Cardinal Archbishop of Toledo apologizing for the presumption of the Archbishop of Dublin, 'without the sanction of your Eminence and of the bishops of your Province of Toledo, to consecrate a certain schismatic named Cabrera to the Episcopate.' It is recorded that on reading this letter Lord Plunket placed his head between his hands and with a sob said. 'To think of it—an English Churchman addressing in this manner the head of the most intolerant part of the Roman Church, because a body of Spaniards wish to have what English Churchmen believe to be a spiritual privilege, and I helped them to obtain it. Surely, surely, there is something very wrong.'

In 1902 a Training College for Clergy was established in Oporto for which a future Bishop of Tuam, Dr. J. M. Harden, then Principal of St. John's Hall, Highbury, prepared the theological course and was for some time in charge of the interdenominational Seminary in Madrid. This sufficiently attests the 'evangelical' character of its teaching. Various Irish Bishops visited the Peninsula from time to time, and the Provisional Council of three from the Irish Bench acted when necessary on behalf of the two Reformed Churches. Their Constitution describes their churchmanship as 'Catholic, Apostolic, Evangelical.' They are supported by the World's Evangelical Alliance together with other Protestant denominations in the Peninsula which, though non-episcopal, are united in opposition to Rome.

It is natural that the cause of minority Protestant churches, standing like the Church of Ireland in the midst of a population predominantly Roman Catholic but claiming to restore the primitive doctrine and practice of the Catholic Church, should strongly attract Gregg's sympathies; and the fact that they had become, so to speak, adopted children of the Church of Ireland was enough to

[2] Mr. W. J. MacAndrew writes: Revd. Fernando Cabrera was the son of Bp. Juan Cabrera. Locally he was considered Bp. elect, but this was never recognized in London, as Revd. Pulvertaft (it seemed to me) was always prejudiced against him, but he stuck out the Civil War in Madrid, and did a deal of travelling when he was only one of the two ministers of the Church after our War ended, when the Bishop of Meath, now the Primate, went to Spain and ordained several suitable men. I always rather admired F. Cabrera, knowing what he had gone through, and against advancing years he got around to minister to the churches.

make their welfare his personal concern. On his accession to the See of Dublin he became *ex officio* one of the Advisory Council of Irish Bishops (the others being Armagh and Meath); and though he did not share the doctrinal liberalism of his great predecessor, he regarded himself, in this as in other matters, as the accredited heir of Archbishop Plunket. The Reformed Churches in the Peninsula were not slow to recognize him as such; their confidence and affection for him grew with every visit he made. The Lusitanian Church was his special delight (its tradition is the more 'Catholic' of the two), and in the Cathedral Church of St. Paul in Lisbon a chapel is shortly to be dedicated to the Glory of God and in memory—jointly—of Archbishops Plunket and Gregg.

Of extant papers concerning Gregg's relations with the Iberian Churches the earliest in date are in the summer of 1922, at which time these Churches had been without a bishop for six years. They are letters from Pulvertaft with enclosures from the Revd. Fred W. Flower, Hon. Secretary to the Synod of the Lusitanian Church. All Pulvertaft's letters to the Archbishop are couched in pleasantly informal and confidential terms, betokening personal friendship. His father lay dying in Cork, but the Irish troubles had made travel impossible. He had attended a meeting of the C.M.S. at which the Archbishop of Armagh (d'Arcy) had 'acted with great wisdom,' but other speakers (including an English bishop) had displayed too much emotion, 'and I have long learned that common sense and sentiment do not always run in double harness'—an opinion with which the recipient of his letter would have cordially agreed. The official news is a proposal passed at the recent Synod of the Lusitanian Church to elect the presbyter Joaquim dos Santos Figueiredo, now its President, to be Bishop.

> In my opinion Senhor Figueiredo has many of the qualities essential to a bishop and has greatly advanced in wisdom and power during the recent years. More than this it would be improper for me to say at the present time. Possibly Bishop Ingham [from America] who will be visiting the Peninsula shortly might be entrusted with the duty of making further enquiry—though for my own part I have little faith in the ability of a visiting bishop during a short stay to obtain full knowledge of local conditions. If he knew the language it would be different, and even then I have on many occasions found to my cost that the impressions I formed needed careful revision.

Unfortunately Gregg's part in this correspondence is not preserved. He replied to all letters in his own hand and very rarely kept a copy. Senhor Figueiredo was never consecrated; but he continued to be the most esteemed member of his Church. On this matter a letter from Mr. W. J. MacAndrew, subsequently Hon. Secretary to the Society, throws an interesting light:

'The Revd. Figueiredo was regarded in Portugal, till the day of his death, as Bishop Elect. In him they had undoubtedly chosen the right man. But from what I know of Dr. Gregg in later years he might well have been hesitant. He was not wholly in favour of Molina being consecrated in Spain, on the grounds of his being a "lone" bishop and, as was then the case, of having only six churches in his charge. It is quite possible that, at the beginning of his office, he might have been even more hesitant. There was therefore no bishop in Portugal until the consecration of the Revd. Fiandor a few years ago, already an old man and now retired; and Dr. Pereira is now Bishop Elect.'

It was not until 1924 that Gregg found it possible to visit the Peninsula. But meanwhile, at the end of a long and often hard day's work which would have satisfied most men as worthy of a full night's respose, he set himself, by sheer effort of will, to acquire a speaker's knowledge of Spanish, in which language he had already taught himself to read. And not only so but also to read Portuguese and—far more difficult—to pronounce it correctly.

Of his love of literature and languages in general his younger daughter writes:

He loved to read Dante, Balzac, Montesquieu and the Spanish classics in the original. His modern languages were mostly self-taught and he delighted to ask questions about grammar and idiom of any expert he might meet, even of the most elementary nature. He would go away repeating under his breath the correct way of saying whatever it might be. Spanish he learnt entirely from books so that he might preach, ordain, confirm and converse in it when he travelled round Spain as Bishop visiting the reformed Church in the Peninsula; he achieved this when he was Archbishop of Dublin, working quietly in his rare spare moments. One of his methods of learning to speak the language was to turn whatever thought might come into his head into Spanish, then reply to it as if he were talking to someone. Next time he met a Spanish speaker he would check his version for correctness, then learn by heart the revised sentence. He often practised on his children and many little phrases that I learnt from him have helped me in Spain. When I was a student in Trinity, a friend of mine who was a Spanish scholar used often to come to the house and he would ask her question after question. Of course his knowledge of Latin gave him a flying start in learning Romance languages.

On his first visit to the Peninsula in September 1924 he was accompanied by Pulvertaft (and incidentally on the boat-train to Boulogne by the home-going Australian cricket team). Having stayed overnight at Burgos they arrived at Oporto where the Archbishop spent an evening practising pronounciation with Senhor Fiandor; next day, assisted by the Revd. Andrew Cassels, he ordained a presbyter in Vila Nova de Gaia, and confirmed many. Thence to Lisbon where Canon Pope was his chauffeur 'along awfully bumpy roads.' They visited the graves of the novelist Henry Fielding and of the hymn-writer Philip Doddridge in the British Cemetery. In the afternoon another Confirmation: 'so great was the interest roused that the chief Lisbon newspaper published a photograph of the Service on its principal page, and an account of what had been done by his Grace.' In the evening he attended a meeting of the Synod in the former Marianos Convent, and was by a spontaneous and unanimous motion at once placed in the chair: a signal compliment from a people so jealous of their national prestige, but a recognition of their debt to the Irish episcopate. The Convent housed a large printing works for the production of Bibles and religious literature, and he was reminded of the times when such establishments were attached to Churches; for example, Caxton's in Westminster Abbey.

Thence to Madrid, to be met by a large number of 'reformers' and among them an old friend, F. Symes Thompson, then Chaplain to the British Embassy. Having viewed the masterpieces of Spanish and Italian art in the Prada he attended and addressed the Spanish Synod. He was allowed by the Library authorities to examine the Toledan Codex of the Bible, and the exquisitely printed first edition of the Mozarabic Liturgy—one of the rarest and most treasured of incunabula. Having spent an evening rehearsing with Senhor Daniel Regaliza,[3] President of the Synod, he ordained a presbyter and a deacon, using the Spanish order; Symes Thompson 'to show his sympathy' robed and sat beside him. The same evening he conducted a Confirmation.

---

[3] Mr. W. J. MacAndrew writes: Daniel Regaliza was the leader of the Reformed Church in Spain immediately after the death of Bp. Cabrera in 1916. He came from a small village in central Spain, Villaescusa, where we owned our own church. Such was his influence that even the mayor became converted, with half the village. This was too much for the R.C.'s who sent a virulent aggressive priest charged to put a stop to this. The protestants refused to be ruffled by persecution; and in the end this priest began to visit Regaliza in mufti 'as an enquirer' and became himself converted. His name was Arenales. Though he never joined the Reformed Church he became a powerful preacher of the Gospel. Regaliza was a remarkable personality—such a *quiet* little man!

He visited Toledo, Saragossa, Barcelona—missing nothing of interest in those cities that opportunity permitted him to see—and spent his last week-end in Sabadell, to consecrate its new church 'largely erected by the people,' and to conduct a Confirmation. Here he met for the first time Mr. W. J. MacAndrew, then Hon. Secretary to the Spanish Reformed Church Aid Society with which he had been connected since 1906, and who now writes: 'I remember addressing him as "Your Grace," but he quickly told me "Sir" would be sufficient. He always placed one completely at one's ease in all contacts.' [4]

He was in fact never so much at ease himself as on these Peninsula journeys. They were for him holidays in which he could completely relax and let go the reins of office. The many photographs taken of him there reveal a genial smiling countenance, in striking contrast to the habitual gravity of his features on public occasions at home.

On his return one of the Reformers wrote in the Lusitanian Church Newspaper:

> In everything he did our illustrious visitor won the hearts of all the people, not only by the amiability of his manner and the worthy simplicity with which he gave his services, but especially by the manner in which he read our Services in Portuguese. He read them carefully before the conduct of public worship in order to acquire the right pronunciation. Only his addresses— which were simple, evangelical and helpful—were spoken in English and were interpreted by one of the ministers.

Protestant newspapers were forbidden in the sister country but *Light and Truth,* the Society's magazine in London, in quoting the above, adds:

> From Spain similar testimony has reached us, and it may truly be said that this visit will long be remembered for the care and pains his Grace took in mastering difficulties of pronunciation that would have dismayed most scholars. Every one likes to think that foreigners value one's native tongue, and all know that to

[4] He adds: Revd. Antonio Estruch was minister at Sabadell. He died in October 1954, having been 56 years in the ministry, 53 at Sabadell. He was converted when an acolyte in the R.C. Church at nearby Monistrol. He married a daughter of Bp. Cabrera. He was a very fine man, and with his brother Juan ran the church day school till 1936, since when all non-R.C. schools have been closed by order. A small charge used to be made to educate children in these schools, as against the R.C. ones that were free. But R.C. parents preferred to send their children to our schools as they were better taught.

acquire proficiency in its pronunciation means the sacrifice of much time and trouble, as well as the possession of a keen musical ear and great linguistic gifts. The Archbishop of Dublin has made a deep impression on the earnest Christian community.

His next visit, arranged for the autumn of 1928 was of necessity a short one. The *terminus ad quem* was the Cheltenham Congress to meet the Patriarchs of the Eastern Church in the first week of October, when he was to be the preacher in Gloucester Cathedral.[5] He had prepared his sermon with special care and read it to his old friend Dr. Newport White, as likely to be the severest critic. But the postponement of the *terminus a quo* was determined by the incidence of a personal tragedy—the sudden death of his younger son.[6] For a week he was writing replies to letters of sympathy, and then travelled once more with Pulvertaft to Madrid.

New scenes and frequent movement and preparation for his duties must have brought a measure of relief. The next day he ordained a presbyter who had been instructed by Dr. Harden, and took the Celebration using the Spanish Liturgy, the whole office lasting for nearly two and a half hours; conducted the rite of Confirmation in the evening and delivered an address in Spanish. Next day he attended the Quadrennial Synod, again being placed in the chair. A discussion ensued on the present position of the Reformed Church in Spain; tolerance under the Monarchy was being replaced under the Directory by a movement which threatened to squeeze the life out of the Protestant churches. But there was no note of pessimism in the speeches. Gregg gave a short address, which was translated by the new presbyter, and spent most of the rest of the day in answering further letters of sympathy which his wife had forwarded.

He left next day for a long train journey to Vilches and thence by road to La Carolina to inspect the fittings of the little church; then on along a pitted and muddy road that sometimes skirted precipices to the model village of Centemillo for another Confimation. After a few hours' sleep he boarded a late night train for Granada. Equinoctial rainstorms had washed away the ballasting of lines in places; at 5.45 he was awakened by a violent crash. The train had collided with a goods train at Jódar—without loss of life but with injury to some passengers. Progress was delayed but he was not pressed for time, and that night in a hotel could enjoy a full night's rest. Back to Madrid next day, and thence to Salamanca

5 See page 166.
6 See page 185.

where the local church had 'passed through vicissitudes,' he took a
Confirmation, and entered in his diary a notice that he evidently
had seen placarded: 'Extirpacion de herejias.' According to
Mr. Pulvertaft: 'The pressure of local representatives of the
Directory aiding the Ultramontane leaders is severely felt.' His last
day was spent in Oporto where, despite a four hours' delay caused
by heavy floods on the rail, he was met by Mr. Flower and
numerous friends, and where the same day he took Confirmation
Services—in Vila Nova de Gaia 'where Senhor Fiandor had not
only maintained but greatly extended the work of his predecessor'
—and in the packed Church of the Redeemer in Oporto where he
addressed the candidates and congregation in Spanish.

His visit had taken twelve days. Conditions demanded that five
and a half of these should be spent in trains or at railway stations.
After many farewells he travelled in comfort by the Sud Express to
Paris; fulfilled his engagement at Gloucester, though with little
time in hand; was met in Dublin by his daughter, and wrote in
Greek in his diary: 'I thank God who leadeth me.'

Mr. Pulvertaft wrote an account of the journey for the *Church
of Ireland Gazette,* ending:

> The gratitude felt by the members of the Reformed Churches
> for his Grace's self-denying work was only equalled by the reti-
> cence of their sympathy with him in the loss of his son. They
> kept silence, knowing that their words could only make more
> acute an ever-present sorrow which had been subordinated to a
> desire to help them in their need.

On his next visit, in the autumn of 1931, he was obliged to go
alone, death having deprived him of his former travelling companion. For the same reason we have no record of this and subsequent visits beyond the bare brief entries in his diary. The week
prior to his departure on 28 September had been one of 'utter
currency chaos'—the franc had fallen; and on arrival at his club,
the Athenaeum, on Saturday the 26th he was still in doubt as to
whether the Society had been able to secure for him the requisite
Spanish exchange. Anxiety was allayed the next afternoon, two
hours before Evensong at Westminster Abbey where he was to
preach, by the club-porter's production of the forgotten packet containing the deposit delivered there some time before. It is of interest
to record that after the Abbey Service he supped with Percy
Dearmer: he would seem to have known all the leading London
churchmen of the 'twenties and 'thirties.

He visited Barcelona, Sabadell and Valencia, where, at the three

days' Synod, 'question arises of fusion with Igl. Esp. Ev. [Spanish
Evangelical Church]. I intervene. Temper good.' (later same day)—
'I speak more fully about Episc. question, and also subventions.
A longish and tiring day.' Thence to Cordoba, and 'walk to
Mesquita which I have long wished to see.' In Seville—'find my
way to Maseo, with Roman antiquities, and a number of Murillos.'
He visits the Cathedral: 'size very impressive; very fine sim-
plicity.' On 7 October news reaches him of the Bishop of Tuam's
death and he wrote at once to Mrs. Harden. The next day he left
Seville for Lisbon in company with the Revd. W. H. Rainy of the
British and Foreign Bible Society and. crossing the Tagus by the
ferry, was met by Canon Pope, Dr. Figueiredo and many others.
A full day in Lisbon ended with two Confirmations in Setubal and
San Pedro, and on the 10th he left for Oporto where he ordained
two deacons and took the Celebration, ending with another Confirmation at Vila Nova de Gaia and an address in Spanish. On his
last day, the 12th, the son of Andrew Cassels consulted him about
ordination. He returned to London in time for the Anglo-Orthodox
delegations' meeting at Lambeth, and sat beside the Archbishop of
Canterbury at dinner. A letter of thanks from the Chairman of the
Reformers' Church Aid Society records their high sense of gratitude for his trouble and kindness, and for his generosity in bearing
a large part of the expenses. 'The Committee also thank your Grace
for your very warm appreciation of our late beloved friend
Mr. Pulvertaft and of its endeavouring to carry on the work without
his guidance and leadership. They truly agree with your Grace
that he is irreplaceable as a Director of operations.'

His fourth visit to the Peninsula, and as it proved his last to
Spain during his primacy in Dublin, occurred in the autumn of
1934. A new Bishop had recently been appointed to the far-flung
diocese of Gibraltar (which includes in its orbit all the southern
countries of Europe), but the Spanish and Portuguese Reformed
Churches were outside its jurisdiction, and Gregg desired a meeting
with the Bishop. They met in the Athenaeum on the evening of
21 September, and Gregg crossed to the Continent the next day.
Bishop Harold Buxton now writes:

It was a happy coincidence for me, having been so recently
consecrated, to have such a distinguished visitor in my Diocese.
We first met at the Athenaeum, to speak about his visits to Spain
and Portugal on behalf of the Church of Ireland. . . . How happy
an occurrence that he who knew Spanish was available for this
function; for no one could have been found anywhere among
the Anglican episcopate so wonderfully qualified, by his dignity

and wisdom, by his evangelical zeal and by his deep Catholic convictions.

How genial he was—and humorous. 'Naturally,' he said, 'as I am *not* visiting your Diocese, and as you *don't* approve of my activities, I shall not embarrass you, and I will not intrude into your Chaplaincies. We shall keep at arm's length if we meet in Madrid.' Then, with a twinkle, 'I'll have nothing to do with *your* Embassy, mind you. *We* have our own.'

His visit on this occasion was very short. It was to ordain one presbyter and three deacons in the Beneficiencia in Madrid, and after a long talk with the heads of the Church the next day he returned to Dublin.

CHAPTER IX

ECCLESIASTICAL COURTS

AFTER ITS DISESTABLISHMENT in 1869 the Church of Ireland continued to use the Book of Common Prayer (with a few very slight alterations) as its manual of public worship, but it appended thereto for its own use fifty-four Canons Ecclesiastical and embodied them in its Constitution. These Canons were expressly designed to emphasize its essentially Protestant or 'low church' character. Only a few years previously the Tractarian or Anglo-Catholic movement in the Church of England had resulted in the secession of some eminent churchmen to the Church of Rome, and this had engendered a sort of panic in the sister-isle and a determination to prevent a similar catastrophe here, where the vast majority of the population was already Roman Catholic. Hence the Canons.

It was felt by several of the clergy then, and has been increasingly felt since, that the Canons are unnecessary innovations and that some of them might with advantage be abolished. But as time went on there were some few of the clergy who were prepared to disregard them without authority and to treat them as though they were non-existent. The first of these was the Reverend Walter Cadden Simpson, Vicar of St. Bartholomew's, Dublin. He had come over from England (where High Church practices were tolerated) a convinced Anglo-Catholic in the tradition of Newman, as well as an ardent Christian Socialist in the line of Maurice and Kingsley. He was a priest of saintly character, and as such will long be remembered; but he was an obstinate and a somewhat turbulent priest. He was not a fifth-columnist in the Protestant camp; he was a valiant and undisguised crusader.

Though the Archbishop was himself a 'high churchman' in the sense that he held an extremely high view of the Church, he was very far from being an Anglo-Catholic. In a sermon on the Tractarian Movement he said:

> The early Tractarians were not ritualists and cared little for externals. Ritual development was perhaps unavoidably carried out with Roman usages, and regard for externals involved the copying of Rome. But there is a ritual of order and decency, a ritual compatible with our Prayer Book, which has nothing to do with Popery.

And he would insist that the Church of Ireland owes nothing to Keble or Newman. At the same time he was far from denouncing those who believed that Anglo-Catholic practices conduce to greater devotion—provided they practised them elsewhere than in Ireland. He too deplored the Canons, but as long as they were in the Constitution they must be obeyed.

I. THE SIMPSON CASE

The extant correspondence connected with this case begins with a letter from the Archbishop, dated Easter Monday 1923, to the Revd. Walter C. Simpson, Vicar of St. Bartholomew's Church, Dublin. The replies to the first series of his letters do not seem to have been preserved.

Dear Mr. Simpson,

I was in correspondence with you in March 1921 on the subject of the use of lighted candles on the Holy Table during Divine Service, and I called upon you to comply with Canon 35 which bears upon the matter.

1. I am now informed by certain parishioners and members of your Congregation that there have been lighted candles upon the Holy Table during Celebration of Holy Communion at various times, and on March 25, 1923, when the same were not necessary for the purpose of giving light.

2. The same gentlemen also inform me that in your Church the provisions of Canon 5 are continually infringed in the office of Holy Communion, in respect of (Par. 1), the minister officiating having his back turned to the people when he is offering up Public Prayer;

3. and (Par. 2) the officiating minister standing at the middle of the Holy Table instead of at the north side.

4. They further allege that the officiating minister from time to time disobeys the same Canon (Par. 4), making the sign of the Cross during the Communion office.

5. They allege further that Canon 4 is infringed from time to time by the use of coloured stoles;

6. and further, that Canon 37 is very commonly infringed by the use of wine mixed with water.

I shall be obliged if you will, without delay, inform me if the allegations are true.

Meanwhile, if and in so far as they or any of them are true, I require you in conformity with paras. 5 and 6 of the declaration made by you upon your institution to your cure, to see that the Canons referred to are faithfully complied with henceforth in the conduct of Divine Service in your Church.

I am

Yours faithfully,

JOHN DUBLIN

April 4, 1923.

Dear Mr. Simpson,

I have your letter of April 3, in which you decline to undertake that no further infringement of the Canons shall take place in your Church in connection with the six points I named.

I am very sorry you refuse to give this assurance, and I would ask you most seriously to consider the meaning of your refusal and where it may lead you, before you commit yourself to a conflict with Church authority.

A question of canonical obedience which you have pledged yourself to render, is involved; also of fidelity in respect of a contract, in virtue of which you were instituted to your cure. You must know that if you had refused to promise obedience to the Canons of the Church of Ireland, institution would have been withheld.

There is further the consideration of the welfare of the Church of God of which you are a priest. If there is public conflict between you and your Bishop, angry passions will be stirred, and stirred far more easily than laid to rest. Are you prepared, by defiance of authority, to increase the disorder in the midst of which we are living, and to create division in the ranks of the Church of Ireland, just when unity is called for?

May it not be that the harm you will do by want of discipline and by the gendering of strife will far outweigh any good inherent in whatever doctrinal principle these breaches of discipline are meant to assert? I ask you to reflect on these considerations very carefully. It is not too late at this stage to draw back.

There is no question of the interpretation of words of doubtful meaning; the issue is of the simplest kind.

If you would care to see me, I shall be at home on Friday, April 6 at noon.

Yours faithfully,
JOHN DUBLIN

April 18, 1923.

Dear Mr. Simpson,

You misunderstood me if, as you write in your letter of April 12, you thought I spoke of myself, *qua* Bishop, as 'merely an official' of the General Synod. I used the expression for the purpose of making clear to you that it is my duty to enforce obedience upon the part of the clergy in this Diocese to the Constitutions and Canons of the Church of Ireland, and that I have no right by virtue of my office to dispense from obedience to them.

It is quite impossible for me to grant you the 'hearing' you ask for. There is no question here of the construction of ambiguous legislation, or of matters of doctrine open to controversy. You have admitted that you have acted in violation of the plain language of certain Canons, and you have declined to give any undertaking that you will abstain from such violation in the future. And since the question is one of obedience and disobedience, I cannot see that any good purpose will be served by further discussion.

Accordingly, I now require you in virtue of the obligation of obedience to which you subscribed as a condition precedent to your institution, to desist henceforth from the practices which I pointed out to you. And I ask once again for an unqualified undertaking on your part that there shall be no repetition of them in St. Bartholomew's Church. Otherwise, I shall be compelled to bring the matter before the Court of the General Synod.

If, from motives of conscience or otherwise, you find yourself no longer prepared to render the obedience you promised, it seems to me that the only honourable course open to you is to resign your cure.

Yours faithfully,
JOHN DUBLIN

April 21, 1923.
Dear Mr. Simpson,

I did want to avoid, if possible, the dangers to the Church attending public litigation; and therefore I suggested that you should put on paper for the Chancellor the main points of your position, in order that I might get for you a lawyer's view of them rather than give you my own.

I doubt very much whether you would be granted by the Court of the General Synod any opportunity of arguing as to the desirability or otherwise of the pieces of legislation we are concerned with. The question would turn, I think, solely on what that legislation means, and whether there has or has not been infringement of its provisions. And I thought that if the Chancellor advised me on your contentions, this point might be brought out for you more strongly than I have succeeded in doing, and might help you to see the relatively narrow issue with which alone the Court would concern itself.

In view of your letter of April 20, is it too late to ask you this question: as you do not intend to defend all the points of complaint—i.e. (I suppose) as you are ready to yield on certain points—can you not bring yourself to yield on all six?

Yours faithfully,
JOHN DUBLIN

April 24, 1923.
Dear Mr. Simpson,

I have your letter of the 23rd. Let me have as early as possible next week the statement you wish me to consider. But do not forget that legislation was framed with the direct purpose of checking advance in the direction in which you desire to move, and was made explicit and absolute.

You mention an interview with Archbishop d'Arcy. He made a memorandum of the conversation, which I have, and writes, 'Simpson promised he would not adopt the Eastward position.'

Yours faithfully,

JOHN DUBLIN

May 14. 1923.

Dear Mr. Simpson,

The Canons prescribe 'the customary scarf.' Until the C. of I. defines what it means by, and includes under, the word 'customary' I do not regard myself as called on to state what the shape and cut of the scarf must be, unless definitely asked for a ruling. It must be the customary scarf of plain black silk.

I do not know by what direction the Canons are printed in our P. Bks. I suppose there is some resolution to that effect. But in many old P. Bks. of the C. of Ireland you will find the 1634 Canons (which are the basis of these) printed.

Yours faithfully,

JOHN DUBLIN

The patience and firmness of the Archbishop had its eventual effect. A letter from the Vicar, dated St. Philip and James, 1923, concludes the first stage in these proceedings.

Dear Lord Archbishop,

Please forgive delay in my reply but the subject has needed my careful consideration. The longer statement will require more time, so this only deals with the points in dispute. I am definitely advised that certain of the Canons were not duly enacted and cannot be enforced. Even though an Ecclesiastical Court were to maintain that consent required compliance, a Civil Court would hold that they were not Law.

Nevertheless as an act of obedience and in order to maintain peace in the Church, I am willing to make the following changes in our custom.

1. To begin the Communion Service at the North side and not in the centre of the Holy Table.

2. To cease from the use of the Mixed Chalice.

3. To cease from making the Sign of the Cross *coram publico*.

4. To limit the wearing of Stoles to such services as will not give 'offence.'

5. To limit the use of altar lights to such occasions as I deem 'necessary for the purpose of giving light.'

K

I have omitted for the present the question of the position of the celebrant at the Prayer of Consecration.

It is reasonable, I hope, to add that my compliance in the points indicated may need reconsideration from your Grace's point of view and from mine, when we have gone more fully into the legal question involved.

Your obedient

W. C. SIMPSON

So matters stood until February of 1926 when the Vicar, in his Church Magazine letter for that month, wrote as follows:

When a question arises about the meaning of Rubrics, a decision cannot be based upon a mere reference to the Canons. All our documents, and the ecclesiastical judgments based upon them, would need to be examined as to their meaning in fact and in history.

Now, I am prepared to stand by this sound principle, and to show that when two laws are in opposition, the higher is operative. Therefore I rule out of my vision certain parts of the Canons. If any one is aggrieved by my decision, the honourable course is to test it in the Ecclesiastical Courts.

In consequence of this letter the entire Select Vestry of St. Bartholomew's requested the Archbishop 'for a ruling on the point made by the Revd. Walter C. Simpson, Vicar, that the direction for the conduct of the Service in the Canons of the Church of Ireland can be overruled if the same directions do not appear in the Rubrics of the respective Offices of the Church.' To this the Archbishop replied, in a letter to the Secretary of the Select Vestry that 'he was fully satisfied that the Court of the General Synod, if appealed to, would maintain the full applicability of the Canons to the conduct of Divine Worship, and their authority where they apply.' At the same time he wrote privately:

March 11, 1926

My dear Simpson,

I am very sorry to get your letter of March 4, as it shows me you do not yet grasp the situation. It has gone beyond a mere matter of accommodation between you and your parishioners. You are taking up the position of one who seeks to make his own laws and to name his own terms.

And this you cannot do; nor can I be a party to leaving matters where they are, consistently with my duty to the Church, my successors and the clergy of the Diocese.

The points in regard to which you claim to be excused from

obedience are relatively small, both ritually and doctrinally, which makes your insistence upon them very difficult to understand; whereas disobedience in regard to them is a serious moral question.

I think it will be better if I tell you as your Ordinary that I require you forthwith to observe the provisions of Canon 5, and (i) not to offer up Public Prayer with your back turned to the Congregation; (ii) in the Communion Office to stand at the North side. Also to observe the provision of Canon 35 to the effect that there shall not be any lighted lamps or candles on the Communion Table, or in any other part of the Church, during the celebration of the Services or the administration of the Sacraments, etc., etc., except when they are necessary for the purpose of giving light.

I confess my extreme dislike to exercising my authority as Ordinary in the matter of these things which, in comparison with the greater things we are concerned with, are minor technicalities. But in this particular case . . . [a page is missing, but it is evident that its contents were simply a repetition of the previously made requirements].

I find it hard to conceive that your continued tenure of the Incumbency is incompatible with a faithful conformity to these requirements, and I shall be glad to hear from you to the effect that you will submit forthwith to the above-mentioned rules laid down by the Church of Ireland.

Yours sincerely,

JOHN DUBLIN

April 8, 1926

My dear Simpson,

I am glad you have gone some distance towards meeting the requirements of the Canons, but I cannot be satisfied until you have complied with what, as Ordinary, I have called upon you to do. And I must now ask you to write and tell me explicitly if you do not intend to obey my direction on the five points named in my letter of March 11, fully and forthwith.

There are one or two points in your last letter which you may bring forward as justifying delay, or non-compliance, which indicate a misunderstanding.

You have misunderstood me, if you interpret me as saying that the Lord's Prayer is not covered by the phrase 'offering up public prayer' at the beginning of the Communion Office. It is to be said in a distinct and audible voice, and said 'at the North side of the Table.' It may have originated in this position as the priest's private prayer, but for our liturgy it cannot be so treated, and may not be said with the back turned to the people any more than any other public prayer.

Let me also quote to you Archbishop d'Arcy's memorandum of an interview with you on the subject of the 'Agnus Dei.'

'Mr. Simpson promised he would limit singing during Communion to well-known Communion hymns, and not introduce Agnus Dei, as he did, between the Communion of the clergy and of the people.

'N.B. I explained this was a special concession, as I would not permit the introduction of new elements into the H.C.'

As to the unauthorized hymn before Magnificat, my view is as it ever was. I have *no* authority to permit it. If my attention were drawn to it, I should forbid it. I do not like its use there, but so far I have not called upon you to discard it.

I have no reason to think that St. Bartholomew's is not 'loyal in principle' to C. of I., but you must not claim that it is loyal *'in detail,'* so long as on any of the five points I have specified in previous letters obedience is not rendered, even after your attention has been called to infringements of Canon or Rubric, and obedience has been enjoined by your Ordinary.

Yours sincerely,

JOHN DUBLIN

June 16, 1926

My dear Simpson,

The main points of attack, so far as I know, are the white stole, *habitual* use of lights on the holy table, and your position as celebrant almost at the centre of the table and with your back all but fully turned to the people.

I make no attempt to defend you in any of these three points; the utmost liberty of interpretation I have conceded you in the third is the Northern end of the West side of the holy table, with your back not turned, but anglewise. And even this you imperil, if you persist in doing what your Ordinary has repeatedly told you is illegal and forbidden you to do.

Mr. Chamney may be concerned with other points than these, such as finance—but this does not affect the question of the vulnerableness of your position, and the strength of his, in respect of these. And you will be defeated, and the cause you think to champion will not be advanced.

Yours sincerely,

JOHN DUBLIN

As my plans are at present, I shall be away on July 4.

Meanwhile the Archbishop was replying to letters from an equally militant Protestant, Mr. William Chamney, who had been for twenty-six years Hon. Treasurer of the Church. However, the Vicar was so far persuaded by the reasonableness of his Archbishop's counsel that in June 1926 he wrote in his Parish Maga-

zine: 'Definite obedience to the Church of Ireland is our clear
duty in St. Bartholomew's'—but added cryptically: 'Obedience, to
be ethical, must needs be co-operative and intelligent.' But, no
change took place in his conduct of the Services.

Mr. Chamney thereupon resigned, because of practices which he
considered 'not merely unnecessary but illegal.' The Vicar replied
that he considered many of the Canons were 'silly.' He did indeed
sincerely think that any Civil Court of Law would regard them as
too trivial to be seriously regarded. The objectors therefore brought
an action against the Revd. W. C. Simpson in the Court of the
General Synod, to the judgment of which (rather than of a Diocesan
Court) all matters of doctrine and ritual must be referred.

The Court consists of the three most senior Bishops (Armagh,
Dublin, Meath—or of others in order of precedence); and of four
lay judges (elected triennially by the Standing Committee of the
General Synod, drawn from Judges of the Supreme High Court in
order of dignity). Charges involving doctrine or ritual may be preferred by a Bishop, or by not less than four Communicants, in the
form of a Petition in writing lodged with the Registrar of the
Court. But it is open to the Archbishop of a Province, if one of his
own clergy is charged to appoint a Commission of Enquiry to
ascertain whether a prima facie case has been established; if in
his judgment and in that of the two senior lay Judges it has not
been, they shall then order further proceedings to be stayed.

The Petitioners had first put their complaints before Dr. Gregg.
They were two: first that Mr. Simpson, when saying the Prayer of
Consecration at Holy Communion, did not stand at the north side
of the Holy Table, but at the west side; second, that he wore a
coloured stole during his ministration of Divine Service. Dr. Gregg
had rejected these charges.

In September 1927 the four Petitioners—William Chamney, Samuel
Haughton, Charles Alexander Rankin and Albert Edward Murphy
—presented a more detailed Petition charging Mr. Simpson with no
less than ten breaches of the Canons and Rubrics in addition to the
two former charges, and at the same time they appealed against
the Archbishop's decision respecting the latter. The remainder of
the Petition contained charges that Mr. Simpson had been guilty
of breaches of the Canons and Rubrics in the following respects:

(1) During the administration of Holy Communion, standing
at the West Side of the Holy Table;
(2) Saying the first half of the Prayer of Consecration with his
back turned to the people;

(3) Making use during the Holy Communion of two hymns
other than those prescribed in the Office itself, or ordered or
permitted by the Ordinary;

(4) Elevating the Paten and Cup beyond what was necessary
for taking the same into his hands, in administering the Holy
Communion;

(5) Bowing to the Holy Table on several occasions during
Divine Service;

(6) Making the sign of the Cross when placing the Alms upon
the Holy Table;

(7) Using lighted candles on the Communion Table when the
same were not necessary for the purpose of giving light;

(8) At Evening Prayer, immediately before the Magnificat,
using a hymn, called by him the Office Hymn;

(9) Immediately before the Prayer for the Church Militant,
asking the congregation to pray for the Faithful Departed;

(10) Carrying a Cross and allowing and permitting persons to
do so through the Church in a Procession as a Rite or Ceremony.

When the Petition had been presented, the Archbishop, anxious
both to shield his disobedient cleric and at the same time to avert
scandal to the Church by publicity, exercised his right of appointing
a Commission of Enquiry. On 3 January 1928 there was made an
Order signed by the Archbishop, by the Rt. Hon. Baron Glenavy
(formerly Lord Chancellor) and by Mr. J. H. Moore, K.C. (formerly
a Judge of the County Court), declaring that no prima facie case
had been established in respect of charge No. 6. The others were
admitted.

Normally in a case of this kind the Archbishop of Dublin should
be summoned as one of the ecclesiastical judges, but in this case
the Petitioners had combined, with their charges against the Vicar,
their appeal against the Archbishop's decision in respect of their
two former charges. He could not therefore sit in a court convened
to hear an appeal against one of his own decisions, but he could
and should do so in respect of the ten charges (reduced to nine)
brought before the Court of the General Synod. Dr. Gregg was
quick to perceive that the Petition was irregular, and wrote to the
Registrar giving notice that he reserved his right to protest (a)
against the form of the Petition, and (b) against the failure to
summon him to adjudicate on the points other than the appeals
dealing with the two original charges, which groups should, in his
view, form the subjects of separate Petitions. This point did not
escape the notice of the Vicar's solicitors, who wrote to object that
the Court had not been legally constituted, since the ecclesiastical
judges had not been taken in order of precedence.

These complications were avoided at the hearing. By consent in open Court of Counsel for the parties, the Court made an Order dividing the original Petition into two: the first to be confined to the two Appeals, and the second to the original charges. Thus, the Court which dealt with the two Appeals included the Bishop of Cork as one of the ecclesiastical judges, but, for the hearing of the original charges, the Court was reconstituted by the inclusion of the Archbishop of Dublin.

The hearing commenced in the Synod Hall on 23 February 1928 and occupied four days, judgment being reserved. The Court reassembled on 22 March to give its decision. With regard to the two appeals the Court held that the wearing of a purple stole by Mr. Simpson was a violation of Canon 4, and that, in occupying the position admitted by him during the Prayer of Consecration, he was acting in violation of both the Rubric and Canon 5. With regard to the charges in the Second Petition (for the hearing of which the Archbishop took the place of the Bishop of Cork), he was judged guilty of a number of these and was admonished in respect of them and of any repetition of them, and he was ordered to pay £220 towards the Petitioners' costs, a sum roughly equivalent of half the costs. The offences of which Mr. Simpson was found guilty were:

(a) That, while saying the Lord's Prayer and several other prayers during the Communion Service, he stood at the West side of the Holy Table and that, when reading the Prayer of Consecration, he turned his back to the people;

(b) That he made use of two unauthorized hymns, contrary to the provisions of Canon 5;

(c) That on occasions he bowed to the Holy Table, contrary to the provisions of Canon 5;

(d) That he made use of lighted candles on the Communion Table when the same were not necessary for the purpose of giving light;

(e) That he made use of an office hymn before the Magnificat at Evening Prayer;

(f) That he asked for prayers for the Faithful Departed, immediately before the Prayer for the Church Militant, contrary to the provisions of Canons 1 and 5.

The Judgment of the Court is reported on page 367 of the Proceedings of the General Synod for 1928. The reasons for the Court's Judgment were given by Lord Glenavy and were published in a Supplement to the *Church of Ireland Gazette* for 20 April 1928. Among these it is recorded that, with regard to the charges of bowing to the Holy Table—

His Grace the Archbishop of Dublin is doubtful whether the appropriate Canon applies to any act save those performed during the actual time occupied in the celebration of the prescribed Service and consequently is not to be taken as concurring in the finding of the Court so far as the acts of obeisance when entering and leaving the Church are concerned.

It is clear that once the affair came into Court (a calamity he had tried so hard to avoid) he did his very best for the turbulent cleric who had scorned his counsel. As Mr. Micks says: 'The part which Dr. Gregg took in the course of the proceedings, which must have been extremely distasteful to him, was one which shows his strong sense of fair play in cases in which clergy were charged with ecclesiastical offences, and also his keenly incisive mind when confronted with any legal question that arose.'

II. THE COLQUHOUN CASE

The Church of St. John, Sandymount, Dublin, was founded and endowed by the Rt. Hon. Sidney Herbert, M.P., under a Deed of Settlement dated 1 April 1850, and erected pursuant to the provisions of the Church Building Acts. The object of these Acts was 'to enable and encourage the erection and endowment by private enterprise of churches and chapels in which the liturgy and rites of the united Churches of England and Ireland as by law established should be used and observed, and which would be subject to the spiritual jurisdiction of the Bishop of the Diocese.' The Vicars were appointed by the Trustees of the Deed of Endowment; and they were by tradition priests whose standards of churchmanship were far from being 'low.'

The Revd. S. R. S. Colquhoun had been appointed by the Trustees and instituted by Archbishop Gregg on 7 June 1930. But the Services as conducted by him had been under close observation by members of the Church who felt that he openly transgressed a number of the Canons—to which he had promised assent at his Institution. It was therefore not surprising that matters were brought to a head on 13 December 1934 when a Petition was presented to the Court of the General Synod alleging this fact and asking that he should be duly brought to trial on the charges which numbered twenty-one in all.

In reply Mr. Colquhoun submitted that, under the Deed of Endowment in 1850, the Court of the General Synod had no authority to adjudicate in this matter. The submission was rejected by the Court at a meeting held in Belfast on 8 March 1935, on the grounds of his vow at Ordination and promise at Institution 'to submit himself to the authority of the Church of Ireland, and to the Laws and Tribunals thereof.'

Mr. Colquhoun next applied to the High Court in Dublin for an Order of Prohibition restraining the Court of the General Synod and its members from 'acting in excess of their legal authority.' The High Court was unanimous in its decision that it was not within its province to give any such Order 'since the Court of the General Synod of the Church of Ireland derives its authority solely from the consent or agreement of the members of that Church . . .' (The case is fully reported in the 1936 *Volume of the Irish Reports*, page 641.)

A final effort to obtain the interference of the Civil Courts was made when the Hon. Mr. Justice Meredith was applied to for an injunction to restrain the Court of the General Synod from hearing the Petition. This application was dismissed with costs on 9 July 1936.

The hearing of the Petition was resumed in Belfast on 7 October 1936. Mr. Colquhoun, appearing for himself in person, raised a preliminary objection to the composition of the Court by reason of the absence from it of Archbishop Gregg. His absence was due to the fact that Counsel for the Petitioners intended to call him as a witness. The Court therefore overruled Mr. Colquhoun's objection. Meanwhile Mr. Colquhoun had filed his Answers in writing to the charges made against him. These charges and his replies are as follows:

That, on or about the 18th of June 1933, and the 11th of March 1934, and on divers other occasions, during a Service prescribed for the Administration of the Lord's Supper, he

(1) Did not say the Lord's Prayer at the beginning of the said Service. Answer: a denial that he failed to say the Lord's Prayer, but an admission that the prayer was not audible to the Petitioners, if present.

(2) Did not rehearse the Ten Commandments or the Summary of the Law prescribed as an alternative. This was admitted.

(3) Remained seated during the singing of the Creed from the words 'Begotten of the Father' to the end. (In answer, Mr. Colquhoun admitted that he remained seated during part of the Creed, but denied that, in doing so, he did anything contrary to the Rubrics or Canons.)

(4) Made the sign of the Cross during the Ascription before the Sermon. This was admitted.

(5) Pronounced the Ascription after the Sermon while standing with his back to the People. This Mr. Colquhoun admitted but denied that it was unlawful.

(6) Being the sole Minister present, did remain standing while he and the people made the General Confession. This was likewise admitted but its illegality was denied.

(7) Made the sign of the Cross when pronouncing the Absolution. This was admitted.

(8) Used a hymn not prescribed in the Office of Holy Communion, and not ordered or permitted by the Ordinary or other lawful authority of the Church. In answer, Mr. Colquhoun submitted that the charge in that form was too vague to admit of an answer and ought to be dismissed on the ground of indefiniteness.

(9) Repeated a prayer, which was inaudible after the Prayer beginning 'We do not presume.' To this Mr. Colquhoun replied that the Prayer of Consecration which follows the Prayer of Humble Access may have been said inaudibly.

(10) Caused or permitted a bell to be rung during the time when he was performing the Manual Acts. This was admitted.

(11) Repeated a prayer which the Petitioners believe to have been the Prayer of Consecration while standing at the West Side of the Holy Table, only moving to the North Side immediately before the Manual Acts were to be performed. These were admitted.

(12) Elevated the Cup and Paten at the Consecration beyond what was necessary for taking the same into his hands. This was admitted.

(13) Did sing or cause to be sung after the Consecration of the Elements the 'Agnus Dei' which is not prescribed in the Office nor ordered or permitted by the Ordinary, etc. Mr. Colquhoun admitted that he caused the 'Agnus Dei' to be sung but denied that was not prescribed in the Office nor permitted by the Ordinary, etc.

(14) Made the sign of the Cross when pronouncing the Blessing. This was admitted.

(15) During the said Service did wear a Biretta which he frequently removed from and replaced on his head, and also wore a Cope and Chasuble and other ecclesiastical vestments or ornaments not prescribed or permitted by the Canons. This was admitted.

(16) Conducted these and other Services with lighted candles in the Chancel when the same were not necessary for the purpose of giving light. This he admitted, but denied contravention of any Rubric or Canon.

(17) Caused or permitted a hanging lamp to remain burning over a side table during the Celebration of the said Services and others, when the same was not necessary for the purpose of giving light. This was admitted.

(18) Allowed a Cross to be on the Communion Table. This was admitted.

(19) Caused or permitted divers acts and ceremonies other than those prescribed in the Book of Common Prayer to be performed by Servers or Acolytes, whose employment is not provided for in it or the Canons. This was also admitted, though the charge gave no particulars of the acts or ceremonies.

(20) Performed acts of obeisance to the Lord's Table on various occasions too numerous to mention in detail. Answer: he did perform acts of obeisance but denied that they were performed to the Lord's Table.

(21) Used incense or permitted its use in the Church during Public Services. This was admitted.

It is of some importance to observe the extensive nature of Mr. Colquhoun's admissions, since Archbishop Gregg was not called as a witness. The Petitioners' Counsel's statement that he intended to call him, however, excluded him from sitting in the Court as one of the Judges. It was as a result of these admissions that it became unnecessary to call the Archbishop as a witness.

Mr. Colquhoun was adjudged guilty of all the charges, except the sixth, and was further found to have been in disregard, neglect and violation of the Canons. The Court further declared that he was deserving of the most severe censure and strictly admonished him to refrain in future from any repetition of any act which the Court had decided to be illegal. He was also directed to pay the costs of the Petitioners. The Judgment of the Court is reported in the *Journal of the General Synod* for 1937, pages 357–9.

Unhappily this did not see the end of litigation in this matter. One of the last of Dr. Gregg's duties as Archbishop of Dublin was to preside in his Diocesan Court on the hearing of a Petition for the issue of a faculty to remove from this Church the following articles:

(1) Stations of the Cross;
(2) A Crucifix set up on the wall behind the Pulpit;
(3) A Confessional Screen;
(4) A Crib;
(5) Six large candlesticks and two smaller ones on the Communion Table and two small candlesticks on the second table;
(6) A Mass Board,

on the ground that each of these articles was in character illegal and had been illegally introduced into the Church.

Archbishop Gregg, with the Hon. Gerald FitzGibbon, LL.D., a Judge of the Supreme Court, as his Chancellor and Assessor, the

Ven. J. W. Crozier, Archdeacon of Dublin, and Mr. R. H. Ryland, Chancellor of several Dioceses, formed the Court. Mr. Colquhoun appeared in person, as before, to oppose the Petition. Notice of opposition had also been given by two members of his congregation.

The judgment of the Court was given on 29 December 1938, and declared that the Stations of the Cross, the Confessional Screen and the six large candlesticks on the Communion Table were unlawfully introduced and should be removed. Since the Crib was not in the Church when the Petition was filed, or afterward, and since Mr. Colquhoun undertook not to introduce any such article into the Church without the Archbishop's approval, the Court made no order in respect of it. As to the Mass Board the Court held it to be an ordinary notice board, and accordingly a faculty for its removal was refused. The two small candlesticks on the Communion Table, and the two on the second table, should be retained, provided that candles in them were lit only when necessary to give light. The Court refused to give a faculty for the removal of the Crucifix, and of the two pairs of small candlesticks; these having been introduced with the Archbishop's approval and being lawful ornaments.

'On the subject of the Crucifix behind the pulpit Archbishop Gregg gave a judgment containing his reasons which displayed a characteristic combination of deep learning and unswerving adherence to what was relevant. The judgment is not widely known and deserves close study by any one who is interested in matters of Church Law.' (Unfortunately it is too technical to quote. But by way of personal interest two facts may be recorded. It was related at the time that when the Archbishop was expounding the reasons for his judgment, his Assessor was about to interrupt. The Archbishop raised a hand and said quietly, 'I did not ask you anything.' He then proceeded to substantiate his judgment by citing precedents in Ecclesiastical Statute Law of which neither his Assessor nor any one else in the Court had ever heard. Further, it was on account of the hearing of this case that he postponed so long his removal to Armagh after his election to the Primacy. He did not wish to leave it as an undesirable legacy to his successor. His diary for December 1938 contains two characteristically brief references to it. '28th. Working a good deal on completing Crucifix-Faculty judgment. 29th. I pronounce re Crucifix that no order is made. Each side pays its own costs.' Then on 30th: 'Cease to be Abp. of Dublin.')

From this decision of the Diocesan Court the Petitioners appealed to the Court of the General Synod, from so much of the judgment as refused a Faculty for the removal of the Crucifix. On 28 July 1939 that Court recorded its agreement with the Archbishop's judgment. Nevertheless it held that a necessary condition for the obtaining of a valid permission from the Ordinary under Canon 40 was the consent of the Select Vestry. Accordingly, the Crucifix having been introduced without such consent under Canon 40, and no Faculty having been given with respect to it, the Court was bound to give a Faculty for its removal.

The application for this Confirmatory Faculty came before the Diocesan Court of Dublin on 23 November 1939, judgment being reserved until 16 December. The Court now consisted of Dr. A. W. Barton (Archbishop of Dublin) with the Hon. Gerald FitzGibbon, LL.D., as his Assessor; the Ven. E. G. Sullivan, Archdeacon of Dublin, and Mr. R. H. Ryland. From the evidence it appeared that in St. John's, Sandymount, the provision in the Constitution for holding the annual Easter Vestry and revising the Register of Vestrymen had been disregarded until the Diocesan Council, in exercise of its powers, had convened a meeting at which a Select Vestry had been elected. This newly appointed Select Vestry had passed unanimously a resolution (a) opposing the grant of a Faculty for the retention of the Crucifix, and (b) nominating the original Petitioners for its removal as its representative before the Diocesan Court.

Against this decision of the Diocesan Court, Mr. Colquhoun and three of his parishioners took an appeal to the Court of the General Synod. After further debate it was decided, in order to put an end to prolonged litigation, that this case should be heard on its merits; and a Confirmatory Faculty was granted authorizing the retention of the Crucifix in the place which it had occupied for many years. 'In the result, the exception taken to the conduct of the services at Sandymount was for the most part justified by the decisions of the Ecclesiastical Courts, and sound and scholarly guidance was given by the original judgment of Archbishop Gregg.'

Mr. E. C. Micks has made a detailed summary of these cases which is now deposited, together with the documents concerning them, in the archives of the Representative Church Body. The above account is a much abbreviated version of his summary. To it he adds the following comment:

An Archbishop of Dublin has plenty to do and little enough time in which to do it, without having his cares increased by cases in the Ecclesiastical Courts. Dr. Gregg was unfortunate in that two such cases arose during the years when he held the See of Dublin, but each case served to show the essential fairness of his mind and its immediate grasp of what was relevant.

He always had a deep interest in the decision of rights and wrongs between people. If he had chosen the Law as a profession he would have been pre-eminent in his time. All the necessary qualities were there—ability to study, a strictly relevant mind, the gift of concise and lucid expression and, above all, a keen sense of what was equitable and what simply would not do. He did not share the frequent misconception that a lawyer's worth was mainly concerned with the defence on criminal charges of persons who inevitably were guilty of whatever offence had been alleged against them and who, while embarrassingly candid in their admission of guilt, nevertheless insisted that their lawyer should conduct a defence on the basis of complete innocence. He read the newspapers and did not overlook the reports of civil actions which raised any point of legal or human interest, and upon several occasions he asked me for fuller details of cases with which I had been concerned. When the amalgamation of the University Club with the Kildare Street Club was proposed he astutely referred—in opposition to the idea—to the decision of the House of Lords given in 1904 in the General Assembly of the Free Church of Scotland v. Lord Overtoun. Nor was a *cause célèbre* in the racing world beneath his tolerant interest and his shrewd comments. On these occasions he was entirely human, charming and witty.

It is seldom that one can say that one has had the honour of knowing a really great man. I can say that I knew Primate Gregg.

CHAPTER X

QUESTIONS OF REUNION

A CELEBRATED LIBRETTIST in light verse has opined, though in other words, that every human child is innately either a potential liberal or a potential conservative, and the generalization may be taken to cover other fields of discourse than the political. A bias in one direction or the other is probably much more a matter of temperament than the exponents of either position would be willing to allow. And it is quite possible to be liberal in the realms of thought and conservative in the sphere of conduct at one and the same time, without inconsistency.

Liberalism and individualism may be said in general terms to be synonymous. Gregg was born in an age of outstanding individualists and, too, of a liberalism in religious thought vital enough to survive the shattering impact of the first Great War and continue into the late 'twenties and even beyond them. As a theologian he very largely shared that liberalism, that individualism; and this because his theology was the expression of spiritual experience: it was concrete and personal rather than abstract and doctrinaire. But as a churchman he was utterly opposed to it. For him, as for most other ecclesiastically-minded reactionaries, liberalism and individualism in that respect were subjective sentimentalism, which from his soul he abhorred. Though as a theologian and biblical divine he was as liberal as any modernist of his time, as a churchman he was uncompromisingly conservative. He stood for that sense of corporateness, of structural coherence, which has behind it the time-honoured observance of established tradition, the sanction of law, the weight of authority. Thus he declared himself both in politics and in churchmanship a constitutionalist—for these are spheres of activity where the individual must behave as a member of a body and conform to certain canons and regulations. Not by any means that he undervalued the stimulus which the individual —the prophet—can and does impart to the general life of the body; on the contrary, he valued this most highly; but such individuals must act as cells within the organism, not as intruders invading and disrupting it; for though the individual has indeed a value which is intrinsic and unique, its value is not so great as that of the corporate whole of which it is an integral part. And for him the visible Catholic Church was such an organism. To others less positive and

159

dogmatic on this point, it might seem that he tended to confound the organism with the organization.

But for him the question of any possible coalescence of that Church with any other religious denominations in Christendom which were non-Catholic, non-episcopal, in short nonconformist, was one of acute—even anguished—difficulty; in fact, without some signs of *metanoia* on *their* part, inadmissible. Holy Faith was for him inseparable from Holy Order, and Holy Order enshrined a three-fold ministry—bishops, priests and deacons—dating back to the apostolic age: this for him was a cardinal article of faith (despite Streeter's *The Primitive Church*).

Yet it would be altogether unjust to let it be inferred that he saw only one side of the question, or that he had not weighed the arguments in favour of a more liberal approach. His fair-mindedness, his judicious, judicial approach to every problem, were the outcome of his reverent, even passionate, devotion to truth. Those who heard him speak on the question of Reunion in his later years might perhaps be surprised that he could deliver himself to the following effect, as he had done on his enthronement in Kildare Cathedral in 1920.

Succession is a law of the Church's life, a law whose ordered working has always counted for much with the historic Christian body. But succession, however continuous, reminds us of the changeableness that attends all things earthly, and it throws us back by way of contrast upon the abidingness we find in the living Christ. 'The one remains, the many change and pass.' . . . We are members of an organism, not rigid by inherited prescription, but adapting itself to the needs of its indwelling life. The Church is not a dead crystallization; flexibility is the condition of its health. . . . The conditions of a true discharge of its duty by the Church are correspondence with the God who lives in it and with the society in which it lives. The Church is sorely tempted to become a creature of established custom, of use and wont. But if it is to be the true interpreter of God to the world it must reconcile the demand for abidingness with the demand for adaptability. . . .

There are those, and they are very many, who rejoice to paint the ideal Church as immutable, A far truer view, to my mind, is that of a Church which can learn and can also unlearn. Take as an illustration the attitude of the Anglican communion to Reunion. The day has gone by when one can be satisfied with an isolation which practically unchurches those Protestant churches which are separated from us. Our isolation is indeed based on principle. We have received what to us is truth, and only by isolation can we guard it. But we have been learning more of Christ and have come to ask ourselves: 'How does isolation agree with Christian charity? Is Christ truly reflected in a divided Christendom? May it not be that if we are outside charity we are outside Christ?' And these heart-searchings have borne their fruit. They have compelled us to ask ourselves if life itself is not a thing of varied form, and if it is not in keeping with the phenomena exhibited by life in every direction that the Church should be multiform rather than uniform; if the true text of life is not quite as likely to be found in connection with the fruit it bears as with the form it wears; if, for example, it is not perhaps as important that worship should be living as liturgical, or if a Church with a technically irregular ministry might not be saving souls unto God as surely as a Church with an unimpeachable episcopal succession. We are asking these questions, and as we beat out an answer we give to our Church a new and more Christlike form. We are content to believe that our particular form of Church life need not be the standard for all Church life, and that it is possible for those who are not of us nevertheless to be of Christ. And so our eyes are turning away from an isolation which sterilizes our Christianity, to a comprehension which may show to the world a Church abounding in love and bringing forth the fruits of Christ.

But this was a speculative line of thought foreign to his natural instinct for clear definition, and he did not pursue it; on the contrary in all subsequent utterances on the subject he strongly opposed it. For it opened up vistas without boundary, of a comprehensiveness altogether incomprehensible.

Seven years later, at the midsummer Synod of his United Diocese in Dublin in 1927, on the eve of the World Conference on Faith and Order to be held in Lausanne that August, we find him warning his audience against undue optimism. It was not, he emphasized, to be a Conference upon Reunion, but one of preliminary study and discussion. What was above all to be feared was *vagueness*. There were seven topics for discussion: The call to unity; the Church's message; nature; common confession; ministry; sacraments; and lastly, the unity of Christendom in relation to the existing churches. And it is clear that he went with his own mind unalterably made up on each of these topics.

Preaching in St. Patrick's Cathedral on 30 October of that year he said:

Reunion cannot rest upon sympathy and good-will only; it will only be real if those who unite in saying the same thing mean

L

the same thing. The great problem of Reunion is to bring different religious organizations into a *visible* unity. . . . It is a great
deal more than Christian individuals fraternizing; it involves
their fellowship in a society—an *external* society. And as soon as
the question arises of the nature of this society, and of the terms
of membership, and of the meaning of its rites, sharp differences
manifest themselves. And therefore, those who are working
towards an external and visible Unity recognize that, although
sympathy and good-will are indispensable, nothing permanent
can be arrived at without a common understanding upon fundamental questions.

And for this reason the Anglican Church has a position forced
upon it which many of the Protestant Churches find it hard to
understand. . . . It is painfully aware that Reunion cannot take
place between itself and them if Reunion involves it in any compromise upon principles which to it are sacred. External Reunion
purchased at the expense of truth would only mean internal
disunion for ourselves.

The Anglican position is a historic one, Catholic as well as
Protestant. . . .

He went on to show that among the principles sacred to the
Anglican Communion is that of the three-fold ministry in unbroken
succession from the Apostolic Ministry, as is explicitly stated in
the Preface to the Ordinal in the Book of Common Prayer. And
the Thirty-fourth Article is severe on any who 'through his private
judgment, willingly and purposely, doth openly break the Traditions and Ceremonies of the Church, which be not repugnant to the
Word of God, and be ordained and approved by common
authority.' But this principle of continuity with the past goes hand
in hand with that of attentiveness to spiritual guidance in the
present.

It is because of our Church's adherence to these two principles: (1) the authority of the Church's Tradition provided it be
not repugnant to Holy Scripture, and (2) the authority of the
contemporary guidance of the Holy Ghost—that she is bound
to move slowly in matters of Reunion, even though she believes
Reunion to be the will of Christ.

The truths she believes and the practices she follows, she
regards herself as holding in trust. And yet, though she sees
patent evidence of the work of the Holy Ghost in other Churches,
she does not dare to surrender, for the sake of fellowship with
these others, anything which she believes to be characteristic of
Catholic Church life.

For these reasons, while there was at Lausanne 'a surprising extent of agreement' on the Church's message and common confession of faith, there were 'equally firmly registered disagreements' on the Church's ministry and sacraments.

In Christ's visible society, we believe that it is by the will of God that the authoritative transmission of the right to minister in the congregation should not be merely inward, but outward; that Ordination not merely registers something already given, but conveys the divine gift.

And similarly the Sacraments to us are means of grace: not merely signs, but effectual signs—signs that convey the grace which they signify.

A sceptically disposed critic might object that on this showing —'conveys the divine gift'—Ordination is another sacrament and should unequivocally be acknowledged as such; and that while much is said in retrospect about the external authority of the Quadrilateral: Catholic Creeds; Holy Scriptures; Two Great Sacraments; Three-fold Apostolic Ministry—nothing at all is said, except by way of mention, about the authority of the Holy Spirit leading onward into further and fuller truth.

At the next year's General Synod, in May 1928, he developed his theme of the need for caution in approaching questions of Reunion—with cogency. Of the Lausanne Conference he said:

It was a very remarkable gathering, notable not so much for the results achieved as for the spirit of unity that prevailed amongst delegates representing the most widely differing religious organizations. It is is not possible yet to say that it has brought nearer the day of general reunion between the sundered Churches, but it has manifested quite plainly that the Person of Christ is a principle of reconciliation—a principle so constraining that it can lead men who know themselves and their Churches to be at variance with one another on serious points of external Church order to transcend their differences, and hold happy converse with one another. But it would be a mistake, for all that, to minimize the serious differences that separate the Churches.

Speaking humanly, I find it impossible to see how certain cleavages which became manifest will ever be bridged. I do not venture, in saying that, either to forget or to limit the grace of God; what I mean when I say that, is that the problem is too vast for rough and ready human solution. I have no doubt that, just as the disciples saw what kings and prophets had desired to see, so there is a light behind the clouds of to-day waiting to break out when the Church is readier and riper to receive it.

He went on to explain that the problem centred round the nature

of the Visible Church, the machinery—the external organization of
which was as necessary as the spirit which informs it; just as man is
not spirit alone but embodied spirit, just as the Incarnation was a
manifestation of the divine within the human—so

> the unity that Christ desired was an earthly and visible unity, a
> unity which the world might see, and so be led to believe. And
> that unity is a thing which must be built; built up of men on
> earth with their differing histories, nationalities, temperaments,
> convictions, built up round Christ. Lausanne, in one sense,
> effected nothing. It will take many years of debate and many
> such gatherings to bring about any such unification of Church
> life. But Lausanne represents a necessary Christian ideal which is
> ever acquiring more strength among the Churches of the modern
> world in which individualism has asserted its revolt against cen-
> tralized authority. It is my earnest hope that the Church of
> Ireland whose tendency, alas, is to shrink into an insularity of
> interest and of outlook, will cultivate the temper which in secular
> affairs would be called international. . . .

He proceeded to contrast the Irish tendency to insularity with
what he called the 'differentiation' of the Church of England, with
its breakdown of the impossible ideal of uniformity.

> Uniformity is attainable where you have a closed system, and
> minds drilled into subjection. But you cannot have it where free
> enquiry, as encouraged by true Protestantism, prevails. . . . For
> what so many who call themselves by the name of Protestant
> forget is this: 'Protestantism did not merely shut a door; it
> opened one.' And the results of the opening of that door are
> manifesting themselves to-day in that process of differentiation
> to which I have called your attention.

Lausanne stood for the far-off ideal of integration: 'that broad-
ened life which is only possible where the Churches of various
traditions bring their treasures into the City of God, and where
they share, each with all and all with each, the riches they owe
to Christ their Lord.' And he ended this portion of his address on
a note of toleration which had been absent from his previous
addresses:

> Room has to be found in our Church for those who, while
> accepting the Church's fundamental faith, differ in regard to its
> expression. It must be so if we believe in the Holy Ghost guiding
> the Church into the truth. We cannot prescribe whither He is to
> lead us. The limits of coercion are narrower than they were even
> fifty years ago. The rights of free men to the exercise of their

conscience are more fully acknowledged. As we come to see how few fixed points there are in the apprehension of religious as of scientific truth, there is greater disposition to allow for and expect differing opinions. . . .

The general homogeneousness of an earlier day exists no longer. The only *regimen* which will enable free men to unite in voluntary religious associations without sense of grievance is one in which differences are allowed for, as men of various types of temperament, with mutual deference to one another's consciences, acknowledge one another's right to Christian consideration in non-essentials.

Nevertheless that note of tolerance is not harmonious with his general thought upon the problem, but rather it is discordant; because he could never bring himself to envisage any concrete formula where it could apply; could never name any tenet of Anglicanism as non-essential to the Catholic Faith; could never yield one jot of what he, with the most earnest sincerity, called its principles—others, cynically, its privileges or prestige; yet others, maliciously, its prejudices or preconceptions or predilections; yet others still, unkindest of all, its wishful even wilful thinking. But with Gregg the problem was throughout his life one of anguished tension: with his heart he yearned for the unity in fellowship of all the disciples of Christ, wherever they might be found; but with his mind Catholicism and catholicity were incompatible; the more definitely Catholic one's creed the less catholic must be one's religious sympathies.

§

But as the Anglicanism which he represented could not yield an inch of ground in *rapprochement* with other Protestant persuasions of a non-Catholic variety, so neither could it advance a step towards appeasement with the great authoritarian 'unreformed' Catholic Churches. In one direction or the other, this would be tantamount to a betrayal of its distinctive heritage and trust. On 5 February 1928 he treated his large lay audience in St. Patrick's Cathedral to a discourse on the Malines Conversations, which had been launched in 1921 by Lord Halifax after his approach to Cardinal Mercier and held thrice subsequently. His sermon would have been appropriate to a seminar of theological graduates. He was careful to point out that these Conversations had not been official; there had been no attempt at 'negotiations,' but only free and frank discussions between individuals who, though eminent in their respective Churches, spoke for themselves. But a difficulty was the 'ham-

pering reticence' of the Roman representatives who were unwilling
to express their personal views on certain points without official
authority. Nevertheless though nothing tangible had been achieved
by the Conversations, and they would not be resumed, they had
served a good purpose. Certain members of the Church of England
had tried to impress on sympathetic ears within the Church of
Rome its own position asserted nearly 400 years ago, namely—

> That the standpoint of the English Church is central, and that,
> while in worship and doctrine it has removed from its office
> books and doctrinal standards certain later accretions which are
> specifically Roman, it has removed nothing from them which is
> truly Catholic according to the standards of Holy Scriptures, as
> interpreted by the early Fathers.

The following sentences are the most significant:

> The great Roman Communion is a solid fact of Christian
> history, and a fact that must be reckoned with, and a fact that
> is not disposed of by being merely ignored. It is impossible to
> rest content in the belief that to the end of time no understanding
> is possible, or even to be sought, with this Church—with its
> essence of order, its love of the past, its extension and its witness
> over so wide a range of humanity. How such an understanding
> can come about, until Rome alters, I cannot see. . . .

Although, in common with many other Anglican high churchmen, he saw brighter prospects of ultimate reunion with the Eastern
Orthodox Church, his attitude was guarded. During the first week
in October 1928 there was held in Cheltenham, under the presidency of the Bishop of Gloucester, the first Church Congress to
welcome the delegates from that Communion.[1] These were the
(much-bearded) Patriarchs, Deissman, Amundsen and Germanos;
and the English Bishops deputed to meet them were those of
Gloucester (Headlam) and of Durham (Henson).[2] Gregg, after his

[1] The Report of the Congress of 1928, entitled *The Anglican Communion*,
was published by John Murray, 1929.
[2] They were friends, but of widely different antecedents, temperaments
and preferences; the one—senior in age and in office, forthright, blunt,
formidable, a conservative; the other—ironic, suave, loquacious, a liberal.
On Henson's arrival at his brother-bishop's Palace the following dialogue
is said to have ensued:
Henson (archly): 'Headlam, do you intend to kiss these persons?'
Headlam (gruffly): 'Certainly not.'
Henson (persistently): 'Well, Headlam, I think you *ought* to kiss these
persons.'
Headlam (still more gruffly): 'I'll leave that to you.'
Henson (in precise tones): 'Well, Headlam, I am told that the efficacy of
our relations with the Eastern Church depends on the fervency of our
osculations.'

tour in Spain and Portugal above-mentioned, crossed the Channel
with little time to spare and reached Cheltenham on the afternoon
of 4 October just in time to hear Dr. W. R. Matthews read his
paper to the Congress in the Town Hall. (The Dean of St. Paul's
is now the last survivor of the noble company of Christian thinkers
who met on that notable occasion: they included other such personalities as Inge, Gore, Streeter, Quick, to name only a few.)
Whether in consideration of his rank or his convenience Gregg was
given pride of place as last of the four special preachers (his predecessors being Bishops Henson, Gore and Warman); and the same
evening preached the sermon, which he had prepared with great
care, before a vast congregation in Gloucester Cathedral, taking as
his text 1 Cor. 1: 10. He stayed the night together with Bishop
Henson and the Patriarchs as a guest in the Palace.

The sermon was printed in full in the *Church Family Newspaper*
and summarized briefly in the *Church Times*. In effect it was a
reasoned challenge to English churchmen to say what they meant
and, even more important, to mean what they said. The Lambeth
Quadrilateral had stated the irreducible minimum of its terms as a
basis for Reunion with other Churches.

It is necessary to agree not merely on the formula, but upon
its meaning. Are the doctrines of the two great Sacraments [as
enunciated in our formularies] to be safeguarded under conditions of Reunion, or not? Does it make no difference whether
the outward signs mean something or nothing? And does acceptance of the three-fold ministry mean that Christ instituted a
ministry and that the Ordinal provides for its transmission in an
authoritative way, or does it not? . . . There is a great need for
Anglicans to rediscover what Anglicanism stands for, and to
reassert the corporate authority of their society.

The *Church Times* correspondent commented: 'The sermon
presented a rather stiffer front towards all sections of English
Church opinion than that to which they are accustomed.' And the
editor, after praising the frankness of the Free Church representatives (Garvie and Lofthouse) but disassociating himself from such
a loose position, wrote:

For our part we must fall back upon the advocacy of principles of which the Archbishop of Dublin proved to be so firm
an exponent; and must deprecate very urgently the proposal of
any concrete steps towards reunion in this country, except upon
the basis of à reasonable and tolerable unity, not only in outward
practice, but in inward interpretation and faith.

This would seem the place in which to allude, though too

briefly, to the convener and president of the Congress, and to compare and contrast his outlook with Gregg's.

Headlam of Gloucester was recognized among his peers as the most learned as well as the wisest divine of his generation in the whole Anglican Communion; by more than one foreign churchman he was called Erasmus *redivivus;* bishops and clergy of all persuasions at home and abroad looked to him as their natural leader in oecumenical councils, even when differing from him, because of his massive erudition, his sober-minded comprehensiveness, balanced intellect, moral integrity and steadiness and firmness in debate—and this in spite of some obvious prejudices. His outlook therefore provides a norm by which to assess the theological temper of his contemporaries. His famous Bampton Lectures of 1920 entitled 'The Doctrine of the Church and Christian Reunion'— when he was as yet Regius Professor of Divinity in Oxford—profoundly influenced the Lambeth Conference of that year and prompted its Appeal to all Christian People. Dr. Jasper's admirable biography of him now enables us to summarize here, though inadequately, some of the salient points in his doctrine of the Church.[3]

1. The two Sacraments are clearly social rites, implying the idea of a society.
2. There was no command of Christ or of his Apostles in favour of episcopacy, but only of ministry. But an historic episcopate is best fitted to provide a basis for Reunion.
3. Apostolic succession, though not proven historically, is most probable. It implies continuity of function, not transmission of grace.
4. No mechanical theory of Holy Orders need compel the Church to deny divine grace to those separated from it.
5. All Christian bodies composed of baptized persons are all imperfect parts of the one true Church. The Church is divided inwardly; it is not a single visible communion with all the schisms outside it.
6. Holy Orders and Sacraments outside the Catholic Church are possibly irregular, but not necessarily invalid. There is no indelibility of Holy Orders. The validity of non-episcopal ministries, if appointed with prayer and the laying on of hands, should be accepted.
7. The church should make no premature attempts at Reunion; no real progress could come through sentimental effusion or ignoring differences which in fact exist. Desire for unity should never interfere with loyalty to truth.

[3] *Arthur Cayley Headlam* by Ronald Jasper. Faith Press, 1960. See especially pp. 111ff. and 140ff.

8. The Lambeth Quadrilateral laid down a solid basis for Reunion, but Creeds and Sacraments may be interpreted by different minds in different ways.
9. He suggested the mutual recognition of Holy Orders as between Catholics and Nonconformists, and a regularization of all future ordinations.

Of these points Gregg would have agreed with No. 1. Of the rest the only one with which he would have agreed emphatically is No. 7. Though he produced no major theological work it is possible to apprehend his doctrine of the Church from his many addresses and papers. The impression is inescapable that Headlam's outlook was more detailed and comprehensive, more conciliatory and charitable, more solid but less rigid, less positive and definite, than that of Gregg. Gregg did not perceive as clearly as did Headlam the impossibility of expecting agreement upon the interpretation of formulas.

A former member of the Church Unity Committee in Ireland suggests that the Archbishop's extreme 'catholicism' may have been partly due to ecclesiastical snobbery.

Any association with non-Anglicans seemed to make him uneasy. If they were not kept at a distance familiarities might take place! On Reunion plans generally he was heard to say, 'The Archbishops in England are pursuing a very dangerous course and I have told them so.' And 'The Church of South India is not a Church, it is merely a society.'

When a tablet commemorating the first visit of John Wesley to Ireland was being placed in the church in which he preached his first sermon here, the Archbishop could not attend the service at which the unveiling was to be performed by the President of the British Methodist Conference in association with several Dublin Methodist ministers. He instructed the Rector: 'You must be present and see that they behave!'

I think it irritated him that non-Anglicans did not admit freely their under-privileged position—they seemed so unaware that they were the deprived children of Christendom. Worse—they seemed to adhere obstinately to their prejudices. I heard him say that butter wouldn't melt in a Presbyterian's mouth.

A prominent Dublin clergyman was a guest at a Methodist wedding and was asked by the minister to assist. He refused but said he would read a lesson. The notice of the ceremony in the *Irish Times* a few days later said: '. . . by the Revd. X assisted by the Revd. Y.Z., Rector of St. A.' The Archbishop sent for the Revd. Y.Z. and reprimanded him, though he explained that he had merely read a little scripture to a gathering of Christian people. However, a year or two later he was given a canonry.

He often spoke in a surprised manner (whether assumed or real) that so learned a man as Calvin should in his reformation have tried to recreate the N.T. church 'without the Apostles.' This easy identification of the apostolate with the episcopate was a little naïve. Had he not become a bishop in early life his N.T. and patristic learning might have led him to more moderate conclusions. He was after all a bishop for most of his life and that remarkable fact was bound to affect his judgment in many matters. As an Anglican watchdog he performed a useful service, but if the entire personality is subdued to the act of keeping guard, a limit is set on one's larger talents.

He was too unduly aware of his dignity. His attitude to junior curates was very much *de haut en bas*. I remember him in animated conversation with an excellent churchwarden after Service. At length he asked the man his occupation. 'I'm a bread-server, your Grace.' Conversation came to an end; he could talk to a man, but not to a breadserver!

A typical remark, as he washed his hands in the vestry after a Confirmation, was 'The boys were more oleaginous than usual.'

A certain Missionary Society required the joint signature of half-yearly cheques by the Archbishop and the Provost (Dr. Bernard). If he went to the Provost first the Archbishop invariably commented 'I see you have been to the Provost.' If conversely, the Provost never failed to say 'I see you have been to the Archbishop.' Neither could easily accept second place.

Dr. C. Beaufort Moss has been for many years and is still one of the most prominent members of the Anglican Church on the side of Reunion with both the Eastern Orthodox Church and the Old Catholics:

On the occasion of the first Anglo-Catholic pilgrimage to Jerusalem in 1924 Dr. Gregg entrusted me with a letter of greetings in Greek to the Patriarch. He told me that the word *theotokos* should be pronounced with the accent on the penultimate syllable; stress on the second gives it a different and absurd meaning. On arrival I was expected to read the letter aloud, but this I declined, since I have never learned how to pronounce modern Greek and those who were present did not know what language I was speaking!

At the Faith and Order Conference in Lausanne the representatives of most of Christendom would have committed themselves to heresy—I think Adoptionism—if Dr. Gregg had not pointed out their inadvertent mistake.

I stayed a night at the Palace at Armagh just after the General Synod had accepted agreement with the Old Catholics. The Primate had feared it was premature, but Bishop Kerr of Down pushed it through. The Primate told me that there was only one clergyman who approved (a Rector from Co. Wicklow) and a small handful of laymen.

He was a generous subscriber to the Friends of the Assyrian Church (now no more) for many years. I met him in Westminster Abbey in 1925, on the 1600th anniversary of the Council of Nicaea, when the Assyrian Patriarch, the Greek Patriarchs of Alexandria and Jerusalem, Archbishop Söderblöm, and many other eminent persons were there. He seemed glad to see someone he knew.

I had the greatest admiration for him. He was perhaps the greatest that ever filled the See of St. Patrick.

On 20 October he preached the Cambridge University Sermon in Great St. Mary's, on the subject of 'Anglican Orders and Prospects of Reunion.' It states his position so fully and concisely that nothing short of a complete reproduction could do it justice. It was printed *in extenso* in *The Cambridge Review* of 25 October.

In 1930 he attended his second Lambeth Conference, and some entries from the Bishop of Durham's diary are of interest:

> *July 21.* I walked with the Archbishop of Dublin (Gregg) from the Athenaeum to Lambeth, and had much talk with him about the Historic Episcopate. He is a much stronger Episcopalian than I am, but *au fond* he is not a little perplexed as to our combination of insistence on the fact and repudiation of the theory it apparently implies.
> *July 23.* There was a considerable rally of Anglo-Catholics this morning, and the excessive hopes of the Evangelicals were mainly dashed. However, we shall give some sort of blessing to the South Indian Scheme. I am impressed by the unyielding episcopalianism of the Archbishop of Dublin. His dislike of what he calls 'sentimentalism' carries him into a curiously close alliance with the 'hard-shell sacerdotalists.' The American Bishops are evidently dominated by the crazy sectarianism of their country. . . .[4]

§

Meanwhile there was steadily growing in the Church of Ireland, especially in the Northern Province and in Belfast where dissension between the three rival churches—Roman, Anglican, Presbyterian —had been bitter, a new movement in favour of reconciliation

[4] *Henson, Herbert Hensley: Retrospect.* Vol. II, pp. 269–70.

between the two latter, and it was championed by no less a person than the Primate of All Ireland, Charles Frederick d'Arcy. The section of his Presidential Address to the General Synod in 1954, of which the theme was Christian Reunion, had been printed as a pamphlet by general request. In it he had said:

> There are new movements which simply ignore the divisions of the churches, finding that human souls can attain the beatific vision, and realize the power of Christ to change the life of man, without any reference whatever to the denomination to which the individual belongs. For us, as for all who belong to the Anglican Communion, the *Appeal to all Christian People* issued by the Lambeth Conference of 1920 is the natural starting-point for thought on this subject.

He went on to remind his audience that on that occasion no less than 252 Bishops, representing the Anglican Communion in all its branches and all its varieties of ecclesiastical outlook, had adopted the Appeal with enthusiasm and as a great manifesto for Christian unity. Having quoted from its main statements, showing that its aim was not absorption but affiliation, he emphasized its special urgency as an Adventure of Faith, and ended:

> The Lambeth Statement was meant to refer to the whole body of Nonconformists. It was not relative specially to our brethren of the Presbyterian Church, with whom we have been carrying on Conferences. Further, apart from the laws of any particular Church, there has been among all great Christian thinkers the recognition that God does not bind Himself to any particular system. The Ministry of His great prophets in all ages is proof of this. . . .
> At the Reformation the Bishops, except in England and Sweden, failed utterly in leadership; and God set them aside and raised up others in their places. Was He going to leave His people without a ministry when there were faithful presbyters to carry on His work? There I see a 'validity' higher than any formal legalism could supply. And this was recognized by leaders of Christian thought who were nearer to the troubles of that time than we are, by Hooker, by Usher, and even by High Churchmen like Bramhall, Cosin and Andrewes. And with their verdict most of our great modern scholars agree. Let us thus determine to face the great problem of our own age, not in any niggardly or grudging spirit, but with a large apprehension of the needs of our time, and of the power of God to lead us on towards that unity for which our great Divine Master prayed.

Though the question of Reunion was not a subject for debate at this Synod, it was thus ventilated with a view to further deliberation. A motion that the report of the Joint Committee on Reunion between the two Churches be received was formally proposed by the Primate and seconded by the Archbishop, as was right and proper. It was carried with one dissentient.

But it was well known that the Archbishop of Dublin did not agree with the Archbishop of Armagh in this matter. And when on 23 October of the same year the representatives of his United Diocese met in the Synod Hall, Dublin, he began his presidential address with these words:

> I think that in view of the position which has been reached in regard to the subject of Reunion in Ireland, something may be expected to be said by me. I do not wish to be controversial, though before the position is settled it may be inevitable that something of a controversial kind should be said. I am rather concerned now to show what is the nature of the proposals for discussion made to non-episcopal churches, based on what is known as the Lambeth Appeal of 1920. As a member of that Conference I am not without some reminiscences of what was intended by the appeal.

He went on to explain that the subject had engaged the minds of the Bishops as far back as the Lambeth Conference of 1908. The *crux* had always been recognition of the 'validity' of non-episcopal ordinations. That Conference, though desiring to respect the convictions of such as were non-episcopally ordained, could not surrender its own principles of Church Order as laid down in the Preface to the Ordinal of 1549. Therein it is explicitly stated that 'From the Apostles' time there have been three Orders of Ministers in Christ's Church—bishops, priests and deacons' and that 'no man be admitted thereto' unless by 'episcopal consecration or ordination.'

> It is not infrequently said that this statement represents a purely domestic rule of the Anglican communion. . . . I cannot follow this argument, although I know that there has been very real goodwill between the Church of England and the Continental Protestant Churches.
>
> Those who drew up this preface were legislating, indeed, for the Church of England, but this view was not restricted to the Church of England. For them the Church of England was part of the visible Church of Christ spread abroad in the world, and of one texture with it through and through; the Church of England was the local presence and organ in England of the Universal

Church, and the rules it was laying down were not merely English and for England; it was reaffirming principles which had governed the Universal Church from the earliest times, and which must therefore govern England; and to those principles it professed an unfaltering adhesion.

The words in the Preface to the Anglican Ordinal are so emphatic as to imply a deliberate rejection of non-episcopal Orders. The Church of England is pledged to continue the ancient threefold ministry, and to acknowledge no other. To do otherwise would be to 'prejudice it in its desire for a reunion with the Eastern Orthodox Church and the Old Catholics—to name only those which seem to be within reach.' But as far as reunion with non-episcopal ministries is concerned, the years between 1908 and 1920 have seen only a deadlock.

> The Conference of 1920 entertained great hopes of finding a way to break the deadlock, and it issued its Appeal to all Christian People, which aimed at piercing the hitherto impregnable walls dividing the separated communions of Christians. The Bishops reaffirmed the fourfold basis of the approach to Home Reunion laid down by the Lambeth Conference of 1888 (commonly called the Lambeth Quadrilateral)—consisting of the acceptance of the Holy Scriptures, the Apostles' and Nicene Creeds, the two great Sacraments of the Gospel, and the historic Episcopate. . . .
> And immediately after the need of a Ministry, which all portions of the United Church may hold and recognize, has been thus stated—may we not reasonably claim that the Episcopate is the one means of providing such a Ministry? We do not deny the spiritual reality of the non-episcopal ministries. We thankfully acknowledge that they have been manifestly blessed by the Holy Ghost. But we submit that both the history of the past and the experience of the present justify the claims that such a Ministry of the whole body can rest only upon the Episcopate.

He then read from the text of the Appeal dealing with reciprocal recognition of ministerial commissions; emphasizing that 'by such action no one could be taken as repudiating his past Ministry' but was seeking 'additional recognition of a new call to wider service in a reunited church.' The proposal was a novel one; difficulties and flaws were manifest; but it had affinities with an experiment which was to be tried elsewhere, namely in a South India United Church, 'in which there is to be a merging of episcopal and non-episcopal elements in a system which should have an episcopal ministry throughout virtually its whole extent in thirty years.' But even in this experiment it was made plain that there was to be no inter-communion or exchange of pulpits, between episcopal and non-episcopal churches.

§

In 1935 he accompanied the Delegation from the Church of England to confer in Bucharest with a Commission from the Orthodox Church of Rumania. His position was that of an Assessor, to represent the Church of Ireland. One of the Anglican delegates was a former Bishop of Gibraltar (Harold Buxton) whose memories of the Archbishop were in 1961 still fresh, chiefly on account of the latter's visits to the Peninsula. Of the Rumanian visit he has written:

> The Archbishop read a paper on 'The Christian Life and the Stimulus of Oecumenicity' at one of the sessions, but he took a minor share in the formal conference. His important contribution was made, so to speak, in the background, where his learning, judgment and facility of expression proved so valuable. The Delegation was sent to Bucharest in order to elucidate certain 'statements' on doctrinal subjects which had been made during the Lambeth Conference, 1930, and at the Joint Doctrinal Commission, 1931, and these subjects were taken up in turn during a week of conferences. Each evening it was necessary to put on paper a brief resumé of the day's work with an appropriate declaration. This was perhaps the most responsible work which the delegates had to perform and the debt to Dr. Gregg was very substantial indeed.

The present successor of Bishop Buxton in the See of Gibraltar (Stanley Eley) now writes:

> My impression of Gregg was that he was a natural successor of the great Caroline divines and in particular Bramhall, and that for him the Anglican Church remained, without any equivocation or doubt, an integral part of the historic Catholic Church, that the historic ministry of the Anglican Church is an essential part of its Catholicity, and therefore that any decision on either faith or order must be strictly loyal to this historic heritage. Anything which savoured of facile accommodation was alien alike to his nature and his massive learning.

There could be no truer estimate, and the reference to his great predecessor, Archbishop Bramhall of Armagh whom he greatly revered, would have been especially pleasing to the Archbishop.

§

During the ten years between 1920 and 1930 representatives of
the Church of England had held various meetings with those of
the Federal Council of the Evangelical Free Churches of England.
But results showed that there had been little advance towards Home
Reunion, if any. And in the Report of the Reunion Sub-Committee
of the Lambeth Conference of 1930 it had been stated:

'In particular, we cannot enter into any scheme of federation
involving interchangeability of ministries while differences on
points of Order which we think essential still remain.' . . . 'There
is at present no ministry which fully corresponds with the purpose of God. Yet we are persuaded that the historic continuity
of the episcopal ministry provides evidence of the Divine intention in this respect. . . .'

Though the Report of its Sub-Committee was not the official
utterance of the Lambeth Conference of 1930, it stood behind the
resolutions which were adopted by the whole Conference.

But there were others who did not interpret the resolutions of
the Lambeth Conference in this sense, and among them was the
Primate of All Ireland. The matter came to a head in a debate at
the General Synod in May 1935. The Dean of Belfast, William Shaw
Kerr (later Bishop of Down and Dromore), moved:

That in accordance with the resolution passed by the Joint
Committee of the Church of Ireland and the Presbyterian Church
in Ireland on Reunion on January 29th, 1934, the General Synod
of the Church of Ireland declare that:
'Without prejudice to the convictions held by either Church
as to the preferable forms and methods of administering the
rite of Ordination and the Sacraments of the Church, and without
prejudice to any future arrangements that may be mutually
agreed upon;
'The Church of Ireland fully and freely recognizes, as a basis
for further progress towards union, the validity, efficacy and
spiritual reality of both Ordination and Sacraments as administered by the Presbyterian Church.'

Before the resolution was proposed, the Archbishop of Dublin
submitted that, to effect the recognition required, the Synod must
pass a resolution this year by a two-thirds majority, followed
next year a bill passed by a two-thirds majority.

The Primate consulted his assessor, Lord Justice Best, and
announced: 'He advises me that, in his opinion, this does not
involve the consequences which the Archbishop of Dublin fears;

that it is not really in any sense an alteration in our standards of doctrine or of discipline. It merely intends to express a view on the nature of the Orders and doctrine of another Church, without in any way altering our own.' (The announcement was greeted with loud applause by a considerable section of the Synod.)

The Archbishop of Dublin—I bow to your ruling, but under protest, and I shall see that the matter is brought further. I give notice accordingly. (Applause from another section of the Synod, and cries of 'Hear, hear.')

Lord Justice Best—I must protest against His Grace the Archbishop of Dublin standing up in the Synod and disputing my ruling, or the ruling of His Grace the President on my advice. ('Hear, hear.') There is a way known to His Grace by which the matter can be questioned, but it is not the proper way to stand up in the Synod and make a speech to give his reasons.

The Dean of Belfast then proceeded with his speech:

It should not be necessary to emphasize that there was no question before them concerning the episcopal constitution of the Church. . . . To each and all of them episcopacy was one of the fundamental conditions of reunion. . . . What the resolution did involve was simply the recognition that their Presbyterian brethren, when they came to the Table of the Lord in obedience to His command, received the fullness of His sacramental blessing. Could that be doubted for one moment?

Remember, it was this Synod that initiated the conferences. So, as a condition of further negotiation, it was required that each Church accept definitely and unmistakably the full authenticity of the other's Orders and Sacraments. We can confer on no other basis. . . .

Let it be clearly understood that this resolution goes not a whit beyond the Appeal to All Christian People issued by the bishops of the Anglican Communion in 1920. The united episcopate explicitly acknowledges the spiritual reality of these ministries and that they are 'manifestly blessed and owned by the Holy Spirit as an effective means of grace.' This was reaffirmed by the Lambeth Conference of 1930. That is all we ask this Synod to agree to.

He pointed out that in the Articles of Religion, and also in the Preface to the Ordinal, two things are made clear; one, that the Church ensures for itself an episcopal constitution; the other, that it carefully refrains from specifying that episcopacy is essential to the nature of a Church. And the Nineteenth Article defines the visible Church without reference to episcopacy. He concluded:

M

We are asked to come into line with the Lambeth bishops, and declare our recognition of the reality—the validity—of non-episcopal ministries. A refusal—which God forbid—means that we stamp these ministries as unreal and delusive. . . .

Does not the present crisis admonish us to heal our divisions, to rise above unnecessary theological feuds, to stand for the great essentials which alone can save the faith? It is fifteen years since the Lambeth bishops warned us that the faith cannot be adequately apprehended, and the battle of the Kingdom cannot worthily be fought, while the body is divided. Each succeeding year makes that message more impressive. I beseech you to take away a stumbling-block in the road to a new realization of unity, fellowship and power.

The Dean's speech was received with prolonged applause. His seconder, Mr. John Bristow, in a shorter but equally forceful appeal, regretted the use of the word 'validity' which was ambiguous, and ended:

The necessity for Reunion was greater now than in 1920, when the Lambeth Conference made their Appeal to All Christian People. If they delayed Reunion they were taking a frightful responsibility. The Christian Church must unite or die. Had the Presbyterian Church suffered in the past from an inferior sacrament? There was no evidence to support that, and they dared not say it.

There ensued 'a lively debate.' There was a full Synod and the galleries were thronged. The Revd. T. Browne, supporting the resolution, said that it sought not compromise for the sake of union, but comprehension for the sake of truth. Dr. Frederick Hatch (later Dean of Down), regarded its phrasing as 'patronizing' to their friends in the Presbyterian Church. The Archbishop of Dublin reiterated that he did not in any way dispute Lord Justice Best's ruling. 'I said I bowed to it, but asked that my protest should be recorded in the minutes.' He added that if the resolution were passed, it would only be by a 'snatched majority.' He thereupon moved an amendment that

The Synod has considered the report of the Joint Committee presented to the General Synod, 1934, and has noted its contents with interest. It has also had opportunity to consider the report of the Committee appointed by the Archbishop of Canterbury to confer with representatives of the Church of Scotland. It has also learned the condition prescribed by the General Assembly of June 6th, 1934, for the Representatives of the Assembly to engage in further discussion on the subject of reunion in Ireland with Representatives of the General Synod. It recognizes, with regret, that approach to the question of reunion in Ireland along the lines of the 'Appeal to all Christian People,' Lambeth, 1920, or the Lambeth Resolution of 1930, offers no present prospect of success, and that further consideration of this important question must, accordingly, be deferred until more promising methods of approach present themselves.

The amendment, he said, would turn aside a direct vote upon the validity of another Church's Orders and Sacraments. The resolution was in direct opposition to the Lambeth principle, which said: 'Ask no questions of the other Church. Give what you have, and take what they have.' We have been separated from the Presbyterian Church for 400 years, and now are proposing to give away the point which had been at issue for that period.

Dr. Oulton (afterwards Regius Professor of Divinity), whose voice was seldom heard in the Synod, spoke in favour of the amendment.

The Primate, Dr. d'Arcy, then descended from the dais and spoke from the floor of the house. The Lambeth Conference, he said, had put aside the word 'validity' as ambiguous, and had substituted 'spiritual reality.' The Presbyterians unfortunately had not done so. But the difficulty was in any case artificial and unimportant, and he was himself in favour of the original motion. But he would rather that the Archbishop of Dublin's amendment were passed than that the motion were rejected. He continued:

Speaking of the matter from the higher side, apart from this fighting about words, the Presbyterian Church is one of the most splendid Churches in the world. From its theologians he had himself learnt much.[5] He would say without fear of contradiction, that in the realm of philosophical theology the Presbyterian Church stood at the head of the whole Christian world. To be in association with that Church was something for which he would thank God.

The Dean of Belfast said that if the amendment were passed it would be the end of all efforts for reunion. It was with difficulty that subsequent speakers made themselves heard. There were continual calls for 'Vote, vote!'—and the Primate had to ring the bell for order. When at last a vote was taken on the amendment, it was carried with large majority. The original motion was then put, but only a few voted for it.

Archbishop Gregg had saved the Church of Ireland from what would have been a perilous lapse into latitudinarianism.

[5] No doubt he had specially in mind the brothers John Caird and Edward Caird.

CHAPTER XI

RES GESTAE PUBLICE ET PRIVATIM

THE YEARS OF THE Archbishop's tenure of the See of Dublin, covering as they did times of acute political disturbance, were marked by public cares of an unusual kind. Both by character and ability he showed himself equal to deal with them; indeed, he appeared to take them in his stride, and in fact did so. But these years were marked also by private griefs which were concealed from the many and known only to the few, and they perceptibly deepened the furrows in a countenance of habitual gravity. It is right, in justice to his memory, that these—if only in part—should now be disclosed. And, happily, lighter interludes were not lacking.

As the occupant of a house in St. Stephen's Green he was a parishioner of St. Ann's Church, of which the Revd. John Winthrop Crozier (son of the former Primate, and himself afterwards Arch-deacon of Dublin and for many years Bishop of Tuam) was then the Rector. He now writes:

> While the Palace was in 50 St. Stephen's Green, the Gregg family as parishioners went regularly to St. Ann's Church, Dawson Street, whither the Archbishop himself accompanied them when he was free. It was rather an ordeal for the clergy to preach on these unheralded occasions, but never by a single syllable did the Archbishop express any criticism or disapproval, no matter how dissatisfied the preacher had been with himself. One Sunday morning on which the choir had sung a beautiful quadruple setting of the Te Deum he hurried into the Vestry after Service to express his pleasure at hearing it again after many, many years, as it was composed by Dr. Mann, the famous organist of King's College, Cambridge, who had taught it to Gregg when he was a Cambridge student. Dr. Gregg sat down at the Choir-master's piano in the Vestry and there and then played the chant through with obvious pride at remembering it. The then organist of St. Ann's had been a choir-boy at King's College under Dr. Mann.
>
> St. Ann's pulpit at that time was a modern one of Caen stone elaborately carved, but much worn by time and the hands of cleaners and decorators. It took so much room as to obscure the south side of the altar and it was out of harmony with the 18th and 19th century furnishings in the chancel and sanctuary. One day in 1922 in the vestry in the presence of the church

180

wardens, the Archbishop remarked: 'That pulpit of yours is a great eyesore. Could you not persuade some friendly I.R.A. man from Belfast to blow it up?' This remark repeated to vestry and parishioners reconciled them to the replacement of their old landmark by a fine carved oak pulpit much more in keeping with its surroundings.

During the illness of both Vicar and Curate on one occasion the Archbishop at once took the whole Service himself, from start to finish, though help then was not so difficult to get as it is now.

At Dr. Hyde's Installation as President of the Irish Republic the Archbishop had asked the then Archdeacon of Dublin to accompany him as his chaplain. On arrival at St. Patrick's Hall the seat reserved for the chaplain was already occupied by a senior official chaplain who had come without informing the Archbishop. But Dr. Gregg would not allow the Archdeacon to withdraw and was prepared to go home *himself* if the man whom he had asked was not provided with a seat somewhere. So all ended well with the Archdeacon in a particularly advantageous seat just behind Dr. Gregg and the Roman Archbishop.

At a Diocesan Council the addition of rooms to rectories by clergy with large families was denounced by successors with small families or none. A man with only one adopted daughter had had to follow an Incumbent of some private means, twice married, with a large family by each wife. Addressing the Archbishop, he enquired dramatically, 'That is my position, your Grace, and what do you think of it?'—'You were left to hold the baby,' was the reply of Dr. Gregg, without a smile.

The reminiscences of another former Archdeacon of Dublin, the Revd. John Tobias, Rector of Rathmines, are as follows:

When Dr. Gregg was elected by the House of Bishops to the Archbishopric of Dublin in succession to Dr. Bernard the news was hailed with mixed feelings by many of the Clergy. During his five years in Ossory he had gained the reputation of being a stern disciplinarian, and many of us thought it was a case of 'my father chastised you with whips, but I will chastise you with scorpions.' True, his very appearance lent weight to these forebodings. A tall man, with massive head, beetling brows and stern jaw, he made lesser mortals to quail in his presence. In later years, shortly after he was translated to Armagh, someone gave him the title that seemed so perfectly to fit the man—The Marble Arch! Yet during his eighteen years in Dublin none of us had ever thought of this!

But, as the event proved, this picture was much overdrawn. True, he was a stern man, but beneath it all he was a man of great kindness and tolerance, patient almost to a fault and absolutely just. I was a member of the Dublin Diocesan Council at that time and I often wondered at his readiness to give every member, no matter how cranky his views, a fair hearing. He was a superb chairman and his summing up of a situation was always sound and often masterly. Indeed he had a quite remarkable grasp of affairs and I could not but feel that he would have made a success as an industrialist, financier, or other high executive. On one occasion when Dr. W. E. Thrift, afterwards Provost of Trinity, was acting Chairman of Finance Committee he told me that a certain document had been received from their financial experts in London. It was so complicated that he and the Secretary decided to take copies of it home for further study. At that moment Dr. Gregg came on the scene, and asked to be allowed to see the document. He took it away to another room and after twenty minutes returned with a complete masterly summary of the contents.

I had been at meetings of the Representative Church Body pressing on several occasions the care of Dalkey Parish Church which had to be almost completely restored through the ravages of dry rot. Time after time the matter was shelved. Finally after apologizing for wearying the members so often I said 'Indeed, your Grace, I feel like the Importunate Widow in the Scriptures.' Quick as a flash came the reply—'And who, may I ask, is the Unjust Judge?'

In a Dublin Synod (Bishop Tyndall remembers) a long and tedious debate regarding the functions of a newly-elected 'City Parishes Commission' was winding to an end. An incumbent, puzzled by the question of the authority of this Commission vis-à-vis the Diocesan Council, jumped up. 'But, your Grace, in the case of a Poor Parish Grant for my Parish what medium of communication am I to use?' Answer: 'I should think the penny post would suffice.'

It is the custom at a certain Committee (said Archbishop Barton) to allocate the sum of £10 to a clergyman whose wife has presented him with a baby, in order to help meet attendant expenses. 'On one occasion we had to deal with a case of twins. Considerable discussion took place as to what should be the amount of the grant. The Primate brought the matter to a conclusion by saying, "Shall we give him £15, and tell him not to do it again?"

'He was, in fact, in his own personal and domestic expenditure severely thrifty and frugal, and he brought the exercise of economy into his administration of public trusts. He was suspicious of appeals for financial help and scrutinized the statements of applicants very narrowly. But he rejoiced whenever able to relieve those of his clergy or others who were really necessitous.'

§

He was on holiday alone in Italy in September 1922, and had
left Spezzia by motor-boat for San Terenzo in the Bay of Lerici
with the intention of visiting the house where Shelley had spent
the last three months of his life, only to find that an explosion of
ammunition had devastated the little place two days before; and
'I could not bring myself to land and move about this place of
mourning as a sight-seer.' In an Italian newspaper he had read
that the damage to Shelley's house was slight, but the surviving
victims of the disaster were in grievous need and he wrote a letter
to the *Times* appealing for relief.

Early in 1923 his old friend Ross, the Bishop of Tuam, underwent
a severe surgical operation. He visited him frequently in hospital.
There appeared to be good hopes of recovery but on 22 May he
was summoned by the physician, Mr. Speares, to the bedside of his
friend who was temporarily released from morphia. There he
administered the last Sacrament, with a whisper from the dying
man, 'Thanks for many memories.' Four days later his diary
records: 'Primate (d'Arcy) and I officiated alone together at grave-
side.' When in February of the following year he dedicated a tablet
in the parish church of Portrush to the memory of Bishop Ross, he
said:

> Sincerity was the outstanding mark of his character, and he
> was as good as he was sincere. Yet, with his goodness and
> sincerity, he had an unusual humility of mind. He was devoted
> to the service of God in the performance of his duty. Everywhere
> he went his influence made for manly strength and a manly facing
> of the tasks of life. The Church indeed can ill afford to lose
> servants of this type, and every one who knew him will feel, with
> the Primate, that Ireland has lost a noble son.

When in 1923 a proposal was introduced into the Dail Eireann
for legalizing sweepstakes organized on behalf of charities (in the
result, for hospitals), he preached on 26 February in St. Patrick's
a sermon which is worthy to take a place in any textbook upon
social morals. He advances all the arguments that can be raised
in favour of the proposal and demolishes them one by one. His
language is reasonable, clear and concise, matching the clarity of
his thought. Even more devastating was the sermon he preached in
the Rotunda Hospital Chapel after the acceptance by its Governors
of this form of revenue. 'We see Ireland's public men seated round
a revolving drum! These are thy gods, oh Israel! The worship of
the Golden Calf has not yet ceased.'

He is less sure of his ground when he comes to deal with another vexed social problem, namely that of divorce. The Irish Parliament had early in 1925 issued a bill prohibiting it (as is natural in the Government of a country whose people are predominantly Roman Catholic, and for whom matrimony is a sacrament). On 15 February Dr. Gregg preached in St. Patrick's on the subject a sermon intended as a definitive pronouncement of his views, but which was, in fact and of necessity, inconclusive. His main point, as is to be expected, is the significance of the so-called 'exceptive clause' in the first gospel, but his discussion of this is too abstract and he gives no guidance as to its practical application. Other exponents of moral theology in the Anglican Church (notably K. E. Kirk, late Bishop of Oxford) have dealt with the problem more fully and lucidly. But no one has found a solution to it.

On St. Andrew's Day 1924 he was the special preacher at the jubilee celebration of the consecration, by his grandfather the Bishop of Cork, of St. Fin Barre's Cathedral on that date in 1870. The occasion had been delayed four years owing to civil war. The concluding sentences of his sermon read like a peroration. This was most untypical of him, and the rhetoric may have been deliberately 'atavistic.'

. . . But there is a higher sense of the expression, 'We are strangers and sojourners,' because we cannot be satisfied with a material world. Our life must be a detached life; we must be visitors, not residents, for our citizenship is in heaven.

Throw your mind back to 1870. Of those who gathered here on that great day there are very few survivors. . . . Here we have a great material construction looking calmly down while the busy tribes of flesh and blood live out their little day; and yet of the great preachers who filled the pulpit that week—the voice of Trench is silent, the silver eloquence of Alexander is still, the oratory of Magee, where is it? Bishop, Dean, architects and builders are all gone. Yes; for all flesh is grass and the glory of man as the flower of grass, and yet death and decay have not the last word. If the builders have gone, they have printed their witness on the stones that survive them. The stones may be dead, but men have made them speak and tell of deathless reality.

On 23 December 1955 he sent to the then Dean of Cork, Dr. H. McAdoo, the sole surviving copy of the Consecration Service of the Cathedral on 30 November 1870.

On 1 April 1926 the Palace, 50 St. Stephen's Green, was sold, and on 1 July the Archbishop moved into the new Palace, 18 Shrewsbury Road.

On 29 August 1927 died untimely, when just past his sixty-seventh birthday, John Henry Bernard, 'whose name is written and written for good—broad across the *ethos* of the Church of Ireland of the last thirty years.' Thus Gregg spoke of him at the Memorial Service in Trinity College, and it may be said that Bernard was the only man of his generation upon whom he looked with unqualified respect. The tribute which he wrote for Bernard's biography—Ciceronian in its diction—is remarkable for the fact that the qualities in Bernard which he signals out for admiration are those which he himself also possessed.[1] It would seem that in Bernard he saw himself reflected as in a mirror.

The next year, 1928, was to bring him a most grievous personal loss.

§

His younger son Claude had passed with credit from Osborne to Dartmouth where he was 'tremendously happy' and excelling in seamanship, study and games. Friendly, cheerful, affectionate, he was a universal favourite and a dearly loved son and brother. On 25 August when stationed at Chatham he was spending a week-end with friends in London. He became suddenly ill and was taken next day to Millbank Military Hospital, where his illness was diagnosed as pneumonia. His mother crossed on the night of the 28th. Her daily messages home were on the whole hopeful till 7 September, when she sent her husband a telegram which reached him at 7.15 p.m. He crossed by the mail boat the same night. But he found time on the way (Bishop Crozier remembers) to call at a Nursing Home to see one of his clergy also taken suddenly ill. 'He prayed with him, and paused to offer financial help, though he was himself in deep distress and great haste.' He reached Millbank Hospital at 10 a.m. the next morning to find his son 'quite wandering and delirious.' He remained all day at his bedside except for meals, and all the following night, till the end came in the forenoon of the next day, a Sunday, just over twenty-four hours after his arrival. His wife went home alone that night, whilst he stayed on to make necessary arrangements.

The page in his diary for that week is headed with three words: *My Little Son.* The date is enclosed between two crosses; and then in Greek the words: *Hallowed be Thy Name.* This, and the stark brevity of the subsequent chronicle of events—business matters of necessary urgency but mercifully filling his days—enhance the poignancy of the page. He returned on Tuesday night. The funeral was held privately on the Wednesday in the plot of ground

[1] *Archbishop Bernard: Professor, Prelate and Provost*, by Robert H. Murray, Litt.D., pp. 228–35.

which he had bought in the churchyard of Enniskerry. The sudden loss of this bright young life was felt as a personal sorrow by a large number of friends: and in his sister's words: 'Inexpressible grief is inadequate to describe the sorrow of his parents and family.' Not till the Saturday could his father write: 'Calmness to-day' and then in Greek, 'I no longer weep.' For a week he was writing replies to letters of sympathy, and then travelled once more with Pulvertaft to Madrid to fulfil his engagements. But he had received a shattering blow. It was not till several months later that he found himself able to say, 'At last—at last—I have been able to let the boy *go.*' And yet he never forgot to enter the anniversary of his son's death in his diary with every passing year.

Another grief of a different kind now struck him and it was an even harder blow. His daughter writes:

How sad it was that two such fine sons could bring grief in such divergent ways. John was never able to fit into the home environment in the same unselfconscious way that Claude did. A strong, independent, highly intelligent boy, he could not accept with grace and humour the restraints inseparable from a clerical household of such unworldly idealism. Handsome, witty, sociable, and the best of company, he found his friends in circles differing widely from the professional and upper-class families which satisfied others in his family.

Inheriting from both parents natural endowments of mind and body as well as strength of will, he gained a scholarship to Shrewsbury from his preparatory school, Arnold House, Llandullas. In School House, under Dr. Sawyer, he was an able student and later went to Christ's College, Cambridge, again with a scholarship in Classics. Here, unfortunately, the tendency to a less scholarly and more worldly life, which had at times manifested itself at school, became a more confirmed attitude. While an excellent athlete (with a half-blue for athletics), a good tennis, squash, and hockey player, his scholastic record declined from a 2nd class in Part I of the Classical Tripos to an *aegrotat* in Part II (following an accident) at the end of his three years. His father, who had hoped that this son of such brilliant promise would like himself graduate with a double first, was bitterly disappointed. This disappointment was not lessened when John seemed unable to settle into some constructive career. He taught for a while in a preparatory school and worked in a solicitor's office for another spell—and was always able to use more money than he earned. It was finally agreed between them that if his father gave him a year in Trinity College to work for the Civil Service examination, John would promise to put his back into it and try to secure a place as a Home, Indian, or Colonial Civil Service cadet. While in Trinity he was selected as a 100 yards sprinter for the Irish Olympic Team, but a leg injury prevented him from accompanying the Team. He was a member of the Achilles Club. His aptitude as a sprinter brought the following attractive limerick to the pages of *T.C.D.*

'Though the latest achievement of Gregg's,
  On the track, for publicity begs,
    He is urged by his pater,
    Himself in a gaiter,
  To take no delight in his legs.'

Happily he passed the Civil Service examination high enough to be offered a Malayan cadetship, just missing the Indian Civil Service. This was a tremendous relief and his father felt that at last the boy could embark on a sound career and that all his years of embarrassed forbearance had been justified. It proved to be a most happy career and John threw himself into his administration, both as a District Commissioner and as a Magistrate, with enthusiasm and efficiency. Malaya at that time provided a full life for a man of a vigorous nature, and it brought out in John his linguistic talents. Besides Latin and Greek and a running knowledge of French he now acquired Dutch, Tamil, Malay, and a considerable knowledge of Cantonese. He wrote home regularly —delightful, descriptive letters—and though he took his last leave in Australia instead of at home, the family at last felt that though he was separated from them by distance and temperament, he was still one of themselves. Despite their very different outlooks John always had a great respect for his father; and this was probably an important anchor in his life, though he might not have acknowledged it.

To these sorrows was added increasing anxiety on account of his wife whose health from the year 1923 necessitated recurrent care both medical and surgical, and therefore long periods of inactivity. To so vital a nature as hers such pent conditions were unbearably frustrating. Her husband could do little to alleviate them. Lacking her company he would take solitary walks to Sandymount by way of Sydney Parade Station, the station-master of which would watch him past the level-crossing and was heard to say: 'Ah, a grand fine gentleman, but a lonely poor soul!'

But these distresses were lightened by the achievements and companionship of both daughters. The elder, Margaret, having left the Manor House School at Brondesbury in North London as head-girl and games-captain, returned to Dublin where she took her medical degree in Trinity, securing high marks and first place in midwifery and surgery, and the Professor of Medicine's prize in

1931. In the same year she won the Hudson Scholarship in the Adelaide Hospital, being the first woman to do so, and was appointed House Surgeon. After qualifying she sat for and achieved the primary and later the final Fellowship examinations in the Royal College of Surgeons in Ireland. While at Trinity she was in the first women's tennis six and in the second hockey eleven. She was also an active member of the Elizabethan Society, and of the Dublin Univ. Social Service Society. In 1936 she married Cecil S. Wilson, M.Ch., of the Malayan Medical Service, and went to Malaya with him when he was appointed State Surgeon, Selangor. She thus saw a good deal of her brother again before the outbreak of war.

The younger daughter, Barbara, after school also at Brondesbury, entered Trinity College and gained a non-foundation scholarship in 1931, graduating with a Senior Moderatorship in Modern Languages (French and Italian) in 1933, and winning the Kathleen Burgess Prize in Italian. Under the nom-de-plume of Barbara Fitzgerald she was the author of a remarkable and brilliant novel, *We are Besieged*, dealing with the Irish 'Troubles' which in her girlhood had left an ineffaceable impression on her mind. It was awarded the Book Society's Recommendation in 1946. In 1935 she married Michael, son of Vice-Admiral Boyle Somerville, C.M.G., of Castle-townshend, and spent several years in West Africa where her husband, a perfect French linguist, was an official in the oil industry, and served through the war in the field and in the Intelligence Corps.

§

In 1931 a Committee was formed, of which the Archbishop was President, to commemorate in the following year the 1500th anniversary of the landing of St. Patrick in Ireland. Like all Irishmen Gregg was an enthusiast for Ireland's patron saint, but like the majority his enthusiasm was untempered by historical criticism. As early as the turn of the present century the validity of the traditional view of the saint was being scrutinized by scholars of Celtic Church origins,[2] despite the popularly undisputed authority of Professor Bury. But Gregg was either unaware of these questionings or ignored them, and held to the conservative uncritical view,

---

[2] An admirable survey of these by the Dean of Christ Church Cathedral, Dr. N. D. Emerson, M.R.I.A., entitled 'St. Patrick in Modern Scholarship,' was read by him at the Southern Conference convened by the Bishop of Limerick, Dr. R. W. Jackson, M.R.I.A., in 1962, and printed, together with the other lectures, as a pamphlet.

allowing sentiment to override accurate scholarship, and this even extended to trivial matters. One who was then a leading member of the Commemoration Committee and is now a dignitary of the Church writes:

In 1931 we engaged an artist to design a coloured poster for display in churches and halls. The design was to be approved by Archbishop Gregg. The poster appeared with St. Patrick wearing a very conventional mitre. At a subsequent meeting of the Committee the Primate (Dr. d'Arcy) was present and vigorously denounced the unhistorical character of the poster and those responsible for putting a medieval head-dress on the saint. Archbishop Gregg remained silent, with his gaze fixed on a distant part of the ceiling, and made no reference to his having himself approved the design.

We also engaged a well-known Dublin literary man as press-agent. He supplied news items to the papers and wrote various articles himself. One of these, in typescript, was shown to the Committee. Dr. Gregg scored out parts of it and altered others. The author was indignant and said that as a professional literary man what he wrote was his, and could not be revised or altered by any one else: the recognized ethics of letters. Dr. Gregg then went to the editor of the *Irish Times* and asked him confidentially whether this was so, as of course it was. But he never expressed a word of regret to the author for not accepting his word.

As another example of his 'temperamental distrust of others' the same writer instances the following:

The United Council of Churches submitted to the Standing Committee of the General Synod a resolution in favour of joint action in the matter of Adoption of Children.[3] It was accepted. But when their Report came before the General Synod, somebody grumbled about 'an equating of the Church of Ireland with other denominations.' Dr. Gregg thereupon addressed a reprimand to the representatives of our Church in the United Council. Our Secretary then sent him word that the impugned resolution had been submitted to the Standing Committee in scrupulous watchfulness of the Church's interests, and had been accepted by it. The Archbishop went to the Assistant Secretary of the Standing Committee and enquired if this was true. He was shown the relevant entry in the minute-book, but he never expressed publicly or privately any regret that he had so baselessly censured people who were as concerned about the Church's interests as he was.

[3] See page 253.

He was keenly interested in the erection of the little church at Saul in Co. Down to commemorate the site of the barn in which St. Patrick is said to have preached his first sermon in Ireland. It was built to the design of Henry Seaver who also gave his services as honorary consultant architect to Armagh Cathedral and in other ways over a long period of years. When this scribe met the Archbishop in 1939 in the Palace, Armagh, his first words were: 'Your uncle has placed the whole Church of Ireland in his debt.'

The compulsory teaching of Irish in Church National Schools was as repugnant to Dr. Gregg as it was to others, and those not only of the Protestant persuasion; but he showed his wisdom in encouraging the young to learn it. The Free State Government had in 1927 sanctioned the opening of two or three Protestant Schools in the Dublin area preparatory for the Church of Ireland Training College. One such was opened in Glasnevin in March of that year. In proposing the Report of the Board of Education before the Joint Diocesan Synod in June, the Revd. E. C. Hodges (afterwards Bishop of Limerick) expressed the view that the compulsory teaching of Irish was, because of the time involved in teaching it, 'unfair to the child and injured the educational efficiency of the school as an instrument for producing efficient citizens.' The Archbishop, following him, said:

I do not pretend to like compulsory Irish in our National Schools. I think it is bad policy, but as long as the Government requires it to be taught, I would rather it were taught well than ill. . . . I want to see our young people holding Government positions, and if the path to those positions is along the thorny track of Irish grammar, Irish cannot be altogether an uneconomic subject of study, when it makes the difference between employment and unemployment.

On 7 May 1934 he opened another such school, St. Moibhi's College in Phoenix Park, in the presence of Mr. de Valera, then President. The Education Department, he said, had agreed to its foundation 'with the greatest readiness and goodwill. He could not have expected anything more in the way of courtesy and goodwill than he had received from the Government of the Irish Free State.' And again he encouraged Church of Ireland children to study Irish 'whatever might be their private feelings' because this was a Government regulation and they could not secure posts without it. Press photographs of the occasion reveal the features of the Archbishop and the President clearly, and both in a most amicable mood.

At the celebration of the centenary of Catholic Emancipation in Ireland, in his presidential address to the Joint Dublin Synods on 25 June 1929, he recalled some historical facts which are all too easily forgotten.

As one who tries to take an objective view of the world upon which he looks, I can only say that I cannot grudge to my fellow-countrymen all the satisfaction which they feel upon the recovery of their political liberties, nor can I do anything but admire the tenacity with which they stood together in adversity ('Hear, hear'). I am profoundly glad that the grievances of Roman Catholics are removed. I recognize and deplore the injustice of their lot before that time. . . .

The penal laws were the product of quite other times and other manners. . . . In some countries one side imposed penal laws; in some countries the other did. It happened that in England and in Ireland penal laws were imposed by a Protestant Government, but the laws they imposed were all of a piece with similar laws enacted against Protestants elsewhere. It was the existence of such laws in France that brought great bodies of French Protestant refugees to find a new home in Ireland. I make no pretence to justify those laws. . . .

I would ask that those who have the teaching of the youth of Ireland should not teach history in a false perspective by concentrating attention on what happened in Ireland to the exclusion of what was happening simultaneously elsewhere in Europe. It is quite easy to inflame passions and to keep prejudices alive by the suggestion that England's treatment of Ireland was cruelly and uniquely unjust. It is only natural to feel most keenly about hardships inflicted on and suffered by those from whom we are sprung. A reading of the history of France and the Netherlands, of Spain, of England, and even of Ireland, would show that positions were in some cases reversed, and that then it fell to the Protestants to suffer. I do not think any one has anything to gain by dwelling on the hardness of those past ages. . . .

This was one of his best addresses, especially in its tribute to Edmund Burke. 'Ireland, as it builds the new State, will do well if it turns for inspiration to that mighty political genius whom Ireland bore, but whom Europe appropriated.' The whole address is well worthy of commendation to those of both religious persuasions to-day, for it is as pertinent now as at the time he gave it.

During the months of July and August in 1932 there was waged in the columns of the *Irish Times* the famous war between Archbishop Gregg and Cardinal MacRory, Archbishop of Armagh, upon papal claims to supremacy and infallibility, known to posterity as 'The MacRory Controversy.' It is impossible in this book to do more than briefly refer to what was in its day a *cause celèbre*. Happily the correspondence between them has lately been given permanent form and can be read in the Library of the Representative Church Body. It is a monument to Gregg's learning. Nowhere does he display with more telling effect the proof of the precept which he used to enjoin upon his clergy that one should '*study one's ground, know one's ground, and stand one's ground.*' On the Cardinal's side, the correspondence ended somewhat abruptly; and a rumour got abroad (unauthentic but not inherently improbable) that His Eminence had received a peremptory message from the Vatican to this effect: 'Stop! This man knows too much.'

It was at his instance that the Library of the Representative Church Body was founded at the end of 1932, and also that the services of Miss FitzGerald, then Assistant Librarian of the Royal Irish Academy, were engaged, and have been retained for thirty years to the benefit of the Church of Ireland. Of their relations in that capacity she has written:

The Archbishop insisted that I should go up to St. Stephen's Green, see the place, and interview the two chief officials before I decided on accepting the post. The first day I went there on duty in November 1932, he made time to call in, to welcome and encourage me. And I never received anything but the greatest kindness and consideration from him; he listened patiently to any complaints and personally saw to it that they were redressed.

I have a vivid memory of his patting the head of the Palace cat as though bestowing an archiepiscopal blessing, while he smiled very kindly at him, and deprecated some mock reproof to the animal with—'Oh, Timmy is not a bad old cat at all.' I was never really afraid of him after that.

He was Chairman of the Library Committee and attended it all the time he was in Dublin, taking the most lively interest in its expansion and progress. As all who worked with him in his prime can testify, he was an admirable Chairman, courteous, patient, but firm and business-like, guiding discussion and grasping essentials with his first-class brain, phenomenal memory, and amazingly varied erudition and culture. I remember best the quick, apt, witty gleams of a quiet yet keen sense of humour that often unexpectedly lightened the routine of business.

He was reserved and uneffusive, but he noticed any effort to do one's best and appreciated it. Two years before his retirement when his sight was failing and his lameness was a severe handicap he wished to consult the standard *Concordance of the*

Septuagint, of which there is only one copy in Ireland, namely in the T.C.D. Library. This would have been most difficult for him; besides which, the work consists of a number of heavy tomes. I happened to know that a copy existed in Dr. Williams's Library in London (from which our Library occasionally borrows). But the Primate said at once that it would be too much in use there to expect them to lend it to us. I thought so too, but unknown to him put in a special plea for the loan. When the volumes arrived in Armagh he wrote to me: 'May I thank you cordially for all the trouble you have taken—and taken so successfully—to help me in this matter. I would never have ventured myself to ask for the loan of so important a reference book.' He referred to the incident at a subsequent Committee, still in wondering terms, somewhat shocked at the Librarian's temerity!

His personal life was disciplined by meticulous attention to each day's routine and scrupulous punctuality. Every letter was answered, in his own hand if possible, on the day it was received. His replies were brief and to the point, beginning in old-fashioned style—'I am obliged by' or 'I have to thank you for.' He wrote 'like lightning' it was said, but in a perfect script, with the fine nib of 'Gillot's super-orb pointed' which could absorb much ink with one dip. Every evening he could be seen hastening down the steps of 50 St. Stephen's Green with a bunch of letters for despatch in the (then red, now green) pillar box near by.

He never cared for what he considered the *trivia* of his office. 14 August, 1925: 'I begin to wear episcopal ring. Purchased *ex* Episcopal Expenses Allowance. Have passed nearly ten years without wearing one, but certain incidents pointed to its desirability, though not necessity.' In the same month he attended the Church Conference in Stockholm.

In the latter part of 1933 he set himself a course in Shakespeare methodically, beginning with the historical plays many of which he appears to be reading for the first time in his life, and before Christmas notes: 'Finish Shakespeare' [!]—'all plays now read.' There appears no further reference to Shakespeare in his anthology of poetry or in any of his manuscripts or printed writings.

In May 1933 he was for some days ill and in bed. On the 10th: 'Synod passes Reunion Resolution "unrestricted" and on "basis of Lambeth 1920." I did *not* approve, as Primate seems to have said I did.' Next day: 'Wrote early to Primate concerning my "approval." ' His diary records the course of his disapproval in the following year.

N

1934. Jan. 29: To Belfast. Meet in Presbn. Church House. Before lunch, Resolution passed to which I dissent, that General Synod be asked to declare Presbn. Orders valid, etc. Four inoffensive Resns. passed after lunch.

Feb. 20: Bishops' meeting. No. 2 on Resn. of Jan. 29. Very little result.

April 19: Joint Committee with Presbns. Draft Report. I fear I was rather too much agitated. More moderation and self-control needed, or else I must give up agitating discussions. [*in Greek.*]

May 4: Call at Lambeth Palace and talk with Abp. of Canterbury (¼ hour) on the Reunion proposals of our Jt. C'tee with Presbns.

May 15: General Synod. All Reunion questions happily shelved by Resn. proposed by Primate and seconded by me.

In 1936 the medical officers for Dublin City and County made public their investigation into the appalling condition of the slums in the city, and the leaders of the Churches took notice. From his See in the north Cardinal MacRory, Archbishop of Armagh, called for a nation-wide effort to secure decent housing facilities. An 'eminent Catholic Prelate' in Dublin suggested demolition of the old tenements and their replacement by self-contained flats. but said nothing about their landlords. The 'Protestant Archbishop of Dublin' demanded a great missionary crusade to end this evil which was the reproach of a great city. It would require great expenditure on the part of its citizens: 'but if we do not pay in money we will pay in health; disease knows no boundaries. Much could be done in the schools; baths should be provided there, and hygiene should be taught; it is to the next generation that we must look.' But it was from the Chief Rabbi, Dr. Isaac Hertzog, that the most forcible and practical comments came, for he spoke, as the others did not, from personal experience of life in the dwellings of the poor, and the lot of Dublin's was worse than any he had known in Europe.

§

It was against the Archbishop's principles that the disestablished Church of Ireland should pursue a policy of isolated self-satisfaction, and he encouraged and prompted interchange of pulpits with the sister churches across the channel. Bishops and well-known preachers in England, Scotland and Wales responded to his invitations to preach in St. Patrick's or Christ Church, and some—such as Studdert Kennedy and P. T. R. Kirk of the Industrial Christian Fellowship—to conduct mission-services or retreats. And he was himself well-known in England, not only as an occasional but authoritative writer in church papers on religious or political topics, but also as a preacher in several pulpits. Thus in 1926 he preached in Westminster Abbey; at the dedication of the War Memorial Library in his old school at Bedford in the presence of Prince Henry; in 1927 in Bristol Cathedral; in 1928 in Halifax Parish Church, and in Gloucester Cathedral. In 1929 he conducted the Three Hours' Service on Good Friday in St. James's, Piccadilly; preached before the University in Durham Cathedral; and in Southwark Cathedral; delivered the University Sermon in Cambridge, and other sermons in two College chapels; and preached again at Advent in Westminster Abbey. In 1931 he again preached in the Abbey. In 1932 he attended, by request of the Archbishop of Canterbury, a meeting of the Church Assembly's Commission on Church and State at Lambeth, to give evidence on matters connected with the experience of the Church of Ireland since Disestablishment. In 1933 he preached in Birmingham Cathedral; in 1934 in Pershore Abbey; in 1936 again before Cambridge University; in 1937 in St. Mary's Cathedral, Edinburgh, during the Faith and Order Conference. In this year also, at the Archbishop of Canterbury's request, he deputized for the Archbishop of Armagh (who was in ill health) on the Consultative Body of the Lambeth Conference. And he had always maintained his personal connections in England. The old home in Eastbourne, where his eldest sister continued to live was still his *pied à terre* to and from his yearly visits to the Continent. In 1929 he was made the recipient of the degree of Doctor of Divinity of Cambridge University. The present Master of Christ's College writes: 'For the higher Cambridge doctorates a candidate submits all his previously published work, and accordingly no special thesis is submitted for the degree of D.D. This in Gregg's case was an "earned" degree, not one conferred *honoris causa.*' Henceforth he invariably wore his Cambridge hood in preference to the Dublin black-and-scarlet. But it is not likely that he thought any longer of a position in Cambridge with wistfulness, as he had when toiling as Rector of Blackrock. It must therefore have been a surprise to him to receive the following letter dated 25 November 1933 from a Fellow of his old College (whose signature is unfortunately illegible):

My dear Archbishop,
    For some little time some people have been thinking about the succession to the Mastership which in the ordinary way McLean will resign in about 2½ years—and one or two have prompted this note to you which is of necessity personal and quite unofficial. Could you in the most private way possible give

me a hint as to whether you would spare a second thought to consider it if and when the need arose? Under the new statutes the Master retires at 70 unless the Fellows ask him to go on before the expiration of his term.

Incidentally, and this is not the cause or the occasion of this letter, the present Master is at the moment seriously ill. He collapsed at a private dinner party but he is better and quite clear to-day. I hope you are well and that you will forgive me for this letter.

Gregg made a note in pencil of the gist of his reply:

Wd. not say that 'in no circs.' wd. I consider it—but as long as health allows Ist duty to C. of I. Shd. need to be v. well assured that duty to go was greater than duty to stay.

The prognosis of the writer of the invitation proved premature, since a year later Gregg received a letter from the Master written in his own hand.

Christ's College Lodge,
Cambridge
14 November 1934

My dear Archbishop,
I have the great pleasure and privilege of informing you that the Governing Body of this College yesterday elected you to an Honorary Fellowship—which may be fairly described as the highest honour it is in our power to confer. We are all so happy and united about it, and your old friends, among whom I venture to include myself, are overjoyed at the well merited recognition of your services to learning, to the Church and to the Country.
With every affectionate wish for your happiness and success.

Yours very sincerely,
NORMAN MCLEAN

There is nothing to show that he ever allowed his name to be considered for an English bishopric. However, there are among his personal letters two which would not be worth mention unless he had thought them worth keeping. One, quite brief, is from the former Bishop of Lichfield, John Augustine Kempthorne, then in retirement in Cambridge, to a clergyman named Nelson; the other, unfortunately a fragment only, is from the latter to Archbishop Gregg. It would seem that during the vacancy in the Primatial See of Armagh in the autumn of 1938 a move was made, though unauthoritatively, towards Gregg's nomination for the bishopric of Durham on the impending resignation of Bishop Hensley Henson.

The first letter, dated 19 October 1938, is as follows:

My dear Nelson,

... I agree with you that the Archbp. of Dublin would be an admirable Bishop of Durham. But would he leave Ireland?

I am certainly not equal to the burden of any diocesan bishopric—least of all to such a one as Durham. ...

Dominus tecum.

Ever yours sincerely,
J. A. KEMPTHORNE,
Bishop

The first page of the other letter being lost, so too is the date. The second page reads:

... and spoke in warm appreciation of *all* that Your Grace has done to promote peace and goodwill between England and Ireland. Like so very many others, they expressed regret that you did not fill a leading position in the Church of England. I fear that the loyal Church folk of Dublin would be shocked if they could hear the strong wishes expressed on all hands that you could be persuaded to accept the Bishopric of Durham. I mentioned this to Bishop Kempthorne, who, like Your Grace is a Cambridge scholar, upholding the Lightfoot–Westcott–Moule tradition.

With Your Grace and our greatly beloved Archbishop, both in the Northern Province, it would give the Church a great uplift.

With much respect and renewed thanks, I beg to remain,

My Lord Archbishop,
Yours obediently,
W. J. NELSON [4]

What Gregg's future career would have been, had he gone to Durham, is an interesting speculation.

The memories of the present Bishop of Derry, Dr. Charles Tyndall, are those of one who entertained towards the Archbishop feelings of admiration and personal affection as well as discernment and understanding. 'He was always,' he writes, 'rather a hero of mine.'

My first encounter with him was in 1925 when I had occasion to visit the Palace in Dublin. The maid had some difficulty with my name. I gave her a visiting card and asked her to present it

---

[4] The writer may be identified with William Joseph Nelson, then Vicar of Fridaythorpe in the diocese of York; formerly Rector of Stratford-on-Slaney (dio. Leighlin) 1898–1904, and of Bannow (dio. Ferns) 1904–9.

to his Grace. The interview ended, he saw me to the door, gave me the rather limp handshake, produced the visiting card and said 'You may need this'!

At the time of my examination for Priest's Orders, I had met my examiner in the Greek of Ephesians the previous night at a social occasion, and had said to him, 'Till me meet, sir, on the plains of Philippi.' At lunch at the Palace next day the examiner (Canon Young) recounted this to his Grace. The Archbishop rejoined genially: 'Oh! I suppose he really should have said, "I go to fight with the beast of Ephesus."'

As a prelate he had within a few years established an unassailable position. In Ossory as the youngest Bishop, and in Dublin as probably the youngest Archbishop, he had won for himself an almost Olympian dignity. But by 1929 it would seem that he felt the need to come down from this pedestal. His own teen-age daughters probably brought home to him the gap between age and youth; and the Youth Conference of 1929 might well be considered an important turning-point in his ministry. In the previous year at a Diocesan Synod he had delivered a remarkable speech emphasizing the need for an infiltration of young life in the councils of the Church. 'We are all or nearly all grey-headed men.' It was as a result of this speech that the Youth Conference was launched and he was invited to be president. He came in for a lot of criticism on the part of the older clergy for supporting us. (I think a sentence in a Synod Speech by the Primate (d'Arcy) deploring 'sectionalizing tendencies' may have been a criticism of the Youth Movement.) But he pushed calmly on and completely won the hearts of the youth in the Dublin Diocese and of his more junior Clergy. People close to him thought that the Archbishop became more human and approachable from this time onwards. I know he was deeply moved by the experience. Night after night he came down to the Metropolitan Hall. He was wonderfully patient even when stupid things were said. When finally we presented him with some kind of remembrance he was visibly touched.

It must be added that the writer of the above was one of the leaders of the Movement, and that the Archbishop's daughter Margaret was another. Their vigorous addresses and those of other members of the Conference were printed in the booklet which preserves a full record of the proceedings. The high-light was Studdert Kennedy's appearance and contribution—only six weeks before his sudden death. It is not known what was the Archbishop's reaction to that independent thinker's vivid and unconventional—and slightly heretical—presentation of the Christian faith, but he was the life and soul of the Conference.

That the Archbishop was deeply impressed by the worthwhileness of this experiment is clear from his address to the Joint Diocesan Synod on 25 October 1932, in which he stressed the importance to the life of the Church of the Youth Movement, and welcomed Youth to its councils. But it is equally clear that he was not carried away by it, since he added a wise proviso: 'While it is right that Youth should have its share in our elective offices, I do not think that Youth can reasonably ask—and it does not ask—for a majority of those offices. So long as human nature is constituted as it is, experience will be more honoured than untried enthusiasm.'

§

On 19 March 1935 a letter appeared in the *Irish Times* as follows:

Sir,

Some months ago my attention was called to a movement in Dublin for the consecration in future of Christ's Cathedral to the service of the Roman Catholic Church. I expressed my strong approval of such a change. During my childhood in Dublin this Cathedral was a roofless ruin. Whether it ever really got going again after its rebuilding by an eminent distiller I do not know; all I can say is that when I visited it last there was not a soul within its walls, neither worshipper nor verger, dean nor chapter, unlike St. Patrick's which had always kept alive more or less, within a few minutes' walk, and is amply sufficient for the needs of the Protestant Episcopal Church.

I also visited the church in Thomas Street which was serving as a Catholic Pro-Cathedral. Both as to site and architecture it was so unworthy of its function that I described it as being 'as ugly as if the Devil himself had built it,' and suggested that if its services could be transferred to Christ Church it could be deconsecrated and the site let or sold for ordinary commercial purposes, with considerable benefit to the church funds.

This letter of mine was communicated to the Press; but, as it happened, I did not see it in print until to-day, in a cutting not from an Irish paper, but from the *East Anglian Times*.

Fancy my horror, when I found that some Handy Andy—no doubt, honestly intending to do his faith a service, by transferring my criticisms of the architecture of the Thomas Street church and my proposals for its deconsecration and demolition to St. Patrick's—had altered the name in my letter, thereby reducing it to revolting absurdity and discrediting the whole project. If the matter should be put forward again as a possible gesture of goodwill in connection with the King's Jubilee, it had better be kept under better direction than that of poor Handy Andy. Meanwhile, I must beg enough of your valuable space to correct a misrepresentation, which must have caused many of my fellow-Protestants to give me up as quite insane.

Yours etc., G. Bernard Shaw

A letter of such import from so distinguished a writer could not be disregarded. Gregg took evident pains over his reply and—what was most unusual—kept a copy of it.

March 25, 1935

Dear Sir,

As letters from you have appeared in the Press concerning our Dublin Cathedrals, and you have associated yourself with certain parties who plan what they call an amicable arrangement as to the handing over to the R.C. Church, in plain English the confiscation of one of them, I wish to point out to you that, if it is the case that you remember Christ Church Cathedral as a roofless ruin, it is a pertinent question how the Cathedral ceased to be so.

And the answer is that a member of the Church of Ireland expended nearly a quarter of a million on its restoration. Our interest in the building is therefore a substantial one, quite apart from questions of legal title.

Your statement that you found no one in the Church when you happened to visit it could be paralleled by a statement of my own experience in visiting some of the greatest R.C. Cathedrals in Europe, for example Toledo and Seville and the Meyquita of Cordoba, to take Spain alone. Choral worship takes place twice a day in the Cathedral, as you would have known had you gone there at the appropriate time.

I could have wished you had remembered the extraordinary difficulties under which the Church of Ireland labours to-day, and had not taken your part in adding to them.

Yours faithfully,

JOHN, ARCHBISHOP OF DUBLIN

Any letter of Shaw is worth preservation, as the following letter certainly is:

29th March 1935. Genoa.

My dear Archbishop,

You are almost as naïve as my friend Dean Inge, who, on returning from a remote place where he had taken a service for an old college friend, said to his wife, 'So-and-so must be a very popular preacher, the church was quite full.'

However, I do not know what the average congregation assembled in Christ's to hear an average preacher amounts to. What is plain to common sense is that St. Patrick's is quite sufficient for Protestant needs in that rather slummy district, where my uncle's church, St. Bride's, has long since disappeared.

Christ's, like St. Patrick's, was rescued from ruin by the pennies spent by poor Irish Catholics on porter and whiskey. Both restorations were transactions that would have made Simon Magus blush. But neither Guinness nor Roe could create a commercial value in the cathedrals. Legally the Ecclesiastical Commissioners (or are they still Church Temporalities?) could sell the site of Christ's for commercial purposes. Morally, that would be impossible. There are only three courses really available: (1) to make a big Christian gesture and offer it to the Roman Church as that of the vast majority of the people; (2) to offer to sell it to the Roman Church, which badly needs a dignified cathedral; (3) to play the dog in the manger, and hold on to Christ's at a loss for the sake of keeping the Papists out of it. It seems to me that No. 1 would be beyond all question the best course. It would raise the prestige of Christianity in Ireland enormously, and give the Protestant Church the lion's share of that prestige.

But I really cannot pretend to have studied the position thoroughly. The proposal did not originate with me. I never thought of it until a certain Mrs. Kilkelly, otherwise unknown to me, wrote to me declaring that there was 'a movement' in Dublin in the direction indicated, and that my opinion would be valued. I saw at once that there was a good deal to be said for it. I said so and pointed out that the Roman Catholics could with great advantage deconsecrate and sell their vulgar church in Thomas St. to endow Christ's.

At that I left it until the other day, when I discovered to my horror that my letter to Mrs. Kilkelly had been published with St. Patrick's substituted for the Thomas St. Church, when I at once wrote to the *Irish Times* to correct the error.

I still think the proposal worth the Church's very serious consideration; but I hardly care to pursue the subject with Mrs. Kilkelly.

I am very much obliged to you for taking the trouble to write to me, thus enabling me to submit my view to your authority instead of turning the heads of people whom I can only guess to be rather impossible.

faithfully, G. Bernard Shaw

The Revd. Canon Robert J. Ross, B.D., a member of the Chapter of Christ Church Cathedral for many years, recalls instances of the Archbishop's vigilance as its Ordinary.

His triennial Visitations were serious and thorough occasions. He demanded the attendance of the complete Cathedral Staff (including the Assistant Organist, which I then was), and each

member of the Cathedral Choir was expected to present himself
and to answer the Roll Call. We all received a wholesome Charge
concerning our duties, and on the importance of the singing of
the Service twice daily throughout the week. We were in no
doubt who was the Ordinary of the Cathedral; nor were we in
doubt that the Archbishop cared deeply and really about the
work of the Cathedral and about the persons who were concerned in it.

He gave full attention to all the details of every special Service
held in the Cathedral, requiring that the proofs of the Order of
all such Services be submitted to him before printing.

His obstinacy was evident one Easter Day when he was cele-
brating Holy Communion in C.C.C. and there was insufficient
Bread. He rejected the suggestion that he should break the bread
into smaller pieces, and insisted on having a knife brought to him
from the Verger's House a little distance away. The one responsible for the inadequacy in the provision of the Bread was
properly and severely rebuked by the Archbishop after the
Service.

His humility was illustrated to me one day as he was leaving
the Cathedral. He was stopped by a rough-looking man who
tipped him on the arm and said, 'Would you tell the Dean that
I want to see him: I'm looking for the job as gardener?' The
Archbishop replied, 'Certainly I shall convey your message to
the Dean. What name shall I say?' And turning back he went
into the Chapter House and told the Dean that a gentleman by
the name of Mr. A. was wishing to speak to him.

I was present as a member of a small sub-committee at which
the Archbishop presided. There were not more than four of us
present with the Archbishop. It was a long, troublesome meeting,
during which hard words were spoken, and tempers more than
a little frayed. After some two and a half hours we reached a
conclusion and a solution of the problem submitted to us. At the
end of the meeting Dr. Gregg said in that peculiar lilting voice
of his, 'Thank God we have reached a solution.' One of the
members gave a slight derisive laugh. Turning to him and
addressing him by name, Dr. Gregg said, 'Why do you laugh?
I see no cause for laughter. At the beginning of this meeting I
prayed for the guidance of God; I meant it; and I believe we
have had God's guidance.' And he then closed our meeting. It is
a clear example and illustration of the fact that his strength of
character and his fearlessness and his wisdom arose from his
practice of relating his life to his prayers.

He was always ready to encourage old students and his clergy
in the pursuit of learning, and in doing so would often surprise
them in his knowledge of by-ways in their own line of study with

which they were themselves unfamiliar. An example of this is shown in a letter to an old student, Cecil de Pauley, then Vice-Principal of Trinity College in the University of Toronto, afterwards Dean of St. Patrick's and now Bishop of Cashel.

18 March 1938

Dear de Pauley,

It was most kind of you to think of sending me a copy of your book on the Cambridge Platonists. The men you write of, particularly Whichcote, Cudworth and More, have been familiar names to me from my College days, though alas! more as names than as teachers. Cudworth came to my College, Christ's, from Emmanuel, and was Master for the best part of 30 years. He and More nearly had a feud, in so far as so saintly a man as More could have a feud with any one, as C. was afraid More was going to publish before he could get his book on Natural Ethics out. It (the latter) never appeared!

More was offered the Provostship of T.C.D. as well as two bishoprics. He seems to have been a real saint, but the life of contemplation had greater charms for him. He writes that he once spent *ten* days *nowhere*, presumably in a kind of automatic state. He seems to have been a real mystic, and some one described him as the holiest person on the face of the earth—but like some other mystics he had a very practical common sense.

You have chosen a very interesting study, and you seem able to move about in the world of ideas with a happy intimacy. You belong to the T.C.D. tradition in this. I have always noticed how much the philosophical side of things has stamped itself on Trinity men and their output. We had philosophically-minded men at Cambridge, but the atmosphere was not philosophical. It was possible to pass through one's entire course without being brought up seriously against philosophy, though of course classical men have to do some Platonic study. I was lectured e.g. for several terms by that distinguished Platonist, James Adam. But for all that, philosophy was not part of the texture of life.

With all good wishes and renewed thanks for your most interesting study.

I am
Yours very truly
JOHN DUBLIN

Full as his days were and conscientious as he was in fulfilling his obligations, he did not allow himself to be overworked. For he was a late survival of the spacious days when churchmen in high places allowed themselves (and were expected) to enjoy times of leisure like lesser mortals. He was not expected to open bazaars or dedicate church furniture or perform trivial functions of a like nature. Others might do this kind of thing because it was a way of bringing them into touch with people. But Gregg was not a good mixer and made no pretence of trying to be one.

He worked to a well-regulated time-table which included intervals for physical and mental refreshment. He was a member of the Fitzwilliam Lawn Tennis Club and played there all the year round, on grass and hard courts. He did not care to play with all and sundry, but had his special associates. And, though he always played all-out to win, he liked to pit himself against a stronger player; especially the redoubtable Professor A. A. Luce who in earlier days (before war service in the Royal Irish Rifles with a M.C. and subsequent election to a Senior Fellowship in Trinity) had been a first-class amateur in this and other games. They regularly played singles once a week during the winter. Luce could always beat him, but testifies to Gregg's keenness and activity on the court. They entertained for each other a mutual though silent regard.

Gregg suffered from abdominal trouble all his life, and to this cause may be attributed his tendency to lapse into sleep during afternoon committee meetings, and also his desire to keep fit by physical exercise. When no tennis was possible he would go for strenuous walks—generally to the Marine Parade in Sandymount to be in sight of the sea, and back by another route: his 'triangular' walk. If prevented from his daily walk he always recorded the fact in his diary—'no walk to-day.'

He was delighted to accept invitations to tennis parties at private houses in Dublin. But he was loth to be seen in the public streets clad in flannels. So, having dressed himself in them, he would wear over the white shirt his accustomed episcopal black garb and don the episcopal black top-hat; proceed secretly to his garage whence he would be driven—the top part of him alone being visible—in splendid state to his host's door; to whose astonished gaze he would emerge in piebald guise, black above and white below, and having peeled off the black proceed eagerly to the tennis courts.

This, which may be taken as no more than an amusing idio-syncrasy, was in fact illustrative of a serious characteristic. It is in line with his sense of the fitness of things, of keeping up appearances, of the importance of setting a good example, and—more especially—of 'giving no offence in anything, that the ministry be not blamed.' In this connection his elder daughter remembers how her parents differed in the matter of games on Sunday.

Mother, brought up in a large non-clerical household, would say, 'I'd much prefer you to bring your friends here on Sunday and play tennis on our own courts, and don't go to the Club.' Father, rejecting from his rational outlook his own Sabbatarian upbringing, yet slow to offend members of his flock who retained these scruples, would say, 'I have no objection to tennis on Sunday, but don't let people see you playing here. Go elsewhere and don't let me know.' The result was, of course, that we rarely did play tennis on Sundays.

When in 1929 he discovered the delights of Castletownshend, this little paradise of the West became for him and his wife and daughters a holiday resort to be preferred above continental excursions. To his younger daughter indeed it was to become a second home. Here the Archbishop embarked, and in a literal sense, upon a new recreation. This was yachting. Having hired a boat and a fisherman to teach him the rudiments of the art, he bought an old trawler from Major Chavasse and would put to sea in all weathers. To pilot his craft and keep it on an even keel required a navigational sagacity equivalent to that of piloting the church through troubled waters; and in either case he disliked the rôle of a mere passenger. He became a regular entrant for the annual regatta in Castlehaven Harbour. Though given a good handicap on account of the rough structure of his boat he never won a race; but he was an object of awed interest to spectators as, reclining in a negligent posture in the stern and with an arm hung limply on the tiller, he let her lean out to the wind.

Castletownshend was at that time still in its golden glory; unknown to tourists, and inhabited mainly by the interrelated clans of Somerville, Coghill, Chavasse and Townshend, whose gardens ran into one another's; and it was from one of them that the Gregg family rented a house—'The Castle' or 'Glen Barrahane' or 'Tally Ho! '—Miss Edith Somerville was the dominant figure in this select little community, and reigned over it at 'Drishane.'

It happened to the present writer, who in 1925 had been a guest there, to have the good fortune to recall with the Primate—not many years before his death—memories of Castletownshend in those days. The talk turned on Miss Somerville's quiet exercise of her unquestioned authority and her combination of so many various accomplishments, literary, artistic, musical, sporting and practical—and the Primate, with that singular graciousness which enabled him to converse with a junior and inferior on terms of equality, wound up the discussion thus: 'Yes, I think we must agree that she was a Remarkable Personality.' (But his daughter who married her nephew explains that his use of this expression was a polite way of veiling—not exactly disapproval—but a sense of temperamental incompatibility.)

§

On New Year's Day 1936 at a time when 'world problems perplex the statesmen of all nations,' a Letter to the People of the Church of Ireland, calling upon them 'both publicly and privately to seek to make the law of Christ prevail,' was published above the signature of both Archbishops. They had collaborated on its composition, and its interest now lies less in its contents than as an illustration of their relationship. When the final draft was agreed upon between them, d'Arcy, with his customary humility, wrote to Gregg: 'Enclosed seems to me sufficient. I like your way of putting things better than my effort. I have added only a few additional words. If you approve of them, I think we may let the statement stand.'

> The strongest power that can be exerted by a human personality is that of believing prayer; and it is our conviction, both, that vast stores of this power remain unreleased through want of faith in prayer generally, and of belief in the significance of our individual prayers in particular; and also that the release of the prayer-energies of the entire body of Christians throughout the world would introduce into the world-situation factors of incalculable potency.

And when the Archbishop of Canterbury (Lang) wrote a grateful appreciation to Armagh, the latter forwarded it to Gregg with the words: 'The emphasis on prayer was your special contribution. All good wishes for the New Year.'

And on 2 May of the following year Gregg received this letter:

My dear Archbishop,

Will you let me say how much I enjoyed reading your Address to the Gen. Synod? Your affirmation of the principle of liberty in relation to personality is tremendously important for the age in which we live. 'The training of free personality' is certainly the true aim of all real education.

I should like your address to be given some permanent form and circulated. It states the principle most needed in our time.

With hearty congratulations,
Yours very sincerely,
CHARLES F. ARMAGH

P.S. Would you object to my saying what I have written above in a letter to the *Gazette*?

In the first week of May 1938 he wrote in his own name to the *Church of England Newspaper* on 'The New Friendship between England and Southern Ireland.' The recent Pact, in which England recognized Southern Ireland as a sovereign and independent state, augured well for their future relations. The handing over of the three naval bases 'will be regarded as the tardy removal of a symbol of alien domination and of a hindrance to taking measures of self-defence.'

It has been said that Irish history is a thing which Englishmen should remember, but which Irishmen should forget. But it is very hard for English people with their world-wide interests to give more than a passing thought to Ireland of to-day, let alone Ireland of yesterday. On the other hand to Ireland England has been the barrier lying between itself and Europe; its vastly richer neighbour, ruling it for centuries against its will, imposing on it an alien religion and alien culture, and an alien language— the intruder and the enemy. Ireland will not forget the past. Only by dwelling on the things wherein she differs from England can Ireland's self-consciousness find its desired nourishment. In this Ireland we need not look for any sudden change of heart.

But, he continues optimistically, 'they can now appreciate (perhaps as never before) one another's viewpoints and good qualities.' And he ends on a note of hopeful prophecy:

Both sides recognize that when questions of national defence arise neither country can do without the other. In a European conflagration England cannot afford to have a hostile Ireland on its flank, and Ireland would never be allowed by an enemy of England to remain neutral; and while Ireland has the wit to see that England is the surest defence of its freedom, England does not fail to perceive that an Ireland which feels itself free is a safer neighbour than one which sullenly repeats the slogan, 'England's difficulty is Ireland's opportunity.'

Unfortunately that was not how things worked out. . . .

In September he received a private letter from Mr. de Valera, then presiding at the assembly of the League of Nations in Geneva, which with his kind permission is here published.

Delegation of Ireland,
Private   to the Assembly of the League of Nations
23. ix. 38
My dear Lord Archbishop,
I thank you most sincerely for your kind letter of congratulations which was duly forwarded to me.
I regret that we seem to be able to do very little here. The

League has lost whatever authority it had. It is little more now than the symbol of an ideal. The ideal however is itself one that cannot die—and it is because of its promise for the future that I am convinced we should not abandon the existing league, however ineffective it may be.

The arrival of the genuine new league will come sooner or later according as the spiritual leaders of the people are or are not successful in bringing home to the individual the real values in life. It is the Churches that will matter.

I am, my dear lord Archbishop,

Yours very sincerely,

EAMON DE VALERA

His Grace
Most Rev. Dr. Gregg,
Archbishop of Dublin

§

In the summer of 1937 he had allowed himself, perhaps somewhat ill-advisedly, to be interviewed by a newspaper reporter. Eliminating the unessential, we find that the conversation revolved round four topics.

'You see,' said the Archbishop, 'people don't read sermons nowadays.' 'Do you think they ever did?' I asked. He recrossed his gaiters and stared at the fireplace for a moment. 'Well, I suppose there was a time when collected volumes of sermons were read,' he said, with that curious upward lift of the voice that I had learned to expect at the end of each sentence. 'In times when books were not so plentiful as now they probably enjoyed a certain measure of popularity. . . . No, nobody reads sermons nowadays. That is why it is so fruitless to make them studied or needlessly erudite. . . . The ideal sermon is spoken in the plainest possible language; it has one theme, which is brought to the surface again and again and driven home by analogies and illustrations. Absolute simplicity is the basis of success.

'All people are really spiritual beings; they may forget this fact now and then, but you can always make them remember if you speak to their hearts. And to do this you must speak to them in the language they best understand. In any case, a plain style is always the best style. And I believe very firmly that one of the finest trainings for speaking pure and plain English is a classical education. A man trained in the classics is known not by the number of Latin tags he uses, but by the purity and vigour of his English.'

Dr. Gregg is a tall man, with gaunt ascetic features and rather untidy black hair. He neither looks nor speaks like an Irishman, although I assure you that he is one. . . . His bookshelves are a mine of interest. Theological works are there, of course, in plenty,

but here and there volumes of essays, plays and slender and
elegant little books of verse catch the eye with their vivid and
secular bindings; for the Archbishop is a man of wide interests
and sympathies: he is fond of travelling, and speaks Italian,
Spanish, French, and German 'with pains.'

He is a student of church music, and used to play the organ
occasionally. He is well versed, of course, in Bach, though he
confessed to me that he used to play him 'more by way of drill
than choice.'

His greatest hobby, however, is English literature; he is rarely
so happy as when he is immersed in the English poets, particularly Browning. . . . 'I admit,' he said, 'that there are things
in Browning which I have not yet grasped. Sordello, for instance,
is a very difficult proposition. . . . ' 'And how many times have
you read "The Ring and the Book"?' I asked him. 'Only once,'
he replied, 'but that, I think, is more than many people have
done. Oh yes, I am passionately fond of Browning; he has tremendous intellectual force, which is so much more than you can say
of Tennyson, his contemporary, who strikes me as being little
more than a marvellous craftsman. My first school prize at
Bedford was a volume of Browning, and I have read him
assiduously ever since. Of all his poems I think I love best "Rabbi
ben Ezra" and "A Grammarian's Funeral"; there is great philosophy in both. Another man with great intellectual force is
Francis Thompson, although I find his language rather too full
of Latinisms.'

We stepped gently from Browning to Meredith. I was surprised that he was not well acquainted with Meredith's poems,
so many of which read like irregular offspring of Browning.
'Well, I think I prefer Meredith in prose,' he said; 'the novels—
most charming. *The Egoist*?—Yes, extraordinarly clever, but I
am not so sure about its charm; I had to work fairly hard at
The Egoist. But every young man and woman ought to read
Richard Feverel; it is surely one of the most beautiful books in
the language.'

Of course, you cannot claim to have interviewed an Irishman
properly unless you ask him what he thinks of the renascence of
Gaelic. . . . 'If our people—that is to say the Protestants—are
to live in this country, they must learn the language,' said the
Archbishop. 'I have never opposed the teaching of Irish; indeed,
I am manager of a preparatory college for national school
teachers, one of five such colleges which were recently established
by the Government and have a definite Gaelic atmosphere. Our
Church is by no means anti-national. Many of our men are Irish
speakers, and at one church we have a fortnightly service in
Irish. After all, the whole medium of life here is Gaelic and it
is only right that Gaelic should be spoken by the people.'

o

His younger daughter gives a more intimate account of his idiosyncrasies at home and abroad.

My father had a disconcerting habit of stepping on to trains as they were in motion, not always because he arrived late, but because he liked to be free until the last possible second. When the family left Kilkenny for Dublin, he brought my sister and me with him by train; we were put into our seats and told not to move, and, naturally, he kept the tickets. As the train left, he was still standing on the platform. Horror overcame me and I jumped up to grab the communication cord, but he swung into the carriage, quite undismayed, as the train gathered speed. It was only later that I learnt from my mother that this was his habitual practice.

He loved trains and everything to do with railways. It thrilled him to see and hear a great express roar through a station and he had quite a collection of railway tickets. Sometimes he bought a ticket for a destination just further than his own so that he would not be obliged to surrender it at the barrier. When we left Dublin on school journeys to England he always handed us our tickets, seat reservations and travelling money in a used envelope with a pencilled note of the contents. Once, the boat had actually left for Holyhead with me on board before the ticket collector discovered that instead of a valid ticket I had only the Dun-Laoghaire-Westland Row section of my last journey in my possession; I had been met by car at the boat and my father had retained the ticket for his collection. How he had come to put it into my journey envelope instead of the new ticket was a mystery. The L.M.S. staff were perfectly charming and I was allowed to proceed to London, after giving them his name and address and sending him a telegram from Holyhead, which, of course, caused him the most dreadful feeling of guilt.

He loved to make jokes without the glimmer of a smile and, unless you knew him very well, it was not always possible to know that he was joking. The Palace of 50 St. Stephen's Green, in Dublin, had double mahogany doors between the main rooms and one day I searched the house for my father, who was wanted on the telephone; finally I located him, between the doors, making his way from the study to the dining-room.

'Oh!' I exclaimed, 'I've been all over the house on a wild goose chase!'

'And who,' he enquired with carefully simulated iciness, 'Is the wild goose?'

One day my mother announced that a friend of her's, whose company my father did not find stimulating, would be coming to lunch on Monday. He looked past us as he said gently: 'Ah, that will be something to look forward to!' Suspicious, I said,

'What will?' 'Tuesday,' he replied, without a trace of a smile. One of his great delights in that house was a mirror, strategically placed so that from his desk he could see who was on the doorstep when he heard the bell ring. His study had two doors, so he could dodge an unwelcome visitor, but as he was the most approachable of men he very seldom did so. The drawback of such mirrors is, however, the fact that those whom you can see can also see you, and his clergy soon came to know whether he was at home or not before they even rang.

It was not until we had been in that house for about three years that I came to regard my father as anything else but an alarming personage. Between the ages of eleven and thirteen I spent a good deal of each winter in bed with various chest complaints, and each summer my parents were advised to take me to Switzerland or Italy. I did not then realize how my father dreaded the possibility of one of us developing tuberculosis, which had killed his own father. It was on these trips abroad that I came to know him, and he me. My mother was not at all strong and could not walk far, but my father and I used to set out by 'bus or train to some point and walk back, or work out a circular route to a certain place and back again. It was on these walks that I discovered his humanity, and he often told me later that it was only then that he found out that I was a person.

Baedeker in one hand and walking stick in the other, he wore an ordinary shirt with a soft collar, an ancient suit of clerical grey and a yellowing panama hat with a black band; his black socks and his tie—the latter more loosely knotted than that of a man who wears one every day of his life—proclaimed his calling. He was so obviously enjoying himself that it did you good to see him.

We talked a great deal, but sometimes we just slogged along the roads, too hot to speak. I discovered that in everything he was a classicist, whereas I had been born a romantic and had to learn to appreciate his point of view. He revelled in classical Italian landscapes, with villages, vineyards, churches and evidence of cultivation from the beginning of time; the wildness of Irish mountain scenery dismayed him, but he loved to watch the sea, particularly if it was rough; it gave him great pleasure to see a ship come into port. The spectacular quality of Swiss scenery made him marvel, and he delighted in the way man had contrived to overcome the appalling natural hazards and build roads and railways through seemingly impossible country. He loved to stand on a bridge over a deep chasm and gloat over the river fiercely fighting its way through a narrow channel below, and the skill and courage of the engineers who had devised and built the bridge. He would dole out bits of chocolate during these pauses. He beamed with delight when he saw trains clinging

to the side of a mountain or threading their way through a series
of rock tunnels, like a string through beads. He thoroughly
enjoyed a trip on a funicular railway. Mountain roads made him
almost breathless as he considered the horror of having to drive
in the outside lane, with nothing between you and perdition but
a few white stones, sparsely placed.

He had a very sweet tooth and greatly enjoyed Swiss black
cherry jam and certain kinds of patisserie. He had discovered
the delights of Asti Spumante when wandering in Italy as a
student, and to the end of his life described it as the most wonderful wine he had ever tasted, though he was no wine drinker.
He never liked dry wines, or spirits of any kind. He did not
smoke. I believe that twice in his life he went to the cinema,
but he had an unmovable suspicion of the film industry, whose
influence he thought to be undesirable.

He kept meticulous accounts in pencil on odd half sheets of
paper. We were advanced money for our daily needs when we
were students, and accounted for every penny. I remember no
complaints of extravagance, but I do remember having sometimes to be very mean in order to avoid such a complaint, or the
fear of it.

He never used a fountain pen, let alone a typewriter. It was
only when my brothers were growing up that he could be persuaded to use a safety razor, instead of a cut-throat, so conservative was he about adopting modern 'gadgets.' Every letter
was written by him, personally, by dip pen, except for occasional
circulars. His erudite hand on an envelope looked like the work
of an educated spider. To his children, he signed himself: 'Ever
yr loving Fr.,' and his letters to us were always perfectly spaced
to cover both sides of a half sheet, without wasted space or over-
crowding. His outward mail was thrown down on the carpet
near his desk, each letter as it was completed, then collected,
stamped and taken to post; he knew exactly when to post letters
for any destination, and was a confirmed 'late fee' user. My small
daughter, whose orderly eye disapproved of papers strewn all
over the floor, once picked up all his letters and put them tidily
in the waste paper basket, causing him great distress.

He was sentimental in many things, like the rest of his generation. Sunsets and the alpenglow filled him with wonder and
delight and brought lines of poetry to his mind, which he would
quote. He treasured small mementoes of either people or places.
He brought each of us a little present whenever he returned
from abroad and loved to see his choice appreciated. He often
recalled early sayings of his children and liked to use pet names.
Certain hymns evoked memories of home, school or college and
he used to play them over, head back, humming, without words.

He was over forty when the First World War broke out, so

found it hard to adjust himself to the instability and insecurity of the post-war world. Life without security—of Government, jobs, income and justice—was unthinkable to him and he would have marvelled, had he been conscious of it, at the courage of the young people of to-day who no more expect it than he could envisage a moment's serenity without it.

My father believed that poetry without nobility of thought was mere verse; lyric poetry made no appeal to him whatever. Since I could not agree that poetry was the proper vehicle for noble thoughts, we could never agree upon the nature of poetry.

He was not young when he decided to learn to drive. One reason for this decision was that his chauffeur might have his Sundays free. He enjoyed driving, as he enjoyed sailing a boat, but his mind used to wander and he would forget that he was driving a fast-moving vehicle. Like his grandfather, of whom it is written—'he used occasionally to drive his own horse in a gig; but this was with him never a satisfactory or even a safe arrangement, for his thoughts were occupied with other things than the horse . . .' it was really better when he allowed himself to be driven.

He walked at tremendous speed and made a point of covering about two miles each day, often after dark and generally with one of his daughters. We used to run along beside him, struggling to keep up. He would go a long way to see a really rough sea, and would time his walk for high tide if there was a storm, then dodge the spray that shot over the sea wall, enjoying every moment of it.

His standards, as I had discovered when I was a tiny child, were, in everything, of the highest. In examinations, merely to be in the first class was nothing; the only thing that counted was to be first of the first. When my elder brother was awarded an *aegrotat* at Cambridge, it was like a death in the family. My father suffered so terribly because of this that he ceased to smile, or even utter unnecessarily, for several months. I think it really broke his heart. Many years later, when I was up for Moderatorship in Trinity, I dreaded hearing the results of my own examination as, owing to the illnesses of both my parents and myself, I had been unable to do anything like as much work as I should have done. When the results were due, day after day passed, and each day I knew that my disgrace was coming nearer. I knew that I had failed. There was no question of it in my mind, but my father would not believe this and still imagined, poor man, that I might be a credit to him and to myself. Then, one afternoon, I walked into the house after having spent the day riding, and was met by my father, who rushed out the moment he heard me coming. His face was sorrowful and he did his best to break the bad news gently. My tutor had telephoned, he said, to say that I had been placed third of the Firsts. 'I hope,' he said, with great feeling, 'that you are not *too* disappointed.' I have always thought that he considered the jubilation with which I received this incredible news gravely misplaced.

He disliked dogs ('white hairs on my clothes'), mistrusted horses and had a horror of touching birds. He loved cats. Ducks, he habitually described as 'the most profane of creatures.'

He loved his home and never stayed away from it a moment longer than was absolutely necessary. My mother used to complain, in fun, that he would never stay away long enough to enable her to empty the Palace and give all the servants a holiday at the same time; even if he said he was going away for a fortnight, he would find a way to cut his journey short and be back in eleven days.

Sometimes emotion nearly overcame him in public and obliged him to turn his mind resolutely away from its cause. He told me that, once, it was only by doing this that he was able to continue with a service of dedication of a War Memorial, so near to tears had he been. The sound of the Last Post always brought him near to tears. When he was moved by the misfortunes of individuals, he had a way of grunting, almost groaning, as he tried to work out some means of helping them. He took care to apply the various legacies and trusts over which he had control with unassailable integrity and genuine charity. His private assistance was of the most personal: a letter, a visit, a little present of money, always a token of the immense compassion he felt and found so hard to express.

He could be wary, non-committal, cagey, when people pressed him to support them in enterprises of whose uprightness he was unconvinced; he could be distant when submerged with friendliness by people who had only just swum into his orbit. 'Now, what did they *want*?' he would ponder; 'it wasn't just for my *beaux yeux* they made all that fuss of me.' He always refused absolutely to give a personal recommendation to any one whom he had not known personally; the practice of doing so was, in his opinion, 'debasing the currency.' When he refused impossible requests of this nature and people showed their displeasure his only comment would be: 'They were very cross with me.'

He did not find it easy to trust strangers; his mother had once been the victim of a confidence trickster, and this inclined him to suspicion. Beggars at the door did not find him altogether an easy prey; he would question them and listen to them at length, trying to assess their genuineness, He had the Victorian hatred of being 'done' and of assisting the 'undeserving.' His favourite way of expressing personal dislike was to say: 'I'm sure his mother is very fond of him.'

As he aged, he mellowed; in his later years he ceased altogether, I think, to be alarming. His smile became more frequent and he rejoiced in the companionship of members of his family as they came and went. As a grandfather he is remembered with affection, and his penetrating intellect caused the young to regard him with great respect. I never once heard him complain of his blindness or of the difficulty he had in moving about during his later years. The blindness deprived him of two things on which all his interests were based and nourished: reading and writing. He was never, at any time, bad-tempered and would take the greatest pains to avoid imposing his will or opinions upon people. 'Who am I' he would say 'to do such a thing?' But he could assess with great rapidity, and lay bare with clarity, the ultimate values of any proposition or decision, however skilfully disguised. He never thought of himself as being anybody special.

Abroad, on two occasions, when I mentioned his name, I was told: 'He is the man to whom the Anglican Communion owes its survival, who held it to essentials at Lambeth; without him we should have been finished.' One of the speakers was a dignitary of the Church in South Africa, the other an Anglican Chaplain in France.

CHAPTER XII

THE PRIMACY

CHARLES FREDERICK D'ARCY, Archbishop of Armagh and Primate of All Ireland, died on 31 January 1938 after an illness protracted for many months during which the affairs of the diocese had been ably conducted by the Dean, Ford Tichborne, assisted by the Archdeacon, Lockett Ford. On 3 February he was buried in the grounds of Armagh Cathedral in the presence of a vast assemblage. The Archbishop of Dublin delivered the 'panegyric' on the composition of which he had spent the whole of the previous morning. It is remarkable for its sincerity in extolling the virtues of one from whom as a churchman he had differed profoundly, but whom, since his curate days in Ballymena, he had always regarded with respect and with some degree of affection.

. . . It is not often that a man is called to serve as bishop in so many Sees; nor again is it often that a bishop is able so successfully to combine his activities as a diocesan with the demands of the intellectual life. He was, in the first instance, a man of thought rather than action, but forces stronger than himself placed him in positions calling for the exercise of the practical faculties, and it is here that he showed his self-mastery and his force of character. He threw himself without reserve into his administrative duties, with many of the enslaving technicalities of which it was not hard at times to see that he was impatient. His faithfulness brought its reward.

His philosophical writing escaped the defect which beset many of those whose work was confined to the study and the lecture-room. In his thinking he never passed out of touch with life. That, to my mind, is the secret of much of the influence which he wielded as thinker and writer. As one who had to do with human souls, he never lost himself in remote abstractions. He was concerned with the close connection between belief and life, thought and action, theology and ethics, and herein he showed himself a true follower of that courageous idealistic philosopher of the eighteenth century, whom he delighted to acknowledge as a master—George Berkeley, himself also a bishop of the Church of Ireland.

His was, indeed, a great mind. He was able to take his place in the company of the finest intellects of our time, and yet he never obtruded his learning upon those whom he met in the ordinary intercourse of life. But for all that, there was only a

216

thin partition separating the twin worlds of thought and action in which he lived.

With those whom he knew, his conversation would spontaneously reveal the wide range of interests which formed the home of his eager and unresting spirit.

I shall never think of the Primate as an old man. The word I always associate with him is the word 'wonder.' The world he lived in was for ever fresh to him; the commonest things awoke his questioning faculty. For the Primate there was no staleness about the world he lived in. Every natural object was fresh, new, wonder-stirring. Life was a joy to him because his interest in it remained ever unspoilt. In the most real sense of the word, he pursued knowledge. To one with such an outlook upon life, religion was a necessity of existence. His perception of God furnished him with the master light of all his seeing, and it was his chief delight to apply his mind to those deep questions which have to do with the being and nature of God and lie behind the relations between God and man. And yet, for all his power of inquiry into the deep things of the mind and the ways of God, his religion was a simple religion. He knelt as a penitent sinner before a holy God. He trusted humbly in a crucified Saviour; prayer was as real for him as for the humblest cottager. His soul rejoiced in the wonder of the love of God. So in his preaching there always rang a note of confident assurance. We heard the voice of one who could say: 'I know whom I have believed, and I am persuaded.' ...

The Archbishop does not seem at first to have considered the almost inevitable consequence to himself of this vacancy at the head of the Church. In any case he was preoccupied with a spate of committee meetings in Dublin. But on 23 March his diary reads:

10.0 R.C.B. I preside. 11.30 H.C. St. Patrick's. 12.20 special meeting of Ho. of Bishops *re* Primacy. I was elected by 8 to 4, having stated I would require good time for consideration.

Next day: 'Have talk with Bp. of Derry [Peacocke] at Club, who discourages my acceptance. Various conversations *re* Primacy.' On 1 April begins a soliloquy:

The Primacy. I had never desired it, and never has it aroused in me the least emotion of desire. In looking forward to the inevitable vacancy, I had always felt I was unconcerned—it was not for me. During the days Mar. 23–31 I had been becoming a little more reconciled to the possibility that it might be right for me to go, but I felt I should be leaving behind all that held my real interest, nor did I think that at 65 I should ever be able to find N. Ireland anything but a strange land spiritually and

politically. However, as there seemed a strong feeling that I
ought to go, I was getting ready to try it. A v. sympathetic call
had reached me from the Armagh clergy.

A large number of the clergy in his own diocese of Dublin and
Kildare desired him to remain and sent him a petition to this effect.
There is no mention of this in his diary and it is unlikely that it
weighed with him in making a decision. But the circumstances of
its composition are of peculiar interest. Mr. Terence de Vere
White, now Literary Editor of the *Irish Times,* writes:

> I happened to be staying at the time for a week-end with Dean
> Craig's family in Kildare. The Dean told me that he was rather
> bothered because he had been asked to write a letter to Dr. Gregg
> asking him to remain in Dublin. The composition of the letter
> was giving him concern. I said that while he was taking Service
> the next day I would write the letter for him. I did so. He then
> took it up to Dublin and had it signed by various prominent
> people, and I was amused on the following evening to see a
> photo of the Archbishop in the evening paper holding a letter
> which he said he had received and which he was considering. As
> a result of the letter he then refused the Primacy. This story
> would hardly be worth repeating were it not for the fact that I
> am a Roman Catholic. It always struck me as rather piquant that
> I interfered in this way. However, my intervention seemed to
> have given pleasure at the time, and to have been set right at a
> later period by a higher power.

On 23 March he had asked their family doctor for an opinion
as to whether a move would be 'without disadvantage' for Mrs.
Gregg, and the doctor had 'quite definitely deprecated it' on the
grounds of high blood pressure and general debility. At his request
a consultant was called in, who on 1 April confirmed that opinion.

> This has virtually settled the question for me. I feel no dis-
> appointment—rather, relief. I only hope I am not yielding too
> readily to my wishes. But I dare to say that I was virtually ready
> to go, if there was no pointing in a different direction. I had asked
> to be kept entirely flexible, and to see things in proportion and
> objectively, and lo! the matter seems settled for me without any
> need for a painful and wrestling decision. God grant that nothing
> may lead me later to think I should have done anything else
> which I have not done.

On 2 April he was himself medically examined and given an
excellent report. On the 4th: 'Go up to Armagh and look round.
PISGAH. Meet Hugh Maude who goes over house and garden, etc.
with me till 4.0. . . . Hearn comes up specially to press me to go.

I urge political difficulty.' On the 5th the doctor called again and said to him: 'To go is a justifiable risk, but you have abundant reason for staying.' The same day he discussed the problem with Canon T. W. E. Drury, and later with Archdeacon J. W. Crozier: 'Both strongly urge going.' The matter was still open until the 10th when he again raised it again tentatively with his wife. In the result, 'I think I must now finally decide against. It seems plain that physically and temperamentally the strain of a move would be altogether too much for her.' *11th:* 'On this day I decline the Primacy. How shall I think of it in later years? It has been the most difficult question I have ever had. I have acted under a constraint I could not resist.'

So on the following day he wrote to the Secretary of the House of Bishops as follows:

I have during the past fortnight examined all the pros and cons that I could put together, and the result of it all is that with all respect and with unfeigned regret I must ask the House of Bishops to allow me to decline their gracious offer of the Archbishopric of Armagh and the Primacy of All Ireland.

Kindly summon Bishops for election of Archbishop and Primate on Wednesday 27th.

In reply to a letter which he wrote to the Archbishop of Canterbury he received the following, dated 21 April:

My dear Archbishop,

I am very grateful to you for letting me know about the reasons why you are not to be the Primate of All Ireland. They do not surprise me: they seem to me very natural—particularly as regards the political Protestantism of the North. I think your position would have been difficult.

On every personal ground I am sorry, but, as I say, I am not surprised. And I admire your self-sacrifice on conscientious grounds.

I only hope a good man may be elected in your place. But I am sorry to hear about Mrs. Gregg's arthritis.

Yours very sincerely.

COSMO CANTUAR:

Strangely, the effect upon Gregg of this letter appears to have been disturbing. It prompted a further soliloquy:

Feeling all right till Cantuar of Ap. 21. Reaction from then onwards to 29th—'Have I made a calamitous mistake?' Sinking of heart—sense of disappointment. I am sure I shall see it more as I saw it previous to decision, as time passes. But at present,

all difficulties seem to be forgotten. I think only of what I lose—
Gen. Synod, R.C.B., presidency. The legitimate climax of a
profnal. life. But these will give way to: The joy of *accepted*
sorrow. 'My choicest wreaths are always wet with tears.' The
practical and satisfying day to day life which remains.
    23rd. An evening of some depression, thinking upon *what* I
refused when I refused Armagh.

On 27 April he records: 'Bishop Day of Ossory elected Primate.
(look back to Mar. 23).' The election had in fact been unanimous.
    Though Gregg and Day had been contemporaries at Cambridge
(in Day's words, 'my partner in many a hard-fought tennis match'),
and though Day after eleven years' service with the Cambridge
Mission to Delhi had, as Vicar of St. Ann's and Professor of
Pastoral Theology in Trinity, been in contact with Gregg in Dublin,
and had then succeeded him in the diocese of Ossory, they had
never been intimate. Gregg shared the admiration of every one for
Day's personal qualities which made him a man so greatly beloved,
but at the same time he mistrusted his judgment in the management of affairs. The day after the election he confesses: 'Suffering
from painful reaction all day. I am beginning to perceive what I
have lost.'
    And on the 28th: 'A fine day physically, ἀλλὰ καρδία μέλαινα
ἔνδον' [a quotation from Pindar].
    For the first two months of his primacy Archbishop Day con-
tinued his episcopal duties in Ossory. (His successor, for a brief
eighteen months, Dean Tichborne of Armagh, was not consecrated
till 24 June, and was himself succeeded in the Armagh deanery by
the Precentor, Thomas James McEndoo.) For this reason the new
Primate was obliged to be absent from the second session of the
General Synod. It opened on 10 May when he delivered his presidential address, and was loyally supported by Gregg who steered
him through the intricacies of procedure. 'Day went off very
quietly.' During his unavoidable absence on the second day Gregg
presided both at the R.C.B. and the Synod. 'During private session,
I asked if it would embarrass any present to pass a Resn. con-
gratulating Douglas Hyde on Presidency. As some 6 demurred,
matter dropped.' On the third day the new Primate again presided.
'The 3 days pass with wonderfully little pain.'
    On 26 August when on holiday in Castletownshend: 'Hear from
R. R. Hartford that Primate is not well—under observation for
recurring sickness.' On the 22nd the Primate returned from his own
holidays at Trearddur Bay in Anglesey to undergo an operation
at a nursing home in Dublin on 4 September. It appeared success-

ful, but on the 17th a second minor operation was performed. On the 20th his doctor called on Archbishop Gregg to say that 'the Primate is dangerously ill, and inclined to wander.' Subsequent bulletins fluctuated between hopes and fears till Sunday the 25th when unconsciousness supervened. It lasted until the following night when the doctor telephoned that all was over. The funeral service was held in St. Patrick's on the 30th and the burial was in St. Canice's, Kilkenny. Once again the funeral oration was given by the Archbishop of Dublin. His diary entry for that day reads: 'Whose turn will it be next? How many men have given funeral address over two Primates, and in one year?' His address is printed in full in R. R. Hartford's biography of Godfrey Day, and it bears witness to the sincerity and sensibility of a mind that could recognize greatness in a character so different from his own, and could pay so glowing a tribute to the possessor of qualities which he knew himself to lack. More concise but no less felicitous in expression is the Foreword which he gave to the biography:

This book is a record not so much of external, as of spiritual, achievement. It is in the realm of the spirit, in the things wrought by prayer and love, that the subject of this Memoir was distinguished.

He lived in a remarkable degree in the lives of others, and many of those whose lives he touched will be glad to know a little more of the manner of life of the man whose impact on their soul they had felt.

Far more effectual and abiding than the skilful use of administrative or intellectual gifts is that vital fruitfulness of influence which is granted to a personality whose chief capacity and joy lie in self-giving and self-spending. Its results, largely intangible, are written not in books and epitaphs, but in human lives quickened and inspired.

What Godfrey Day was cannot be conveyed by any printed or spoken word; but this Memoir, a tribute from one who was admitted to his confidence, will tell and preserve something of what his devoted life meant to those many who rewarded him with their answering love and trust.

Gregg must have known that the question of his succession to the Primacy would again be raised in the House of Bishops, but there is no mention of it in his diary till 17 October when the Bishop of Derry among others was present at a special meeting of the R.C.B.

After meeting Derry speaks to me re Primacy, and says he has been asked by 3 Bps. to stand and he is prepared to do so. What is my attitude? Tell him I do not personally look beyond Dublin, but if wanted will consider matter v. seriously.

19th.—Bp. Tichborne says that the majority of Bps. wish for me.

On this day, 19 October, to his great satisfaction his old friend R. T. Hearn (since 1934 Archdeacon of Cork) was elected Bishop of the Diocese nearly unanimously.

The election for the Primacy was delayed by the necessity of appointing an *ad interim* Bishop of Armagh. The redoubtable Dean of Derry, R. G. S. King, was at first elected, and on his refusal Archdeacon Crozier, who requested time to consider it. He was however himself elected Bishop of Tuam on 23 November; and it was not until 13 December that a dignitary could be found to fill this temporary office in the person of Canon Hughes, of St. Patrick's Cathedral.

Two days later the Bishops met to elect their Primate.

15 Dec. 12.0 Bps. meet a/c Primacy. Hughes there, but not Crozier, Bp. elect of Tuam.

I am elected PRIMATE, the 2nd time, by 7, 3, 1. Will accept when Court Case ends.

This case concerned the final stage of the 'Crucifix-Faculty' judgment in St. John's Sandymount, and it was given on 29 December: 'I pronounce that no order is made. Each side pays its own costs.' On the 31st he signed the Court orders of Judgment, and the same day wrote in his diary: 'Cease to be Abp. of Dublin.' He was succeeded in that office on 7 February 1939 by Arthur William Barton, Bishop of Kilmore (who was himself replaced automatically by the temporary Bishop of Armagh), one who as pastor, bishop and archbishop, was a man universally beloved. In the words of Dr. G. O. Simms, now his successor in the See of Dublin: 'His wide human sympathies, his outstanding pastoral gifts, his warm and winning eloquence as a preacher, his genial unaffected approach to men and affairs, commended the life of the Church to many in Ireland and abroad who were not of his communion.'

There is no further note in the Archbishop's diary to account for the reversal of his decision respecting the removal to Armagh. Two reasons are sufficient to explain it. The first is the certainty of his wife's agreement that, the sacrifice having been once made and the call having been repeated, it was 'something that was meant to be,' as well as that of the doctor's repeated assurance that the risk was justifiable. The second is the fact that their elder daughter had recently returned home from Malaya and was able to relieve her parents of all effort by superintending the removal of the whole household herself.

PART THREE

ARCHBISHOP OF ARMAGH

CHAPTER XIII

'THE CHURCHMAN'S BISHOP'

THE THEME OF HIS SERMON on his enthronement was the historic continuity of the Archbishops of Armagh since St. Patrick.

There had been a Bishop of Armagh at the end of that half century whose preceding years had seen the deaths of St. Ambrose, St. Chrysostom, St. Augustine and St. Jerome. . . . This continuity with the past is an awe-inspiring thing. . . . This great ceremony which has spoken to us all of historic continuity, should speak to me of humility. It tells me of the greatness of the trust and the unimportance of the individual.

Of the three successive Primates, d'Arcy with his large philosophical outlook and scientific interests had been called 'The Layman's Bishop'; Day with his sanctified humanity and touch of mysticism was 'Everybody's Bishop'; Gregg with his emphasis on doctrinal orthodoxy and ecclesiastical discipline became known as 'The Churchman's Bishop.' But there was another and more personal reason for this. No one in his office was ever a more loyal friend to his clergy. All felt that they knew exactly where they were with him; that if he said a thing he meant it; that if he made a promise he would keep it; that he had their individual welfare, both spiritual and material, on his mind and heart. And as he gave the clergy his loyalty he won theirs. Sometimes one or another of them, guilty of some fault of commission or omission, deserved and would receive a reprimand. He used to confess in private to his family; 'If only I could lose my temper with them it would help; but I can't!' Nevertheless his disapproval was probably more effective by an awesome silence or a mordant comment than it would have been by any display of anger.

It was said of him by some wit: 'He casteth forth his ice like morsels: who is able to abide his frost?'

But the essential tenderness of his nature was a quality known to few. His sympathy for suffering or trouble or distress of any kind was acute, though his natural reticence and restraint imposed a ban on sentiment.

Once one of his junior clergy came to see him by appointment in great distress. His wife's illness had necessitated on medical advice a year's absence from Ireland. So he came to offer his

225

P

resignation, but added a halting request that perhaps some niche in the diocese might be open to him when they returned. 'It is difficult to say which of the two of us was the more deeply moved. He gave me his promise at once about coming back, and after my interview was over he came out with me and stood with me for awhile on the Palace steps, his arm over my shoulder, not able to speak. I loved the man. I worshipped him this side of idolatry.' There are others, especially among the junior clergy or any one in sorrow, who would say the same.

A priest for some time on the Staff of St. George's Cathedral, Cape Town, Ronald McFadden, was ordained by the Archbishop in Armagh in 1954.

I remember vividly the interview on the eve of the day he made me a deacon. He stood all the time—about an hour—behind his desk, while I sat in a chair in front of him. On the desk before him lay a piece of paper, yellow with age, on which were ten headings; and three sermons I had written in College. In one of them I had quoted from 'The Hound of Heaven' somewhat extensively; he pointed out that such quotations were inadvisable, as most congregations could not on first hearing grasp their implication; he then drew out of one of his rows of bookshelves the *Poems of Francis Thompson* and began reading, to clarify what he meant. He became quite carried away as he read quite a part of the poem. Before I knelt for his blessing he pointed out how often in my ministry I would have to take a stand for what I knew to be right, in the face of opposition, at a vestry meeting or with an individual, and ended, 'Always speak the truth in love,' repeating the words twice.

At my ordination to the priesthood he had forgotten the inscribed Bible, and asked me whether I could perhaps come one day to the Palace and get it. But I was going immediately on a tour on the Continent on my motor-cycle with a friend. I told him so, and for how long. He said, 'I will write to you on your return.' He seemed most interested in my holiday and suggested places and things I should see, and even some wines in France that I should taste! Sure enough, soon after I got back, came a letter asking me to tea at the Palace and to bring any photographs I had taken. I spent a very pleasant hour with him and Mrs. Gregg; he took a great interest in all I had to say and in the photographs. None of the places were unfamiliar to him. He gave me the inscribed Bible. At the door I asked him not to come out, but he wanted to see the cycle on which I had done the trip. (I had parked it well out of sight.) He was interested to know why I preferred a motor-cycle to a scooter. He always made one feel that one's opinions mattered and were of use.

I was always perfectly at ease with him, as I have not always been with much smaller persons. In his company I always felt that even I mattered!

When I thought of coming out to South Africa my rector, Canon Cooke, spoke to the Archbishop and asked him if he would have a chat with me about it. He gladly consented, but added, 'Of course, I won't act God for any man.' He was much feebler than that day five years before. He lay on a couch to rest his leg which gave him considerable pain, and asked me to sit beside him on a chair on his right side where he could hear better. I was amazed at his grasp of affairs in South Africa. He did not try to influence me at all. He did stress the mental strain of living in a crisis-country, and thought it unlikely that I would return to the life of the Church of Ireland. And he said that the Armagh diocese would shortly be opening out for young men like myself. However, when he saw that my mind was set upon it, he wished me well and gave me his blessing; and a few days later wrote: 'I have written to the Archbishop of Cape Town. I was able to tell him that I lived in the same house with Jan C. Smuts. We were both freshmen 1891–2.'

I can truly say that I have never loved a man so much, and never came away from the Palace without longing to serve Christ more faithfully.

I can recall amusing incidents caused by his fussiness about little things or by his original wit. Before a Confirmation Service his asking for his chimere and, there ensuing a pause, his adding in a rather irritated tone, 'It's the big black thing!' And in response to a request from my rector for permission to broadcasts from St. Anne's: 'I don't like broadcasts; however, they are, I suppose, an ordinance of man to be endured for the Lord's sake.' And his making towards the hall where soup and coffee were being served after a Diocesan synod: 'Is this where the wild asses quench their thirst?'

The Revd. W. J. McCappin writes from Belfast in similar terms:

I was ordained by the Archbishop for the Parish of Armagh, and from the very beginning found him a kindly and humane person, and not at all the Marble Arch of fame and legend. I was the only ordinand and was bidden to spend the few days prior to Ordination at the Palace. I still remember the devastating experience of sitting opposite the Archbishop while he delivered his ordination lectures to me across the vast desk in his study. I marvelled that he was prepared to give up so much time in his very full life to one who was about to become the most junior cleric in his diocese.

During the time that I was serving as an army chaplain in

Europe and the Far East I had a letter from the Archbishop about every six months. I was still part of his care and concern.

This was manifest again after demobilization when the Archbishop wrote him a line of welcome back and encouraged him to apply for nomination to a parish in the Armagh diocese then vacant. But, through a misunderstanding on the part of the nominators, this fell through and he accepted another offer. Dr. Gregg wrote that he was 'very glad that, things being as they are, you have decided to go to Ardoyne. It is a sphere of work that will exact from you all you have to give, and it will give you something back. . . . I hope you will be very happy in your busy city life.' Later he wrote an enquiry to Mr. McCappin about a book which he had lent him (which had been duly returned), and upon its discovery wrote a letter 'which is but another example of his wonderful courtesy and humility.'

My dear McCappin,
    I am very sorry for the trouble you have had over the Congreve book, and still more sorry that I did not write immediately when it came to light in an unexpected place a few days ago. I apologize for its having slipped my mind, and for not having destroyed the original slip, recording that I had lent the book, on its return. . . .

It was due not only to his temperamental reticence and reserve, but also to a deeper quality of character, namely personal humility and reverence for the conscience of others, that he would never intrude into what he conceived to be another man's sacredly private concerns, even when asked to do so. For this reason he shrank from proffering 'ghostly counsel.' There was no trace of the sacerdotalist in him. He would never, as he put it, 'act God for any man.' An instance of this, and also of his sound judgment as a mediator in practical affairs, is afforded by the Bishop of Down.

My election to the See of Kilmore, Elphin and Ardagh, was such a surprise—not to say shock to me—that I went at once to see the Archbishop and to tell him that I did not feel called to the Episcopate. He replied: 'But the Diocese has called you. GOD has called you.' I then asked him for advice. The advice which he gave me was by no means what I expected, but it was nothing if not practical. 'You should not undertake more than two special duties on any Sunday. It is so easy to be physically present and spiritually absent.' (I cannot claim to have followed what, I am sure, was excellent counsel. Few Bishops can hope to limit their Sunday ministrations, other than Holy Communion, to this wise measure. It is so much easier to do many things poorly.) His next advice was that I should steep myself in the Regulations of the Book of Common Prayer and the Constitution of the Church of Ireland!

On the retirement of Bishop Kerr in 1955 I was translated to Down and Dromore. In 1956, on the retirement of Bishop King-Irwin who had formerly ruled the United Diocese of Down, Connor and Dromore, the Dean of Belfast, Cyril Elliott, succeeded to the Bishopric of Connor. A curious situation then arose. By an act of the General Synod promoted by Bishop King-Irwin in 1952, Lisburn Parish Church had been made the Cathedral Church of the Diocese of Connor. But St. Anne's Cathedral in Belfast is territorially in the Connor Diocese. The question then arose: in which Cathedral was the newly appointed Bishop of Connor to be enthroned? In this dilemma both Bishops went together to Armagh to seek a ruling from the Archbishop. He gave it without hesitation and it was immediately accepted by both of us. The Diocesan Cathedral of Down and Dromore, and the Diocesan Cathedral of Lisburn, be regarded as respectively the centres for the Enthronement of the Bishops of the two Sees.

§

He always encouraged 'sound learning' wherever found. An example is provided by the Revd. F. R. Bolton, then a clergyman in the Norwich diocese, who later came over to Ireland to complete and publish his book *The Caroline Tradition in the Church of Ireland*, and is now Dean of Leighlin. In sending the Archbishop's three letters he writes:

With the first Dr. Gregg enclosed a transcript, in his own hand, of Peter Browne's eucharistic devotions for 'my reading and kind return.'

The second is in answer to my letter returning the transcript and telling him of my interest in the Church of Ireland, and of my attempt to write a book with special reference to the Caroline form of consecrating Churches.

The third is about an article on Bishop Mant in the *Church of Ireland Gazette*.

I send them as illustrating not only Dr. Gregg's keen interest in the history of his own Church, but also the encouragement he gave to a person entirely unknown to him and in another part of the Anglican Communion. At the time I had misgivings about continuing with my book. I doubted whether a member of the Church of England should presume to write about a sister Church. But the Archbishop's second letter encouraged me to go on.

Oct. 31, 1947.

Dear Sir,

Your note on Bishop Wilson's *Short and Plain Instruction* has interested me greatly, and I venture to enclose for your reading and kind return the Private Eucharistic Devotions taken from a MS. volume now in Cork Cathedral written by Peter Browne. They seem to belong to the same tradition as the ones you quote on p. 382 of *Theology*.

I wonder if you know of *The Exemplary Life etc. of James Bonnell, Accomptant General* (who died 1699) by Wm. Hamilton. It is a book which is referred to at least three times by Mr. Keble in his volume of *Spiritual Letters*—the 3rd edn. which I have was published in 1707. It is a remarkable picture of a Churchman's religion in Dublin in the first half of Bp. Wilson's lifetime.

Sincerely yours,

JOHN ARMAGH

Nov. 12, 1947.

Dear Mr. Bolton,

I have to thank you for your letter of Nov. 3 in reply to mine. The references to James Bonnell's Life in Mr. Keble's *Letters of Spiritual Counsel* are pp. 3, 68, 155.

I have only a slight knowledge of the Irish Consecration Forms of 1666, and still less of their authorship.

I know well and am greatly impressed by the Form in Use in the early eighteenth century, with its curious use of *Lavatory* and *Dormitory* for κοιμητήριον (not used there for the first time),[1] and its delightful language regarding the ministerial altar and the earthly imitation of the eternal Sacrifice. I am sorry more use was not made of the latter form, when our present Form was drawn up.

I am glad you are interesting yourself in Irish Church History. With our independent episcopal succession, our Canons of 1634 including that remarkable one on the call to confession, and such names as Ussher, Bramhall, J. Taylor, Wilson, King, Bonnell, Jebb, Alexander Knox and Wm. Palmer (ordd. deacon for Limerick), our little Church has something to give as well as to receive. But it is hard to overcome the prejudice aroused by the austerity of our ritual canons of 1870—and yet, they do but reflect the widespread feeling existing in England as well as here, at the moment when we were disestablished and compelled to set our affairs in order, regarding the unregulated developments then taking place. A worse hour for ecclesiastical reorganization could hardly have been chosen.

Sincerely yours,

JOHN ARMAGH

[1] Dean Bolton observes: Jeremy Taylor, in his Funeral Sermon on Bramhall (VIII, 402), uses the word in this sense: 'Charnel-houses are but κοιμητήρια, cemeteries or sleeping-places.'

Feb. 12, 1949.
Dear Mr. Bolton,
   This is just a line to say that I have been reading your 'Bishop Mant' in the *C.I. Gazette* with much interest. I am very glad you are doing something to show what a very solid Church idea existed here during the 18th and early 19th centuries—going back even to James Bonnell, who must have learnt *his* religion in Ireland. It is of course not to be denied that a great many good Irish Bps. (side by side with at least as many bad ones!) were sent over from England, e.g. Bramhall and Jeremy Taylor and later, Mant—but they found a Church here and were not merely foreign bodies.

Sincerely yours,
JOHN ARMAGH

   Look out for a book of some quality by H. R. McAdoo, *The Structure of Caroline Moral Theology.*

The postscript in the last letter has reference to a work which earned for its author the rare distinction of a Doctorate in Divinity in the University of Dublin. He was then one of the younger clergy in the Southern Province of whom the Archbishop had taken note, and to whom he was now writing on another matter: namely the vexatious possibility of having to revise parts of the Irish Prayer Book in view of the Republic's renunciation of allegiance to the British Sovereign.

Private
20 Dec. 1949
Dear Dr. McAdoo,
   I am engaged with a small sub-Committee of the Gen. Synod in trying to find a solution of the problem of (so-called) State Prayers for Eire. There seem to be very curious differences of opinion on the subject of how much (if any) space, or rather time, should be occupied with reference to King George.
   I should be glad if you—without going into any details—would kindly give me a rough notion of how things stand at your end of Co. Cork. Does any one mind about it at all? are any of your young people fervently republican? is there much difference of opinion on the subject between the different social strata?

Yours sincerely,
JOHN ARMAGH

It may be added that when he found (to his secret dismay) that not a few of the rising generation were 'fervently republican' and that therefore changes in the suffrages must be made, he rejected the proposal of 'O Lord, save the State' as being too abstract and impersonal, and insisted on substituting 'O Lord, guide and defend our Rulers.'

When a short time later Dr. McAdoo, now Bishop of Ossory, was elected to the Deanery of Cork, the Archbishop wrote him an impromptu letter of congratulation. It shows his continuing interest in and affection for St. Fin Barre's Cathedral.

15 November 1952
Dear Dean-elect,

I was reminded that I ought to write you a line of warm congratulation, when last night I was reading the Bishop of Exeter's words on his notice of your book in *J. Theol. Studies* 199/200, p. 245, 'By its publication C. of I. has put the whole Anglican Commn. in its debt.' Such words from so competent a writer must have gratified you.

You are indeed happy to be going to serve at St. Fin Barre's. For hereditary as well as for personal reasons . . . I love the Cathedral—some of the happiest associations of my life are with it.

Your position as Dean offers you a great opportunity for all kinds of usefulness and influence—*quam Spartam nactus es, hanc exorna.*[2] But I hope the busy life in the parish will not hinder your writing on Anglican Moral Theology.

With all good wishes,
Very truly yours,
JOHN ARMAGH

Canon Bothwell recalls his keen interest in the proceedings of the Armagh Clerical Union:

He regularly attended the afternoon sessions. He would make his way to a chair by the fire behind the President. There he would promptly close his eyes and go to sleep. Towards the end of the discussion the President would look round and say, 'Would your Grace like to say anything?' Then he would rise slowly and in a short speech would clarify and summarize all that had previously been said. This habit of sleeping and waking up at the psychological moment was sometimes disconcerting. I remember the Dean telling me of an occasion when the last hymn was drawing to a close in the Cathedral and the Archbishop was asleep in his throne. The Dean in the Sanctuary was wondering whether he should pronounce the benediction. But the Archbishop woke up just in time to do so.

---

[2] SPARTA. In Greek form, Cicero, in allusion to Euripides, has the word twice proverbially: Σπάρταν ἔλαχες, ταύταν κόσμει—i.e. Sparta is your country, make the most of it. Cic. Att. 4, 6, 2; cf. id. ib. 1, 20, 3 (*Lewis and Short*).

This proneness to instantaneous slumber, in which however some part of his mind was fully conscious of what was going on, was a characteristic well known to his clergy; to others it was a matter for surprise. Lady Granville (sister of the Queen Mother), whose husband Lord Granville was Governor of Northern Ireland 1945–51, wrote in a letter to Mrs. Wilson after the Archbishop's death:

> I met him so seldom, and only on official occasions, and always wished I could have known him better, for he inspired one with real affection and a joy in his dry sense of humour.
>
> One of the first times I met him was at a big University Celebration dinner, when he was seated beside me, and at which many speeches were made—supposed to be limited to a few minutes each. However when one of the Professors rose to speak the Archbishop sighed, sat back and went fast asleep. The time signal went, but the speech went on. The Archbishop suddenly opened his eyes, and looking at me with a twinkle murmured, 'I think I have another ten minutes,' and relapsed into sleep again. His judgment was absolutely correct.

Canon Bothwell continues:

> It is a pity that he did not publish more. His lectures on 'The Creeds and Authority' are a masterpiece. And his commentary on the Book of Wisdom in the Cambridge Bible shows what he might have done in Biblical criticism. His knowledge of the Psalms was as intimate. They were, he said, the Bible of our Lord. 'In the prophets we read what God has said to men; in the Psalms what men have said to God.' He recommended us to read them in the Greek version; and he pointed out to me that in the Hebrew, curiously enough, the word for *faith* occurs but once.
>
> St. John's Gospel was another of his favourite books; and he stresses the fact that it is more concerned with the revelation of the Father than of the Son. I think that his own mysticism was always more Theocentric than Christocentric.

Canon Bothwell's observations are confirmed by an article of Dr. Gregg's in the *Expository Times*, August 1951, entitled 'The Old Testament Approach to Religion.'

> The Fourth Gospel is commonly treated as that Gospel which more than the others witnesses to the Divinity of Christ. But I think its purpose is primarily to witness to what the Father is, as seen in and through the Son. 'He that hath seen me hath seen the Father.' And I am reminded of the words of a well-known mystical writer who passed from our midst only two or

three years ago.[3] 'You see,' she writes, 'I came to Christ through God, whereas lots of people come to God through Christ. But I can't show them how to do that—all I know about is the reverse route.' Yes, but what she calls the reverse route, the approach to Christ through God, is the historic Christian order of approach. The disciples learnt of God first, and then learnt more fully of Him in Christ. . . .

Belief in God—belief in the One living and self-revealing God—was possible for many years before ever Christ appeared, and is the working faith of the pious Jew to-day. And, as witness to that quite solid fact, we possess this practical consideration, namely, that with all our greater knowledge of God that has come to us in Christ, the Christian Church has never outgrown its use of the Psalter, the hymn-book of post-Exilic Judaism, as its manual of public as well as private devotion.

One of his sincerest and most affectionate admirers, from ordination to consecration, whose tribute has been quoted in these pages, writes:

One could not be blind to faults, however. His humour was not infrequently biting and to some people must have seemed rather cruel.

I think he took unnecessary dislikes. He may for example have appreciated old . . . 's excellent gifts, but he never concealed his feeling that the man bored him to distraction! And he intensely disliked men who appeared to him to be common. In fact quite honestly it must be admitted that he was rather a snob! Whether socially or intellectually, he tended to look down his nose at lesser mortals.

I think his inability to mix with his fellow-men was a real handicap. It was sheer inability and drove him into a kind of splendid isolation. He confided to me once how much he envied Bishop Godfrey Day's gift of being able to help people. He apparently longed to have Day's approachability. (I made bold to say how much we would appreciate a book giving the gist of his pastoral ministry. He said rather sadly, 'Impossible. So many letters to write each day. And then, the running of a large Diocese.') That is one of the major impressions I had about him —that he was a very *lonely* man. But his intellectual resources prevented him from feeling his loneliness. What was it? Shyness? self-centredness? self-sufficiency? He was certainly no man-pleaser. Did he err on the opposite side?

At my pre-Consecration I was struck by two remarks. One concerned the frustrations one had to endure as a Bishop. Situations

[3] Simone Weil.

arose in which one was held up from bringing in adjustments which were obviously right and one had to leave them aside. And then quite suddenly in time the whole thing came right. Hidden forces were at work. He used the analogy of the darkness of the tomb suddenly illuminated by the Light of the Resurrection.

The other point was the joy he had found in being able to alleviate harsh circumstances from time to time amongst his clergy, or to reward merit through resources at his disposal.

This time I felt the serenity of a real saintliness about him. The long years had brought a gentleness and certainty of touch that were enormously helpful. There were always hidden depths of tenderness and humanity in the man, and a *longing to help*. The *simplicity* of his faith was the central factor all through. He was an example of the practice of daily living in the sight of God.

But though he had a message to the converted and could confirm their faith, he had none wherewith to convince the honest doubter or 'bring back the wandering to the fold.' Two examples will suffice for illustration.

The first concerns a lady who had already made a great name in the realm of ecclesiastical art, and who had for many years found in Anglo-Catholicism her spiritual home and had worshipped in St. John's, Sandymount. In the course of years however this failed to satisfy her religious sense and after a long period of inner struggle she found satisfaction for her personal need in Roman Catholicism. During many months of conflict and indecision she sought the help and counsel of her Archbishop, and though it cannot but be that a person of her intelligence, sincerity, and sensibility found in him a sympathetic listener, it is equally certain that he was constitutionally incapable of understanding her difficulty. Only one letter of their correspondence survives: it was her last to him, after his elevation to Armagh.

Dower House, Marlay,
Rathfarnham

February 12th
Your Grace,

It was kind of you to send me the Intercession paper and I shall use it. I hope you are pleased with the new appointment in Dublin; also that you will be happy in Armagh. We shall all remember with thankfulness your time here, and I should like again to thank you for your great kindness to me personally during these last 3 years. I have often wished that I could dismiss the doubt and question which has troubled me for so long now, and think of it as mere speculation, but I cannot in truth do so. Perhaps I am mistaken; if so I pray that I may be given light to realize my mistake. If I were to consider my own feelings and affections only, I should be glad to find I was mistaken, for the thought of what the action which I shall probably have to take before long, will cost, often overwhelms me with sorrow; yet I know this bitterness and sadness is wrong, and springs from a lack of trust. I can only pray at present for a right judgment. It seems as though whether I am meant to go on or remain is really not my choice.

With best wishes and thanks,

Yours very sincerely,

EVIE HONE

Late in the year 1950 the Archbishop, concerned by the increasing number of lapsed in the churches, caused to be printed and widely disseminated a short paper which he had written on 'Non-Churchgoing.' Though simply phrased and reasonably argued it cannot be called an inspiring document. A week later he received a long letter from a Dublin lady, whose husband (a peer) had for years acted as the Archbishop's assessor at Synods, informing him that she had read it and promptly torn it up. She had in youth been a keen church-worker but had grown out of it as from a 'nursery,' having found that the complexity of Christian theology was a hindrance rather than help to her real faith which defied doctrinal definition. She believed that she spoke for very many who were no longer church-goers. Not that she had completely lost interest in the church; when in London she often went to St. Martin's in the Fields, and never missed a chance of hearing Dr. Matthews preach —'a wise and understanding man.'

There are three letters from this lady, and of one of his replies the Archbishop kept a copy which is as follows:

Thank you for your letter. May I write these few words in reply? I think you have thrown over the basal realities of the Christian faith too readily. When you remember that the faith in God-made-man changed the faith of Europe, and that our outlook even to-day is conditioned by its principles—when you admit your veneration of Christ, and yet forget the tremendous dilemma that the man who made those claims is either God or else an impostor—when you think that it is only because of what He taught about God that God is for you a Being of truth, justice, love and beauty—is it not for you to re-think the rejection of the Incarnation and the truths for which the N.T. stands, and ask if you have not hastily thrown away too much?

I can well understand the stubborn intellectual integrity which will not profess to believe what it does not believe, but are the grounds on which you have rejected the belief that God has revealed Himself in Jesus Christ—are they really solid grounds? When so serious a thing as our life is in question, and when there presents Himself to us so gracious a figure as Jesus Christ, claiming to reveal God to us and to show us the way to God, does not mere seriousness require us to face the issue?

You write that you appreciate the Dean of St. Paul's. Will you let me lend you a book of essays, edited by him, on the Christian Faith? I should be very glad if you would let me lend it to you.

The lady, having already thanked him for his kind forbearance, wrote again:

Again I must thank you for your letter. It was good of you to suggest sending me the book, but I think I can get it, so don't bother—thanking you all the same.

I must have expressed myself very badly. I believe Jesus Christ is a revelation of God to man; but I cannot believe in the Immaculate Conception, the Resurrection, and the Atonement. I feel He is one of many revelations of God to man, and I think my point of view is that of many Protestants who don't go to Church. I wonder whether you would read a book called *The Magic People* by Arland Ussher. At the end of it he calls himself a Christian. I think I am the same sort of Christian as that; perhaps you would not call that being a Christian at all. I believe God is beauty, truth, mercy, justice, and that God reveals himself in many different ways; in music, art in great and noble human beings, and in one unique moral genius, Jesus Christ.

Therewith the correspondence appears to have ended.

§

On 11 December 1939 there appeared in the *Belfast Telegraph* an account of a sermon preached in the Presbyterian Church in Newcastle, Co. Down, by the minister the Revd. A. C. Anderson, B.D., challenging certain claims made by Archbishop Gregg in St. Mary Magdalen's, Belfast, the previous Sunday. He asked for historic evidence for the claim which Archbishop Gregg made for the Church of Ireland of unbroken continuity with the ancient Celtic Church, and for the assertion in respect of Holy Orders: 'We trace the stream of succession back to Christ in the upper room.' Where, he asked, is the historic evidence for either of these statements? He further criticized the statement that 'since the New

Testament was the product of the Early Church, it must be understood in the light of the Church's teaching.' This was equivalent to the familiar Roman assertion that tradition was of equal value with Scripture. He ended: 'At a time when the world needs Christian action, it is deplorable that a responsible Church leader should engage in a childish renewal of that dispute as to which should be greatest, that the Lord himself had rebuked.'

The Archbishop kept a press-cutting reporting this sermon, but made no reply to it.

§

Though distant and reserved with his brethren on the episcopal bench (Hearn excepted) and with the clergy generally, he was more inclined to unbend in the company of laymen and of women, and, in some cases, of the junior clergy. He responded, perhaps too ingenuously, to two different lines of approach: frankness and flattery. When these were conjoined his response could be warm. In later years, in Armagh, he became more easily accessible than formerly. But he was not by nature affectionate. His friendship was not lightly given; there were no more than three in his life who won it: Bishop Hearn was one, Archdeacon Sullivan another, and with both of them his associations dated back to early days in Cork. The third was of the younger generation, and one of whom it may be said that he regarded him almost as another son. This was Richard Randall Hartford, a brilliant scholar of Trinity, whose early appointment as Archbishop King's Professor of Divinity was due very largely to Dr. Gregg's patronage, and whose succession years afterwards to the Regius Professorship was solely due to him.

Dr. Hartford was close to the Archbishop both personally and officially, since he served under his chairmanship as secretary or as a member on several committees and was much in his counsels and confidence; the contributions in this regard which he had promised to this book would have been important and enlightening. Death, untimely and unexpected, has deprived the Church of Ireland of his unique services as its delegate at Oecumenical Conferences and in many other ways, and these pages of much that would have been of value. During his last few days in hospital, however, he contrived to commit to paper some personal reminiscences as well as some notes which he intended to explicate later in conversation. Lacking this verbal interpretation the notes are unfortunately now valueless; the memories (though disconnected and incomplete) are here transcribed:

I first saw him, and heard him, in the summer of 1916 when he preached in Abbeyleix. He was the new Bishop of our diocese, and I vividly recall his striking appearance, raven black hair, tall and young and vigorous, and commanding. The following year I went to school at Kilkenny College and so I heard and saw him often. We boys vied with each other in imitating his unusual voice, but we had for him unbounded respect and admiration. Incidentally he disliked mimicry of any kind and I remember years later, when I knew him well, talking with him about it. 'A very dangerous gift,' he called it. 'No,' I said, greatly daring, 'you have to distinguish between mimicry and burlesque. You can only successfully mimic people whom you hold in esteem, whereas you burlesque those whom you do not hold in esteem.' He smiled and said, 'Well, you have made a point, and in any case it is a comforting doctrine!'

He confirmed and ordained me and I remember clearly the practical wisdom of his advice to us before Ordination. From my very first contacts with him I found him easy to talk to—not an experience shared by all. He encouraged me to talk frankly and he talked frankly to me. Indeed, one of his axioms of conduct was to respect the individuality of every person with whom he had to do, and he consistently lived up to Kant's second form of the Categorical Imperative: 'So act as to treat humanity, whether in thine own person or that of another, as an end withal and never as a means only.'

He appeared to many, even to the end, to be aloof, austere, even forbidding. The truth was that he was a shy man with a deep, almost inquisitive, interest in people. Perhaps too with a curious distrust of his fellowmen, for he once said to me, 'I always rate a man who is a friend as one who might become an enemy.' It was of course, partly, his way of saying, 'Don't be over-trustful' (and looking back I wish I had, in one or two cases, taken his advice). I think he had few intimate friends, but to them he was unswervingly loyal. He disliked easy familiarity and would not pander to the modern fashion of calling people by their Christian names. 'I wish he'd call me Godfrey,' said his saintly predecessor in the Primacy. They had been friends at Cambridge and retained a life-long respect for one another. But Archbishop Gregg was not a man to tamper with the proprieties. And he was truthful and accurate almost to a fault. 'I was glad,' he wrote to Archbishop Day, 'to be able to officiate at the funeral of my old acquaintance, the Bishop of ———.' 'He might have said friend' (said Day), 'but he couldn't have.' But though he didn't bandy about Christian names he admired people who were generally thus known. 'It shows,' he told me once, 'that they *count* in the estimation of many people.' I was honoured by his confidence and friendship, and yet the formality of his letters was invariable—till towards the end, when he would write, 'My dear R.P.D.'

I suppose people often thought him over-conscious of his dignity and he did sometimes speak and act in a way that suggested this. Once when a famous cricketer was visiting Dublin the Archbishop was somewhat unwisely asked, 'Would your Grace care to be introduced to Jack Hobbs?' 'No,' he replied tartly, 'I do not like meeting celebrities.' Godfrey Day was present and was asked the same question. He replied with enthusiasm, 'I'd love to. I have wanted to meet him for a long time.' But Archbishop Gregg was basically kind, and he often wrapped up his rebukes in a kindly sally. 'O your Grace,' a lady once gushed, 'I'm sure you don't remember *me*?' 'Is there any particular reason why I should?' was the rejoinder, with a disarming smile.

It has been said of him that he had great wit but little humour. I think there is truth there. Story after story can be told of his quick repartee. Once at the Standing Committee of the R.C.B. we were discussing nominations for the Youth Committee of the Irish Churches. Nine names had been proposed for eight places and none of us cared to suggest the name for exclusion. There was a long silence. It was broken by the Archbishop with the remark, in slightly bored tones, 'Well, gentlemen, which kitten shall we drown?'

As an example of his inquisitiveness and interest in people. At a garden party in the U.S.A. Embassy once, he said to me: 'Who was the lady to whom you were speaking just now?' 'I'm afraid I don't know.' 'But I saw you having an *animated* conversation with her.' 'Yes, but I didn't give myself away.' 'But, then, tell me how you do it?' 'Well, as a curate I learned to ask how old is the baby when I had forgotten the sex.' 'No,' he said, 'you should ask, how old is *baby*?—leave out the article and the enquiry becomes much warmer.'

He won the hearts of hundreds by his deep and sincere sympathy for sorrow and suffering. When I lost with startling suddenness a well-loved sister he wrote a letter which moved me deeply, bidding me to remember that there is such a thing as 'the joy of an accepted sorrow.' And when a little later he was himself stricken with grief at the sudden loss of his second son, I wrote, and by return received a reply: 'Claude was a very dear son and his mother and I had great hopes for him. But God is good and the Hope is with us still.' And when his elder son John lost his life in the Second World War he wrote: 'They say that it is unnatural for a father to follow a son to the grave, and I am following two.'

To his intimates he gave himself generously and when he relaxed in their company all the sweetness of his nature came out and, sometimes too, the most forthright and even robust speech. 'Here,' he said to me once, 'is this paper sent to me by X, and I believe he has sent it to you. Will you tell me, is there anything in it at all?' I replied that the old saying, 'what is true in it is not new and what is new in it is not true,' about fitted the case. 'Well, there you are!' he said with an impatient gesture; 'and he is going round crowing about it like an old cock on a dung-hill!'

He had always been a merciful man in his dealings with erring men and women. But this became more marked as the years went by. He told me once that it was only in his middle years that he found out that people did wrong things more because of weakness than because of a perverted love of wickedness.

He admired the philosophical mind, yet was distrustful of it. He was suspicious for example of what he called d'Arcy's 'luminous mind.' 'Arguing from infinite premisses is perilous logic.' The regular, the conventional, the time-honoured observances—these were all part of his profession, and he only slowly accepted new ideas. 'We should not tamely surrender all that our long history has taught us.'

He greatly admired what he called Day's 'redeeming work.' Once they were together in private conversation with a Presbyterian minister who said in the course of it, 'But you do not recognize our Orders.' Day said instantly, 'Of course we do.' Gregg, who would have said 'We do not,' said nothing; and though he disagreed with Day was grateful for his impulsive intervention. 'One could not be cross with him as one would with others.'

As as example of his temperamental distrust. He found it difficult to think that if any one was spontaneously kind to him there was no ulterior motive behind it. 'And yet he doesn't *want* anything from me' he would say in a surprised tone. He was frightened of being accosted by ladies at the end of a public meeting. 'That lady with the pink hat in the front row—protect me at the end!' And also of being found forgetful. 'Quick please —in capitals—the name of the speaker!'

He once told me that in early life he had had a passion for preaching, but that it passed off when he became increasingly immersed in administration.

'Are you not frightened when set in the midst of a great railway station in the United States—what tips to give, etcetera?'

It has been said that he was a poor judge of men. This is not so. It was part of his generous yet shy appraisal of human nature to think the best, and he often softened the harsh judgments of others with one that was more balanced. Once I thought I had been unfairly attacked by a colleague and in his presence. 'It was caddish,' I said to him afterwards. 'Well,' he said, 'it certainly wasn't fraternal.'

Q

He was above all things a just man. 'The fairest-minded man that ever sat in this Synod,' said a Northern Protestant angered by the suggestion that he had been dictatorial in his judgment of a certain issue in the General Synod. But of course he was a master of assemblies. I doubt if any Synod over which he presided ever made a decision which he didn't want it to make. He quickly sensed the mind of an assembly and when he spoke his mind it was always at the end of a debate, after allowing every point of view to be aired. He could lead in another direction when he thought that the deepest interests of the Church were at stake. 'Holding the position that I do, not by your votes, I deem it my duty to warn you that I cannot approve of this,' he once said at a School Board meeting. 'There are,' said the late Dr. T. G. Moorhead, 'very few leaders in the world. Part of what is called leadership is merely a summing up of the view of the majority. But leadership means getting people to accept what you know to be right. And I think I have only known one leader in the true sense of the word and that was Archbishop Gregg.'

But together with his capacity for leadership there went always an exquisite blend of courtesy and consideration—and with this a startling humility. Many years ago when I was a very young chaplain at Trinity and was laid aside by a sudden illness, he came immediately to see me; it was his unvarying custom with sick clergymen. 'There must be many things that you have had to lay aside. Would you not let me help you in some way?' I told him of a student slowly dying in hospital whom I visited regularly and how much I regretted the temporary suspension of such visits. The Archbishop asked me, might he go to see him? He did, several times, and to the great comfort of the dying student.

As a speaker, whatever the occasion, he always prepared what he had to say. Extempore speaking frightened him. At a gathering of Anglican delegates in Edinburgh in 1937 he was suddenly called upon to speak. Of course he did it to perfection, but he showed his dislike at being called on suddenly all the same.

I spoke of his humility. This was never more apparent than in his refusal of the Primacy early in 1938. He asked some of his friends their advice and I was one whom he honoured. He was terribly and uncharacteristically unsure of himself. 'Why should I not give the same service to the Church even though I be number two and not number one?' When later the same year he did succeed to the Primacy he was still a little bewildered. He found a formula: 'If Dublin is a very hard place to leave, Armagh is a very nice place to go to.' He slowly but surely made his way into the hearts of the men of the North. This was due to their appreciation of his sense of justice.

He seldom spoke of his early ministry. Once he told me that in his curate days he had met Sir Roger Casement. 'I took an immediate dislike to him.' He very rarely dismissed a name so curtly, though he was never afraid to say what he thought about celebrities. Of Ronald Knox, his first cousin, he spoke more than once. He didn't dislike him but he didn't like him either. He had a regard for Abp. Cosmo Gordon Lang, and though he recalled with merriment Henson's 'proud, prelatical and pompous' quip on seeing Orpen's portrait of Lang, he thought that basically Lang was a holy and humble man of God. He admired William Temple's gifts, and was shocked by his early death, but he doubted the wisdom of many of Temple's public utterances. He often said that Archbishop Fisher was a very wise man and he came to admire and respect him. I told Archbishop Fisher this and he said, 'I am glad. I always thought that he slightly disapproved of me.' At Lambeth Conferences he impressed many besides Henson with his 'unyielding episcopalianism.' When it was maintained that the Lambeth Quadrilateral was embedded in the South India Scheme he is supposed to have said, 'You might as well compare four pounds of butter with four o'clock.'

Though a high churchman he disliked undue ceremonialism. He refused to knock on the Cathedral door when enthroned at Armagh. He disliked the title of Primate.[4] He had a nostalgia for academic dress. He had no use for the use of abstract terms: e.g. not 'the State' in the changed suffrage, but 'our Rulers.' His mind was keen and incisive and sometimes devastatingly quick. In reply to a confession of Louis Crooks that he had only two good Harvest sermons, the Archbishop countered innocently, 'Have you *two*?' . . .

The second part of the following letter refers to a difference of opinion between the Archbishop and Hartford at a meeting of the Incorporated Society for Protestant Schools, and is of further interest as marking a change of administration in that Society.

June 27, 1944

My dear Hartford,

Many thanks for the copy of your lecture on Erigena. I am very much pressed this week and cannot read it till next week, but I look forward to studying it then.

Thanks too for what you write about last week's Incd. Soc. meeting. I am very glad you said what you did and expressed your mind according to what was in it. I am, like you, sorry our

---

[4] It may be added that he also disliked wearing what is called a 'pectoral' cross. His diary shows that he adopted the habit later than the other bishops in Ireland, and would then wear it only on what he considered appropriate occasions.

ways crossed, but certainly I do not regard what I consented to as the ideally best: but it seems to me that in view of two things—(a) the necessity for sharp reduction of expenditure, and (b) the absence of the man to replace Mayne and be really efficient in a difficult position, the proposal put forward by Mr. Vigors enables us to carry on for a while till we see our way more clearly. It will have to succeed very well indeed, if it is to be regarded as a permanent settlement. Tate will find the extra work a serious strain and the Hon. Sec. will have a heavier task than he yet appreciates. I am very glad you were to be with him for the week-end—his enthusiasm is most valuable, and I hope he may allay even a little of your by no means unnatural doubts. . . .

I hope I may see you at your new home before very long.

With all good wishes,

Yours very sincerely,

JOHN ARMAGH

A further letter is an encouragement to the recipient to pursue the study which he later submitted as his thesis for the D.D., and which was in fact, after revision, accepted.

Nov. 22, 1944

My dear Hartford,

. . . I am very glad you are doing some more work with Erigena. More ought to be made of him and known about him. He was a most extraordinary 'e-mergency' in his day—but maybe, if we knew more, we should find he was not an isolated figure. But I am sure people in his day were afraid of a mind with an Origen-like freedom and range.

Yours very sincerely,

JOHN ARMAGH

Private. What do you think of a country parish in N.I. with joint Sunday evg. services; all to C. of I. one Sunday, all to Presbns. the next, and all to the Methodists the next, right through the winter?

What about pandenominational chaos?

The last of these private letters is remarkable in its unqualified admiration of the stature of a great Christian thinker and leader—the greatest Anglican of his age—of whose liberalism and practical judgment however the Archbishop had often personally disapproved.

Nov. 6, 1944

My dear Hartford,

The Church's tragedy of the last ten days has been uppermost in one's mind. Notwithstanding the difference of one's line of policy on Reunion questions, it was impossible not to admire the amazing gifts of Wm. Cantuar: —his grasp and his mastery of his material, and his felicity of expression—his courage and independence and the appeal his personality made, and the moral authority he exercised. And the natural man in us asks 'Why, at this, of all times?'

Perhaps he outshone all his brethren to such an extent that it is well that others should have a chance of using their gifts, to a fuller extent than was allowed them in the presence of such a natural ascendancy.

Yours very sincerely,

JOHN ARMAGH

CHAPTER XIV

RELIGIOUS EDUCATION AND OTHER MATTERS

THE ARCHBISHOP need have had no misgivings about his reception by the people of the North of Ireland. If any had suspected him of having nationalistic sympathies, his obvious loyalty to the Crown at once disabused them. He showed that he was ready to accept the powers that be as of divine ordinance, whether in south or north; he was never an extremist politically; his moderation was known unto all men. And his integrity, straightforwardness and fairmindedness appealed to the forthright Ulster folk; they knew where they were with him; he said what he meant and he meant what he said. And when he in turn showed how much he admired their disciplined restraint under extreme undisciplined provocation from violent and lawless attacks from across the border, their confidence in him grew into affection.

From the outset he made it plain that his main concern was not with forms of government but with the welfare of the Church. And in 1946 an issue arose which involved him in direct conflict with the Government. Of those with whom he entered the lists in the Education Controversy, as it came to be called, the most distinguished survivor is the Very Reverend William Corkey, D.D., of the Presbyterian Church in Belfast; and it is to him that we owe the following summary of its course, and testimony to 'the wise guidance and weighty support' which Protestant Churches of all denominations received from the Primate during their campaign. (It must be noticed in passing, though Dr. Corkey does not mention it, that the Primate seldom or never appeared at their meetings. His support was given behind the scenes; but it was felt by them as a tower of strength.) Dr. Corkey's tribute is as follows:

Archbishop Gregg, like his illustrious predecessor Archbishop Bramhall, was an inflexible believer in the principles of Anglicanism, and because of his strong convictions in this regard was often considered to be difficult and distant.

But his action in so strongly condemning a breach of faith on the part of the Government of Northern Ireland with the transferors of Protestant Schools was very greatly appreciated not only by members of his own Church, but by all who were concerned about religious instruction in those schools.

246

As to what had transpired before he became involved :

When the Government of Northern Ireland in 1923 passed an Education Act prohibiting the statutory Education authorities from making any provision for religious instruction in State-provided or transferred elementary schools, the Church of Ireland united with the Presbyterian Church, the Methodist Church, and the Orange Order in protesting against a secular system of education; and after a long and intense campaign an amending Act was introduced in 1930 by Lord Craigavon (then Prime Minister), making provision for Bible Instruction to be given by the teaching staff in schools attended by Protestant children, due regard being paid to the rights of conscience.

In view of this settlement, which the Prime Minister stated would be permanent so long as a Unionist Government was in power, almost all the schools under the management of Protestant Churches were transferred to the local Education authorities under conditions ensuring that Bible Instruction would be given by the teaching staff on a syllabus approved by the Protestant Churches.

To their amazement and bitter disappointment the Government of 1946 for some unknown reason introduced a Bill to repeal the provisions of the 1930 Act.

The United Education Committee of the Protestant Churches then organized a series of protest meetings which received large public support. The first meeting was held in the Wellington Hall, Belfast, and was attended by some 1,500 persons. A letter was read from the Primate, Dr. Gregg, apologizing for his absence, and emphasizing his opposition to the plans of the Government. He said he hoped the meeting would demand: 'The full observance of the solemn agreements made with the transferors of voluntary schools after the passing of the 1930 Education Act.'

At another largely-attended protest meeting in Portadown another letter was read from the Primate. He urged that the following points in the Bill be resisted very firmly: 'The proposal to draft every child of eleven-plus, whatever its ability or progress, into a central intermediate school, as the transporting of young children for 220 days in the year was most unsettling; the needless scrapping of the 1930 Act which, with its provision for Bible instruction had worked without a hitch for 15 years; the consequent one-sided breach of the agreements of 1930 with those who transferred on the basis of a solemn agreement resting on the good faith of the provision of the Act; and the form of the conscience clause.'

Fortunately the situation underwent a swift change through the passing of the Butler Act by the Imperial Parliament in 1944, for it embodied almost all the principles for which the Protestant Churches were contending. Subsequently in 1947 the Government of Northern Ireland followed suit and embodied in their Act most of the provisions for Religious Instruction which are found in the English Education Act of 1944.

It is of interest to notice, however, that the transporting of eleven-plus children to central schools is still part of the present system, and the force of the Primate's objection to this has become clearer with the passing of time.

Though it cannot be said that the Primate's intervention directly affected the favourable issue of the controversy, it certainly strengthened the hands of those who were actively engaged in it. His objection to the transportation of young children from the country to large urban schools would be shared by most teachers who have had experience of both. And, from a general point of view, it is another aspect of the evils of undue centralization.

As to his notorious absence from these united Protestant meetings, this must be ascribed partly to his intense dislike of being, or of being seen, in the company of Presbyterians or of nonconformists; it was all of a piece with what can only be called ecclesiastical snobbery. But it was also largely due to the fact that he had among his own clergy one who could speak for the cause more vigorously and effectively than he could himself. This was Chancellor Quinn, Rector of St. Jude's, Ballynafeigh, Co. Down. Concerning him Dr. Corkey writes:

> The Primate had profound confidence in Chancellor Quinn's judgment and rightly so, for no one had a more all-round knowledge of the matters relating to education, and in particular to religious instruction in the schools, than he. He took most meticulous care to get his facts as accurate as possible and then he pondered deeply on the issues at stake; but once he had made matters clear in his own mind no power on earth could move him, and of course he was blamed for being obstinate and often for being a trouble-maker. I have seldom met a more honest or determined man.

The correspondence of the Primate with the Chancellor deals with technicalities and need not be quoted. But his first letter, 5 May 1939, is very characteristic, as showing his caution and conscientiousness.

> I shall be glad to give some thought to the important questions you raise, and may find an opportunity of some conversation with you next (Synod) week.

But first of all I must get my ignorance enlightened.

Can you give me the exact terms of the relevant legislation regarding religious instruction, which legislation, I think you say, presupposes joint action *in re* programme of the Protestant Churches? Is it obligatory or optional for the teachers to teach this programme? do unitarian teachers, as well as trinitarian, teach our Church children? what provision is there in the system for entry into the schools at Rel. Instrn. periods of the clergy, or authorized catechists, of the various denominations for the teaching of their own children and the teaching of their own denominational subjects?

When he was completely cognizant of all the facts, and not till then, did the Archbishop enter the fray—with the skill and generalship of the experienced campaigner. Sometimes when the Chancellor was in favour of direct frontal attack on the Ministry of Education, the Archbishop counselled diplomacy; at other times he encouraged attack and suggested details for the disposal, so to speak, of the forces available. At all times his suggestions were adopted without question. Finally, on 16 January 1946, he wrote a stiff letter to the Minister of Education, in the course of which he accuses him (politely) of equivocation.

I fear I cannot agree with your interpretation of the agreement to preserve the rights enjoyed by School Management Committees under the 1925 and 1930 Acts. The transfer of schools does not mean merely the transfer of buildings; it implies the transfer of the teaching system in an area, the access to the children through the P.E.S. To change the status and designation of pupils over 11 from Primary to Junior Secondary, and at one stroke to subtract from the scope of the agreement *re* Primary Schools all the *children* over 11 by calling them Secondary pupils, bears to me the appearance of a very dubious method of nullifying a proclaimed agreement, in respect of perhaps half the children in an area, by the arbitrary use of terminological labels. I do not see how the rights enjoyed by the School Management Committees under the 1925 and 1930 Acts can be said to be preserved when the representatives of the Churches find their representation reduced from one-half to about one-third.

There is unfortunately no reply to this letter to be found among the Archbishop's papers; but no doubt a copy of a reply exists among the Government files in Belfast.

The Archbishop's Presidential Address to the Armagh Diocesan Synod on 3 July 1946 is almost entirely devoted to a reasoned criticism of the Minister's action, and it appears unanswerable. It is happily on record in the Journals of the Synod.

He took occasion, at nearly every annual meeting of the Synod, to refer to the importance of Religious Education, mentally in the school, morally in the home. He called it 'the truest form of Church Sustentation.'

Merely to inform the mind is not enough. Children might be taught from the skilfully devised programme and yet might be virtually heathen. For a child is not to be thought of merely as a vessel to be filled—it is fire to be kindled.

As the post-war years advanced he became increasingly concerned with the decline in morals and a sense of spiritual values, and the prevalence of juvenile delinquency. He blamed for these evils, partly the Welfare State, partly lack of parental control.

We belong to what we call the 'Welfare State,' and the Welfare State concerns itself with the welfare of the bodies of its citizens. It meets their bodily neds from the cradle to the grave. And in doing so much to protect them, it weakens their sense of self-reliance and initiative. And so the human beings who are the beneficiaries of this system of planned materialism become lost behind the workings of this almost inhuman machine, for all its apparent benevolence. The engine which carries them tends at the same time to crush them. It is not concerned with the citizen as a man, as a child of God and a pilgrim of eternity. . . . A system which has to deal with individuals by the ten thousand makes them little better than cyphers. . . . It robs them of the spirit of enterprise and of forethought with which they were born. They belong to the crowd, and life in the crowd saps their independence and their personal sense of moral responsibility. Think of the amount of dishonesty and gambling around us. . . .

If it is in Church and Sunday Schools that [our children] are taught about God and eternal things, about the duty they owe to God and the duty they owe to their neighbour, it is in the home that they should see this teaching applied to daily life and put into regular practice.

We do owe an unspeakable debt to those who carry on voluntary organizations, such as Sunday School, Lads' Brigade, Girl Guides, Scouts—they help to suggest to boys and girls ideals of character and discipline which in countless cases abide with them through life. But they cannot take the place of a good home, and only too often home influences are anything but a help; the juvenile delinquency, of which the Courts have so much to say, is traceable in very many cases to a total want of responsibility for their children by fathers and mothers.

He recurred to the gravity of this subject again in his last Presidential Address but one, in 1957, the year of the Wolfenden Report:

> The tragic stories of juvenile delinquency are only too often due to the absence of the Christian example and the Christian atmosphere which grown-up Christian people should be expected to provide. . . .
> I feel compelled to make some reference to the recently published Wolfenden Report dealing with certain aspects of vice. I am very glad that one member of the Commission stood out firmly against the proposal to remove the penalty upon homosexual practices between consenting adults. To remove this penalty is not merely a negative act—it is a positive one. The existence of the penalty reflects the determined public judgment upon a certain line of unnatural conduct. This line of conduct is not simply private and personal. . . . The removal of the penalty upon detection substitutes condonation for condemnation. It suggests that the individual's choice, involving as it does more than himself alone, is a matter of indifference to the community. He may go as he pleases. He may lead others to share in his anti-social practices. There is no object in self-control. Too much would be sacrificed to the so-called liberty of the individual —a liberty for which too many are unripe, and which they do not know how to use when it is granted to them.

And in his last address of all, when he could no longer see to read it from a script and spoke extemporally, in dealing with the Report on the Diocesan Board of Religious Education, he said that he could not express too strongly its importance.

> With it lies, to a great extent, the future—the future generation and the future of the Church of Ireland.
> All must be aware of the great amount of laxity in the younger generation, and the responsibility lies with the older generation who have not done all they should in implanting religious and moral principles in the minds of the young. Do that before they are seven, and it is possible you will alter their whole way of life.

The Archbishop was concerned also with education of another kind. This was the education of members of the Church of Ireland in Queen's University, Belfast, which is an academy of Presbyterian foundation. He was largely instrumental in the appointment in 1951 of a full-time Dean of Residences having a pastoral charge of Church of Ireland students. It is to the first of these, the Revd. J. M. G. Carey, B.D., that we are indebted for the information that the Archbishop was personally interested in the establishment of the Annual Theological Lectures, but was unable to attend the first lecture, given by Bishop Wand; that he indirectly supported the transaction whereby the Catholic Apostolic Church was made over to the University as an additional building; that he performed the Act of dedication at the opening of the Students' Centre in 1955, having previously played a large part in obtaining the necessary grant of £5,000 from the Representative Church Body. He had commended an appeal in May 1953 for this enterprise to the Diocese of Armagh:

> I commend most heartily the Appeal which is being made to the members of the Church of Ireland on behalf of the Centre which is now being established for Church of Ireland students (of whom there are now over 600) in the Queen's University of Belfast. The student community in a University is of first-rate importance, in view of the positions of authority and leadership which await those who year by year enter the professions or public life in the walks of industry or commerce.
>
> If our Church people are wise they will recognize, as other denominations have done, how much, for good or ill, depends on the influences surrounding the University population during its most formative years, and will give that liberal support which a strong industrial and commercial community can give to the long-needed Centre, the opportunity for providing which has been placed in our hands.

On 8 July 1949 the Queen's University honoured the Archbishop with the honorary degree of Doctor of Divinity.

§

The Archbishop had also been requested to help with the work on the New English Bible in the section on the Apocrypha. All his knowledge, especially of the Book of Wisdom (of which he drafted a complete rendering in modern English), was placed unreservedly at the disposal of those engaged in the translation. The Irish representative of the General Committee appointed by the United Council of Churches in Ireland is the Revd. Professor J. L. M. Haire, M.TH., D.D., who writes:

> He had been present at some of the earlier meetings of the Apocrypha panel, and both the Chairman of the General Com-

mittee (Dr. Williams, formerly Bishop of Winchester) and the Director (Professor C. H. Dodd) expressed their high regard for him, their recognition of his remarkable courtesy and the incisiveness with which he could put his view when he had made up his mind.

The point at which I came myself to appreciate Dr. Gregg's interest was in connection with the New Testament. Between 1948 and 1954 I sent him the drafts of the books as I got them (from 1954 he received a draft in his own right as a translator) and within a fortnight the draft would return with the most careful detailed work written in his own hand on the margin—and this I would then send on to the Director. He worked over the translation verse by verse and he did it very promptly; and in this work he constantly showed how he had kept his scholarship up to date. The letters I received from him also showed his remarkable courtesy; there was always a note of thanks and appreciation for my keeping him informed.

I came to know his courtesy and promptness in two other ways. When I was convener of the Inter-Church Relations Committee of the Presbyterian Church I had occasion to write to him about a proposed Adoption Bill in 1952, in the first draft of which it was proposed that there should be no inter-denominational adoptions—not only between Roman Catholic and Protestant but between the various non-Roman Churches. We wrote to say that this seemed to us to be an impracticable proposal in the Irish situation. The Archbishop replied in his own hand by return of post (as always in my experience of him), but he also undertook to reconsider the proposal and wrote a fortnight later to say that he had changed his mind and agreed to our suggestions. This seemed to me a sign of his open-mindedness.[1]

At Amsterdam in 1948 I had two long talks with him, and he seemed to me a very fine example of the school of theology that one associates with the late Bishop Gore. We discussed the place of the apostles in the Church. He said it surprised him that so good a scholar as Calvin had found no place for the apostles in his understanding of the government of the Church. I (being 13 years younger, and not often accustomed to argue with Archbishops) countered by urging that Calvin did have a great, though temporary, place for the apostles, and I raised the question as to why no successor had been appointed to James, the brother of John. The Archbishop with a most friendly and open smile agreed that we had now started on a vast subject which would require more time than that between two sessions of the Amsterdam Assembly!

[1] See page 189.

§

On 13 July 1952 died his old friend Robert Thomas Hearn, Bishop of Cork, and the young Dean, George Otto Simms, destined to succeed him for a brief reign before elevation to the Archbishopric of Dublin, preached the memorial sermon and sent a copy to the Primate, who replied:

July 31, 1952

My dear Dean,

I am much obliged to you for sending me your memorial sermon on my old friend, your Bishop. I have read it with great appreciation. In your short intercourse with him you have been able to learn a good deal of what made him the personality he was.

I enjoyed a 50 year friendship with him, and I learnt more than I can say from his way of approaching public affairs. Without ever being assertive he made himself heard, and seemed to possess an intuitive sense of where the real point at issue in any discussion lay. His life was as simple as it was transparent— governed by principle. I shall miss him sadly, and I am sure you will too.

I am glad you quoted those lines in the ambulatory; I think it was I who made him aware of them. I don't know if they were written *ad hoc,* or quoted; anyhow, they are most happily apt, as you used them.

Very sincerely yours,

JOHN ARMAGH

The lines inscribed in the ambulatory of St. Fin Barre's Cathedral are (as the Archbishop was himself to discover almost exactly a year later) a quotation from some verses by an otherwise unknown writer, R. H. Baynes, and are to be found in the anthology *Lyra Anglicana.* And they were, as will be seen, the lines for which he was searching his memory just before he himself died.

'His life . . . was governed by principle.' No words could more fitly describe his own life; they might even be an epitaph. He was as faithful in little as in much.

His sense of principle sometimes went beyond the boundary of what was right or reasonable, when it became identified with a punctiliousness in matters of procedure—professional etiquette— which quite overrode any personal considerations. Archbishop Barton, the most charitably-minded of men and unassuming of dignitaries, recalled with some exasperation cases in point:

Whenever he, as Archbishop of Armagh, was consecrating a Bishop for a diocese in the Northern Province he invariably asked me not to be present. The only explanation which I received was, 'I do not know what I would do with you.' This suggests that his reason was not entirely legal, but was based on the memory of happenings in the past when the Archbishops of Armagh and of Dublin were at bitter variance over their supposed respective rights, each determined to assert his dignities. But his decision was certainly due in part to courtesy. (There is of course no second throne in Armagh for the Archbishop of Dublin as there is in St. Patrick's, Dublin.) I was quite ready to take a place inferior to all the Northern consecrating Bishops, but he felt that it would not be giving me due honour.

When Cyril Elliott was consecrated Bishop of Connor he asked the Primate if I might take part, being one of his oldest and most intimate friends. I was permitted to robe and was assigned a place of dignity outside the Sanctuary, but when I asked if I might enter the Sanctuary just to share in the laying on of hands, I received a quite definite though kindly expressed refusal.

And other cases with amusement:

He once told me on his appointment to Dublin that his predecessor, Archbishop Bernard, said to him, 'You will be burdened with innumerable committees. I can go on taking the chair at the Alexandra College Board, and you need not come.' 'Oh!' replied Gregg, 'I look upon work in that connection as one of the most important of my duties.' 'So' (he continued) 'I used always to arrive five minutes late for the meetings. Bernard would offer me the chair and I always asked him to carry on. So we were both satisfied!'

When I was Bishop of Kilmore I discovered that a collection of Communion silver belonging to Lanesborough Church was deposited in a bank in Longford. We were offered £1,000 for it, for a museum in America. I felt, rightly or wrongly, that this would be a more reverend use for it than deposit in the dark underworld of a bank. We brought the matter up at an R.B. meeting. The Primate went off the deep end and swept away all our arguments. We would have no guarantee that, at some future time, it might not be taken from the museum and put to secular uses. So it has remained ever since in the dark, forgotten and unused.

When Sean T. O'Kelly was to be instituted, for the second time, as President we were both invited to the ceremony. The Primate discussed with me, very seriously, what we should wear for the occasion, so as not to be outdone in the matter of colourful effect and dignity. We solemnly decided that we should wear purple cassocks with pectoral crosses and our Doctor's gowns. The Bishops of the Church of Rome, in considerable numbers, occupied seats below the platform on the right, opposite to members of the Government. We sat a little lower down. The ceremony was brief and dignified, conducted by the Taoiseach, Mr. de Valera. Then the platform party descended to the body of the hall on their way out. The President smiled and bowed, but when he saw the Archbishop of Armagh he stopped and his hand went out. But then he bethought himself, and went back to shake hands with the Bishops of his own Communion whom he had just passed. Then again he came to Armagh and both hands went out and he thanked him with considerable feeling for having come. He spoke to me afterwards about it and evidently was much touched by the Primate's having come all the way from the north to pay his respects on the occasion.

The President's sense of gratitude is most courteously and gracefully expressed in the following letter written in his own hand on 26 June.

Uachtarán na hÉireann
(President of Ireland)

Baile Atha Cliath
(Dublin)

Meitheamh 26^{adh} 1945

Dear Lord Archbishop,

I humbly ask to be excused from not having acknowledged earlier Your Grace's kind letter dated June 21st. I received it only to-day. I found it on my table here when I entered formally on my duties this afternoon.

It gave me infinite pleasure to receive your congratulations and good wishes, and I assure Your Grace that I am most sincerely grateful for them as well as for your very great kindness in graciously assisting at the inauguration ceremony in Dublin Castle yesterday.

With renewed expressions of profound thanks to your Grace and with every good wish.

Believe me,

Most respectfully and cordially yours,

SEAN T. O'KEALLAY

§

It was the Archbishop's custom to write each year in the *Belfast News-Letter* a 'Christmas Message to Ulster.' None is in the least repetitive of another, and all are on a consistently high level of discourse. One may be reproduced here, because it is a reminder of an exegesis of the Gospel story which was taught to divinity students of an earlier day, when he was a Professor of Divinity, but has since then been largely forgotten or ignored; namely that the evangelists were projecting backwards into their records of the

8
VISIT OF THE
ARCHBISHOP OF
CANTERBURY
AND MRS. FISHER,
THE PALACE,
ARMAGH, 1952
(*Belfast Telegraph*)

9. THE LAST GENERAL SYNOD. With the Archbishop of Dublin *(Irish Times)*

WITH (NOW ARCHBISHOP) BISHOP ANTHONY BLOOM, EASTERN ORTHODOX CHURCH *(Irish Times)*

historical life of Jesus conceptions of His personality which they had not formed until after that life was ended.

As we contemplate the Birth of Jesus on this day, we do well to note the contrast between His humble earthly beginnings and the place He ultimately won in human veneration. It is very hard for us of to-day to see Him in the reserve of His primitive simplicity, just as it was hard for those who wrote His story in the Gospels not to throw back upon that story, both in its beginning and in its progress, some reflection from all that He finally came to mean to the circle of those who learnt to worship Him as the Son of God.

And yet it is only when we can appreciate this contrast that we begin to appreciate the wonder of that earthly life. But the sharpness of the contrast is in danger of being missed by readers of the Gospels. They know, as it were, the end at the beginning, in a way in which those about Him did not. The Gospels of St. Matthew and St. Luke begin with introductions which prepare readers for a notable Conception and Birth, while the preface to St. John's Gospel carries our minds back to the beginning, when the Word who in time was made flesh, was with God before time was. And so it is psychologically impossible for us to recreate in our minds the perplexities of those who were forced to ask 'Who is this?' We cannot share the indignation of those who heard this young man saying 'But I say unto you,' or who experienced His masterful handling of the Sabbath tradition, and were driven to ask 'By what authority doest thou these things?' Nor again can we share the sense of blank disappointment with which the Crucifixion frustrated the hopes of His followers. But all this doubt, this uncertainty, this unknownness, this guessing were real facts once, and make us marvel at the patient self-restraint which shrouded this hiddenness of Godhead, and delayed its slow manifestation till there were hearts ripe enough to receive it.

No imaginative writer of that or of any day, creating the story of God incarnate, could ever have thought of painting so unpretending a picture. Would he have joined the universal claim, 'Come unto Me all ye that labour and are heavy laden,' with the subdued admission, 'I am meek and lowly in heart'? Would he have written as Paul did, 'He made Himself of no reputation, and humbled himself'? But it was this unlikeness that made the reality so hard for the eye-witnesses to interpret when it was enacted in their sight. But we of later days who know the sequel as we read the beginning, have this advantage over them: the humble Birth, the obedient Childhood, the unrecorded thirty years, the three years of misunderstood and finally rejected Ministry, can stir our wondering faith by showing the unfathomable depths of Divine Love and Condescension in Him who for our salvation came down from Heaven and was made Man.

R

The war years brought him bitter personal sorrow. Since the Japanese conquest of Malaya and seizure of Singapore, tidings both of his son and of his son-in-law were long in suspense. The fate of the latter was known first: a prisoner in Singapore. Thanks to an excellent constitution and physique, and even more to his invincible morale, Cecil Wilson survived death by starvation and worse, and after long recuperation continued to fulfil his vocation as one of the most skilled and beloved surgeons in the North of Ireland.

Not until 25 January 1944 did he receive word about his son: a telegram from the British Red Cross while the family were at breakfast. His face became ashen, he said nothing because he could not speak, and presently left the table. Later news amplified the brief message. His son John had been thrown with other British prisoners into the hold of a Japanese vessel bound for Japan. Sighted by an American submarine, whose crew were unaware of its freight, it had been torpedoed and sunk on 29 August 1943, with no survivors. The Archbishop's diary has an entry in Greek: it is the text of Rev. 7: 16–17.

The shadow of death had long hung over the Palace. Mrs. Gregg had never recovered strength to enjoy the gardens or meadows or woodlands in those spacious grounds. Her condition became progressively worse. On the night of 8 August 1945 her husband never left her side. After a day of much restlessness and distress, the end came just before midnight on the 9th. Next day his daughter Margaret joined him, and that night he got some sleep. Saturday was 'a day of sad thoughts and memories.' On Sunday his wife's niece, Margaret Jennings, arrived from Cork. He tried to tell her of the circumstances, but his voice broke and he wept. On Sunday, 'I did not go to church. Sat by her bedside during morning and afternoon. *Ave, Ave.*' The funeral service was held in the private chapel; the committal in the grave at Enniskerry. He spent several days replying, briefly and with restraint, to multitudes of letters.

Very many thanks for your kind message of sympathy.

Mrs. Gregg and I were married for over 42 years, and the ending of so long a companionship leaves one with a sense of utter impoverishment. And where one of the two has long been ill, I think the sense of dependence, and the constant visits to the sick room and the carrying of little bits of news, make two lives grow more deeply together than when both are well and strong, and can go each their own way as they will.

God has been very good—one has happy memories and the great Hope.

CHAPTER XV

LAMBETH CONFERENCES AND GENERAL SYNODS

DURING HIS LONG EPISCOPAL CAREER of nearly forty years Archbishop Gregg attended no less than four Lambeth Conferences. Consultation of the documentary records being as yet unpermissible, recourse must be had to the memories of some who sat with him in these assemblies for information as to any contributions which he made to the debates. Unfortunately none carry so far back as 1920, the year of his first attendance; nor has it been possible to elicit any memories of 1938; in 1958 he was too handicapped by deafness for any active participation in the proceedings. But in 1948 his seniority, prestige and stature as a leader in the counsels of the Church were already such that he made a marked impression on the assembly.

It was remarked at Lambeth by more than one of the English and American bishops as a curious thing that, when any motion came to be voted upon, the Irish bishops invariably voted *en bloc*. Those who remarked this did not know, though they could guess, that such unanimity was due not so much to personal conviction as to loyalty to their Archbishop. It was a testimony both to his leadership and to their good sense.

The late Archbishop Barton, his loyal but by no means always sympathetic colleague on the Bench for many years, was among the private dissentients. His memories of Dr. Gregg went back a long way—from their association in early years, the one in the rough and tumble of life as leader of a mission in the slums, the other in the sequestered vale of academic life as honorary treasurer of the mission; on through their middle years as members of the Bench of Bishops; and finally for nearly a score of years as fellow Archbishops. Fellows rather than brothers; for they seldom saw eye to eye, and they were by nature temperamentally incompatible. It is a testimony to the good sense of both that they avoided collision; and as public personalities the one supplied what the other lacked. During his last illness Dr. Barton unselfishly and with difficulty communicated to the writer, verbally and in writing, his reminiscences of Gregg at Lambeth and at Synods.

He did not speak frequently but was always listened to with

profound attention. It was perhaps due largely to the viewpoints which he expressed so forcibly and in such flawless diction, that many English Bishops came to realize, with surprise, that there was sound churchmanship in the Church of Ireland. Some of them had formerly looked upon us as being outside the pale. With Archbishop Fisher his relationship was entirely friendly. He may have felt that Fisher's views on many points were too liberal, but the latter, true to his responsibilities as chairman, was cautious. This conscientious and fair-minded attitude Gregg well understood and appreciated. (It was not always so in his relations with his former Vicar, Dr. d'Arcy, whose liberal views in the matter of Church reunion were anathema to Gregg.)

He got great *kudos* at Lambeth in 1948 for a somewhat long and carefully reasoned speech on the Church of South India. But, as his outlook on this question was quite different from mine, I was not so impressed as some others were! I felt that he had not changed his outlook for thirty years and was somewhat oblivious of the winds of change. If it had been his lot in his University days to be connected with the Student Christian Movement his outlook on many subjects might have been less static.

Of all his work I think he most enjoyed conducting affairs at Synods and Committee meetings. He could clarify confused issues with wonderful skill, and could lead us quickly and surely through a long agenda. But sometimes when there seemed to be few matters to discuss, and we expected a short meeting, he seemed almost to encourage delay and to revel in dissecting finer points of law. As was often said, he would have been superb as a judge. His keen legal mind combined with an unshakable impartiality would have eminently fitted him for such a calling.

It was only under stress of necessity that he would hand over the chairmanship to another—and with obvious reluctance. His lunch at the Synod would be brought up to him on the platform when the rest of us had adjourned. There were times when during a dull discussion at a Committee meeting he would fall asleep, really asleep. But he had an astonishing knack of waking up and at once grasping the point of a discussion. This was quite uncanny at times. There might be brief intervals of unconsciousness during a missionary meeting at the end of a long day. Conscious of the possibility he would sometimes ask the man in the next chair to him to give him a nudge if he showed signs of slumber. I once asked him if he found it difficult to remain awake during the sermon in St. Patrick's Cathedral on a Sunday afternoon, when cut off from sight and (to a large extent) from sound by the curtain of the throne. 'Quite impossible,' he replied.

When the General Synod requested the House of Bishops to draw up a statement defining our relationship with the Church of South India, Dr. Gregg asked me to draft a preliminary statement as a basis for discussion. I toiled at it for many hours and finally concluded that it would be quite impossible for me to suggest the contents of such a statement that would be agreeable to my own conscience and acceptable to Dr. Gregg. I reported this to the House of Bishops and it was agreed that no further action should be taken in the matter. I think that Dr. Gregg was rather relieved in his mind and he certainly accepted my report with his usual courtesy.

Though differing from him in many points, I always realized his great qualities of leadership, his strength of character, high ideals, goodness, and our own good fortune to work under his leadership for so many years. And I had a real affection for him and valued his friendship.

Archbishop Barton's impressions of his impact at Lambeth are confirmed by those of Dr. Gregg's successor in the Primacy, Dr. James McCann:

It would not be contrary to the facts to describe Dr. Gregg as one of the very outstanding figures at the Lambeth Conference. His words were received with marked attention, and his wisdom and learning enhanced the reputation of the Irish Church.

It was my happy experience to hear the speech which he made on the proposal for the South India Scheme of Reunion debated by the Bishops in 1948. He had prepared it with his customary care. Every word had been considered, and the facts of the historic Episcopate as not only the *bene esse* but the *esse* of the Christian Church were placed before us calmly and dispassionately. The statement delivered with his accustomed judicial air of scholarly authority made a deep impression on the Conference. Many who had been unable to make a decision were convinced by the Archbishop's arguments.

It was on this occasion that Dr. Gregg is reported to have brought the House down by a memorable witticism. At the end of the debate on the Church of South India a motion for or against intercommunion with it was put to the Conference. The atmosphere was tense: a large number of the conservative wing voted against; a large number of liberals voted in favour; there was also a large number who abstained from voting. The votes having been counted and recorded, Dr. Gregg rose again and, indicating those who like himself had voted against, said in his high, somewhat querulous, tones: 'We know who *we* are. The *Sheep*— within the fold.' Indicating those who had voted in favour: 'We know who *they* are. The *Goats*—outside it.' Then indicating the abstainers: 'But who are these?—*Angoras*?' [1]

[1] His diary for this day has a characteristic entry:

Archbishop McCann's memories continue:

Ten years later at the 1958 Conference by reason of age and
failing eyesight he was unable to play the same leading part as
formerly, but his interest in the proceedings was undiminished.
He had the Reports of the various Committees read to him, and
his mind was so clear that he invariably noted the crucial word
or phrase which was the embodiment of the suggested change.
On more than one occasion it was decided to read to him in
private the implications of certain resolutions in connection with
schemes for reunion. It was realized that unless Dr. Gregg was
satisfied that the historic Episcopate was to be firmly placed in
a reunited Church, his great influence would jeopardize the
acceptance of any reunion proposals.

There were many sides to his character, some of which were
known only to a few persons. I travelled with him in a London
bus during the 1958 Lambeth Conference when he spoke to me
with emotion of some personal happenings in his early life. Later,
on the same bus, an old woman entered into conversation with
him and he tried hard to hear what she said, and was apparently
happy to talk with her on matters far removed from his accustomed life. I had seen 'emotion,' and I had also seen 'the common
touch.'

It was his last year at Lambeth and he was recognized, by right
of seniority, as the 'Father' of the Conference. The most moving
incident occurred when the subject of some alterations in the word-
ing of the Psalter came before a plenary session after the special
Committee appointed to consider these had presented its report.
Dr. Gregg rose and amazed the Assembly by repeating from
memory phrase after phrase of the Greek version of several different Psalms in support of a certain suggested English rendering. He
had, he said by way of apology, made a private study of the Greek
version for many years. Thereupon the whole Assembly spontaneously stood and accorded him round after round of acclamation.
It was a proud moment for the Irish Bishops, and a *climateric* in
the whole Conference.[2]

Dr. McCann, then Bishop of Meath, who was his *liaison* with
Bishops of other Churches, constituted himself as the Primate's
escort and lent him the help of an arm as he moved with difficulty
from place to place; but it happened after one session that he was
unable to do so, and his place was taken by the Bishop of Limerick,

30 July. Lambeth 11.0 till 6.30. S. India. 'Majority' 135. 'Minority' 97. I
spoke agst. tampering with priesthood. My instances amused the Confce.
Did I err in overmuch mirth?
[2] I owe this account to Dr. Tyndall, Bishop of Derry.

Dr. Hodges. They were proceeding slowly and in silence, the Primate offering no remark, when the Bishop volunteered a question. 'Your Grace, this is your fourth Lambeth Conference. How does it compare, in your opinion, with the others you have attended?' 'Not favourably.' 'Oh! but why?' 'No *pep*, no *pep!*' In view of his well-known abhorrence of vulgarisms, especially any of a trans-Atlantic variety, the answer was astonishing.

At the conclusion of another session the Irish Bishops stood waiting, in extended formation, on the Palace steps for their respective wives to come and lead them to their several destinations. Archbishop Gregg, with head erect and thrown a trifle backward (a characteristic gesture) was heard to murmur, as if addressing the universe at large: 'Some say—wives are desirable. To me—a Necessity!'

Despite his long association with the English Bishops, not only at Lambeth but also on less august occasions, he was never on terms of familiarity with any of them. In earlier years the one of whom he saw most was probably Henson of Durham; in later years Rawlinson of Derby. Both were very different from himself in character and in outlook; but both, it would appear, took pains to try to draw him out of his shell. Henson, it is evident, regarded him with respect mixed with curiosity, though dissenting strongly from his views; and there exists a delightful newspaper print of a photograph of Rawlinson with his arm thrust through Gregg's among the pilgrims in Philippi; both are in cassocks and both are happily smiling, Gregg wearing a straw hat and Rawlinson a biretta. A request to Mrs. Rawlinson for any memories brought the following reply:

> My husband happened to be billeted with Archbishop Gregg in the same hotel (the Eccleston) for the six weeks of the Lambeth Conference of 1948 and they saw a good deal of each other.
>
> Then he was with him when representing the Archbishop of Canterbury on an Oecumenical Pilgrimage 'In the Footsteps of St. Paul' which went in 1951 round the Mediterranean Pauline sites.
>
> He didn't tell me very much about their friendship except that he admired his sincerity and friendliness, but the rigidity of his mind made him a difficult person to know.

By not a few of the Bishops at Lambeth he was regarded as another Nestor. In the words of one of them: 'When we are confronted with any difficult problem, we always say, "We can ask the Archbishop of Armagh." '

He had known personally no less than four Archbishops of Canterbury. Of these he had admired for their church statesmanship, though in different ways, both Randall Davidson and Cosmo Gordon Lang; he had distrusted the philosophical temper of William Temple's mind; and he had liked Geoffrey Fisher and admired his chairmanship.

Finally and fittingly comes this tribute from Archbishop Lord Fisher:

> . . . I fear that I have nothing significant to contribute to your work on the great Archbishop Gregg. . . . I knew him only in his later years when the abiding impression was, of course, of his dignified presence and occasional utterance full of strong conviction based on vast knowledge and experience. He was heroic, but to my generation a survivor of Heroes of old! He spoke but rarely at the two conferences over which I presided, always with great power, but no longer with fresh thinking. At the last in 1958 he was as impressive as ever, though lameness and blindness were affecting him. In later years when I was able to visit him in Ireland, we all thanked God for the wonderful way in which Mrs. Gregg cared for him.

§

No words could more fitly introduce a section on the Primate's conduct of General Synods than these of his younger colleague on the rostrum in later years, Archbishop Simms, who, when sight and hearing had grown dim, was his 'eyes and ears' in the surveillance of that large assembly.

For many, especially in the years between 1939 and 1959, the popular image of the Primate was the stately figure presiding at the General Synod. The elevated rostrum in the solemn Synod Hall emphasized the magisterial mien of the chairman at these annual gatherings of the Church's governing body. Archbishop Fisher, a very different type of personality, was appalled by the loftiness and awe-inspiring build-up of the rostrum when he presided in April 1961 at the Dublin meeting of the Council of Churches. Archbishop Gregg, however, fitted into the setting of the former St. Michael's Church which had been converted into a Synod Hall, with a natural dignity and an apparent relish for a measure of remoteness and detachment in the conduct of the Church's business.

Here he concentrated upon the routine business of bills to be debated and passed, reports to be discussed and received, motions on topics of moment or else (at times) of absurd triviality. The frowning countenance of the 'primatial image' may have at first sight suggested irritability and impatience, but in fact the corrugated brow marked the concentration of the chairman, and those who knew his powers of sitting firmly and immovably through the long procedure and the tedium of tiresome debates could have no doubt about the measure of his patience. He did, however, exercise discrimination in the imparting of his attention to what went on in the somewhat unwieldy assembly of over 600 members, of which two-thirds were laity and one-third clerical. He could doze when detailed attention to a matter in the hands of a clumsy or irrelevant pleader did not seem to be urgently required. His gift for sudden wakefulness as a speech limped to its close, or when a point that needed rapping was irresponsibly made, had for years been recognized at meetings small and great. Eyes were closed at other times to aid concentration in the massive granite-like countenance of the chairman who never fidgeted or fussed, who could not be stampeded into hasty decision nor ruffled by party cries or threats of resignation or a walking out on the part of those who did not see the problem whole as the chairman saw it.

He enjoyed meetings. The ordered progress of a long agenda paper seemed to attract him. As someone remarked, he looked forward with keen anticipation to each item of business with something of the eagerness with which the experienced diner-out scans a menu. He mastered the constitution at an early stage of his episcopate, and advised all bishops to become familiar with the ethos and principles of that charter of the Church. A bishop, he often repeated, is neither a prelate nor an autocrat; he is a constitutional bishop and it is his duty to work the constitution. He knew accurately where the powers of the bishop began and ended, in dealing with the Church's administration: thus he was often consulted by his brother bishops and during his primacy his judgments were considered as wise and final, such trust did those who asked his advice put in his cautious consideration and his judicious way of working and thinking from first principles.

He sensed the atmosphere of the Synod in his vigorous days with an astuteness which surprised many of those who mixed more freely and easily among the laity and clergy. He may not have known individuals very intimately; as a bishop since 1915, with a natural reserve, many of his interviews and personal encounters were formal and far from relaxed. He did, however, capture with shrewdness the mood of a meeting and knew how groups or types of people would react to opinions expressed and reforms proposed. His thorough understanding of the religious controversies in the Ireland of his day enabled him from his work in Connor and Cork, in Ossory, Dublin, and Armagh, to appreciate the emotional content of a dogmatic phrase or a party catch-cry. His mastery of the English language, his gift for exact definition, his ability to say in crisp often epigrammatic utterance exactly what he meant, with no ambiguity or *double entendre* in the pronouncement, inspired trust in his hearers. Those who disagreed with him appreciated the quality of consistency in his statements; his sallies into the thickets of controversy won admiration from those who respect a person who speaks with conviction and reasoned judgments. His courage and his forthrightness had Athanasian qualities. In the Synod there were whiffs of party spirit from time to time. Very often Gregg let the firebrands burn themselves out. He felt that he preferred them to be seen for what they were in full synod. The open forum served as a safety valve and Gregg believed that the average member of the Synod was unlikely to tolerate extreme opinions born of negative bitterness or inspired by the kind of fear which a minority feels when jostled into a tight corner, under pressure. His handling of the diffident speaker from among the laity was fascinating to watch. If he thought that such a member had something worth while to say, or if he grasped that the comment from the floor was in essence just the sort of comment that he might have made himself, he showed with the kindly smile that lit up the set firm features the most courteous consideration, while the untried speaker, unused to the overpowering assembly, tried to express what was on his mind. With the clergy, he seemed occasionally less patient and accommodating. Those who frequently jumped to their feet for interventions of a petty kind were discouraged by a look or a quiet groan. He felt that the clergy should have known better; their training made their crudities in debate less pardonable. 'May I add a word, your Grace?'—the plea from some insistent clerical member not easily suppressed—could be devastatingly met with a weary throaty '*Must* you?'—which the responsive members, anxious to get on with the business, would follow up more directly with shouts of 'No, no!'

Gregg rather suspected the kind of speech which swayed the house with stunts or oratory and flowery passages tinged with sentimentality. Such courting of popularity was thoroughly distasteful to him. At all times he was reluctant to pay compliments in public; he recoiled when personalities clouded the objectivity of an argument.

Each speaker who advanced to the rostrum was given ample opportunity to voice his opinion, but Gregg was chary of catching the eye of the hesitant or the faltering, and he only gave positive encouragement to the few well-tried members who could be relied upon to clear the mists of debate. Synods were thus characterized by their orderliness rather than by their homeliness. Yet the President was keenly interested in the names and the dioceses of those who spoke and often asked *sotto voce* questions about them from nearby members of the platform. He was specially pleased when a younger member showed promise and practical commonsense, but despaired of the rambler and wondered why such a one did not perceive more readily that he had lost the attention of the house.

He will be remembered best at the opening sessions of the Synods, delivering the Presidential address. The house was crowded for this. The laymen looked for something encouraging and constructive in these statements and were rarely disappointed. In these utterances he kept a worthy balance. Home affairs as well as world affairs would be surveyed with the Christian judgment he was wont to apply to all that took place. Every address contained some meaty teaching, some exposition of doctrine which indicated what the Church of Ireland had to say about this or that problem. The result was that what he wrote was far from transitory but served as a deliberate pronouncement of his own carefully weighed reflections upon the matter in hand. When the Second World War was raging, it was typical that he refrained from listing disasters but recalled his listeners to the doctrine of the Church and the promise of God. It was his way of concentrating at such a time upon the things which cannot be shaken. When news came of his own son's death by drowning in a torpedoed ship as a prisoner of war on his way to Japan, with grim fortitude the father observed 'It is better to fall into the hands of God than into the hands of the enemy.' So closely was his belief allied to his practice that such remarks issuing from a deep Christian conviction made many of his asides precious and memorable for those who heard them. Education of the Church's children was a favourite subject for presidential treatment; appeals for candidates for the ministry revealed the simplicity of his own life and the humility of his approach to his own ministry.

The week before the General Synod would be devoted to a careful examination of every Bill to be debated and every notice of motion on the agenda, as well as any issue that was likely to arise, so that no detail was left unforeseen. During this week he undertook no engagements and suffered no interruptions.

For the three or four days of Synod Week it was his invariable custom, in common with most of the Bishops and many of the clergy and laity from outside Dublin, to reside at the University Club, though indeed he would have enjoyed more privacy in a hotel. But he would take his meals at a small table with Bishop Hearn or, after the latter's death, preferably alone. In the evenings he would sit at a window in the reading-room, withdrawn from the circle round the fireplace, reading the newspapers; or else in the adjoining writing-room, answering letters. He was temperamentally incapable of engaging in general conversation; and it was thought that he desired solitude in the intervals of long fatiguing meetings. But this was not so; though he never himself made an approach, if an approach was made to him he responded; once the ice was broken, a thaw rapidly set in.

Synod Week finds time, not only for morning and afternoon sessions of the General Synod, but also for other meetings of sundry organizations which can assemble conveniently at no other time. On an evening after one such meeting, it befell to a little group chatting quietly in the reading-room to be startled by the sudden appearance in their midst of a furious archdeacon who began to declaim, and in no measured terms, his opinion of an address by a fellow-member of the cloth to which he had been obliged to listen for the best part of an hour. So carried away by his theme was he, that the urgently repressive gestures of his audience were unheeded. The address was so bad, he said, that he could think of no word wherewith to describe it. There a momentary pause; then the rustle of a newspaper in a distant corner, and a well-known voice—in slightly bored and petulant tones—volunteered solicitously, 'Would *tripe* do?'

His appearance, especially in his latter years, in St. Patrick's Cathedral for Evensong on the eve of Synod week, when the Cathedral is always packed to capacity by representatives of the Church from all parts of Ireland, was both striking and impressive. The nave-long procession winding down the south transept and up the central aisle and, at the last of all, his Grace of Dublin by his side, the tall imposing figure, tense and indrawn, striding forward, valiantly disguising his limp and concealing his pain, with crozier in right hand and rubber-shod ash-plant in left supporting his steps; head held high and a trifle flung backward, the large brown eyes magnified by thick-lenses glasses, gazing trance-like before him to a point above the distant altar, like a General consciously on parade in the presence of his Commander-in-Chief—High-King of Heaven —whose he was and whom he served. After exchanging a bow with the Dean he would disappear into his curtained stall, to emerge at the end and pronounce with solemnity the entoned Benediction. But for the space of that disciplined hour he seemed silently in his very posture to express all that he had stood for, all that he had striven for, in the course of a dedicated life.

His presidential addresses during nearly twenty years' Primacy are on a consistently high level of discourse, indicating his reaction to the course of events year by year, international, national, ecclesiastical. They are models of their kind in precision of thought and expression, of austere and often astringent eloquence in the severely classical manner. Whole passages in them cry aloud for quotation, but, even were this possible, one would miss the dignified presence and high authoritative voice of the speaker—the measured matter-of-factness in his tone—as he stood on the dais like a schoolmaster among his sixth form with all the lower forms below them in the auditorium. Such was his prestige, such the effect of his personality, that there was none among them, senior or junior, that 'dare bat an eyelid' on those occasions. His intellectual and moral force gave to his personality its special magnetism, so that it is no exaggeration to say that one listened spellbound when he was speaking.

Though his patience was monumental in allowing the rein to a speaker whose verbosity was 'drawn out finer than the staple of his argument,' he made no pains to conceal his irritation when some recognized bore approached the rostrum. Then the spasm of anguish which crossed his generally inflexible countenance would be visible from the auditorium. He did not suffer fools gladly, even though others might; and he was exasperated by facetiousness. Yet his self-control was such that he never allowed his personal feelings to get the better of his patience and fairmindedness. Sometimes indeed, to relieve the tedium, like a naughty school-boy he would scribble a note and pass it to his neighbour on the right or left. Mr. Micks recalls one such:

No matter how strongly he felt about any topic, he was incapable of not giving fair play to every speaker of the other way of thinking. He never used his position or his intellectual pre-eminence to weigh down any one. It was true that a diffuse or a persistently irrelevant speaker could produce suppressed moans. I recall that once when I sat as his Assessor, one dignitary of the Church was recounting the incidents of his early life with a wealth of detail which was both irrelevant and lacking in general appeal. The Primate stood it with quizzical fortitude for a while, and then passed me a note upon which he had written a quotation from Addison's hymn:
'And nightly to the listening earth
Repeats the story of his birth.'

Or it might be a Latin tag with a 'howler.' Archbishop Simms, himself a classicist, and aware of the Primate's penchant for this kind of amusement, once started the game himself with *Vis consili expers*—'Brawn without brains.' The Primate grinned and, whispering 'I can do better than that,' riposted with *Splendide mendax*—'Lying in state' (admittedly a chestnut).

It is probably true, as has been said, that the Synod never made a decision which he didn't want it to make. And there were times when his determination to prevent such a happening caused him to take action which might be construed as very nearly *ultra vires*. Under the Constitution of the Church of Ireland there are two houses in the General Synod: (1) The Bishops, (2) The Clergy and Laity. Furthermore, the Bishops, voting as a separate house, have the power to veto any resolution passed in the General Synod. On one occasion a resolution was put before it for full communion with the Church of South India. The Primate, foreseeing this possibility, had previously secured from the Bishops an assurance that, if pressed to a division, they would unanimously vote against it. The resolution was duly proposed, and was seconded by the veteran Dean of Christ Church, E. H. Lewis-Crosby, then in his nineties, in a long and impassioned appeal of such force and feeling that he sat down to an ovation. The Primate rose and said quietly and firmly: 'Gentlemen, before I put this resolution to the vote, I must warn you that if you pass it you will have the whole Bench of Bishops against you.' He put it to the vote, and those who voted in favour were in a minority.

Archbishop Barton, commenting on this, said:

> He certainly feared all movements towards amalgamation. I have heard him criticize the Ceylon Scheme which seemed to many of us to have got over most of the difficulties which troubled others with regard to the C.S.I. Scheme. He was not satisfied with the sufficiency of conferring Episcopal Orders by the laying on of hands of the Anglican Bishops. He held that we have not only to take into consideration the act of laying on of hands, but the mental concept of Episcopacy which accompanied it.

The mental concept—or doctrine—is that of the actual transmission of authority, and with it of grace, in Holy Orders, by means of the episcopal imposition of hands on priests at ordination, continued in unbroken historic continuity from the apostles. The clearest exposition is to be found in the Archbishop's address to the Scottish Episcopal Church at Glasgow in 1949 (shortly after the Lambeth Conference of 1948), which appeared as Pamphlet 15 published by Pax House for the Council for the Defence of Church Principles. It attracted the attention of Dr. E. L. Mascall who, though himself of quite another colour doctrinally, refers to it in his book *Corpus Christi* (1953) and quotes a long passage from it as 'an admirably lucid statement.'[3] It is difficult not to associate it with the doctrine of the Indelibility of Holy Orders—perpetuated, as Dr. Mascall himself holds, beyond the grave. He would certainly not have agreed with his brother of Canterbury in an exposition of 'Beliefs of the Church of England' (printed in the *Sunday Express*, 14 September 1947): 'There are matters which the whole Church has not and never can define finally in precise terms of human language; over-definition leads to error on one side or the other.'[3] And when Archbishop Fisher in a sermon on Christian Unity, which was widely circulated, made use of the expression 'growing together'—Archbishop Gregg grumbled: 'How *can* things grow together unless from the same *root*?'

§

No President could have been more efficiently and unobtrusively served that he was by his Assessor who sat on his left, Mr. J. R. Lindsay (a nephew of Lord Chief Justice Best), for whose personal qualities no less than for his outstanding legal ability he had a very high regard. In sending his tribute, Mr. Lindsay says truly of the Archbishop: 'He is difficult to imprison on paper. So much of what he said was transformed by his manner of saying it.'

I had the privilege of sitting with Dr. Gregg as legal assessor at eight General Synods of the Church of Ireland and nineteen Diocesan Synods, five of which were concerned with the election of Bishops. As Chancellor of the Diocese of Armagh I was also brought into close consultation with him on a multitude of legal matters affecting the Church's interest, organization and administration. As year succeeded year I became more impressed with the extent and versatility of his genius and with his calm, sound and penetrating judgment. Among many gifted legal people whom I have known none could excel him in seeing the relation of the elements in a complex matter and in getting swiftly to the heart of a problem. The scrupulous care and skill with which he presented his facts and arguments, his clarity and felicity of expression, his capacity to see all aspects of a problem, his realism and acumen all lightened the task of advising him.

As President of the meetings of the Synod he exercised effortless control over its members. His scrupulous fairness to all who took part in the debates won the respect of every school of thought. Even those far removed from his outlook paid tribute to his strict impartiality. Sometimes the adherents of the most

[3] I owe this and the following reference to Dr. Simms, Archbishop of Dublin.

divergent traditions within the Church learnt tolerance in argument with each other from his example. Occasionally his patience was tried by perennial orators who spoke often and at length about very little. Sometimes as these approached the rostrum one would hear coming from him a gentle moan. Now and then he would say to me 'Do me the kindness to record the time and tell me when to ring the bell.' In such cases, on the time limit being reached, the bell rang with a repeated clang. Sometimes there was no need to ring the bell for on occasion the General Synod has its own method of self-protection against a boring or long winded speaker—a subdued tramping of feet—an effective and disconcerting form of protest, which I have not heard in any other assembly.

In the Synod Dr. Gregg enjoyed the combat of lively minds. He grasped every point in debate and often helped the Synod by contributions from his own great store of knowledge and experience. In summing up at the end of a debate he sifted the essential from the superfluous and so illuminated the problem under consideration that issues which appeared complex during discussion were made clear and plain to average minds.

It is customary for the Primate to give an opening address at each General Synod on matters of concern to the Church. Year by year these addresses were awaited with interest and were listened to with rapt attention. They revealed his deep spiritual insight, his many-sided scholarship and his intimate acquaintance with the administrative and financial affairs of the Church.

As Archbishop of Armagh he presided over episcopal elections for the Northern province. These were of absorbing interest to him. In close contests he shared a little of the excitement which prevailed. Once while the results were being awaited in the tense atmosphere of a crowded Synod he quoted to me an apt passage from Lucretius' *De Rerum Natura:*

> *Suave, mari magno turbantibus aequora ventis,*
> *E terra magnum alterius spectare laborem;*
> *Non quia vexari quemquamst jucunda voluptas,*
> *Sed quibus ipse malis careas quia cernere suave est.*
> *Suave etiam, belli certamina magna tueri*
> *Per campos instructa tua sine parte pericli.*

> (Sweet it is, when on the great sea the winds are buffeting its waters, to gaze from land on another's great struggles: not that it is a pleasure or joy that any should be distressed, but because it is sweet to see from what misfortunes you yourself are free. Sweet it is too, to behold great contests of war in full array over the plains, when you have no part in the danger.)

10. WITH ARCHBISHOP PANTELEIMON BEFORE THE IKONOSTASIS, SALONICA, 1951

He had reached land some forty years before, when he had been chosen Bishop of Ossory, Ferns and Leighlin.

One memory of Dr. Gregg will remain with me always. It was connected with an episcopal election for the diocese of Kilmore, Elphin and Ardagh. The meeting of the Synod was as usual preceded by the service of Holy Communion. Ordinarily the Primate would have been the celebrant. The train by which we came from Armagh to Cavan was late. On arriving we were met at the station and Dr. Gregg was told that it had been arranged by the clergy concerned that he should robe in the vestry and go into the chancel where the service was proceeding: but he said 'No, as I am late I shall sit with the people.' When we arrived at the church he slipped quietly into the back pew and in due course made his way towards the altar with the rest of the congregation, kneeling with them to partake of the Sacrament. I felt much moved at the sight of this prince of the Church, kneeling unrobed among his people, a frail and gentle figure receiving with them the Sacrament.

We often discussed the question of the reunion of Christendom. Frequently he emphasized that in essence there was an inward unity among Christians of all communions. As he once put it in an address to the General Synod—'the dividing lines between the separated churches are much thinner than the great dividing lines which separate all those who acknowledge God in Christ from those who either ignore Him or deny Him.' With regard to corporate unity he was eager for closer communion with the Eastern Church which he felt had affinities to the Anglican position in its continuity from Apostolic times and in its refusal to deviate either by addition or substraction from the wholeness of the Apostolic faith. He regarded the Church of Ireland and other members of the Anglican Communion as trustees of a historic inheritance of Scripture, Creed, Sacrament and Ministry which they were not at liberty to disclaim. He believed that to secure a union with other communions by forfeiting this inheritance would lead to ultimate disillusionment. His hope was that in time episcopal government would be brought into harmony with the convictions of those not now subject to it; but he knew that this would be a slow and laborious process calling for infinite charity and patience. He held that there could be no real unity without agreement as to the full meaning and significance of the Episcopate and he foresaw tragedy if agreement were reached based on a formula to which the parties ascribed different meanings. Dr. Gregg realized that although the Anglican Communion had been vindicated by its unique place in history, its mediating position among the Christian Communions and its unbroken continuity of faith and Order with the Church of the Apostles, its ultimate goal was to become merged into a world-

S

wide communion of the One Visible Body of Christ. He was always aware that there could never be One Visible Universal Church that did not include the Roman Catholic Church, but he could see no prospect of success in healing the breach with that Church in this era of history without some fundamental change in its attitude to other communions.

In his own diocese of Armagh Dr. Gregg was held in respect amounting to reverence by clergy and laity. When he first came there as Primate many thought him remote, formidable and aloof, but soon they experienced the attracting power of a great personality—human, gentle, sensitive, scholarly, strong. The discipline which he exercised effectively was never a barrier to friendly and kindly consultation. To him could be applied the tribute which he once paid to another bishop: 'he knew how to rule his Diocese and withal to teach it to love him.' As he moved through the quiet country parishes of his diocese, preaching and administering the rite of confirmation, the people flocked to hear him and listened eagerly to his profound message delivered in language of beauty and precision. He himself came to feel at home in the lonely eminence of Armagh. There he found pleasure in the companionship of others. His gentle courtesy, delicate scholarship, subtle humour, and shrewd judgment of men and events made his conversation enthralling. He had the humility of a great scholar who never disdained an addition to his store of knowledge. Occasionally I lent him a book: invariably he wrote a kind note of appreciation. A few of these I have preserved. Thus when I sent him *John Cassian: a Study in Primitive Monasticism*, by the Revd. Owen Chadwick (now Master of Selwyn College, Cambridge) this note came:

Dear Mr. Lindsay,

I am now returning *John Cassian* which I have read with the greatest interest. It is not a book that can be read at once, but it is full of matter, and especially of interest as having to do with an absolute contemporary of St. Patrick, and possibly even an acquaintance of his. The only literary point of contact which suggests itself to me is in the monastic humility impressed on the coenobite and the reference in St. Patrick's Confession to 'my rusticity' and similar inadequacies.

May I thank you warmly for having caused me to read the book. Mr. Chadwick has put an infinity of learning and labour into his work.

Sincerely yours,

JOHN ARMAGH

As the General Synod of 1958 drew to its close there was an evident tenseness among its members, for many thought that before the Synod ended an announcement might be made of the Primate's retirement. There was relief when the Benediction was pronounced without an indication of any such intention. As the members of the Synod dispersed the Primate remained seated on the dais for a while. He turned to me, laying a hand affectionately on my arm, and said, 'We have travelled a long way together, you and I': then, after a pause, 'I think that this is my last Synod; next year I shall not be here.' The words had the sadness of the tolling of a bell. 'You feel that you *must* leave us?' I said. He replied, 'Sometimes when a person does not know when to go, God tells him, and He is making it plain to me.' We sat in silence in the emptying hall for a few minutes that to me seemed timeless.

I was with Dr. Gregg a few months before his death. His poor body was weak, but his heart glowed with spiritual intensity. He told me that he had been meditating for days on a single theme —The Grace of our Lord Jesus Christ, the Love of God and the Fellowship of the Holy Spirit. 'If only,' he said, 'mankind could realize the unfathomable depth and wonder and glory of these words! '

CHAPTER XVI

PORTUGAL AGAIN: GREECE AND
EASTERN ORTHODOXY

THE ARCHBISHOP'S LONELINESS since his wife's death in 1945 had caused his daughters deep concern, since neither of them was in a position to go to Armagh and look after him. 'The huge, isolated house was no place for a reserved, companionable man. It was therefore a source of great satisfaction to us when he remarried in 1947, and was cared for with such devotion and affection by his second wife, Lesley, daughter of the Dean of Armagh, until his death. His happiness and her support enabled him to continue as Primate many years longer than would otherwise have been possible.'

The secret had been well and wisely kept between themselves and the Dean for the best part of a year, till 11 January 1947 when the Archbishop gave notice of a Marriage Licence to Canon Bloomer, Rector of Armagh, upon whom he so straitly enjoined the strictest secrecy that the Rector was said to be in dread to venture forth from his house till the marriage had taken place. It was solemnized on the 22nd in the Cathedral by the aged Dean in the presence of a few members of the family. Next day the world was astonished by the announcement, which appeared in the Irish and London papers.

The Archbishop had a recipe for a successful marriage:

> He ruled, because she would obeying be;
> She, by obeying, ruled as well as he.

So it proved, and it brought a brightness into his life which continued steadfast and undimmed to the end of his days.

He was able to revisit the Lustitanian Church in Portugal thrice from Armagh, in 1947, 1949, 1950, though Spain was ecclesiastically out of bounds. On each occasion he was accompanied by Mrs. Gregg and was delighted to introduce her to well-remembered scenes and former friends. She writes:

> On our first visit to Lisbon, Dr. Pinto Ribeiro, a very fine
> linguist, translated the Confirmation addresses, sentence by sen-

tence, as the Archbishop delivered them; but on other occasions, as when we were in Oporto, the Archbishop would hand a copy of his address, in Spanish, to one of the Portuguese priests, to be translated on the spot into Portuguese. On every occasion he took the greatest pains to ensure that the Services would be conducted perfectly, and he spent a great deal of time in preparation to this end.

Our *pensione* in Lisbon had once been a convent, and was built round a charming paved garden, with pepper-trees and a tiled goldfish pond. There had been so many monasteries and convents in Portugal, and the monks had acquired so much wealth and power, that in the middle of the last century the Government stepped in and suppressed them all. Our convent had been a big affair, with many buildings, including a beautiful old church. Nowadays this church, the Marianos, has passed into Protestant hands, and it was here that the Archbishop held the first of his many Confirmations.

In Oporto the Lusitanian Church was a much stronger body than in Lisbon, and owed a great deal to three English port-wine merchants who built churches and established Sunday Schools; so that here the Church has a close association with the English colony.

The Archbishop was keenly interested in every aspect of Church life in Portugal, and in the music which accompanied the Services. The singing of the hymns was inspiring in its wholeheartedness, and he liked especially to hear the whole congregation singing the hymn, 'Vem! visita a tua Igreja' to the tune of Ton-y-botel. A prominent Lisbon layman, Dr. Leopoldo Figueiredo, was an accomplished organist as well as a musical composer. At an Ordination in the Marianos Church in Lisbon the choir rendered a beautiful setting of music, specially composed by him.

Dr. Figueiredo and his English wife were very kind in treating us to excursions to many different places, such for example as Mafra, Ericeira, the great monasteries of Alcobaça and Batalha, and even Fatima! When in the chapter-house at Batalha, the Archbishop was interested to see a bust of a 15th century Bishop of Ossory, Hacket, who had also been an architect, and who had been commissioned by the then King of Portugal to attempt to do what other architects had failed in—the feat of re-roofing the chapter-house by a single span. In previous attempts the roof had collapsed, killing some workmen. Bishop Hacket did not want this to happen, but the King assured him that he would give him condemned criminals to work for him! However, Bishop Hacket completed the work without mishap, and the roof is standing to-day. This story the Archbishop was able to tell to our hosts!

He enjoyed everything he saw on our travels with the keenest interest, and knew all the clergy and many of the laity by name, and remembered the names of their families, where they lived, and what their particular problems were, from visit to visit.

The Bishop-elect of the Lusitanian Church, Dr. Luíz Pereira, who was also a doctor on the railways, had at the time of our last visit built at least two churches with the help of local labour at and near Vila Franca de Xira. The Archbishop was deeply impressed by the devoted energy of this priest who, after his busy days of work for the railways, could give his evenings to his work for the Church.

Mrs. Gregg encloses a letter from Bishop Fiandor, written from Vila Nova de Gaia on 9 March 1959, at the time of the Archbishop's retirement:

My very dear Archbishop,

I acknowledge receipt of your letter of the 3rd instant for which I thank you very much.

I was saddened to read that you have suddenly been prevented, by failure of sight, from reading and writing, but I am quite sure that your steady faith will help enduring such a situation and that God will give you the blessing of a calm life softened with the deserved rest of so many years of hard labour.

I am very glad indeed to read that your successor is the Bishop of Meath who assisted at my consecration in Lisbon and whom I was very pleased to know personally. May God want him to maintain in future the close connection between our Churches as they have been maintained in the past.

I very often recall your good and fatherly friendship which was never found wanting whenever we had any difficulty either spiritual or doctrinal to be solved. I take this moment to express to you once more the heartfelt gratitude of our Church. I also pray that God continue pouring His Holy Ghost upon you and the Church of Ireland for His Honour and Glory.

With all good wishes and kind regards from my wife and myself for you and Mrs. Gregg, believe me to be
Yours very sincerely,
ANTONIO PEREIRA FIANDOR,
Bispo

His successor Archbishop McCann has written:

Dr. Gregg came to know and to have a very special affection for these small scattered groups of Christians in the Lusitanian Reformed Church in Spain and Portugal. He visited them in their homes, spoke to them in their own language, and kept up a correspondence with several of them between his visits. Those who could know him only as the somewhat severe-looking and formidable Prelate in the Church of Ireland would have wondered to see how he had won the hearts of the simple good souls of the Lusitanian Church. I fancy they appealed to him in a singular way, because they reminded him of the small scattered communities of Christians in the first two centuries of the Christian Era. The grave difficulties with which this little Church has had to struggle throughout the whole of his episcopate made an appeal to his own high regard for justice, and freedom from tyranny. The loyalty and devotion of these Chistians for their Church is outstanding, and they found in Dr. Gregg a leader whom they could trust, and for whom they formed a deep affection.

When he sent me to visit this Church as his representative I found that he had made a remarkable impression on them all. They loved him as a true father-in-God. They felt that they were linked through him to the Irish Church. To them he was as one of themselves, who spoke their language, used the same Prayer Book, sang the same hymns, and above all shared in the Holy Communion. One felt on this soil that the Archbishop was the missionary, the evangelist, the pastor (as he is called by them), and very specially the man with the 'common touch.'

The Right Reverend Dr. Luíz C. R. Pereira, since consecrated Bishop by Archbishop McCann, now writes:

Archbishop Gregg exercised a great influence in two ways:

First, because the authority of his opinion was always completely accepted by our Church authorities. When a recent generation appeared in the Lusitanian Church with a more Catholic mentality, Archbishop Gregg manifested profound sympathy towards them, understanding fully their intentions and, with wisdom and diplomacy, upheld them in the Church.

Second, because his authority was strong enough to break down preconceived ideas that existed in the Anglican Communion regarding the Lusitanian and the Spanish Reformed Church. We are sure that it was due to him that the Lambeth Conference in 1948 took such favourable decisions regarding these Churches.

Although the Archbishop was not our Diocesan, and his episcopal acts were performed at our request, he never failed to make careful recommendations as to how the Liturgy was to be conducted, and on the discipline of the Church. Particularly do I remember his recommendations about the Eucharist and the care he showed, by word and example, about the reverence with which the ablutions should be performed, reflecting his teaching on the subject given in his Charge at his Visitation on November 9th, 1927, as Archbishop of Dublin.

The Portuguese Prayer Book contains alternative forms for the laying on of hands in the ordering of priests. One is like the Anglican; the other does not contain the traditional words and is more in the form of a prayer. When Dr. Cabral was ordained Priest, he asked that the more 'Catholic' form might be used. Dr. Gregg smiled and answered that it was the only one he would ever use.

When I was ordained Priest, the Archbishop, knowing the great ties of friendship existing between Dr. Pina Cabral and myself, insisted that I should be near him, and, on the occasion of the laying on of hands, took hold of his hand and placed it on my head under his own hands, whilst he proffered the sacramental words of the ritual.

In 1950 the Archbishop and Mrs. Gregg were invited to be present at the dedication of a new vestry at St. John's, Vila Nova de Gaia. Somebody was asked to unveil a plaque in memory of a member of the Cassels family, and the Archbishop, who could not see or hear very well, asked Mrs. Gregg to explain what was going on. He joined in the clapping heartily. Then Mrs. Gregg was asked to unveil a portrait of His Grace who, not having heard what had been said nor being able to see that the portrait was of himself, clapped again enthusiastically and, in the silence that followed, turned to his wife and asked in a loud whisper, 'Who is that one?' Obviously amused, Mrs. Gregg answered, 'It is you!'

Dr. Cabral having, at her request, administered Holy Unction to a lady who was dying, and his action having been questioned, wrote to the Archbishop for guidance. The Archbishop answered that he did not know what was written or unwritten in the Lusitanian Church about Holy Unction, but that Dr. Cabral had acted, in his opinion, as a Catholic Priest should have acted under the circumstances. Later, when he was officially asked, as Chairman of the Council of Bishops, his opinion about the use of the Unction (already adopted by the American Church) he entirely approved of it, giving most helpful advice on the subject.

As far as I can remember, the last time his advice was asked was on the subject of the Bishop's vestments (1957–8) before our first Bishop was consecrated. Far from imposing the Anglican model, he fully approved robes more in accordance with the primitive use of the Peninsula.

The new Baptistry in the Cathedral Church of St. Paul, Lisbon, is to be dedicated to his memory in gratitude for the loving care he always showed us.

His last letter of counsel to the Lusitanian Church was written
to Bishop Fiandor after his own retirement, from the Woodhouse,
Rostrevor, Co. Down, on 21 July 1959.

My dear Bishop,
If you wish for my personal opinion in regard to the question
in your letter, it is that the Roman Catholic Confirmation, with
the use of Chrysom, is a valid Confirmation, and may be accepted
as such.

But if it distresses our converts, who were confirmed according
to the R.C. rites, that they cannot be confirmed again by you,
then *on your own responsibility* you might use a conditional
form of words, viz. 'If thou art not already confirmed, I confirm
thee, in the name of the Father and of the Son and of the Holy
Ghost. Amen.'

With regard to your second question, concerning the man and
woman who are living together as if they were husband and
wife, and who desire to be admitted to the Sacrament of Holy
Communion. If the original marriage of the man was never con-
summated, and if the two persons in question are observing complete mutual fidelity, I suggest that they may be admitted as
suitable persons for admission to H.C.

I am sorry that I could not reply by return to your letter as
I was unwell at the time it came. I am now much better, thank
God.

Mrs. Gregg joins me in warmest good wishes to you and
Senhora Fiandor.

Most truly yours,
JOHN A. F. GREGG,
Abp.

§

In 1951 the Archbishop was requested to lead the Anglican delegation to Greece, to commemorate St. Paul's mission to its cities
nineteen centuries before. Later in the year he read a paper to his
clergy in Armagh describing this visit. It begins in characteristic
style:

It was in February of this year that I heard from the Archbishop
of Canterbury about the projected commemoration by the
Church of Greece of St. Paul's arrival in Europe in A.D. 51. He
invited me to lead the Anglican delegation in which I should be
accompanied by the Bishop of Derby and the Bishop of Gibraltar.
I found it hard to resist a proposal which offered a rounding-off
of a life which had been concerned with classical studies from its
earliest days, and which had also felt for many years the vital

importance of a proper understanding between Orthodoxy and
Anglicanism. My relations with Orthodox Churchmen had begun
as long ago as the initial meeting of Faith and Order in 1920.
After some searching of heart, for I am far from young, I
agreed to go, and, furnished with a diplomatic passport, left
London by B.E.A. plane for Athens on June 14 at 8 a.m. in
company with Bishop Rawlinson, whom I found a most agreeable
and helpful companion during the fortnight.

In what follows, excerpts from his letters to Mrs. Gregg, which
she has kindly copied for this chapter, are supplemented by relevant portions extracted from his paper for his clergy. The latter
are inserted in square brackets. Many apposite allusions—classical,
scriptural and literary—are necessarily omitted.

                                    Hotel Grande Bretagne, Athens.
June 15, 1951.
    We got here about 7.0 last night, after a perfect transit. I had
a double seat to myself all the way. It was coldish at first out of
London, and got hotter and hotter as the day went on.
    This is a very fine hotel, on a big scale, and so far (noon)
excellent food in it. The weather is quite warm, but by no means
overpowering. The sun is bright, but I have not needed dark
glasses yet. The clans are gathering from all quarters, and we are
due to embark to-night after all (to avoid a port strike beginning
at midnight) instead of to-morrow morning.
    I have a comfortable room with a bathroom, but there is vir-
tually a water-famine and we are implored to go very lightly on
water, which is supplied to the city for 2 hours a day, or every
other day.
    First impressions are quite agreeable. We were met at the
airport by an old acquaintance, Prof. [Hamilcar] Alivisatos [the
moving spirit of the entire celebrations. I had first met him 31
years ago at Geneva, and had renewed acquaintance with him
on many subsequent like occasions. He is a theological professor
in the University of Athens, and a *layman*. The lay professoriate
in theology is a feature of the Orthodox Church of Greece.] . . .
and by the British Chaplain. The latter drove me in his car to
this hotel. He piloted us—Derby and me—to the Secretariate,
where we were treated with due politeness. We *do* seem to be
in some degree guests of honour. I can't yet make out if we have
free hotel keep, but we are told that the voyage is 'O.K.'—which
apparently means is the gift of the gods! Derby and I are getting
on perfectly happily—he has been here before, but is just as
much at sea as I am.
    Grande Bretagne is still popular here, although the Americans
are pouring money in. But I think they like the old lot best! I

had my elevenses—lemonade—in front of a café in a square reminding me very much of Lisbon. . . . The street crossings need watching. . . .

[The weather was exceeding hot. Constant changes of one's clothes became inevitable.

On Friday, 15th, I stood for the first time on the Acropolis, looking over the neighbouring Areopagus and trying to take in the general lay-out of the city.

In the evening, after dinner, the whole body of pilgrims gathered at the Y.M.C.A. buildings and received marching—or rather sailing—orders. There was a substantial contingent of Orthodox ecclesiastics—Bishops, Archimandrites and Priests, collected from the Orthodox Churches of many nations. But the great majority were laymen (and some women), of whom a considerable number were young people of college standing, a good many of them from America. All kinds of non-Roman Churches were represented by these lay pilgrims, while four Roman Catholics were of the number, one a white-dressed Dominican friar, and three priests from Belgium, as observers.

When we had been greeted by our Hellenic hosts, we proceeded *en masse* to St. Paul's Church for a religious service. We were timed to embark on our pleasure cruiser the *Aegaeon* at 11.45 that night. A harbour strike was due to begin at midnight, but *most considerately* we were allowed to clear before it began, and thus the crew were unaffected by the strike orders.

A six-mile drive through half-lighted streets, at a pace hectic enough to satisfy any one's thirst for adventure, brought us to the Piraeus, whence we set out at once to steam up the eastern coast of Greece. By 7 p.m. we were passing Mount Athos and were able to catch sight of a few of the monastic buildings perched on its slopes. 6 a.m. on Sunday brought us to the Port of Kavalla, the ancient Neapolis. I could see from my cabin window that crowds were collecting, and we got word that we were expected to land.]

                                                              Kavalla.
Sunday, 17 June, '51.

. . . What is left of me after a busy day writes this at 3.30 p.m.

We had to leave the boat—about 120 of us—at 8 a.m. On the quay the local soldiers with a band were awaiting us and, after courtesies of the usual kind, we proceeded in a long procession along the streets lined with the local population, preceded by the band and the local clergy with all sorts of ecclesiastical symbols, to the Cathedral—a very long walk, after a very light breakfast.

Then came the Liturgy which lasted for well over 2 hours. Mercifully I was provided with a chair, as being a *très vieux homme*, and I sat it out. A Swedish ecclesiastic collapsed. The Bishop of Philippi gave an allocution in Greek, which then had to be translated. It was a little hard to realize that we were assisting at what was to us Holy Communion. There was interminable singing by a hidden, well trained choir.

Service over, we took our seats in buses and were driven to Philippi, ten miles away. There we were ushered into a large tent covering the site of the first Christian basilica, 4th century, ruined down to the ground. Then we walked on, after greetings and prayers and hymns, to the site of a 5th cent. church, and were given a talk on Philippi, all in a hot sun!

We then 'bus'ed back to the Mayoralty where we had light (very) refreshments, and then Derby and I escaped, and strolled to the boat by 2.45. I was very hot, and changed, and now I write from the steamer in harbour. We leave for Thessalonica to-night.

[The local Bishop, the Mayor, the Town Council, all made speeches of glowing welcome to the grouped visitors, and the local garrison presented arms. A procession was then formed, partly civil and partly ecclesiastical, with the troops and their band leading the way, headed by cross-bearers and waving banners. The popular interest was intense, and the enthusiasm quite spontaneous. Now and then a little boy, or an old man or perhaps a woman, would run out of the crowd, and seize one's hand and kiss it. They knew by one's Cross that one was a bishop, even though we surprised them by not having the customary flowing beards. During a light stand-up luncheon at the Mayor's house some young maidens did a few dances for us. It was on this occasion that a photograph was taken which some of you may have seen in the public press, and which may have led you to think that a pilgrimage in Greece was not altogether without its diversions.]

Just through the Corinthian Canal.

20 June 1951.

. . . We had two great days at Salonica. On the 18th we were driven 30 miles to Beroea, and received with every demonstration of good will a long service, with an address; then we proceeded to the place where (local tradition says) St. Paul preached. Then an *al fresco* lunch overlooking a far-reaching plain; then back in a bus to Salonica.

There are a good many churches at Beroea with disguised fronts to hide their existence from the Turks. The Turks were only got out about 1920 and since then quite a lot of early churches, which had been turned into mosques, have been recovered.

Tuesday was spent in Salonica. Panteleimon is now Archbishop, and was charming. I told him of your message, and he gave a special message back to you.

9.0 Solemn Liturgy at St. Demetrius, 4th cent. de-mosquized. Then reception at University with interminable speeches. The day was swelteringly hot. At 2.30 I got back to the boat and changed. After tea we took a taxi and visited 4 of the ancient churches, and at 7.30 we got to a monastery where we were received by the Archbishop. He gave me a signed photo of an occasion that morning which was photographed, showing *him* talking to *me!*

9.45—the boat left, band of the Greek navy playing vigorously, and orderly demonstrations of good will. We steamed down a peaceful Aegaean till we reached the Corinthian Canal which we negotiated in 38 minutes. . . . The day at sea was tedious, but heat not too great. All well so far. We are due back in Athens late Monday night, for a very strenuous 4 days.

[Archbishop Panteleimon acquired great *Kudos* for the firm front he maintained, while Bishop of Pella and Edessa against the Communists, and his elevation is thought to be due to an appreciation of his success. . . . My prevailing impression of Salonica is that of liberation, ecclesiastically from the Turks and politically from foreign occupation; and this sense of liberation was reflected in the happy enthusiasm which greeted us at every public occasion by the street-crowds awaiting us.]

Hotel Grande Bretagne, Athens.
26 June. 8 a.m.

. . . I could not get my last letter out of my hands till Crete, 23rd. We had three days at sea—perfectly calm, but pretty hot, with a break at Prevezm (or Nicopolis), very near to the battle of Actium (31 B.C.). Then Crete on Saturday, and we rambled over the ruins of Minos' Palace, and saw the frescoes and the museum with all the articles dug out. It was all rather a rush and not the way to do it—one ought to go quietly and browse. Still, everybody was amazingly kind and attentive.

Crete furnishes grapes to the London market. We were given lovely ripe (green) bananas, and oh! such apricots.

4.30—we left for Rhodes. Rhodes is charming. We had an early Service (Orthodox) at the chapel where St. Paul is supposed to have landed (Lindos), and were given refreshments in an open-air café, before our 40 miles bus drive to Rhodes (ville). There we were entertained to a beautiful lunch in a superb hotel—and oh! what cantaloupes, luscious and big. We left this gorgeous place about 3.0 and were back at sea till the 25th. Rhodes has only been given back to the Greeks 2 years, and their joy is intense.

An expedition was planned to Athens, but Derby and I decided

not to go—too long, too hot—and we went on to Athens by boat
and so arrived by midday, and had a quiet afternoon and
evening.

26th. Actually a fortnight since you saw me off, and little more
than a week to go. I enjoy it, but I count the days!

[You may remember that St. Paul wrote to Titus in Crete,
bidding him make haste to get to Nicopolis, 'for I am determined
there to winter.' If this was the Nicopolis that he visited (there
are several towns or sites of that name), I imagine he must have
gone overland. There are substantial remains of a surrounding
wall, but very little excavated so far of the city itself. We were
shown the remains of two or three churches with fine mosaic
floors. Here, as in so many places, I was puzzled by the question,
'Where is all the stone that city and churches were built with?'
and the answer given me was that the Turks *burnt* the stone for
lime. But what they wanted all the resultant lime for, I was not
told! My curiosity is not yet satisfied.]

Having reached the little harbour of Fair Havens they steamed
past the full length of Crete on the south and doubled back along
half its northern coast to Heracleion, whence they were driven
to the Minoan remains at Knossos. Thence to Lindos, a tiny cove,
on Rhodes, and 'up a rough track in the steep cliff to the little
shrine of St. Paul' for a sung litany and an episcopal address. Then
on to the town of Rhodes, a forty mile drive; 'and one could easily
become lyrical on the subject of its beauty.' Then westwards
through the close-packed Cyclades to the Isthmus of Corinth. Here
on ship-board the Archbishop delivered an address on St. Peter
and Paul which he had already prepared at the request of Bishop
Buxton of Gibraltar.

The last four days in Athens were 'one long series of receptions
and sight-seeing.' The Archbishop of Athens, Spyridion, 'an elderly
and apparently fatigued man,' received the delegations and pilgrims.
'It fell to me in my turn to present the felicitations and the thanks
of the Anglican visitors.' They visited the Crusaders' Church at
Daphne, and the massive ruins of Eleusis. They were entertained
by the King and Queen of Greece 'at a most agreeable Reception
at their country house of Tatsi,' and the same evening by the Mayor
of Athens.

There is a street in Athens named after a distinguished Irish
cousin of mine, Sir Edward Fitzgerald Law, who presided over
the finances of Grece about 1890, and married a Greek wife.
The Mayor of Athens, on being told of my kinship with him,
bade me return to Athens as the guest of the municipality—an
offer which I fear I cannot hope to take advantage of.

He took part in a service in the British Church in Athens at which the Patriarch of Greece unveiled a memorial to Archbishop William Temple. This was followed by a reception given by the Theological School of Athens, and then at 7.30 on 28 June 'came the highlight of the whole celebrations'—Solemn Vespers of the Acropolis.

Athens—or as much of its population as could be contained on the hill and the boulevardes leading up to it—*Athens* flocked to the open-air service, and among those present were the King and Queen, and representatives of all the public services. Vespers were sung by the choir, with the public joining in at the proper places. On account of my age (and obvious senility) I was accommodated with a chair very thoughtfully provided, as we were to be on our feet for an hour and a half. Where I was standing, I could watch the sun—right in front of me—sinking lower and lower to the horizon—*and then,* just as it sank behind the hill, the choir broke into the familiar evening hymn which we know as 'Hail, gladdening Light of Thy pure Glory poured' . . . The spectacle was as emotionally dramatic as anything I have ever known.

But for him the day was not yet over. An entertainment by the Government at the Yacht Club and a reception by the President, M. Venizelos. On the last day, the 29th, the name-day of King Paul, a Solemn Liturgy followed by the Deum was celebrated in the Cathedral, the thronged worshippers standing in the aisles. 'I was astonished at the way in which even the women stand for indefinite periods during these very long services. Very few churches have chairs, much less pews, for the comfort of their worshippers.' Finally, a reception by the British Consul and his wife. The Archbishop summarized his impressions thus:

For open-handed hospitality provided by a country which is financially straitened, it would be hard to beat the people of Greece. It is plain that Orthodoxy has a very powerful hold on the Greek mind. I suppose this is *partly* due to the fact that their religion was a kind of rallying-point for the Greek people during the four centuries of their subjugation by the Turk. But at the same time there is little doubt that the commemoration of St. Paul gave the opportunity for a demonstration of the solidarity of Christians of all nations, whether orthodox or not, by way of reaction against communistic atheism.

His address on St. Peter and St. Paul (reprinted as a pamphlet in Athens two years later) deserves perpetuation. It collates in scholarly fashion all that is known of the scriptural and traditional association of the two great apostles, protagonists respectively of the Christian mission to Jew and Gentile. It may however not be erroneous to read into the Archbishop's words another thought, latent but unexpressed, which was always at the back of his mind; the thought namely of the dual ancestry of the Christian Church— looking back for its catholicism to the authority traditionally vested in the Apostle of the Keys, and for its protestantism to the liberalism which Luther and the Reformers rediscovered in the Apostle of Freedom; and, beyond this, to the concept of Anglicanism as the pontifex or bridge-builder destined at long last to reconcile these apparent opposites in a new and enduring synthesis.

§

But though the commemoration celebrations in Greece were thus happily terminated, and the Archbishop was tired and was looking forward to nothing so much as home, this was not to be as yet. 'For some weeks the question of a visit to the Yugoslav Church had been mooted, as the Orthodox Patriarch at Belgrade had learnt of the Anglican delegation to Greece, and did not wish to be left out.' Neither the Bishop of Derby nor the Bishop of Gibraltar could go, and to them the Archbishop 'rather sadly' said farewell; and, accompanied by Dr. Oliver Tomkins of the World Council of Churches (now Bishop of Bristol) as his chaplain, he boarded an airplane of Hellenic Airways on 30 June and reached Belgrade at noon. He expressed himself as unusually fortunate in being allowed to enter a country under a Communist régime; and as greatly indebted to 'that keen Anglican' Sir Charles Peake, the British Ambassador, 'who smoothed my path in every way.' He was the guest of the Patriarch, to whom he presented a letter from the Archbishop of Canterbury. 'We exchanged the customary compliments. We had not yet reached the stage of embracing, though that was to come later. By the way, I might say that the exchange of kisses is not nearly so trying as might be expected. The Greek clergy having never shaved, their beards are soft and silky.'

At this point the story is best continued by Bishop Tomkins, who has generously allowed the writer to take extracts from his travel-diary:

June 30th. The Archbishop and I got a lift to the airport from Christopher King (our W.C.C. refugee agent in Greece, whose station-wagon has also twice been the blessed chariot which whisked us away for a bathe) so that the Abp. had not too early a start. Bp. Scaife of West New York and J. J. Post, his chaplain, were on the same plane. We stopped only at Thessaloniki and, by leaving out Skopje, arrived in Belgrade nearly an hour before schedule. We were wrestling with a man who wanted us to fill in complicated currency forms when the U.S. Embassy car arrived, quickly followed by the U.K. one. Sir Charles Peake and his first Secretary, John Priestman, then took us in hand and no more was heard of such trivialities as customs. . . .

We were taken first to our Embassy to rest J.A.F.G. who is getting a little restive about being treated as though 'in complete senile decay.' But he made such a fuss at the Embassy in Athens about his fatigue etc. that every one here has treated him as though marked 'Fragile.' Certainly he *is* tired, for he fell sound asleep over the last course at dinner last night.

The Peakes are delightful. The Ambassador is a very keen high churchman and Lady P. has a gay inconsequence in conversation which lightens the normal atmosphere of diplomacy. It's their silver wedding on Tuesday and they have a houseful of friends and relations; but even if they had had room for us it is better to be here at the Patriarchate, for it gives chances of little talks with the English- and French-speaking bishops and priests of all kinds at odd moments. Our first audience with His Beatitude was formal but friendly. Armagh presented a letter from Cantuar and compliments were exchanged about the friendly relations of the two churches in the past, etc. . . .

After our audience we were shown to our rooms. The Patriarchate is a vast building—solid granite front and spacious formal rooms. Then alongside, the guest-wing which seems to be a minor hotel. We each have two rooms and a bathroom. . . .

Sunday, July 1st. I have an unexpected hour because J.A.F.G. found 1½ hours in church as much as he could bear of the 3½ due. We stayed only for the episcopal consecration; it starts with ½ hour of the equivalent of the 'electus' reading a long profession of orthodox faith. Then the Holy Liturgy begins—after the Trisagion; the 'electus' is led 3 times round the altar by the two co-consecrators; next he kneels before it, whilst an enormous metal-bound Gospel-book is laid, face-downwards open, on his head and the three consecrators lay their hands on it. I confess the poor man emerged as from a rugger-scrum. . . .

At this point Scaife woke Armagh, whose chair was fortunately behind one of the heavy brass Holy Doors in the centre of the ikonostasis, and I brought him back to our rooms. The old man is very game, but plainly dead tired after this hectic fortnight and we have to face what will doubtless be a very long official lunch here at the Patriarchate and after it the Ambassador is getting him to baptize one of the Embassy babies, since they rarely have a priest here, let alone a Primate! (Later.—We

T

paid a visit to the impressive memorial to the Unknown Soldier at Avala. . . . The Patriarch drove with Armagh who is now more rested and is tackling it all with great zest.)

It was certainly a strenuous performance for a man of his age. On 3 July he rose in time to breakfast at 5.30 and board a Jugoslav plane for Zurich, where he transferred to a Swiss plane which landed him in London at 6 p.m.

And so the expedition ended. Looking back, I feel that Orthodoxy desires to be on really friendly terms with Anglicanism, but anything more than that is *as far off as ever*. Orthodoxy is as exclusive as Romanism. It has passed through neither Renaissance nor Reformation. The Anglican formularies, particularly the 39 Articles, speak in doctrinal categories which are foreign to it, and Anglicans are not even at one with one another in their interpretation of them. And so, whatever approximation may be permitted by way of 'economy,' intercommunion—much less reunion—*is a long way off*.

That was his last word. He had seen Eastern Orthodoxy at close quarters and found it as intransigent, as stubbornly unwilling to concede one jot or tittle of its ancient tenets, as Romanism—or as Anglicanism. Dr. Hartford told the writer that the Archbishop, in his 'conversations' with Orthodox divines, 'would give nothing away—not even an Article.' Yet he expected very considerable concessions from them if they—whether Roman or Greek on the one hand, or Lutheran or Genevan or Nonconformist on the other —were ultimately to unite and find a common home in an Anglicanism that was at peace with itself.

He had, as Archbishop of Dublin, been elected President of the Irish Branch of the Anglican and Eastern Churches Association in 1929, and continued to be such till his retirement thirty years later. The minutes of the annual meetings, in which the substance of his remarks was duly recorded, and letters which he wrote to the honorary secretaries of the association, show a gradual change in his point of view from optimism to caution.

1930. The controversy between ourselves and the Roman Catholic Church has been so strong and pressing that we had almost shut our eyes to this tremendous witness to original Catholicism. This Association sought to do what it could to restore relations with Eastern Orthodoxy.

1934. The validity of Anglican Orders was to be examined in Rumania next year. It was in some respects a disadvantage that our Anglican formularies had been developed from a Latin controversy. . . . The Eastern Church was not so tangible as the Roman which was centralized in the Pope. We must remember also that it had suffered the most appalling misfortunes.

1935. During the Conference in Bucharest they had gone minutely into the main points of difference between the Eastern and Western Churches, and found it extraordinary how the points supposed to divide them were points of statement rather than of fact.

1937. Although the position of the Anglican Church had been defined with the greatest and most careful straightforwardness under the Reformation, its relation with the Eastern or Orthodox Church had been almost entirely ignored. But it had never been separated from these ancient bodies of the Catholic Church, with a tradition unbroken back to the very earliest days, and it was to pursue investigation into the belief and practice of the Eastern Churches that the Association existed.

1939. The reason why we were so interested in the Orthodox Church was because it was the Church which had changed least since early times. One of its great advantages was that its legislation was small, and the number of its fundamental documents very limited.

1943. Among the Serbian clergy whom he met when he had visited that country after the 1914 war, he mentioned especially Bishop Iriney who impressed him by the nobility and sanctity of his character. Others whom he met had since suffered persecution and death, among them Bishop Dosifey, who had been invited in 1939 to become a Vice-President of our Branch.

In October 1947 there was held in Dublin a Conference between delegates of the Orthodox Church and the Irish Branch whose honorary Secretary, then Canon W. E. Vandeleur, was in charge of the proceedings. He kept the Archbishop who was unable to attend in person, informed of these well in advance. Upon one point the Archbishop found himself bound to raise objection: his letter shows his wisdom and his courtesy. (He had at first mistakenly assumed St. Columba's College Chapel as the *venue*; hence its deletion, and substitution of the Divinity Hostel.)

Jan. 7, 1947.

My dear Canon,
The General lay-out of the proceedings seems suitable and gives excellent opportunity for discussion, but I am bound, *with the deepest regret*, to point out that the movement is endangering itself in a serious way, if it takes responsibility for a celebration of the Orthodox Liturgy in a Church or Chapel licensed for

C. of I. worship. Look at Canon No. 1 with its painfully decisive words—'and no other.'

It was to meet this difficulty that recourse was had to the Chapel of the Convent at Sandymount. And it would be a grave precedent, which if followed by any parish priest in C. of I. might entail very grave results for him, that a number of parish clergymen should take part in what is, I fear, indubitably illegal.

I do not think any Bishop or Archbishop could dispense the authorities controlling St. Columba's College Chapel, if it is licensed for Divine Service, from observance of the law. It is to me most regrettable to have to write this, but I would suggest your consulting the Ordinary of the place before you commit yourselves.

(*Later, same date.*) I had written enclosed letter thinking that the venue for the Conference was St. Columba's. On referring again to your letter I saw that the Hostel is to be the place. Nevertheless, I still send you what I wrote, as (whether the Hostel is licensed or not) the point I raise calls for serious consideration. The Hostel is a key-place in our system, and it would be deplorable if agitators were given an opportunity for attacking its management. Until I get more information on the point from you, I think the question of accepting the kind invitation to act as Patron had better remain in suspense, unless it is desired— as may be the case—to withdraw it altogether.

Sincerely Yours,
JOHN ARMAGH

Late in October the Archbishop could write again:

My dear Canon,

Good reports come in from every side of the Conference. You and your Committee are to be congratulated warmly on its good success. It has opened a window into a wider world of Oecumenical life to a good number of C. of I. people and clergy. . . .

Yours very sincerely,
JOHN ARMAGH

Three years later a similar Conference met in Drogheda.

Confidential

April 10, 1950.

Dear Vandeleur,

Thank you for the prospectus of the Conference, which all seems carefully arranged. . . .

I do not know—and I do not ask—*where* the Liturgy will be celebrated. But as Mr. K. has no authority for the use of the

Orthodox Rite in his Church—nor have I, technically at least, authority to permit it—I think it would be wiser not to make public announcement in his Church of the 10 a.m. Liturgy. To do so is virtually to invite his people to attend, and he would be courting trouble, if any troublesome person took the matter up.

May 20, 1950.

Many thanks for sending me word about the Conference at Drogheda. It must have been successful even beyond your hopes. . . .

If only the Orthodox had not been *forgotten* by the West, it would have been very much harder for Papal Primacy to grow in Papal Supremacy!

Sincerely Yours,

JOHN ARMAGH

20 September 1950

My dear Canon,

I could not hope to be in Dublin at the time you mention. . . . But by all means have the A.E.C.A. on a day when you can get Fr. Bloom.

I am glad you were at St. Alban and St. Sergius. I have Dr. Mascall's book on the [*illeg.*], being lectures given at a Conference of the Society in 1948.

The Orthodox must feel themselves very moderate by the side of such forthright Mariologists as Mascall and Parker! But even so, our very simple attitude towards the B.V.M. makes any thought of real Reunion with Orthodoxy very remote.

Sincerely Yours,

JOHN ARMAGH

Canon Vandeleur was succeeded by the Revd. Albert Stokes, B.D., Rector of Enniskerry, to whom we owe thanks for these letters and a perusal of the minute-book of the Branch. These show that the Archbishop continued his championship of Eastern Orthodoxy, but now his emphasis was less on an understanding with Anglicanism than on its superiority to Romanism.

1954. He pointed out how a great deal of Roman Catholic doctrine which percolated into the theology of the Greek Orthodox Church during the 17th and 18th centuries was now being eradicated.

1957. We live among an overwhelming majority who have succeeded in completely eradicating from people's minds the existence of the great Orthodox Church in the East. The impression was that the Church which largely controlled Europe was the ancient Church. It is necessary to remember that something much more ancient than the Roman Church in its present form exists, and with a continuity that cannot be spoken of by the Roman Church.

He would seem to have been slower in *rapprochement* with the Old Catholic Party; it may be because he felt that they had yet more to unlearn doctrinally than the Orthodox. Dr. N. D. Emerson, now Dean of Christ Church, writes:

At a clerical meeting Hartford, then Secretary of the Unity Committee, read a paper on the Old Catholics. I was the main speaker, as a devotee of Port Royal in many ways, and upbraided our Church for not entering into communion with the Old Catholics, as the Church of England had done. In particular I blamed the Bench of Bishops (i.e. Archbishop Gregg). Hartford said that he would take the matter up with the Archbishop. He did so. Dr. Gregg then acknowledged that they had been cowardly in not doing anything. A Bill came before the General Synod, proposed by Bishop Kerr and seconded by me. It was carried almost unanimously.

Because in things pertaining to sound churchmanship he had the rule and governance in his particular domain, his public utterances on the subject of Reunion give the impression of one to whom any suggestion of progress was dangerous, and who conceived it as his duty, whenever ideas of movement were mooted, never to press the accelerator but always to apply the brakes. His ideal of Anglicanism as the Bridge-Church in which the extremes of Catholicism and Protestantism would ultimately meet and merge, or as the catalyst which would resolve their differences without itself undergoing any essential change, seems altogether utopian. What would have been his reaction to the last paragraph of Bishop Wand's *Anglicanism in History and To-day* it is impossible to say.

The Ultimate Aim
To the Great Church of the future Anglicanism is ready to commit much more than this [its forms of worship], even itself. It has no desire to perpetuate itself in isolation, still less to subdue others to itself. It looks forward to a reunited Church in which itself and all it has stood for will form but a part. It expects a world-wide Church which will be truly Catholic and Evangelical but not necessarily Anglican. That was the spirit of the Lambeth Appeal in 1920 and that is the spirit in which the negotiations over South India were undertaken. Certainly Anglicans will want to take steps to prevent their communion from becoming dis-membered and distributed piece-meal among existing Christian

bodies. There is no existing body that, as it now is, stands for all the things in like proportion for which the Anglican Church stands. They are a great heritage and they should certainly form a part of the united church of the future. It ought not to pass the wit of man, under the guidance of the Holy Spirit, to find a way in which they can be preserved within the framework of the universal church.[1]

---

[1] I owe this reference to Dr. C. de Pauley, Bishop of Cashel.

CHAPTER XVII

ALIA PIGNORA OBSERVANTIAE

MR. T. G. F. PATERSON, O.B.E., M.R.I.A., is not only the Curator but virtually the founder of the Armagh County Library and Museum, as yet the only institution of its kind in Ireland. His researches stimulated the County Council many years ago to purchase an eighteenth century building in the Mall as a repository for his collections. These grew to such an extent that recently it has been extended to cover a much larger area, and in recognition of his valuable services to the whole Province he has received a decoration from the Government and an honorary degree from the University of Belfast. He writes:

I always felt that the Archbishop sacrificed much when he relinquished the social and cultural amenities of Dublin for the comparative seclusion of a country life in Armagh. Very soon after his arrival he paid a visit to the County Museum; it was the first of many, in which he showed a keen interest in archaeological and antiquarian matters—an interest not always evinced by church dignitaries.

There are certain carved stones in the Cathedral, some of which are survivals from earlier churches. Built in 1268, its shell is still intact, despite the many structural alterations that have taken place through the centuries. Tradition states that, when erected in that year its walls were adorned with carvings of earlier days—mostly from the walls of the three small pre-thirteenth century churches that occupied its site within the inner ring of the great earthwork which enclosed the hill in pre-Christian days.

On one of the Archbishop's visits to the museum the story of the stones came into our conversation and I mentioned that—though some of them might possibly have been found in grave-digging operations—there was the traditional acceptance that they had been built into the walls of the present edifice for preservation in the 13th century but removed in 1837 by Cottingham, the Architect employed by Archbishop Lord John George Beresford to restore the building. This, I explained, was confirmed to some extent by the fact that we know that Cottingham (who had a private architectural museum) took some to England, and that others had been given to subscribers to the Cathedral Restoration Fund. The Archbishop was much perturbed that the Cathedral Chapter had allowed any of the stones to be removed and immediately said: 'We must trace those that Cottingham carried off, and then we shall look for the others that you say are in gardens in my own archdiocese. We must not rest until we get them back.'

In England we discovered some information about Cottingham's private museum, together with a catalogue which verified the local tradition as to the removal of a few stones from Armagh. We also learned that these had been sold after his death, but were quite unable to trace the names of the purchasers of the Armagh items.

Having failed there, the Archbishop's next command was that we should examine the properties of all the subscribers to the Restoration Fund. Our first visit was to the parish of Ballymoyre where an old mansion, formerly the property of the Synnot family, had passed into the hands of a new owner. A visit was agreed upon. The Archbishop said: 'I have no engagements on Saturday afternoon. We must begin somewhere and if, as you say, the place may change hands again in the near future, we must act speedily.' When I thought of the Archbishops, deans and other cathedral dignitaries who from 1837 onwards had not given the matter a thought, I quickly agreed.

The Archbishop drove. For some reason the ever faithful Totten was not available. We found a figure in what once had been a rock-garden enclosing a small pond. We had to purchase it, but the price was very moderate; our main trouble was lifting such a heavy object into the car. The Archbishop took a firm grasp of one end (no mean effort for a man of his years) and I of the other, and thus we achieved it. I thought we might well be contented with the one treasure for that afternoon.

Unfortunately I had mentioned on the way that I had been told of some stones from the same house having been given to the father of three old ladies in Newtownhamilton, but had not suggested a visit to them since I felt it would be unfair to bring the Archbishop to call upon them without warning. He was so pleased, however, with our first success and was in such an adventurous mood that we proceeded. We found the three ladies at home and were received most kindly. Their father had been a rector in a County Armagh parish. We were given an excellent tea which we much appreciated, stayed much longer than we should have, and eventually left with a parting gift of several animal figures and one carved head. On our way home the Primate said: 'They remind me of the ladies of my grandparents' days and of those delightful characters one reads of in early Victorian novels.' From time to time when in Newtownhamilton I had called upon the ladies in question, when doing research on folk-lore and local traditions there, so when next passing I dropped in to see them as usual. I found that his Grace had been in their neighbourhood again for some function, had called and had delighted them by explaining some scientific problems which they had been unable to resolve.

Our next expedition was a more difficult one. A certain gentleman with archaeological leanings had secured a number of carved stones in 1937. He was of course long deceased, but one of the most interesting carved figures had been removed from his old home at Portneligan to Derrynoose Rectory, and from thence to Tanderagee Rectory, and eventually presented to the Belfast Museum by a later Rector. He had not, however, reckoned on the Archbishop's knowledge of ecclesiastical law. The figure had been bequeathed to the parish by its earlier owner, and should not have been given away without the consent of the Vestry. Having ascertained these facts we approached the Belfast Museum, and in due course the Archbishop received a courteous consent from the Museum Committee agreeing to the return of the figure to the cathedral. We arranged to accept delivery personally, A few days later the Archbishop had to go to Belfast to a reception held in honour of Lord Granville upon his appointment as Governor of Northern Ireland, and he had arranged for the car to pick him up at a certain hour. The function lasted longer than anticipated and cars were going up one side of Royal Avenue and down the other, stopping only for seconds at the Grand Central Hotel to pick up their owners. Totten had been up and down many times and the pre-arranged hour was long past, so he took refuge in a side street nearby. Eventually the Archbishop emerged, waited for some time without avail, and concluded that the car had been stolen and poor Totten either kidnapped or hurt. We were to meet at the Belfast Museum at 5 o'clock and about half-past his Grace arrived in a taxi, very worried indeed. Together we went back to town and called at the Reform Club where messages were to be left for him. Nothing had been heard of the car and we were about to return to Armagh by rail when it was discovered not more than a hundred yards away. Totten had been found by Mrs. Wilson. It was then almost six o'clock, at which hour the Museum closed, but the Archbishop insisted that we should try to retrieve the promised figure. We hastened to Stranmillis but, alas, the place was closed and the night-watchman could not let us have the stone without instructions from the Director. Without delay we got into communication with him by telephone. He gave the necessary instructions at once; the stone was delivered into our hands and it too was of an excessive weight. We drove slowly home thankful that the floor held and inwardly delighted by the Archbishop's pleasure and immense relief that despite all accidents the stone was safely back in Armagh, in the place where it rightfully belonged.

The Archbishop had a way with him as regards museums! One of our most interesting exhibits here in Armagh was a carved stone candlestick, probably 13th century, that had survived the Cottingham restoration of the Cathedral. It had passed through various hands before it came into the possession of the Armagh Natural History and Philosophical Society from whom we inherited it in 1935. I had a special pride in this particular item, but noticing the Archbishop's obvious interest in it on several of his visits I resigned myself to the thought that I was likely to lose it in the near future. This made the loss more bearable when the day arrived on which he said: 'I am going to ask a favour. I know the candlestick cannot be given to the cathedral by you personally, but I feel that if you were agreeable your Committee would recommend my request to the County Council, and that you in your heart must feel that the candlestick would be happy to wend its way back to its old home.' I was by then reconciled to parting with it and approached both the Museum Committee and the County Council. The matter was finally approved and I handed over the coveted candlestick.

When the Archbishop came to Armagh he settled down in his spare time to inspect the treasures of the archiepiscopal Registry where, besides the mediaeval registers of the Province of Armagh, there was a most important visitation of the diocese of Derry made by Archbishop Colton, one of his predecessors, in 1397. This he discovered was missing. At first he was inclined to think that it might have been amongst the documents demanded by the Government at the time of the Disestablishment of the Irish Church. I knew, however, that it had been missing earlier. It had been loaned to the Rev. William Reeves (afterwards Bishop) in 1850 and safely returned by him. I also knew that when the Rev. Robert King was preparing his 'History of the Primacy' the Visitation could not be found. Pressed by the Archbishop, I was forced to say that I had suspicions as to how it went astray but not actual proof. I was willing, however, to try to discover its present whereabouts, and eventually ran it to earth in the British Museum. It had been part of a collection purchased by that institution at the sale of a well-known manuscript collector. The Archbishop made a gallant attempt to recover it from London, but it had been too long 'in custody' to permit of its being returned. He was, however, presented with a photostatic copy.

Another rather similar episode comes to mind. This concerned the parish of Ballymore. I had been trying to persuade him to sponsor an exhibition, in the Church House, of 17th and 18th century church plate from the diocese of Armagh. I had prepared a list of such plate as I thought suitable. He decided however that the cost of collecting, transporting and safeguarding it would be prohibitive. In Ballymore, however, there was a silver chalice and paten that I had never seen. It had been presented to the parish in the year 1686 by Oliver St. John, the then owner of a large property that afterwards passed to the Montague family. I got in touch with the rector and to my surprise found that he was unaware of its existence. That worried me considerably. I knew that both had been placed for safe-keeping in the strong room of the castle in 1836, and I had assumed that when the mansion was no longer a residence of the Dukes of Manchester they would have been handed back to the rector. Alas, they were forgotten and found their way to England with the family silver. Subsequently there was a sale at Kinbolton and amongst the items listed in the catalogue were the Ballymore chalice and paten. There were difficulties with the vendors, but when the facts were laid before the Archbishop he acted promptly and demanded that they should be returned forthwith. This had the desired effect and they are now again in their original home.

I last heard him preach at the centenary celebrations in St. Saviour's Parish in 1958. His sight was failing, and he needed assistance to and from the pulpit. But his mind was as clear as ever. He addressed the parishioners without notes in simple but scholarly language, and ended by reminding them of the significance of the name borne by their parish. His physical frailty combined with the vigour and sincerity of his utterance made it a memorable and moving experience for those who were privileged to attend it.

His scholarship sat lightly on him and he was always willing to share with others less well equipped the large stores of his wide knowledge. As a conversationalist he was a source of delight, dispersing intellectual wisdom with an easy grace, and enlivening serious discussion with a sparkling wit that never had any unkindness in it. In the church he was supreme not only in rank but in ability. He had the gift of clarity in all his judgments and his decisions had a legal quality which made one aware that he would have been equally distinguished in law had not the church been his true vocation. Some people, especially the clergy, professed to find him somewhat intimidating, but he was never a figure of awe to me. Great as his stature was, the quality about him that most impressed me was his kindliness. I had always for him not only a deep respect but a very warm affection.

It has been well said that the Archbishop contrived to know as much or a little more law than his Chancellor, and more of finance than his financial advisers of the Representative Church Body. He gave proof of the latter ability in 1946 when the question of reinvestment of Church funds came up for discussion by that

Body and in the General Synod. Sir Cecil Stafford-King-Harman, who as a prominent member of the Standing Committee was intimately concerned with this difficult problem, thus recalls the Archbishop's personal intervention in the matter.

Archbishop Gregg possessed a remarkably versatile mind and a great gift of grasping the essential facts of a problem even when it might be supposed to be outside his scope. One of the most striking examples of this occurred in 1946 when the investment policy of the R.C.B. was becoming a matter of controversy and anxiety. It was clear that we were approaching a grave financial crisis.

At that time most large and important trusts were governed by strict clauses limiting them to investment in 'gilt-edged' securities. And the Primate himself held strong views on both the legal duties and the moral obligations of trustees. On these points he was adamant. Suggestions that trustees might be allowed to invest in the ordinary shares of commercial companies were regarded with suspicion, as being highly unorthodox. But a proposal was now put forward that investment in equities would be a sound policy and it might help to solve the crisis.

The principal advocate for this policy was Captain Prior-Wandesforde of Castlecomer whom the Primate had known as a leading member of his Diocesan Council when he was Bishop of Ossory. He was a masterful personality and brushed aside all opposition firmly and fearlessly. It did not matter whether the objections were advanced on legal grounds or pleas of speculation. By sheer force of character he succeeded in silencing most of his opponents. There were times when the opposition were inclined to become impatient, but the Primate had little sympathy with interrupters when the speaker was talking sense, and he always made sure that Captain Prior-Wandesforde was allowed to advance his views without interference. It was in fact obvious that the Primate, who had at first been sceptical of these views, was becoming impressed.

It was surprising to find that he had himself good contacts among astute business men in the City of London, and he now decided to go to them in person and obtain their views at first hand. In doing so he displayed excellent judgment and great shrewdness in selecting the persons whose advice he sought. The R.C.B. having obtained powers of investment beyond the scope of the Trustee Act appointed the firm of de Stein and Co. as their Investment Manager, and Mr. George Butler, then Chief Officer and Seceretary was instructed to go to London and explain our position and requirements. The Primate accompanied him, and returned from London with a perfectly clear appreciation of the whole situation in his mind.

The proposal which he now placed before us was to divide up the capital of the R.C.B. into five separate categories, so that the risks inherent in all forms of investment would be widely spread. This would not only provide the greatest security for the capital, and a hedge against inflationary tendencies, but it also gave good hope of a substantial increase in income and a reversal of the adverse trend which had seemed inevitable.

In order to appreciate more fully the situation which confronted Archbishop Gregg it must be remembered that the British Chancellor of the Exchequer had pronounced that any higher rate of interest than $2\frac{1}{2}\%$ was 'exorbitant.' The Primate probably realized that it might not be possible to maintain such an idealistic policy of cheap money in the post-war period and that particular rock was clearly charted in his mind, so that he understood the perils to which the Church of Ireland's finances could become exposed in a period of inflation. No capital was invested in '$2\frac{1}{2}\%$ Dalton's!'

In retrospect we must be full of admiration for the way in which the Primate's quick brain penetrated into the depths of this difficult subject, for it must also be remembered that he had to decide this highly controversial issue many years before the Trustee Act was altered to allow trustees to invest in equities. His decision was made, moreover, a long time before those in charge of the finances of the Church of England arrived at a similar conclusion.

There was of course no lack of opposition from the cautious-minded who were still convinced that it was preferable to ride out the storm in what they believed to be the safe haven of gilt-edged stocks, rather than put to sea and face all the terrors of the unknown. But Archbishop Gregg was no timid captain; he charted his course with care and when he took the helm he was prepared to bear the weight of it. It was due to this initiative, acumen and great influence that the R.C.B. evolved a financial scheme which has benefited the Church of Ireland in bounteous measure, and has provided the pattern for many similar projects.

Nor should it be forgotten (for men's memories are short) that he never, unless otherwise prevented, missed taking the chair at the meetings of the Finance Committee, and showed a keen understanding of every little detail of that Committee's work. It is probable that few men, if any, understood the finances of the Church in all their many ramifications better than Archbishop Gregg.

Recalling the meeting with the financial experts in London, Mr. George Butler adds: 'The Archbishop courteously asked me if he might join me. One of his many good qualities was that of acting correctly on all occasions, and he did so at the meeting. We sat in with three members of the firm from 10 a.m. to 5 p.m. He listened carefully but said nothing till the last half hour when he joined in a general discussion on investments and astonished the members by his knowledge of the subject.'

It has been a tradition in Armagh Cathedral that the organist (and formerly the choristers) should be chosen from English musicians unless, as has occasionally happened, an Irish musician of outstanding ability was available for the post. Tradition was followed in the case of Mr. Frederick Carter, F.R.C.O., who writes:

I first became personally acquainted with Archbishop Gregg in 1951 when I was appointed to succeed R. H. West as organist and choirmaster in Armagh Cathedral, though I was well aware of his high standing as a scholar of the Church long before then. It was to him that I now became responsible for the choice of music. I could not have wished for a more sympathetic and understanding superior, and will always remember his great kindness and wise judgments in helping me to tackle some of the problems of those early years.

From the outset it was clear that he was a great champion of full choral services; and if, for some very good reason, prayers had to be said rather than sung, this was not to be taken as a precedent. He was at first a little suspicious of some sets of responses which I introduced, but his doubts were dispelled when he realized that these were used in cathedrals and collegiate churches in the early days of the Reformation. When, after perhaps having established a leaning towards the music of the Tudor composers, we began to introduce some anthems and services by contemporaries, intending in this way to link the present with the past, the Archbishop was heard to remark: 'I cannot understand Carter introducing that music. I thought he was confirmed in the Tudor tradition.' By this time I had established a musical affinity with the Primate, and among the discussions we had concerning the music played and sung in the Cathedral, the subject of modern music came up from time to time. He would agree in principle that every age must add to the artistic contributions of the past, but I felt that the Archbishop found it difficult to accept some of the more modern trends in musical composition. It is thus easy to account for his love of Mendelssohn's music, and it was at his request that we restored some of this composer's work to the repertoire, principally 'I waited for the Lord' for which he had a deep affection, as he had also for Oakeley's 'Evening and Morning.'

He loved also the singing of the psalms, and one felt that they had a special message for him. I remember the intensity with which he quoted from Psalm 139 in one of his sermons, and to hear him was to make it live anew.

Having played the organ as a young man he had acquired an intimate knowledge of its repertoire, and he was consequently a regular attender at he various recitals in the Cathedral and could always be seen sitting in the nave after evensong when some organ music was regularly played. Besides Mendelssohn he loved the music of J. S. Bach, and some of my most cherished possessions are his volumes of Bach's organ works which he gave me on his retirement. Of all Bach's organ works I think the Fugue E♭ (St. Ann) was his favourite, and it might be of interest to record the music which was sung and played on the Sunday before his retirement, the first Sunday in Lent, 15 February 1959 —a Sunday which provided a good measure of psalmody.

<table>
<tr><td>Matins</td><td>Evensong</td></tr>
<tr><td>Psalms 61, 62</td><td>Psalm 78</td></tr>
<tr><td>The Service was sung to</td><td>The Service was sung to</td></tr>
<tr><td>Gibbon's Short Service</td><td>Weelke's Short Service</td></tr>
<tr><td>Anthem—I waited for the</td><td>Anthem—Beati quorum via</td></tr>
<tr><td>Lord (Mendelssohn)</td><td>(C. V. Stanford)</td></tr>
<tr><td>Hymns 108, 499</td><td>Hymn 498</td></tr>
<tr><td></td><td>Organ Music after Evensong</td></tr>
<tr><td></td><td>Fugue in E♭ (J. S. Bach)</td></tr>
</table>

This, apart from the Mendelssohn, was all unaccompanied music and one may add that in spite of his love of the organ and its music, the Archbishop took great delight in the unaccompanied singing of the choir, and with our increasing repertoire of Tudor music he was able to enjoy it more and more.

It was during the reconstruction of the Cathedral organ that I came into that close association with the Archbishop which enabled me to assess to the full his knowledge of the intimate details of construction whenever these were discussed, and it was a great joy to him when the restoration was completed. He dedicated the organ on 25 January 1955 and one could sense his feeling of pride that we now had an instrument worthy of the Cathedral. But it was a matter of regret to him that the full specification could not then be entirely completed, and it would be fine to contemplate this completion as a memorial to him.

These meetings at the Palace were full of interest, for at their conclusion the Primate would often recall his early days at Cambridge and at Bedford School, from which school he had attended the Services in St. Paul's Church which then represented the so-called high Church party. Whatever this may imply, there is no doubt that those Services had a lasting impression on him, and instilled in him that love of the dignity of the Anglican rite which

never left him. During his Cambridge days he had association
with many of the musicians there, and had a very high regard
for two of the leaders of the University music, Garrett and
Mann.

His humility was apparent to all, and it would be easy for
those of us who worshipped regularly with him in his Cathedral
to have his real greatness hidden from us through familiarity;
but that history will place him among the truly great Archbishops
of the Church of Ireland none of us will deny.

When in York in 1948 he met Canon G. W. O. Addleshaw, F.S.A.,
then Precentor of the Minster, now Dean of Chester, who writes:

He was, to my mind, the last and finest product of Anglo-Irish
culture. In 1948 all the Archbishops attending the Lambeth
Conference came to York for the dedication of our new pulpit
in memory of Archbishops Lang and Temple. He stayed the
night with me and attended our Solemn Evensong in the Minster.
Afterwards I asked him what he thought of the Service, meaning
the music, ceremonial, etc. His answer was: 'It does not matter
what I think, but what GOD thinks.' This remark made an
extraordinary impression on me, as it put a finger on a fundamental weakness of Anglican worship with all our talk of liturgy
and liturgical reform nowadays: our undue sensitivity to what
people think. If one approaches it in the light of Gregg's remark,
of course one's whole criteria are changed.

In some ways he was the greatest ecclesiastic I have ever come
across; but the magnificence of his personality lay in the combination of greatness with a disarming and childlike simplicity.
His conversation had the grace and precision that one finds in a
Jane Austen character. He lamented the removal from Kilkenny
Cathedral of its old choir stalls and showed me an old photograph of them. When I was in Armagh he showed me the print
of Mrs. Alexander on the wall, and regretted that she had never
lived in the Palace. When I remarked upon the wonderful grasp
of theology that comes out of her hymns, he said that in her day
there was an understanding of theology among the educated laity
which is very rare nowadays.

One of my cherished possessions is Jebb's sermons, entitled
Practical Theology. He pulled the volume out of my shelves
and opened it at the page where Jebb speaks of 'chastened
hilarity' as a characteristic of Anglican Liturgical prayer. He
enjoyed this phrase.

I suppose he is one of the architects of the Irish Free State
owing to his influence with de Valera; and I have been told,
when Temple died, 'they'—i.e. the P.M. and his advisers—
seriously thought of him for the Archbishopric of Canterbury.

U

His successor in the primatial See, Dr. James McCann, had been, as Bishop of Meath for many years, a member or chairman of several important committees, some of which affected the Church of Ireland as a whole; and he was thus associated with the Primate directly and indirectly in a number of ways. He writes:

I was brought into close relations with Archbishop Gregg in 1945 when I became a member of the Irish House of Bishops. Calm and judicial at all times he carried through the routine of the Episcopal meetings with marked attention to detail. Nothing was too insignificant for his careful consideration. He was a methodical and painstaking worker, who neither spared himself nor his fellow-bishops when important questions required solution. Often when business was pressing we were obliged to adjourn our deliberations and meet again late in the evening when work would be continued till 11 p.m. or even later. But this was not the end of Dr. Gregg's day: he would be found writing letters after midnight.

For fourteen years I had the privilege of sitting under his chairmanship at many Boards and Committees, as well as of having to consult him on matters requiring his advice and guidance. Certain words come to my mind when I think of him: a great gift of expressing his disapproval by silence, a stern refusal to be influenced by the 'temper of the times.' He was quite unperturbed when his views were rejected, even should he be in a minority of one.

I think he dreaded 'emotionalism' in any form. He once expressed to me his distrust of those who were in any way moved to action by their 'feelings.' Popular movements of every kind were therefore regarded by him with 'grave suspicion.'

A certain austerity and dignity of bearing separated him from those who had no opportunity of meeting him in private life. He was forbidding and unapproachable to them, but behind his outward mask—the aloof scholar and exalted ecclesiastic—there was a deep understanding of human beings and a practical sympathy with the struggling and poverty-stricken.

He was not given to words but rather to deeds. He had known days in his boyhood and young manhood when life was 'plain living and high thinking' because money was scarce. This left a mark on him all his years. He abhorred waste and extravagance and had no sympathy with those who brought themselves to poverty through foolish behaviour, but his heart was touched deeply by cases of genuine need and he would do everything possible to give assistance to such people.

In the years of his later life he appeared to give all his time to his episcopal duties. He delighted in committee-work, and for that reason he had much happiness in the See of Dublin where there was such work to be done almost daily; but he really lived for his work of every kind, and life apart from work had little meaning for him. Such leisure as he had was given to study and reading. His knowledge covered many fields.

When I was engaged on the work of the Church Hymnal Committee he wrote to me and spoke to me on countless occasions about the words and tunes of certain hymns. He studied meticulously any new hymns that were proposed and would find time to write fully on anything of interest to him. His interest in architecture, too, was shown when I asked his advice about converting the Parish Church at Trim into a Cathedral for the Diocese of Meath. As always he took great pains to study the problem in detail, and finally gave the suggestion his approval and support.

He had a great love for trees and delighted to walk in the woods in the Palace grounds at Armagh. When a forestry expert came to report on the trees there after his resignation, it was interesting to learn from him that Dr. Gregg had himself acquired an expert's knowledge of all the trees in the Palace wood.

This great man who was steeped in theological learning was withal a person of simple childlike faith in God. His religion was at the very heart of his life. I think it would be true to say that he worshipped Almighty God as Lawgiver and Judge. His life was disciplined and lived according to rule. 'To keep God's Holy Will and Commandments' would perhaps best express the living day-to-day religion of the Archbishop.

He was a life-long student of Law; and obedience to Divine Law was always for him the thing that mattered most.

The real humility of the man was also a striking trait. It was very evident on the day in January 1958 when he was presented with a Primatial Cross. He spoke then of his own sense of failure, of his consciousness of much work left undone. This humility was also shown when he spoke to the members of the Standing Committee, after their congratulations on his appointment to the Companionship of Honour. He was completely overwhelmed by the award of such a high mark of distinction, and his sincerity was evident to all who heard him.

I think of this great man with his diversity of gifts as in many ways unique —but above all as a servant of God, simple in faith and wise in counsel.

CHAPTER XVIII

HOME LIFE: ROMAN CATHOLICISM

IT WAS APPARENT TO ALL that the Archbishop's second marriage had given him a new lease of life. In public he was found to have mellowed and become relaxed, though with no diminution of mental vigour and strict attention to detail; at home, aided by so cheerful and capable a hostess, he delighted to entertain guests. Mrs. Gregg recalls the day's routine:

He read Family Prayers every morning, at which the C. of I. servants, when we had them, were present. After his sight failed him, I read the Bible portion and later the Prayers as well.

After breakfast he would go to his desk in the morning-room, which he preferred to his rather gloomy study, and answer letters, always in his own hand and always—unless prevented—on the day they were received. He took as much trouble over his letters as he did of everything else. Not till his sight failed did I write them for him, and then at his careful dictation. When we went on holiday he had 'chunks' of letters forwarded to him twice or three times a week.

He would work at his desk till lunch-time. There would also be a daily reading, sometimes quite prolonged, of his Greek Testament and of the Septuagint. Just before lunch he would read the *Belfast Newsletter,* and after lunch the *Irish Times;* a short siesta, then back to his desk till tea-time.

Aftea tea we would go for a good walk by a triangular route: generally up to the Obelisk and back, or in the Palace grounds when he would discuss with his steward the trees to be marked for felling or things connected with the farm. (Mr. Beale always appeared after breakfast for each day's orders, if anything special.) He loved those walks—evening walks had been the habit of his life-time, and it was sad when increasing lameness obliged him to give them up.

After dinner he read the *Daily Mail,* and after the 9 o'clock news the *Times.* He read the legal reports with great interest, after world affairs.

He took in a variety of journals, including the *Journal of Theological Studies,* the *Expository Times,* the *Illustrated London News, Life* and *Punch* (until he disapproved of certain matter in it, when he wrote to the editor), and he enjoyed a series of strange short stories in *Truth,* and was very pleased when I had one published in it.

He introduced her to Browning, and she him to Agatha Christie (!) for reading on journeys by train (but his diary confesses unashamedly that he sometimes finished these thrillers at home). They read together also several of the great nineteenth century prose-writers and poets. Herself a talented artist of original technique, Mrs. Gregg tried to interest him in the modern vogue of abstract art, and showed him Gertrude Stein's work on Picasso. He read it through with interest but was not converted. His comments, which she noted, are sincere and characteristic:

'If he is, as Gertrude Stein says, a mirror of things as he sees them, either the world is as he sees it—a very horrible and happily unrecognizable one; or else he is a distorting mirror. Could anyone—could he himself—reconstruct a year later either the world as he draws it or the figures of hideous men and more hideous women, from his curves and triangles? I don't believe he or anyone else could. His atrocious females, when in a style that makes them recognizable as women, remind me of the figures in the prehistoric Altimira Caves in Spain. There he is indeed a true Spaniard, if early man is a better Spaniard than Zurbaran or Velasquez or Ribeira, or even Murillo.

'Of Abstract painting I confess to having an untutored mind. Artists, it seems, feel that they have to take refuge in the abstract. But how far such intellectualization and its products can be called Art, is a very serious question.'

He had, said Mrs. Gregg, a very real appreciation of the great painters of the past, especially of Turner and more particularly of his water-colours; and among modern water-colourists whose work he admired he mentioned especially Russell Flint.

He loved the music of the great composers, Church music most, and took deep delight in the afternoon services in the Cathedral.

He used to say that if he were 'allowed to come back' it would be to be present at these times. From time to time he introduced to the organist's attention some beautiful hymns and tunes. 'That little French melody "Picardy" which was done last Sunday to "Sing all ye faithful"—I heard it at Cambridge a good many years ago, and am glad to find it in our book. The Dean and Mr. West kindly conspired to have it to please me.' And of Crotch's 'Star-led Chiefs' he said, 'It grows on me the more often I hear it.' He loved the Anglican liturgy, and was very happy when able to attend Church Services in England. I have never heard them read, whether in the Cathedral or in country Churches, so beautifully and sincerely as he read them, before or since.

Of personal traits and opinions Mrs. Gregg writes:

He enjoyed meeting and talking to royalty. Once he mentioned to Princess Marina, Duchess of Kent, that a street in Athens was named after a cousin of his, and was pleased that she knew it.

He said of Roman Catholicism that it is 'the religion of the natural man,' but that it is 'very difficult to be a good Protestant.'

While he respected pietistic people who could bring God into their ordinary conversation, he himself could not do so. I remember when at the London air-terminal a group of men of some (to us) unknown nationality engaged together openly in prayer before the departure of one of them on his journey, the Archbishop was much impressed by their lack of self-consciousness, and regretted that we as a people could not pray so spontaneously in public.

He took infinite pains over all his addresses and sermons—revising and cutting—or 'gouging out' as he would say. And he was infinitely patient in his dealings with people, both in public and in private. Highly sensitive and perceptive himself, he respected the feelings of others and was always courteous, even when most provoked. He had a wide and wise tolerance of people's failings. He would quote, 'To know all is to forgive all.' He was himself absolutely free of self-conceit, though he had a just measure of family pride.

He could admire pretty women, but with qualifications. They must have a degree of 'espièglerie,' and not be too 'intense.' They must also walk well, and articulate distinctly. He had no time for sloppy speech. 'There is no such things as an English accent,' he would say. 'I speak English.' And he was not amused by people 'muttering into their beards' at public meetings.

His freshness of interest made him say, 'I am never bored.' His interest covered virtually every aspect of life. Once anything was over and done, he went on to the next. He didn't like any subject being 'camped on.' 'Life is a series of new beginnings,' he would say at his Confirmation addresses. 'Get on with the war' was another of his expressions.

He was a small eater, but he appreciated good food, and he had a sweet tooth. (But he would allow himself only one sweet or piece of chocolate a day.) He didn't like anything over-seasoned: 'like a torch-light procession all the way down.'

He sometimes spoke of the Italian lakes with nostalgia, and hoped that he would visit them again before he died. But there was never time enough for such a journey. He loved coming home after being away for a day or longer, but he also loved his work. 'My work is my play,' he would say. It was because he loved his work so much that he dreaded the thought of retirement. When I suggested that he should take more rest he said, 'Rest? I shall have an eternity of rest.'

God was close to him always in his everyday life, and closer than ever during his last months of retirement.

In the enormous mansion which has been the seat of the Archbishops of Armagh since the eighteenth century, he strove to maintain the state due to his office and to the 'prestige' which the 'Protestant Ascendancy' in Ireland had enjoyed since the Reformation. But it was a losing battle and he knew it, and perhaps he was not sorry. Mr. MacAndrew, happening to be in Belfast in August of 1953 and being invited to Armagh, found him a 'most amiable host and Mrs. Gregg clearly of the greatest help to him.'

Apparently in his large lordly home he had no domestic staff, or at least none were visible, but was faithfully served by a sepulchral-looking chauffeur, who was sent to the station to bring me up, and to bring me back, but it was beneath his dignity in the service of the Archbishop (I supposed this to be the reason) to accept the customary gratuity. The whole order of things at the Palace was one of dignity, and yet, in company with the Archbishop and Mrs. Gregg, of the utmost friendliness.

Among his oldest friends in Dublin and advisers on matters of church estate had been Mr. Anthony Maude of Belgard Castle, Clondalkin, and his son Hugh. To the latter he wrote on 29 December 1955:

The Palace, Armagh.

My dear Maude,

Very many thanks for your kind and understanding letter. The Palace is, as you see, becoming a real problem. As long as wages were at a reasonable figure, the farm met its own outgoings, provided the house with milk and vegetables, and supplied the labour needed to keep the grounds and avenue in fair condition. But, as you are aware, our arable land is only a few acres, and has to be supplemented with the 92 acres I hold from the Trustees . . . and so it is now a hardly solvent undertaking.

What I am concerned with is what my successor will be faced with, when he takes stock of the concern, without Beale to carry on with—he will see me through and then drop out!

If we could get the Palace, with about 1 acre to stand on, and get rid of all the land (and pay rates of £185), and could (as you suggest) live in a flat in the Palace and let, say, the upper floor as a flat, the house might still be kept, which I greatly hope will be, for the [next] Primate.

The Dio. Council are considering the future, but they have many other things to attend to. With all good wishes for 1956.

Very sincerely yours,
JOHN ARMAGH

Mr. Maude recalls a visit to Armagh in 1946.

Going upstairs one night at the Palace we paused before the portrait of Mrs. Alexander. I remarked how good it was to have her portrait in the collection. 'Yes,' said His Grace. 'Perhaps she is more famous than any other here. She is known by her hymns all the world over. She may well have had a greater influence than any Primate.'
Once the Primate, Mrs. Gregg, and I were at Holy Communion in the Cathedral. On leaving, the Primate stayed behind, and we waited at the car for several minutes. When he came to us Mrs. Gregg said, 'What detained you?' The reply was so simple. 'I stayed to pray. I have an important sermon next Sunday.'
Another time I was staying at the Palace when the Primate had been having a long correspondence with a well-known Anglo-Catholic, who was related to me. His Grace showed me the letters. I shall never forget his brief and simple comment. 'We may not agree. But we all set ourselves on the same road. We all hope to attain the well-promised end of that road.'

Mr. Maude had taught him the meaning of the North of Ireland expression, 'a man of corn.' Meeting him later after a General Synod Service in Dublin, the Archbishop said: 'When you come North again, come to us at Armagh. I would like you and Beale to talk about farming again. He is a man of corn.' Mr. Beale, now retired, has served four successive Primates as farm steward. He was largely responsible for enlisting Archbishop Gregg's interest in the lore of trees—an interest which, like everything else he gave his mind to, became an absorbing study. Mr. Beale, when asked to tell something of his relations with the Archbishop, replied simply and with tears in his eyes, 'He trusted me, and I trusted him. We never had a cross word.'

§

In November 1950 there was promulgated by the Roman Catholic Church the dogma of the Assumption of the Virgin Mary. Soon afterwards letters were sent from Archbishop Gregg to his clergy peremptorily forbidding any of them to reply to it; adding that it was of profound theological significance, and that he would deal with it himself.
Accordingly on the second Sunday in Advent the clergy found themselves possessed of a Pastoral Letter from the House of Bishops which they were directed to read from their pulpits. It was

signed by the two Archbishops on behalf of the whole Bench; but the words are the words of Gregg and of none other. It shows well how he could outmatch the dogma-makers on their own ground and defeat them with their own weapons. It begins by tracing the origin of this belief to an imaginative Oriental document of the fourth century, which had been classed as apocryphal in a decree attributed to Pope Gelasius. Nevertheless—

Acceptance of the belief proceeded with an ever-increasing fervour, as pious meditation, not unmixed with fancy, occupied itself with the venerated figure of the Mother of our Lord.

As the ages passed, an uncurbed religious sentiment came to exalt her to a position in the heavenly world, entirely different from, and out of all proportion to, that which is accorded to her in the New Testament and in the earlier centuries of the Church's life.

He proceeds to show how, despite the reverent silence of Scripture and of the early Fathers, the cult grew 'both in popular devotion and in pictorial art' so that she came to be venerated as co-Redeemer and Mediatrix of all graces, 'until this Marian exaltation has attained such dominance, that theology is called in to justify it. Infallibility has received a mandate and proceeds to obey it. *Vox populi vox Dei.*' Yet Pope Benedict XIV in 1740 emphatically denied it as an Article of Faith (the relevant passages from *de Festis* are quoted). Yet again Pope Pius XII in 1950 asserts 'that it is a truth revealed to the Church by the Holy Ghost.'

By its various enlargements of the ancient Catholic Creed to contain the twelve new articles of Pope Pius IV's creed, the two new articles of Pope Pius IX in 1854 and 1870, and this new dogma of 1950, the Roman church is shutting itself further and further away from the rest of Catholic Christendom into being a self-enclosed corporation . . . which those who are content with the ancient Rule of Faith . . . can only reject as heretical. But inasmuch as the Papal Church claims . . . to speak in Christ's Name for the Universal Church, we are deeply concerned. For it misrepresents the Catholic Faith and exposes it to ridicule.

He concluded with an exposure of papal claims as devices to fabricate doctrine out of human speculation and falsify the faith, so devastating, and a vindication of the original Catholic belief in One Mediator between God and Man, so eloquent—that the whole edifice of later Roman 'accretions' are seen to any rational view of Christianity to be without foundation.

The Roman Catholic Dean of Residences in Belfast University had arranged a course of lectures in January 1954 on the subject of the Blessed Virgin. These lectures were public and many non-Roman Catholics attended. In an endeavour to state the Anglican position the Revd. Robert Edgar Turner, then Dean of Residences for Church of Ireland students, reissued the 1950 Pastoral to all Anglican students. This caused some controversy in the University; and in reply to a letter from Mr. Turner keeping him informed of the course of events the Archbishop replied:

The real gravamen is the definition. It is difficult to limit pious speculation, but to make it *official* doctrine is nothing short of heretical. We must be careful to distinguish between what *has been* said, what *may be* said, and what *must not be* said. I think our Pastoral states the position very fairly and truly. We have to distinguish between the Mary of history, and the Mary of (R.C.) faith. They have concentrated on the Mother-Baby relation— *vide* Madonna pictures. Also, in stressing the Divine Sonship, they have weakened recognition of His abiding Humanity—and the penalty of this is what (*illeg.*) . . . Other human beings have to be brought in as intercessors, i.e. the saints.

In private conversation concerning the dogma in question—that of the Assumption of the Blessed Virgin Mary—he was heard to say with ironical and studied moderation: 'After all, it is only an *assumption*.'

Bearing in mind the Archbishop's well-known polemic against Roman Catholicism, and particularly his famous conflict in the public press with Cardinal MacRory, it is pleasant to be able to record that when in Armagh, which is the seat of both Primacies, his personal relations with the Roman hierarchy were never other than friendly. In this he followed the tradition set by his great predecessor Archbishop Alexander, who was among the first to congratulate Cardinal Logue on his return from receiving the Cardinal's hat in Rome. So in fact the Cardinal told his own clergy. And it was said that the two Archbishops, Logue and Alexander, were sometimes seen in Armagh walking arm-in-arm together! Cardinal Logue was succeeded by Cardinal O'Donnell who maintained this fine tradition, and he by Cardinal MacRory with whom Archbishop Gregg had waged a famous paper war.

LETTERS FROM CARDINAL MACRORY TO ARCHBISHOP GREGG

Ara Coeli, Armagh

(undated)

Your Grace,

It will be a pleasure for me to come to you for tea and meet your daughters on Sat. next, the 25th inst., at 4.15 p.m.

Yours very sincerely,

✝ J. CARDINAL MACRORY

Ara Coeli, Armagh

Your Grace, May 7th, 1944

I hope it will be convenient for you to come over in the afternoon of Saturday next, May 13th, at 4.30 p.m., for tea and a talk. I expect Col. Clarke will be with us.

I have been much engaged recently with Confirmation work.

Yours very faithfully,

✝ J. CARDINAL MACRORY

Ara Coeli, Armagh

My dear Lord Primate, Sept. 11, 1945

Many thanks for your letter and its most interesting comments on various points. I'm glad I called your attention to the articles in the I.E.R.; Fr. Gannon's is a triumph of hard work! The two copies of the I.E.R. reached me safely of course.

I am up to my eyes in work these days, in preparation for my Golden Jubilee.

Believe me, Your Grace,

to His Grace Yours very sincerely,

The Lord Primate ✝ J. CARDINAL MACRORY

Ara Coeli, Armagh

Sept. 25, 1945

My dear Lord Archbishop,

I am very grateful for your kind congratulations on the Golden Jubilee of my priesthood, and thank you most sincerely. It has been a rather trying time, especially as I wasn't at all in good form; but thank God the fuss is all over now and I can take a little rest.

I read with pleasure Your Grace's comments anent the discussion on Mark 3: 20–1. The question has been turning up periodically since 1600 at least; I am hopeful that the ghost is now laid! I trust I am not too sanguine.

Believe, me, my dear Lord Archbishop,

Most sincerely yours,

His Grace ✝ J. CARDINAL MACRORY

The Lord Primate

All these letters are hand-written. The last shows signs of failing strength. Within a few days the Cardinal died.

Parochial House, Armagh
19.10.1945

To His Grace
   Most Reverend Dr. Gregg,
      The Palace,
         Armagh

Your Grace,
   I am writing to acknowledge with much thanks your kind message of sympathy on the death of His Eminence the Cardinal. While regretting your Grace's inability to attend the funeral, we were pleased to have as your representative the Dean for whom we have the greatest respect and affection.

I am, Your Grace,
Respectfully yours,
JOHN QUINN, Adm.

At the next meeting of his Diocesan Synod the Archbishop took occasion to say: 'I shall long remember this distinguished and learned Irishman. He called on me at the earliest moment after I had taken up my duties here.'

Cardinal MacRory's successor was Cardinal D'Alton, who among other gifts was a classical scholar of international repute and a specialist on the Works of Horace. With him Archbishop Gregg found a kindred mind in the love of Greek and Latin literature.

On 24 September 1957 died at the ripe age of 93 the well-loved Dean of Armagh, Thomas James McEndoo, whose younger daughter had become the Archbishop's second wife more than ten years before. She received next day the following letter from the Cardinal.

Ara Coeli, Armagh
25 September 1957

Dear Mrs. Gregg,
   In my own name and in the name of the Catholics of Armagh I wish to offer you sincere sympathy on the death of your distinguished father. I had a great admiration for your father as an outstanding churchman and a man of the highest principle. I can assure you that he was not only respected but beloved by all the members of my flock. I am sure he is already enjoying the reward of a long and devoted life of generous service to God.

   With kind regards to the Archbishop, and with renewed sympathy,

I remain,
Yours very sincerely,
✝ JOHN CARDINAL D'ALTON

Such a tribute, and from such a source, was, to say the least, noble. But the Archbishop's reaction to it was typical of his mental precision and instinct for the strictest veracity. 'How *can* he say it?' he reiterated in genuine wonderment; 'holding the beliefs he professes, how *can* he?' Yet he was visibly moved—and softened.

The following letters were found in 'The *De Sacramentis*—a work of St. Ambrose: two papers by Dom R. Hugh Connolly. Oxford, 1942.' Inscribed 'Presented to His Grace the Archbishop of Armagh, with the writer's respectful compliments (three copies).'

Downside Abbey
12 Sept. 1945

Dear Lord Archbishop,

It is very kind of you to send a postal order for the copy of my pamphlet which you asked for. Will you kindly give the other copies to any friends who may be interested in the subject? So far it has not had much circulation, and my only wish is that the evidence collected should be made known as widely as possible.

At the end of his paper referred to Dom Morin says he has just heard (i.e. in 1929) that the Vienna Corpus have decided to issue the *De Sacr.* among the genuine works of St. Ambrose; and in the last volume of the Corpus that has appeared (1932) it is advertised as in preparation in a list in which it stands *before* the *De Mysteriis.* That, I am convinced, is its proper place, as being the series of spoken lectures (taken down verbally by a stenographer) on which *De Myst.* is based: the latter being a 'boil down' into a *single* tract of *De Sacr.*, or some nearly identical *series*, delivered on successive days in Easter Week—with omission of all liturgical forms which could not be divulged in a writing meant for publication.

I am told that old Dom Morin died last year, somewhere about May or June; but before that I had managed to send him a copy of my pamphlet, and I had a letter from him (from Frieburg in Switzerland) dated 24 March, in which he said that the editor of *De Sacr.* for the Vienna Corpus (Otto Fuller) had published in *La Revue d'Innsbrück,* 1940, a study entitled *Ambrosius der Verfasser von De Sacramentis: die inneren Echtheitsgründe.* That of course I had not seen, and have not yet been able to see; but I expect to find that the evidence he has produced will coincide to a large extent with that which I have collected.

Your Grace's humble servant,
R. H. CONNOLLY

Ara Coeli
Armagh
July 15th, 1947

Your Grace,
I wish to thank you for lending me Dom Connolly's Pamphlet on the Ambrosian authorship of the *De Sacramentis*. I found it very interesting. Though I cannot speak as an expert, the case he makes seems to me on the whole convincing.
With kind regards to you and Mrs. Gregg,
I remain,
Yours sincerely,
JOHN D'ALTON,
Archbishop of Armagh

To a request for an appreciation of the Archbishop for this book, the Cardinal, at that time ill and in his doctor's hands, very generously dictated and signed the following:

Ara Coeli, Armagh
25 October 1961
. . . It was a privilege for me to enjoy the friendship of Archbishop Gregg during my years in Armagh. I always looked forward with pleasure to paying him a personal visit. One felt one was in touch not only with a charming personality, but with a fine scholar of wide intellectual interests. His Grace was always interesting to meet, for he was widely travelled and had a good memory of all that he had seen and experienced. I heard with great regret that owing to ill-health he was compelled to resign his high office. I have the happiest memories of my intercourse with him.
✠ JOHN CARDINAL D'ALTON,
Archbishop of Armagh,
Primate of All Ireland

The presentation of a Metropolitan Cross to the Archbishop to mark his long episcopate, for use by him and his successors, was made in Armagh on 24 January 1957. The proposal had been initiated and the appeal for subscriptions circulated by the Revd. Noel Mackey of Belfast. The appeal was widespread and the response instantaneous. The design produced by Miss Helen M. Roe was based on a conjectural reconstruction of the ancient Market Cross in Armagh. That the Presentation should assume this form was due to the suggestion of the Dean of Armagh, the Very Revd. H. W. Rennison. An old Alms Dish from the Cathedral, too heavy for use, provided 7¾ lbs. of silver. A Latin inscription was worded by Professor Wormell, the Public Orator of Trinity College, as follows:

REVERENDISSIMO JOHANNI ALANO FITZGERALD GREGG, ARCHI-
EPISCOPO ARMACHANO, HOC OBSERVANTIAE PIGNUS AMICI EX
OMNIBUS HIBERNIAE PARTIBUS IPSIUS SUCCESSORUMQUE IN USUM
DONO DEDERUNT.

A balance in the funds was invested to provide a Prize, in the Archbishop's full name, for the best Choir Boy in the Cathedral, to be chosen by the Dean in consultation with the Master of the Choristers and the Senior Vicar Choral.

On the occasion of the Presentation tributes testifying to the veneration and affection in which the Archbishop was held all over Ireland were paid by Dr. McCann (then Bishop of Meath); by Dr. de Pauley (then Dean of St. Patrick's); and by Major Garratt (representing the Standing Committee of the R.C.B.) The Presentation was then made by Mr. Mackey. The Archbishop, after thanking them all for this tribute of which he felt unworthy, went on to say:

One knows, better than anybody else, the utter failures that there are in personal character, and often in performance. In the mercy of God, a good many of them are not observed by other people, but one knows them oneself, and therefore one bends in shame when one thinks what kind of things people say of and attribute to one. If they only knew the weaknesses, the inadequacies of the man, one feels that their tribute and their respect might be a little more chastened!

Perhaps no words that he ever spoke in public better became him than these. He went on:

Forty-two years is a very long time. One appreciates it as one looks back. A real change has taken place, not only in the situation in Ireland but all over human society, and one feels that at the age which one has reached, one is living in a world which one can no longer claim to understand. There are so many differences taking place in outlook, in practice, in thought, that one really feels one is living outside a great deal of what is going on—and it is time that a man should be moving on, to make room for people who are more fully in touch with things.

He spoke of the past that he had lived through; of his hope to attend one more Lambeth Conference; of the status of the

Church of Ireland; of the meaning—historically—of a Processional Cross.

On 13 June 1957, the Queen's Birthday, appeared the announcement that the Archbishop of Armagh had been made a Companion of Honour. He was astounded, delighted and bewildered. He had on infrequent official occasions met members of the Royal Family; twice it had been his privilege to present the Irish Bishops to the King and Queen at the reception in Buckingham Palace which precedes the Lambeth Conferences; he had attended functions at Stormont in Belfast at which they were present; on one of these occasions at luncheon in the City Hall his companion at table had been the Princess Elizabeth: 'Get a nice impression; entirely unspoiled and simple; pretty smile'—so his diary. But he had never courted favour in high circles, and he could not imagine what he had done to merit so signal a mark of royal regard. For more than a week he was answering letters of congratulation; when these were verbal he lifted his hands with a helpless gesture and exclaimed, 'A bolt from the blue! A bolt from the blue!'

When in the following year, frail and worn but still erect, he again made his formal presentations, this time to the young Queen, it was noticed that she with gracious and thoughtful tact detained him in conversation for some time after, and was heard to say to him: 'I am glad to be here, your Grace, on this occasion when you are here.'

Apart from the access of increasing physical infirmities, life dealt gently with him in his latter years. He was noticeably less formidable, more accessible, especially to the young. He would be seen, for example, sometimes in the County Museum with a small group of children round him pointing out to them and explaining some curio or other in the cases. He took pride in the reports of his grandchildren in school and college, and affectionate pleasure in their visits to Armagh whenever possible. It rejoiced his heart that each one of them proved to be a credit to the family.

Brian Wilson. His brilliant scholastic and athletic achievements are remarkably similar to his grandfather's. Having served two years short service commission (N. Ireland) in the Royal Irish Fusiliers, in 1957 he entered Christ's College, Cambridge, from Sedbergh School with the Otway Exhibition (at Open Standard) in Classics, and took a first in Part I and a second (first class) in Part II of the Tripos. He was elected to a Scholarship at the end of his second year. In his first year he gained a half-blue for Fives, and ended as University Captain. He was also remarkable in personal resemblance to his uncle Claude Gregg, so much so that his grandfather, when sight and memory were failing towards the end, sometimes mistook him for that dear long-departed son and would inquire, 'How's Claudie?'

Audrey Wilson. Captain of Tennis at Wycombe Abbey School and in the Lacrosse XII. At Southampton she played Lacrosse for the English Universities and twice for Ireland. At St. Thomas Hospital, where she qualified as a nurse, she was again Tennis Captain.

Julian Somerville. Head of his House at King's School, Canterbury.

Christina Somerville. B.Sc. first division (Horticulture), London University. Vice-President of the Wye College of Students, and Secretary of the Beagles Club. Married, 18 August 1962, the Revd. Simon Hoare.

Canon F. A. G. Willis, editor of the *Church of Ireland Gazette*, gave expression to the feelings of all Church people when he wrote in its pages a valedictory tribute for 19 December 1958:

> It cannot be said that the announcement of his impending resignation by the Primate was unexpected. Eighty-five years is a heavy burden to carry and while Dr. Gregg has given little indication of its effect upon his faculties no one will begrudge him the rest he has so surely earned. We of this Church of Ireland can but be thankful to Almighty God for the length and strength of his ministry and pray that it may be an inspiration to us in the years to come. For many of us his passing from the active scene marks the end of an epoch in the Church's life, for he has been with us to guide and counsel in two of the most critical periods in our history. It is surely something for which we have to give thanks that it was in 1920 that Dr. Gregg was translated to the Archbishopric of Dublin and again in 1939 that he became Archbishop of Armagh. In the first case it was imperative that the Church of Ireland should have in the South a Metropolitan whose strength of character, moral courage and wisdom could match the strains imposed upon her people at a time when despair for the future could so easily have taken hold. History may record and posterity assess the contribution of John Allen Fitzgerald Gregg in the peaceful assimilation of the religious minorities in the new Ireland but it is in the hearts of men and women for whom his very presence was a symbol of stability and permanence that the real assessment was made. In 1939, with another World War imminent and with the prospect of Ireland's being once more acutely divided, he came to Armagh. Here, too, the same qualities of strength and wisdom helped to bind the Church, North and South, against sundering pressures. In either case, the right man was in the right place.

x

Much has been and will be said about the Primate's scholastic attainments, the esteem in which he is held within and outside the Anglican Communion, his ability as an administrator and his uncanny—and perhaps unexpected—appreciation of human nature in all its aspects. These appear to us as no more than useful adjuncts to what has really been at the back of his domination of the ecclesiastical scene for so long, the rare personal integrity that marks him among his fellows. . . . Almost exactly twenty years from his enthronement as Archbishop of Armagh the Primate will lay down his task as the Church's first bishop and it is impossible not to regret that he has felt impelled to make this decision. But he leaves with us all, bishops, priests, deacons, laymen and women, the memory of a lifetime spent in the service of God and of a personal character whose strength and consistency were the inevitable products of its oneness. We pray that he may find the rest and refreshment he so richly deserves.

He had for years been hypersensitive to cold, and when officiating in Armagh Cathedral in the winter had always worn a wide cassock over his greatcoat. For retirement he therefore chose the warmest place of abode in Ulster, Rostrevor, in a wooded corner of the Carlingford Lough. But the peculiar warmth of that lovely village (not shared by its near neighbour, Warrenpoint) makes it relaxing; and the Archbishop loved his long morning drives with Mrs. Gregg, she at the wheel, in the fresher air of the Mourne Mountains. In the evening she would read to him, and his eager mind was thus kept abreast of events and refreshed by treasures new and old from the world of books. Occasional visits pleased him if they were not too long, and visitors were touched as much by his bodily frailty and mental alertness as by his complete dependence on the cheerful selfless devotion of the kind companion who was at his side or within his call.

It happened that early in December 1960 his elder daughter was at Woodhouse for the day, and it was a day of momentous news. The following entry in her hand is in the Archbishop's diary for 2 December:

Father wants it specially noted what a tremendous event he considers the visit of the Archbishop of Canterbury to Pope John to be. Perhaps the most important event in potential, certainly in our time, and indeed could be one of the greatest in the history of Christendom—if men of good will can make out of it the union of minds which those who hope for unity, feel can be achieved. The danger is the bitter determination of the bigoted elements in both R.C. and Protestant circles to queer the pitch!

It is the last entry.

His consciousness became gradually detached from the world about him; he slept long and peacefully. On 2 May 1961 without a sigh or struggle he gently slipped away.

A Last Prayer:
said aloud, overheard by his wife:

Into Thy hands, O God. That is the farthest human mind and will can go—into Thy hands.

CHAPTER XIX

CREED AND CHARACTER

PEOPLE'S CONVICTIONS ARE STRONG, it has been somewhat cynically said, in proportion to their ignorance. This is not true of Archbishop Gregg. He is an example of one whose convictions were strong because of (some would say)—in spite of (others might think)—his erudition. So strong indeed were his convictions and so forcefully expounded that they reinforced the faith of others who were less sure of their ground because they had not studied it so carefully.

In general however it is only for those who are themselves already half convinced that strong convictions carry weight: only those already predisposed towards a doctrine who can be well and truly indoctrinated. But there are hosts of other minds, equally learned and equally thoughtful, who remain unconvinced. Why is it that they are so blind? Are they guilty merely of crass perversity?

In a world so vast and various as this there are manifestly whole areas—continents—of thought and experience excluded from the view of those who are convinced that theirs alone is right. The light of truth shines through a myriad of facets. There are a multitude of aspects to every single situation. Archbishop Gregg was not unaware of this: he welcomed the expression of individual and independent points of view; he valued the interplay of diverse minds on points of doctrine; and he preached on the limits of human reason. Two of his most reverenced poets had written, the one of our 'little systems,' the other of our 'broken arcs.' But he conceived it as his commissioned duty to safeguard and delimit the boundary of his own. He 'knew his ground, had studied his ground, and stood his ground'—none better or more faithfully than he; it was a definite plot of ground, strongly entrenched, four-square. And from it he would not yield an inch in any direction whatsoever.

The theological content of his religious faith was comprised within the frame of the 'Lambeth Quadrilateral'—Bible, Creeds, Sacraments, Ministry; and to this he refers again and again as the norm of belief, not only for the Anglican Church of to-day but for the Universal Church of the future. What appears as anomalous is the flexibility of his attitude towards the first two of its basic tenets, contrasted with the fixity of his attitude towards the fourth.

1. *The Bible.* 'It is in the Scriptures that we get the nearest to an arbitrary authority, from which there is no appeal.' They represent 'bedrock fact, together with the divinely taught interpretation of the same.' 'This then was the authoritative deposit committed to the Church.' It may be objected that there is inconsistency in this description of the sacred record as 'authoritative' by one who, in the front rank of biblical scholars, subjected 'the deposit' to such rigorous critical scrutiny as to cause him to conclude, for example, that the fourth Gospel cannot be regarded as history since in it facts are overlaid by symbolism; that the argument in 1 Corinthians 13 is illogical; that much of the phrasing of Pauline and Johannine Christology is derived from a book in the Apocrypha. But there is no real inconsistency in this. It is true that Gregg employed all the scientific apparatus the textual critic and the acumen of the higher critic in evaluating the contents of 'the deposit.' But the deposited Scriptures are, he said, 'the quarry to be dug': they are not therefore the smelted mineral itself. And the Church that received the deposit was, he insisted, from the first a *teaching* Church.

2. *Creeds.* 'A Creed is the embodiment of the traditional witness of the Church upon its basal historical facts and upon the interpretation of those facts. A Creed is not an effort to present ultimate truth.' The Church has the right to revise its Creeds—or any of its other formularies. There is much truth in the criticism that the Creeds suffer from a lack of balance; that they overstress some aspects of the faith to the neglect of others. They are not to be regarded as sacrosanct.[1]

3. *Sacraments.* He seems to have accepted without question the definition of the two dominical Sacraments as stated in the 25th and 28th Articles and in the Catechism, without minutely examining the several eucharistic doctrines; though he rejected outright the metaphysical concept of transubstantiation. His doctrine of the Sacraments was quite simple: Baptism is the 'initiation,' and Holy Communion is the oft-repeated 'fellowship act' on the part of the members of the Visible Church, which is the Body of Christ extended in time and place. And though his celebration of the Holy Communion was austerely simple and restrained, devoid of any act or posture other than is prescribed by the rubric, it was marked by a solemnity which impressed upon the worshippers a sense of the numinous.

---

[1] For both these sections see *The Church: Creeds and Authority,* Lecture I

4. *Ministry.* It is when we come to the fourth of the cardinal articles of his theological belief that we encounter real difficulty, because he gave to Holy Order an unalterability, a 'sacro-sanctity,' which he withheld from Holy Faith as given in the Scriptures from which he maintained that Holy Order is derived. The historical accuracy of the Gospels may in some minor particulars be questioned; there are a few obvious interpolations; Pauline and Johannine theology may be contrasted and evaluated; but apostolic succession trans-mitted unbroken through bishops, priests and deacons is a fact not to be disputed, and is indispensable for the very existence of a true Church.

But apart from the inherent improbability that the same 'order' prevailed in the widely-scattered Christian communities in the first and second centuries, ecclesiastical functions in the sub-apostolic age are too obscure to substantiate a direct proof of an episcopate through apostolic succession in all or any of the Churches. Its claim must therefore rest on other grounds than history can adduce: it must rest on the theological necessity for such a belief in order to validate the continuity of an organized, visible, external Church.

And if the claim for apostolic succession perpetuated in a three-fold ministry be granted as a theological necessity, and the spiritual grace of Holy Orders recognized as having been actually conferred by an episcopal laying on of hands, it should follow that ordination to Christian priesthood is a sacramental act, no less 'valid' than the sacrament of Baptism into Christian membership and the sacra-ment of Holy Communion into Christian fellowship. In acknow-ledging it to be such the Roman Catholic Church and the Eastern Orthodox Church show consistency. By them Ordination is held to confer an ineffaceable *character* (stamp or seal) upon the recipient, and the doctrine of the 'indelibility' of Holy Orders is after all the logical outcome of that of apostolic succession through the imposition of a bishop's hands.[2]

The Archbishop's 'unyielding episcopalianism' was a source of encouragement to those of his brother-bishops who were like-minded with himself on the matter, and an embarrassment to those who were not, both on the Irish and the English bench. It is im-possible that it could commend itself to all, or that others outside the fold could be persuaded to embrace it on the strength of bare assertion. It is hard to see how the efficacy of a faith which claims to be universal, accessible to all races of men on the face of the

[2] But yet it is to be noted as a somewhat anomalous fact that in neither of the two great Catholic Communions—Roman and Eastern Orthodox— is the act of episcopal consecration itself a sacrament.

earth, could be fettered within so narrow a channel; such a claim must delimit the preserve to the elect whose minds are so constituted as to receive it. It has been said that reason is the faculty which finds reasons for what we wish to believe; but the ultimate Truth must lie beyond the range of our human reason and surpass the highest hopes we cherish here.

And the Archbishop was himself too fair-minded a churchman not to recognize this. He says (in his Glasgow address) that at the Faith and Order Conference held at Amsterdam in 1948 he found 'a tension so far quite unresolved.'

For Anglicans, Holy Order comes, and must only come, by transmission from those who have received transmitted authority to transmit. To us, Christ is the ordainer or consecrator of priest or bishop, Himself acting through human hands as truly as faith sees Him as the consecrator at our Eucharists. But the nonepiscopal Churches emphasize the direct and contemporary action of Christ as the ordainer, which direct action in their view needs no limiting restraint confining that action to Bishops. The direct action of Christ, for them, overrides all human interventions. And who would dare to deny that grace comes in that way within that sphere?

But is it the grace of Christ's priesthood? Is it the grace of the Apostolic ministry? In sacramental matters we need to be able to speak with sureness. And in the one we can, and in the other we cannot, speak with sureness either to ourselves or to our people.

But ecclesiastical beliefs concerning the correctitude of Holy Order are less important than theological beliefs concerning Holy Faith, and theology itself after all is no more than the integument of collective religious experience. As an intellectual concept theology is but a segment of the full orb of consciousness. Religion is one's living response to the totality of experience, in which the mind is inextricably engaged together with the feelings and the will.

And indeed the Archbishop's inner life was nourished, not on mental concepts but on prayer. It was as necessary to him as breathing. 'We kneel how weak; we rise how full of power.' He loved to quote the verses in which that line occurs, written by a great predecessor, Archbishop Trench. And because we know not how to pray as we ought, and yet need language of some sort to articulate our aspirations, when at a loss for words he would have recourse to the language of the Psalms (with which he was as familiar in their Greek version as in English) and of the Collects (which he could repeat in Latin). It was his prayer-life that gave to his character its stability, integrity and strength.

Externally, the office which he filled was the one to which he was pre-eminently suited. It fitted him as a glove fits a hand; the man was the Archbishop and the Archbishop was the man. It is difficult to envisage him in any other situation unless the judiciary. And it brought him too that splendid isolation which was congenial to his temperamental shyness and reserve. For though he was very much a man of affairs he remained all through his life unworldly, because his exalted position placed him beyond reach of the badinage to which lesser mortals subject one another. There was thus, for all his business-like astuteness, an air of guilelessness about him. For example: in youth he had been a keen billiards player, but one cannot see him exchanging banter with half a dozen men round a snooker table.

And though his concept of the ideal Christian society (and he never ceased from stressing it) was that of corporate fellowship, of inter-relatedness, of *sobornost,* in which the unrelated individualist was an alien intruder—he did not in his own person exemplify this; for in outward demeanour he appeared to be detached from his fellows, a lonely individual. Yet inwardly this was not so; inwardly there was a feeling of human kinship, of personal outgoing, and the longing—rarely gratified—to realize it and express it.

Undoubtedly he had an undue sense of his dignity—of the respect that was due to him as a person, and still more as a prelate. And on his side he gave, in Pauline words, to every man his due. But he could also when necessary administer a rebuff. He strove to embody the definition of a gentleman: 'never to give offence unless you intend to.' An amusing story serves to illustrate this. A prominent layman of the Church called at the Palace one winter afternoon on a matter of diocesan business. The Archbishop was alone and he was courteously invited to stay to tea. He found his host so genial and charming that when he felt it time to go and the Archbishop with expressions of regret opened the door and stood aside to allow him to pass into the hall where his greatcoat was hanging, still chatting gaily he held the coat out armslength towards his host— as he would to any other man—in order to be 'helped into' it. What was his consternation to find that his host had swung round and turned his back on him! He had forgotten—and needed to be reminded—that the man with whom he had taken this liberty was not only a charming host, but was also the Primate of All Ireland.

Being the representative of the most ancient Christian Church, as he believed, in the British Isles, he bore himself with a dignity befitting that high office; and as a man among other men he could not but be conscious of possessing powers far beyond the ordinary; but inwardly he knew himself to be among the humblest and least worthy of the servants of God. The Cathedral of Armagh and the graveyard on the south-west side of it is the sepulture of many of his illustrious predecessors, and of some there are recumbent effigies in the nave. Judged by any standard—whether of learning or of rule or of piety—Gregg must be reckoned as among the most illustrious of any; but to him there is no sculptured memorial, and his mortal remains rest by his own desire not there, but in the obscurity of a country churchyard in Co. Wicklow with those of his wife— his wife and son.

But dignified as he was, and even at times majestic, he had no self-importance. For one thing, he was too sane, had too strong a sense of proportion, to be puffed up; for another, he was spiritually too humble-hearted. Natural dignity he had and he wore it as his garment; but simplicity and humility were his inner clothing. He did justly, loved mercy, and walked humbly with his God. A lady writes that she met him briefly in a hotel in Sidmouth in the spring of 1957, when he and Mrs. Gregg came to convalesce after influenza, 'The *one thing* I have never forgotten was the Archbishop's silent witness of standing and saying a short Grace before each meal. It was so quietly and reverently done that I can see him now, even after the lapse of time. It is so rare for any one to say Grace these days. But he was obviously such a saintly person.'

His life had been from youth unreservedly dedicated to God's service, and he brought every thought into captivity to the law of Christ. To this end it was severely self-disciplined; he eschewed both stimulant and narcotic. He had no taste for tobacco, though he wondered whimsically at times 'whether perhaps I ought to have learned to smoke; smoking is said to be conducive to sociability.' But he would have nothing to do with any sort of drug, even the mildest soporific. In reply to a request for elucidation on this point his daughter, herself a doctor, writes:

This horror of taking drugs (even the humble aspirin, to the family's despair!) was due, I am sure, to his determination to be master of his mind; *anything* which tended to diminish his control of himself was not permitted. Hence, besides drugs, alcohol was most sedulously rationed, though it was a real pleasure to him on rare occasions to drink a glass of wine— *such* a pleasure, indeed, that it was virtually cut out, to avoid any chance of indulgence. Smoking he never enjoyed, I think, and financial stringency more than moral dictation would have eliminated it in early days.

And upon another point, not unrelated to the other:

His curious apprehensive fear of dying was, I think, due to his sympathetic *personal* feeling for suffering in others. I really think he *feared* that, if great pain or distress were to be his lot at the last, his powers of endurance, even with God's help, might not stand extreme suffering. We were so happy that he was not called on to suffer much.

He would not himself forget, nor wish his people to forget, 'that in all the cares and occupations of our daily life we are ever walking in God's sight,' that all we have is a gift from Him, and all we do is some slight service that we can render Him. Every morning he set forth to his day's work with these lines in his heart of Charles Wesley's noble hymn, composed as they were to the text in the Psalms which he loved, '*I have set God always before me; for he is on my right hand, therefore I shall not fall*':

> *Forth in Thy Name, O Lord, I go,*
> *My daily labour to pursue;*
> *Thee, only Thee, resolved to know,*
> *In all I think, or speak, or do.*

To one whom he had thanked for some service, and who showed his letter of thanks to his daughter, she replied:

If he thanked or praised any one, it was because he felt they had given unstinted and unselfish service, and he wanted them to know that he would see that it was done for God. This pleasure in giving praise where it was due brought much almost tear-stained gratitude from people to whom praise was not a daily diet. I welcomed your expression of this attribute of his because, in talking recently to people, I have found that so many felt his austerity and his business acumen and his scholarship were his keynotes, whereas to us who really knew him it was his humanity and affection that were so outstanding.

Many, especially candidates for Ordination, have written of the graciousness which was so marked a characteristic of his later, rather than his middle, years, when age had softened angularities. Perhaps the following, from a Vicar in Yorkshire, the Revd. J. W. Latham, may speak for them all:

I happened to be staying at the Prince's Hotel, Torquay, in April 1953, when he was staying there too. Some of us were engaged in a religious conversation of some kind which had sprung up spontaneously in the lounge (this was before I was ordained). After a while Archbishop Gregg came in and sat down near the group, but without actually joining it. He said nothing for a while but sat listening; then he said, 'I hope you don't mind my joining in—it's very rude of me.' He then made comments from time to time, but in such a way as to let the discussion drift on, without in any way wishing to lead it or even to prompt it. After a while he said: 'Would you be so kind as to excuse me, as I have to take a rest. Thank you very much for letting me join your conversation; it was tonic and a privilege.'

Such humility from one of the Princes of the Church needs no comment; except that one needed to observe the manner in which he spoke to realize the extent of his humility.

Not only did he long to give expression to the sympathy for others which he felt, but he longed also to receive it. Accustomed as he was to formal thanks on public occasions, what he valued more was the gratitude and encouragement of private individuals whom he had been unwittingly able to help. An example of this comes from the Revd. W. McDonald, a combatant in the Second World War, then Rector of Mullaglass:

I attended Matins in Armagh Cathedral on Easter Sunday 1944, when on leave, with D-day looming ahead. It was four months since I had been to Church, and it was to be five months before I had another chance to do so. What the Archbishop said I don't remember—it was to do with asserting the moral nature of man, and the purpose of the war lay in that. But what I keep in mind is the impression of a man who was himself the embodiment of what he was putting into words; man and message were one. I went in the strength of that realization, of what the Christian faith had performed in one character, for the rest of the war.

When I returned to Trinity in 1946 I told Professor Hartford of this experience, and he said it was something I ought to tell the Archbishop myself.

At one of those gracious interviews which he granted me when I was a curate in Armagh Parish I did tell him; and his gratitude and humility in expressing it is something I can never forget.

If he was thought cold on occasions when a manifestation of emotional warmth might have been expected, this may have been because his feelings were so intense that he had deliberately to

restrain them. This was always so when he preached on Good
Friday; the apparent stiffness of his utterance masked an effort of
self-control to prevent himself from breaking down in the pulpit.

It happens not seldom to a prominent public figure upon retirement, when all the many interests which had sustained him in office
like the props of a building are suddenly removed, to find himself—
bereft of outward support—in a state of interior collapse; and if
he be a great churchman, when he can no longer exercise his
ministry, and the limelight which had high-spotted his every appearance is switched away, to experience within him a deplenishment
of spiritual resources. Such a condition, though sad, is natural.
But with Archbishop Gregg it was otherwise. His work had been
his life, it had completely absorbed his energies; for that reason
he had dreaded retirement and had postponed it as long as possible.
But when it came, and he was laid aside, scarce able to see or
hear or walk, his inner life underwent an intensification. 'In those
last months,' says Mrs. Gregg, 'he was very much with God.' And
this was apparent to all who visited him in Rostrevor. Near the end,
repeating to his wife one of his favourite collects, the fourth after
Trinity, and commenting that the word 'finally' does not occur in
the original Latin, he said: 'Eternity is here and now.'

Many contributions have gone to the making of this book, each
of them a facet reflecting from the view-point of the observer some
aspect of a personality great in stature but difficult to know. The
fact, that despite the variety of these view-points there is such
similarity in their impressions, testifies to the integrity of the
subject. But because of their point of observation they can of
necessity do no more than record aspects of the outer man. There
remains one left to the last, given by his daughter Margaret, which
reveals the nature of the inner man, and it is in the light of this that
all the others should be read.

To our whole family he was always *there*—a tower of strength,
understanding and great wisdom. It was not until my later years
that I realized that the strength of character, which we appreciated but without discernment, was not an innate gift but an
acquisition, by a soul who had from very early days dedicated
himself by a most conscious 'deed of gift' to the whole and utter
service of God. If the phrase the 'utmost for the highest' was
ever applicable to any one, it was to him. And so, having accepted
and bowed his neck to the yoke of the Christian life his formidable mental equipment was then bent to living it immensely
and expounding rationally to those who had ears to hear the
good sense of the Gospel.

In his personal life he regarded himself as God's servant, in his public life as God's priest.

As God's servant, he knew that his submission to his Master's will entailed a rigid and complete self-discipline. Acceptance of this discipline by a personality fully alive to the joys and pleasures of this life, fully sensitive to human emotions and fully liable to the temptations of human frailty, necessitated a code of conscious examination of impending action and adjustment of his performance to accord with what he perceived to be the way of the spirit—this perception came to him through his habit of prayer. How fervently he would tell those who pleaded frailty in the fight, 'you cannot do it in your own strength, only in the strength of God.' And how constantly did he himself wait upon God. Prayer was putting himself into the climate of God's radiance, so that when he returned to the work of the world, his mind was turned to see the answers in the light of God's wisdom. Faith to him was not just believing, it was a certainty and consciousness of that world of the spirit, whose rule had to be the rule of life because it was the only way that made sense.

Those who knew him less well seem to have been impressed by his apparent austerity. The deep lines on his face spoke of the sternness with which he disciplined himself, but those who knew him better found that beneath this was a depth of feeling for sorrows and sin, which showed itself in fearless advice and gentle encouragement, and an almost agonized sympathy. To him each human soul was some facet of the Divine image. When even his forbearance was sorely tried and he had looked in vain for some glimmering either of grace or of mother wit, he would to our great amusement exclaim, 'I am sure his mother was very fond of him.' This valuation which he set on human personality showed itself in many ways. His courtesy was no mere veneer of accepted good manners but an expression of his respect for individual personality—every one was treated alike—'like a gentleman.' Of all his many sermons to which I listened (and when he was Archbishop of Dublin, I was habitually his Sunday chauffeur, and 'sat under' him when he preached in the many churches of the diocese) the one which has always remained with me more insistently than any other was on the text 'Whosover shall say "thou fool" shall be in danger of hell fire.' To him, to take away a man's self-respect by mistrusting him wrongly, demeaning him, lowering his status in the eyes of his fellows, was a base deed. An interesting contrast to this attitude, though both are so very consistent with rational good living, was his insistence that 'thou shalt not bear false witness *for* thy neighbour.' If he gave a reference as to character, it was completely fair, both to the man concerned and to the prospective employer.

Many of his aphorisms, the truth of which I myself appreciate in my daily life, have a bearing on this respect for the individual. 'Withdraw thy foot from thy neighbour's house lest he be *weary* of thee' was a practised rule. Perhaps the one which delighted him most—possibly because of its permissible malice, was a description of a well intentioned woman. 'She was very kind to her friends. You knew them by their hunted look.'

The balanced nature of his outlook was immeasurably helped by his reading and memorizing massive chapters of scripture and pages from the poets. He was a voracious reader and had a habit of marking in pencil the date he completed a book or poem, and often the place, even in the train between *a* and *b*. As children we were trained to learn by heart many chapters of scriptures and poems. Isaiah 55 and 53, 1 Corinthians 13 and 15, Psalms 91, 23, 121, 72, St. John 14 and 15 and many other portions are still in my memory. The catechism we learnt and repeated each Sunday word perfectly; nothing else would do. His habits of work, as of his reading, were systematic and ordered. Meals had to be punctual and he would disappear afterwards into his study and work or read until a visitor, a meeting or the next meal interrupted. Letters were replied to as immediately as possible; how often have I been told, with astonishment, that the Archbishop had sent a carefully thought-out reply, in his own hand, by return of post. When the family had gone to bed, he would work far into the night. I remember feeling that he and God had the house to themselves, when the rush of the day was over.

Absolute integrity and absolute independence of thought characterized him. This integrity extended to everything—accounting for the last halfpenny, exact phrasing of his meaning, not only abhorrence but despising of lies—lies were irrational, they debased the currency, and were unpermissible on grounds of reason as well as morality. His independence of thought was a result of his powers of reasoning. He studied the case from all available sides and arrived at a decision, to which he committed himself unless some unexpected factor altered the situation as previously presented to him. So in his way he was profoundly amenable to reason, and, rather proudly, unswayed by considerations of light sentiment. This determination to maintain his independence of thought leading to independence of action was the reason why he steadfastly refused to join either the Freemasons or the Orange Order. He considered a member of either organization forfeited independence of judgment. Often he quoted the story of two masons during an appointments board. One pompously announced that '*ceteris paribus,* we will appoint a mason.' A voice came from down the table, 'damn the *ceteris paribus.*' This story carried great weight with him and he often regretfully found what truth it contained. He prized tremendously intellectual achievement—or indeed any achievement, manual or moral, which came as a result of unremitting toil. It was not the honours of success that appealed, but the tremendous satisfaction of what had actually been acquired by dint of industry and dogged determination. People who were 'feckless' met with little sympathy, while the hard workers who failed met with understanding.

There can have been few men who entered on their Ministry more sincerely or more humbly. He grew with his work, more able in administration and more mellow in his understanding of human frailty. As a priest, he felt his public example was immensely important, and so his demeanour, his public utterances, the things from which he refrained, the causes to which he committed himself, were selected and adhered to with the same rational sense of deliberate purpose. Things of potential for good were of prime importance and so perhaps his keenest enthusiasms were for the education of the young and the training and selection of men for the Ministry.

Fundamentally to his mission as God's priest was his profound reverence for the inexplicable wonders, grandeurs and beauties of God's Universe. It was to him unthinkable to explain life and the wonders of creation other than by acknowledgment of the supreme creative mind. And so reverence, adoration, amazement and humility were the natural outcome of this profound belief. He just couldn't reasonably contemplate taking in vain or blasphemously the name of God, the Master Mind. Even his pronunciation of the Holy Name as 'Gord' (so often commented upon and ridiculed) was an expression of feeling, deeper than the more usual, or to him more flippant, 'God.'

In all his pastoral ministrations and public appearances and utterances he strove to maintain the dignity of Church worship and the sense of reverence in its conduct. Very specially was he concerned that the service of confirmation and the ordering of priests and deacons should convey to the participants the sense of solemn importance and the idea of a life-decision, which he trusted it really did mean. He never failed to conduct these services himself—he never delegated them unless it was impossible for him to be there. The greatest care and thought went into his addresses. The essence of his priesthood and episcopacy was exemplified in these forms of laying on of hands.

And so it was with much sadness that those of us who loved him dearly realized how physical infirmity was diminishing his ability to carry on the work he loved. The loss of his sight was quite decisive and though he tried to carry on by memorizing his part in the services and his addresses, this effort was too much for his ageing brain. When he retired Feb. 19th 1959 he was anxious and worried to find he was in a state which he himself described as 'brain fag and brain fog.' He never regained his full vigorous capacity, though he enjoyed talking and being read to and hearing about all that was going on.

He seemed to realize not so very long before he died, that he was failing; he slept more and was strangely peaceful. One day I was sitting with him and he was trying, trying to remember some lines of a poem and sent me to find them in his book of quotations. These were the lines:

What though he standeth at no earthly altar,
Clothed in white vestments on that golden floor,
Where love is perfect and no step can falter,
He serveth as God's priest for evermore.

As he repeated again and again 'God's priest,' I realized that this was the full meaning of his life and work.

INDEX

Contributors' names are asterisked: the pages of their contributions in italics

337

Y